DREAMING IN ENSEMBLE

DREAMING
IN ENSEMBLE

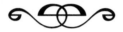

How Black Artists
Transformed American Opera

LUCY CAPLAN

HARVARD UNIVERSITY PRESS

Cambridge, Massachusetts

London, England

2025

Publication of this book has been supported through the generous provisions of
the Maurice and Lula Bradley Smith Memorial Fund.

First printing

Library of Congress Cataloging-in-Publication Data
Names: Caplan, Lucy, author.
Title: Dreaming in ensemble: How Black artists transformed American opera / Lucy Caplan.
Description: Cambridge, Massachusetts ; London, England : Harvard
University Press, 2025. | Includes bibliographical references and index.
Identifiers: LCCN 2024001380 | ISBN 9780674268517 (cloth) |
ISBN 9780674299511 (epub)
Subjects: LCSH: Opera—United States—20th century. | African American
composers—History—20th century. | African Americans—Music—History
and criticism. | Music and race—United States—History—20th century. |
Race in opera—History—20th century. | Black people in
opera—History—20th century. | Racism against Black people—
United States—History—20th century.
Classification: LCC ML1711.9 .C36 2025 | DDC 782.10973—dc23/eng/20240517
LC record available at https://lccn.loc.gov/2024001380

TO MY PARENTS

Emily Green Caplan and Jeff Caplan

Contents

DREAMING IN ENSEMBLE

Introduction

On a still, hot summer evening in July 1925, a line of young Black women formed outside the 135th Street Branch of the New York Public Library. As the clock struck seven, they filed through the doors of the elegant limestone building, descended a staircase to the lower level, and entered a subterranean auditorium, where a panel of judges waited to hear them sing. These women were entrants in the Ferrari Fontana Vocal Trials, a singing contest for African American sopranos who hoped to "train for a musical career in grand opera."[1] The winner would receive free vocal lessons with the Italian tenor Edoardo Ferrari Fontana; the announcement also noted, tantalizingly, that "one of the ambitions of Mr. Fontana's life is to hear the opera 'Aida' sung in the noted Metropolitan Opera House with a Negro soprano in the leading role."[2] The contest was so "swamped with applicants" that it required three nights' worth of auditions as "voice after voice was tested for its quality and range."[3] The judges eventually heard more than 250 singers, many of them extraordinary. Forty-two women advanced to the semifinals, and twenty-four appeared at a public final recital. From this abundance of talent, two winners were chosen: Marguerite Avery, who sang an aria from Massenet's *Le Cid,* and Jessie Zackery, whose selection was from Verdi's *Aida.* An exhilarated Fontana addressed the crowd: "I feel absolutely certain that before long you will hear of some of the singers you have listened to tonight conquering huge audiences on the operatic stage. I promise you that I will do all within my power to bring this about."[4] But soon the hubbub died down. Fontana did not make good on his promise. Neither winner went on to an operatic career.[5]

Singers like Marguerite Avery and Jessie Zackery contended with profound constraints, including the racist ideology and practices that barred them from major US operatic institutions. Fontana's evasive claim that the winner might sing in the "noted Metropolitan Opera House"—that iconic space that often functions as metonymic shorthand for opera itself, and did not engage a Black singer in a principal role until Marian Anderson's debut in 1955, thirty years hence—was one manifestation of this fraught racial politics. So, too, was his apparent failure to provide the winners with the opportunities he promised.[6] Yet institutional segregation never prevented Black artists from engaging with opera in creative and complex ways. The sheer number of participants who entered the contest illuminates an extensive, sustained interest in operatic singing among Black women in 1920s Harlem. Invested in opera's possibilities as a locus of artistic achievement and social significance, these women devoted untold hours to honing their voices, practicing their craft, and making opera part of their daily lives. Opera shaped their dreams, too, becoming a venue for individual and collective aspiration. "I was determined to sing my best," said Avery, recounting her journey from a rural southern childhood to the New York stage. "I made up my mind to go someplace where I could get my voice trained. I wanted to sing."[7]

The Ferrari Fontana Vocal Trials upends a conventional narrative of opera's relationship to Black culture. By foregrounding not the few artists who reached the art form's upper echelons, but rather the many who sang opera in a library basement, it reveals that although African Americans' engagements with opera were often relegated to the symbolic and actual underground, separate from the respective mainstreams of the US opera scene and Black cultural life, they maintained a persistent, dynamic presence. Nor did these voices stay underground. From that basement, the sounds of Avery's voice, Zackery's voice, and hundreds of other voices may well have floated up the staircase and into the library stacks above.[8] On May 7, 1925, just two months prior to the Vocal Trials, the 135th Street branch library formally opened the Division of Negro Literature, History, and Prints, a vast collection of books, manuscripts, and artifacts. The convergence is striking: opera, sung by Black women, resounded through this nascent repository and wove itself into the very warp and woof of African American history.

This book tells the story of how, during the first half of the twentieth century, Black artists created a culture of operatic music-making that flourished even as they were excluded from the art form's most prominent institutions. Across the fields of performance, composition, criticism, and

pedagogy, African Americans engaged with opera in kaleidoscopically varied ways. Those who did so were geographically, artistically, and ideologically diverse. New York and Chicago were central hubs of Black operatic activity, but it also flourished nationally and transnationally in Boston, Cleveland, Denver, Paris, Philadelphia, and Rome. Some participants were members of the African American elite, and others were young working-class men and women seeking out new forms of cultural expression; many lived lives marked by economic precarity. The primary agents of change and creativity were often women whose artistry exemplified a radically modern version of Black womanhood: one that was dynamic, cosmopolitan, and aesthetically and conceptually expansive.[9]

Black artists aspired to far more than literal and figurative inclusion within the opera house. Rather, opera was a collective cultural practice and a rich vein of lived experience under Jim Crow, an endeavor that powerfully expanded the parameters of Black cultural production by facilitating new modes of self-making and world-making. Through creative acts of transgression and imagination, African Americans redefined opera as a wellspring of aesthetic innovation, collective sociality, and antiracist activism. Their work was fundamentally transformative, both for the individuals who took part in it and because of the contributions it made to Black cultural production, the art form of opera, and the modern culture industries writ large.

A presumption of absence haunts the study of Black opera's history. The topic has been described as "profoundly absent" from the scholarly literature, a little-explored "last frontier of black music research."[10] But this phenomenon results from a lack of attention rather than a lack of historical material, bringing to mind Toni Morrison's observation that "certain absences are so stressed, so ornate, so planned," as to demand inquiry into the "willful oblivion" that has produced them.[11] The obfuscation of the longstanding Black presence within opera—and the longstanding presence of opera within Black culture—reinforces the notion that there is something incoherent, even impossible, about the concept of "Black opera," and gives credence to narrow ideas about the relationships among race, music, and genre. In doing so, it obscures alternative and more multivocal histories of Black cultural life.

Within opera studies, scholars often have examined Blackness as a representational object rather than considering Black people as subjects—performers, composers, critics, or listeners. This focus may reflect the prevalence of white-authored depictions of Blackness within the repertoire, a

trend brilliantly described by the writer Samuel Delany: "From *Aida* and *Otello* to *Porgy and Bess* and *Lost in the Stars,* we as blacks have been opera-ed, have been operated upon, have been operationalized by white composers so that there seems to be a kind of massive charge running from white musicians to us as black subjects."[12] Yet as scholars including Samuel Dwinell argue, a disproportionate focus on representation risks re-centering the (white) composer and (white-authored) work as central objects of inquiry, thereby discounting the lives, labors, and ideas of those who have been "opera-ed" as racialized subjects.[13] In addition, scholarship on racial representation in opera tends to subsume Blackness under the rubric of broader frameworks like exoticism and Orientalism.[14] While such inquiries usefully elucidate the art form's overarching investments in racial and national hierarchies, their collective departicularization of Blackness risks reproducing the logics it seeks to critique. Much as the historiographic bias toward representation reiterates a composer- and work-centric approach, a focus on the flattening impact of exoticism and Orientalism reiterates these strategies' minimization of difference among the people they putatively depict.

Within Black music studies, opera's place remains ambiguous. Institutionalized in the academy during the 1960s and 1970s alongside and in conversation with African American studies, ethnic studies, women's studies, and other interdisciplines, and similarly animated by an interest in highlighting people and cultural practices historically deemed unworthy of scholarly attention, the field has focused overwhelmingly on popular and vernacular musical traditions. Generations of scholars have provided definitive answers to the racist question that Eileen Southern was infamously asked: "Besides jazz, what is there?"[15] But opera is rarely part of the response. This absence reinscribes the limiting notion that African American musicians participate only in popular music, and it naturalizes the notion of opera's "assumed whiteness."[16] The further assumption that Black music functions as a generic "voice of the people" also devalues opera: how can the exceptional "voice of the century," as Arturo Toscanini famously referred to Marian Anderson, also be a voice of the people?[17]

Although scholars of Black musicians and the Western art music tradition have long noted that, as Kira Thurman has written pithily, "to be black and a classical musician is to be considered a contradiction," that contradiction is often undertheorized.[18] One scholar, for instance, posits that early twentieth-century African Americans considered classical music "morally positive and politically inoffensive," an apt "vehicle for cultural vindication."[19] This perspective adheres to two conceptual paradigms that have come to dominate studies of twentieth-century Black cultural production.

One is the class-oriented concept of racial uplift ideology, or the idea that the achievements of a few—the "Talented Tenth"—could catalyze Black social progress writ large. The other is the politics of respectability, a strategy by which individuals behaved in a socially sanctioned manner to contest degrading representations of African Americans and improve the standing of "the race."[20] While both ideas refuted dominant notions of Black inferiority and proved that white supremacy's racist premises were logically indefensible, their focus on individuals' behavior meant that they necessarily maintained a conditional view of racial progress; in other words, social equality had to be earned, and was not something Black people deserved on the basis of their inherent humanity. Uplift and respectability offer analytically useful mechanisms for thinking through some aspects of Black opera, but they go only so far. Overemphasizing opera's symbolic cachet, they fail to account for the art form's collective impact on Black culture, its aesthetic and historical specificity, and the meanings it held for participants on the level of experience.

This is not to say that Black opera has gone wholly undocumented. James Monroe Trotter's *Music and Some Highly Musical People* (1878), the first work of music history by an African American author, gave pride of place to the Western art music tradition, including substantive attention to opera.[21] A treasure trove of information appeared nearly one hundred years later in Eileen Southern's radically wide-ranging *The Music of Black Americans* (1971), which offered a meticulously researched look at Black American music across the boundaries of genre and style.[22] Equally significant, yet too rarely acknowledged, are many other Black women scholars of Southern's generation—including Willia Daughtry, Hansonia Caldwell, Celia Davidson, Mildred Denby Green, Antoinette Handy, Doris Evans McGinty, and Josephine Wright—who undertook the project of documenting Black operatic artists' lives and work, often orienting their research toward description and bibliography.[23]

As a cultural practice, Black opera was never lost, and it does not need to be recovered or rediscovered.[24] Yet the cumulative effect of these academic absences, coupled with a citational politics that has neglected the foundational work of a generation of Black women music scholars, is that scholarship on Black opera has only recently begun to flourish. The important collection *Blackness in Opera* (2012) offered a wide-ranging perspective that focused primarily on twentieth-century operas by Black composers and the presentation of Blackness in canonical works.[25] Other scholars have taken up the subject in the context of broader inquiries into race, music, and sound, in works ranging from Kira Thurman's *longue durée* history of

Black classical musicians in twentieth-century Central Europe, to Nina Sun Eidsheim's exploration of how listeners ascribe racialized qualities to vocal timbre, to Naomi André's transnational analysis of Black opera in the United States and South Africa in the twentieth and twenty-first centuries.[26]

The figures at the heart of this book—African American artists whose transformative impact on opera took place within the cultural and social context of the early twentieth-century United States—have been largely absent from these scholarly conversations. There have been important biographical studies of celebrated figures in concert music from this era, like Roland Hayes; but, while these are individually valuable, the methodological overrepresentation of biography reinforces the notion of the Black classical singer as an inherently exceptional figure.[27] In lieu of profiling a single artist's life or focusing primarily on operatic representations of Blackness, this book takes a holistic approach to the study of Black operatic artistry, locating the activities of composers and solo performers alongside those of amateur ensembles, laborers, and listeners.

This book is about opera, but it also tells a more expansive story about music, race, and genre in the twentieth century. It joins a number of musicological studies of opera, race, and ethnicity that have examined the relationship of early twentieth-century Jewish, Italian, and Asian Americans to the art form.[28] In foregrounding the entwined aesthetic and political goals of Black operatic artists, it builds on work in popular music studies, particularly from scholars who have revolutionized our understanding of Black popular music by conceiving of Black musicians as intellectuals, archivists, and activists.[29] In framing opera as a culturally rich practice in its own right rather than an assimilationist endeavor, it is inspired by Black feminist scholars such as Imani Perry, who proposes "black formalism" as a useful analytic for moving beyond the paradigms of respectability and uplift.[30] Ultimately, in showing how Black artists identified opera as a generative source of aesthetic and political creativity—despite white supremacist conditions that denied them access to the art form's mainstream—it offers an alternative history of Black cultural production in the early twentieth century.

Even as a young girl, it was said, Sissieretta Jones "showed possibilities as a singer and would fill the air with melody on the slightest provocation."[31] The most acclaimed African American soprano of the late nineteenth century, Jones was a concert singer who aspired to sing in fully staged opera—a goal she would never attain. Advertisements billed her as the "Black Patti," a sobriquet that compared her to a white counterpart, the

Italian diva Adelina Patti. She purportedly disliked the term, preferring the elegant "Madame Jones." Nevertheless, she molded it to her advantage. Willia Daughtry, a pioneering scholar of Jones's life, wrote that Jones used the Black Patti moniker "as a weapon—a kind of boomerang—which drew the predominately white audience to her—an audience which expected to find a freak, a comical, awkward, unusually strange creature before it, but which found instead an artist who exhibited the same training known to the white singer of her time as well as a decorum which gave new dignity and finesse to the Negro image on the concert stage."[32] Excluded from mainstream opera houses, Jones created alternative opportunities. When she began performing with a vaudeville troupe, the Black Patti Troubadours, in 1896, the group regularly concluded their evening-length program with a thirty-minute "operatic kaleidoscope," in which Jones starred in a potpourri of scenes and arias drawn from works by Verdi and Wagner.

Performers like Jones have been characterized as part of a vibrant yet short-lived phenomenon.[33] In the freewheeling culture of the late nineteenth century, Black concert artists who sang operatic music had a chance of success: opera was still a crucial component of popular entertainment, and cultural life more broadly thrived on the spectacle of racialized novelty performances. But they found themselves pushed aside as new musical and theatrical forms arose, and as the fleeting hopefulness of the Reconstruction era was crushed by the virulent, violent rise of Jim Crow. Consequently, Black performers in opera are thought to have effectively disappeared until the "golden age" of Black operatic singing during the 1960s and beyond—a development made possible by the desegregation of mainstream stages during the long civil rights era, as well as a resurgence of interest in the art form among American audiences.

I argue here that Black opera, in fact, flourished precisely in the gap between those two historical moments. It did so at a moment of definitional flux, characterized by vigorous debates regarding the relationship between music and race as well as the significance of emergent cultural hierarchies. As Ronald Radano and David Gilbert have explained, the category of "Black music" gained new cultural legibility at the turn of the twentieth century. With the advent of ragtime and Black vaudeville, both popular with white publics, Black music began to be understood as a mass-market commodity predicated on the notion of essential, "authentic" racial difference.[34] In parallel, opera was rapidly losing its nineteenth-century status as an integral part of US popular culture and becoming sequestered in the elite space of the opera house.[35] The very notion of "Black opera" interacted with and mounted an implicit challenge to each of these classifying schemes. By

defining opera in racialized terms, Black artists necessarily departed from the prevailing trend toward the "sacralization" of opera and its ensuing associations with middle- and upper-class white identity. They did so in a society marked by the constricting grip of Jim Crow, the political and economic disenfranchisement of African Americans, and the omnipresent threat of white supremacist violence. To participate in opera under such tyrannical circumstances could be a way to cross the sonic, cultural, social, and legal color line and claim full artistic citizenship.

Entanglements between Blackness and opera, both globally and in a US context, have a long history. Recent scholarship reframes opera's emergence in early modern Europe alongside systems of capitalism, colonialism, and slavery as not simply coincident, but also as a co-constitutive event, one in which opera's spectacular extravagances were made possible through the violence of transatlantic slavery.[36] The first known performance of opera in North America took place in Charleston, South Carolina—an occurrence inseparable from the wealth generated by that city's status as the capital of the American slave trade. A more immediate relationship emerged within the context of the minstrel show. Like opera, blackface minstrelsy was an exceedingly popular form of entertainment in the nineteenth-century United States, so it is unsurprising that the two often overlapped. T. D. Rice, the white performer who was one of the founders of blackface minstrelsy, popularized his creation using the term "Ethiopian opera," and the venues in which these performances occurred often were called "Ethiopian Opera Houses" or "African Opera Houses." Parodic versions of Italian arias by Bellini, Donizetti, Verdi, and others abounded, as did full-length burlesques of entire operas.[37] In its insinuation that connecting Blackness to opera was absurd, this strategy constituted what Marvin McAllister calls a "metaphorical assault on black expressive culture," rendering the notion of a legitimate Black operatic artist unthinkable to white audiences.[38]

In other corners of the nineteenth-century white racial imaginary, opera and Black singing were figured as strangely similar. White music critics often described Italian opera and Black music in similar terms, as Jennifer Stoever has shown: both were "*too* emotional, *too* bodily, *too* unrestrained."[39] The British actress and memoirist Fanny Kemble, in her diary of life on a Georgia plantation, listened to enslaved people's singing and responded by musing, "With a very little skillful adaptation and instrumentation, I think one or two barbaric chants and choruses might be evoked from them that would make the fortune of an opera."[40] Walt Whitman, a devotee of both opera and minstrelsy, proposed the theory that Black southern dialect carried within it a "future theory of the modification of all the words of the

English language, for musical purposes, for a native grand opera in America."[41]

What such predictions failed to perceive was that Black performers, composers, and listeners were already engaging with opera in meaningful ways. Elizabeth Taylor Greenfield was born enslaved in Mississippi in 1819 and spent most of her childhood in Philadelphia, then toured the northern United States and Canada, interspersing arias with parlor songs and ballads in her recitals. As Daphne Brooks has argued, Greenfield initiated a "genealogy of black women's cultural play within classical music forms," and many would follow in her footsteps.[42] Along with the celebrated Sissieretta Jones, the sister vocalists Anna Madah and Emma Louise Hyers also sang operatic music, as did Marie Selika Williams, Nellie Brown Mitchell, and a host of others. Collective efforts were rarer. The Colored American Opera Company was founded in Washington, DC in 1873 by a white conductor, John Esputa, who directed an all-Black cast in the comic opera *The Doctor of Alcantara;* it lasted only a single season. The Fisk Jubilee Singers, founded at Fisk University in Nashville, Tennessee, broke new ground by creating a musical genre, the concert spiritual. Transcribed using Western musical notation and performed in a bel canto style, these songs established a profound connection between Black performers and classical singing; they became the cornerstone of the Jubilee Singers' wildly successful national and international concert tours, which began in 1871.[43] These endeavors were products of the Reconstruction era, and their success was animated by that era's widespread hope in the possibility of multiracial democracy. Arriving on the cultural scene at the height of blackface minstrelsy's popularity, they offered new models for Black expressive performance.

The Fisk Jubilee Singers performed regularly in spaces known as "opera houses," then a catchall term for entertainment venues that featured traveling opera troupes alongside various other types of performance. This nomenclature reflected the art form's ubiquity in the nineteenth-century United States.[44] But by the turn of the twentieth century, that landscape was changing. The establishment of permanent opera companies, along with institutions like symphony orchestras and art museums, was a hallmark of Gilded Age culture, championed by elites who saw cultural hierarchy as an expression of order in a society beset by social fragmentation.[45] Opera's redefinition as "high culture" was thus bound up with its institutionalization—a shift that exemplified a broader reconfiguration of economic and cultural structures via consolidation and incorporation. The development of the Theatrical Syndicate in 1896, for instance, concentrated

power in the hands of a few managers such that by the first decade of the twentieth century, six men collectively owned thirty-three theaters and controlled bookings at more than seven hundred across the country. Since opera was less profitable than other entertainments, the syndicate booked fewer and fewer companies.[46] An important distinction emerged: although operatic *music* continued to circulate widely via recital performance, parodies, and new media technologies from phonographs to movies, fully staged operatic *productions* were pushed into the opera house, a shift that would inextricably link opera as an institution with whiteness and elitism.

Black operatic artists in the late nineteenth and early twentieth centuries, then, were multiply marginalized. Their race located them at the periphery of a historically Eurocentric musical tradition, while their focus on opera set them apart from African American artists working in popular and vernacular traditions. Those factors were compounded by the increasing marginalization of opera itself. But although each of these conditions might seem to be a deradicalizing or disempowering development, in fact the opposite was true. Instead of diminishing the significance of these artists' work, especially in comparison to their counterparts in popular culture, these efforts became what might be thought of as an expression of "high culture on the lower frequencies"—to borrow a line from Ralph Ellison's novel *Invisible Man* ("who knows but that, on the lower frequencies, I speak for you?"). Embracing what Stuart Hall famously called the "productive space" of marginality, Black operatic artists acknowledged the existence of the hierarchical cultural arrangements that produced the concept of "high culture" without accepting them as static or inevitable.[47] Instead of seeking incorporation or acceptance into such arrangements, they embraced their status on the lower frequencies, within what Gayle Wald calls a "sonic register of subterranean power."[48] They used opera to contend with the dislocating conditions of modernity, the violent terrors of white supremacy, the immense possibilities generated by the rise of mass culture, and the radical imagination vital to Black freedom struggles. Together, they transformed opera into an aesthetic and social vantage point from which to perform, interpret, teach, research, document, and theorize their own lives.

In the title of this book, *Dreaming in Ensemble,* I have sought to evoke the fundamentally generative and fundamentally collective nature of these artists' work in opera. They often voiced their relationship to the art form in aspirational terms. For composer William Grant Still, opera was "the dream of my life." For impresario Mary Cardwell Dawson, establishing an opera company was a way to "further the realization of the dreams of our

racial group." For soprano Anne Wiggins Brown, "It was opera of which I dreamed when I thought about the future." Opera was a "dream" not because their artistic goals were naïve or utopian, but rather because structural realities often hindered the attainment of these goals. ("Not a chance!" lamented Brown, just after explaining her ambitions. "The opera scene . . . was closed to me.")[49] By calling attention to the trope of the dream, I aim to link these figures' artistry to a familiar rhetorical tradition in African American letters. But I also use the gerund "dreaming" deliberately. This move "from noun to verb," as Nathaniel Mackey has written, "linguistically accentuates action among a people whose ability to act is curtailed by racist constraints," and is meant to emphasize the active, imaginative ways in which Black artists engaged with opera.[50] And while these figures' ambitions were often deeply personal—core to their individual senses of artistry—they are ultimately best understood as occurring in ensemble: independent, yet interwoven. Some Black operatic activities were crafted by actual ensembles (a performance by a company of singers, for example), while others were collective in the sense that they were fostered by broader musical and social communities. Moreover, individual aspirations were bound up with a commitment to structural change: Black artists paired opera's extravagantly creative aesthetics with a conviction that the art form's cultural and social significance could be remade. Their shared efforts transformed the landscape of American opera, dreaming into being a world in which the art form could yield new artistic and political meanings.

To convey the scope and significance of this endeavor, I introduce a new conceptual term: Black operatic counterculture.[51] Black artists' engagements with opera were far more than a reactive response to white supremacy; as they built institutions and communities, reinterpreted existing works, and composed new ones, they crafted a distinct cultural formation with its own coherent logic and parameters. I argue that by claiming the art form's grand aesthetics as creative resources for the project of Black world-making, African Americans radically theorized and enacted opera's generative potential. Composers, performers, and critics collectively showed that opera's sonic grandeur and dramatic maximalism equipped it to express the complexity of Black life. Largely uninterested in assimilationist conformity, these artists embraced operatic aesthetics in a spirit of reclamation and generation by asserting a historical relationship to the art form, embracing the expressive power of the operatic voice, and repurposing operatic composition to interpret the Black diasporic past.

Black operatic counterculture facilitated creative self-making, enabling African American artists to step outside the conditions that shaped their

lives on and beyond the stage. It not only functioned as an alternative to a US-based tradition of Black stage entertainment rooted in blackface minstrelsy and evolving into other harmful, exploitative representations, but also freed its participants from returning perpetually to the pathos of the spirituals, or presenting realist art that offered sociologically legible evidence of Black suffering.[52] Eschewing the narrow representational frameworks so often bestowed on Black performers, operatic artists embraced the art form's spectacular, even fantastical nature. Opera is characterized by its patent unreality, as recent criticism has emphasized: it is an "impossible art," per Matthew Aucoin; one "that encourages us to dream, fantasize, and transform ourselves and the world," per Alison Kinney.[53] This aesthetic quality converged with the speculative conditions under which Black operatic artists worked, insofar as their hopes and visions far exceeded the possibilities available to them within the crushing constraints of Jim Crow and white supremacy. Taking seriously what Robin Kelley might call these artists' "freedom dreams," and the possibilities that emerge therein, I emphasize the affective contours of these artists' experiences, as well as the breadth of their aesthetic ambitions.[54]

Such endeavors rested on another of opera's signature qualities: its collaborative praxis. Moving away from the familiar story of the exceptional Black singer who overcomes structural obstacles to enter a predominantly white cultural space—what Farah Jasmine Griffin terms the "spectacle of the singing black woman"—I focus less on individual careers and more on collective efforts.[55] As a result, narratives of "groundbreaking" acts of desegregation do not animate my inquiry; while I am interested in these activities insofar as they were an important avenue of Black artists' ambition, my primary focus is how these artists conceived of opera's significance within their own lives. Another meaning of the "lower frequencies" is useful here: frequency's etymological root is the Latin "frequentia," meaning a crowd or multitude. Although sometimes associated with solitary figures like the (male) composer and the (female) diva, opera is an intensely social art form that necessitates creative collaboration among its participants.[56] Like their counterparts in other corners of the Black classical music world who, as Samantha Ege has argued, "shaped a network that gave them space to thrive as individuals, as well as space to thrive in ensemble," Black operatic artists embraced the art form's intrinsically collective qualities as a way to forge new solidarities, both with one another and with the broader communities that their efforts reached.[57] As they created various ensembles—companies, choruses, audiences—opera not only circulated within the Black public

sphere but itself *became* a public sphere, one where new social arrangements could be generated.

Black operatic counterculture's aesthetic and social imperatives were entwined with its political significance. Although opera's dominant whiteness meant that Black artists consistently faced racist barriers, it is not the case that participating in opera was an *inherently* oppositional act. To the contrary, Black participation in opera might be—and often has been—interpreted as a way to seek access to the perceived advantages offered by the genre's elite associations, or a class-based iteration of respectability politics.[58] ("A race that hums operas will stay ahead of a race that simply hums the 'blues,'" sniffed an editorialist in *The Messenger* in 1924.[59]) Yet opera's political connotations were distinctly malleable: inclusive of, but ultimately far more capacious than, a commitment to uplift and respectability. Enacted by socially constituted ensembles that were committed to challenging cultural norms of race and genre, Black operatic counterculture created the conditions for opera to become an arena for activism and dissent.

No singular ideological outlook emerged; nor was its political potential limited to the singular goal of demanding inclusion in the operatic mainstream. Rather, Black artists used opera to unsettle the color line in creative ways that were meaningful within and beyond Black communities. Singers and listeners embraced opera's associations with cosmopolitanism and mobility, imagining themselves as subjects whose aesthetic and political aspirations reached beyond the parameters of the US cultural scene and its reductive conceptions of Black artistry. Critics and intellectuals elucidated the art form's complicity in extant systems of white supremacy and demanded change, framing the opera house as a key battleground in the Black freedom struggle. Thinking beyond the context of the Jim Crow United States, composers and performers also marshalled opera's grand aesthetics in service of diasporic cultural citizenship, remaking the art form as a modern venue for Black liberation.

Black operatic counterculture thrived over the course of several decades, and its trajectory was not determined exclusively by the decisions of white institutions and tastemakers. Challenging the typical periodization of Black participation in opera as beginning in earnest during the civil rights era, I reframe iconic events such as the premiere of *Porgy and Bess* (1935) and Marian Anderson's Metropolitan Opera debut (1955) as culminations rather than beginnings, showing how they emerged from and relied on decades of operatic activity. While this temporal reorientation excavates the deeper historical roots of African Americans' engagement with opera, it

also makes possible a shift in focus toward efforts that did not attain mainstream recognition: the ephemeral events, minimally documented happenings, and ambitious but unrealized ideas that were crucial to Black operatic creativity. This broad temporal scope also illuminates opera's interconnectedness with other facets of Black creative and political life. Like the voices that resonated beneath and through the 135th Street branch library in July 1925, operatic undercurrents reverberate across African American history and culture. Note that in 1853, the young abolitionist Sarah Parker Remond took an activist stance by purchasing a ticket to the whites-only section of a Boston theater for a performance of Verdi's *Don Pasquale*. Consider that W. E. B. Du Bois's short story "Of the Coming of John" in *The Souls of Black Folk* (1903) and pivotal scenes in James Weldon Johnson's *The Autobiography of an Ex-Colored Man* (1912) take place at the opera. Listen for the quotations from *Rigoletto* and *Carmen* in Louis Armstrong's "West End Blues"; the classically trained timbre of Odetta's voice; or Mahalia Jackson's recounting that she listened to Roland Hayes to learn how to sing.[60] As these examples suggest, an analysis of opera predicated on its supposed difference from other creative practices is bound to be inadequate. To consider Black artists' engagements with opera is thus an opportunity to consider the whole of African American culture from a newly elucidating vantage point.

My choice to frame opera as counterculture is also meant to disentangle the art form from its associations with cultural hegemony. Other scholars have emphasized the vitality of Black opera beyond the art form's mainstream: most notably, Naomi André characterizes Black opera as a "shadow culture" whose "parallel, yet obscured, lineage to the dominant tradition" endures across a wide range of times and places.[61] The particular experience of early twentieth-century African Americans—who not only lacked access to the operatic mainstream, but also worked at a distance from other, newly popular genres of Black music and theater—might also be understood as what Raymond Williams calls residual culture: more aligned with past cultural formations than presently dominant ones, it nonetheless remained an active, and thus potentially oppositional, cultural practice.[62] Building on these insights, I argue that not only was Black operatic counterculture of equal importance to the "dominant tradition," but also that its shadowy, residual, lower-frequency status—its removal from mainstream view, its partially realized nature—was precisely what imbued it with radical, countercultural potential.

In its commitment to remaking the intellectual and aesthetic terrain on which opera was created, Black operatic counterculture was a characteristi-

cally modern project. Previous studies of twentieth-century Black musicians in predominantly white genres have tended to describe their work as proceeding along two parallel but distinct paths: one that confronted segregation by securing a place for African Americans within existing institutions, and another that sought to create an autonomous cultural sphere.[63] Black artists working in opera were interested in each of these objectives, yet I argue that their goals were more complex and, ultimately, more expansive. Following Paul Gilroy's paradigmatic work on transnational Black artistry as a "counterculture of modernity," as well as Daphne Brooks's theorization of Black women's "confounding" role in the making of modern popular music, I consider opera as a counterculture in, but not of, modernity—an endeavor distinguished by visionary ambition and "firstness" while also maintaining deep connections with the past.[64]

Yet in an era defined by the rise of the modern culture industries, opera was also, importantly, *not* popular culture—a fact that demands critical inquiry. Put simply: why opera? What compelled Black composers, performers, critics, and audiences to devote their time, attention, labor, and thought to this work? Ardently loved by its proponents, the art form never enjoyed truly widespread appeal during these years. If Black popular musicians made a remarkable impact on public culture under conditions of duress—they were, as Brooks writes, figures "whose country gave them nothing and who, in return, gave the country the defining popular art of the twentieth century"—then operatic musicians worked under more ambivalent circumstances.[65] Opera's peripheral status meant it lacked the mass visibility that often motivates quests for cultural representation; yet this under-the-radar status enabled participants to evade the spectacularizing, even traumatizing pressures faced by Black artists on popular stages. Opera's prestigious connotations bolstered its appeal to elite audiences in an era of Talented Tenth ideology (and arguably decreased its ability to reach broad constituencies); yet this status also enabled it to skirt the racialized demands of culture industries that gobbled up Black artistry for profit. Opera's high financial cost made it difficult to produce; yet the aesthetic possibilities enabled by that expense—elaborate sets and costumes, large casts and orchestras, opulent venues—were fundamental to its creative appeal. Opera's Eurocentric origins fostered a perception that it was divorced from other facets of African American culture; yet the collaboration intrinsic to the genre facilitated meaningful intellectual and artistic exchanges among its participants, enabling them to make bold claims about Black politics and sociality. These paradoxical conditions are vital to understanding both the art form's limits and its oppositional potential.

This book's narrative of Black operatic counterculture spans six decades. Although it begins with the premiere of an opera by composer Harry Lawrence Freeman in 1893 and concludes with Marian Anderson's Metropolitan Opera debut in 1955, I do not mean to present a list of steps in an inexorable progression toward the ultimate goal of desegregation. Instead, I show how African Americans maintained a consistent presence in opera throughout the first half of the twentieth century. This approach has an ethical basis: it refuses the logic of exceptionalism that was and is still used to justify opera's disproportionate whiteness, namely the idea that only extraordinary individuals are truly deserving of a place in either the opera house or the historical record. The story that I assemble is panoramic rather than comprehensive. It shows how Black operatic counterculture emerged in churches, schools, theaters, and stadiums, in living rooms and music studios, on the pages of newspapers and in the realm of its creators' imaginations.

One corollary of Black opera's absence from the scholarly literature is the assumption that Black operatic musicians, if they existed at all, went unacknowledged in their own time, treated as novelties at best or pariahs at worst. Yet not only did Black operatic musicians exist; they were also both celebrated within their own communities *and* invested in the project of recording theirs and others' achievements for posterity.[66] Narrating their lived experiences, intellectual contributions, and visionary theoretical work as fully as possible requires a wide variety of sources. While I draw on scores, libretti, sound recordings, correspondence, oral histories, programs, photographs, scrapbooks, and memoirs, I am especially indebted to the archive of the Black press. If white-authored journalistic sources tended to propagate voyeuristic narratives that framed Black participation in opera as racialized spectacle, the Black press offered a fuller perspective by way of reviews, essays, criticism, social announcements, and advertisements that illuminate the quotidian texture of African American cultural history in abundant detail. Other crucially important facets of Black opera—lost manuscripts, unrecorded voices, unrealized dreams—lie beyond the scope of print, inviting more speculative methods of engagement with the archive.[67]

In fact, Black operatic counterculture thrived in the archive, a paradoxically generative condition that can be attributed partially to these artists' marginalized status. Lacking access to traditional institutions like the opera house and the canon, many artists aimed to secure their legacy via print, fashioning a rich textual resource in the process. Indeed, a (counter)historical impulse was at the core of Black operatic counterculture. History-making was a key facet of opera's broader canon-building at the turn of the

century, enacted via a commitment to staging a standard repertory via increasingly standardized productions. Black operatic counterculture remade that canonical practice, too, with participants taking care to document their own labor and artistry. Like the jubilee singers whose renditions of the spirituals embodied Frederick Douglass's assertion that "every tone was a testimony," they imagined opera as a site for the creation of Black historical narrative.[68] They understood that to articulate a theory of Blackness in relation to opera was also to offer myriad counterhistories: of the relationship between Blackness and Western art music; of a centuries-old art form; of what Black creativity had been and could yet be.

The book's opening chapters focus on how Black operatic counterculture was theorized and enacted in its earliest stages. Chapter 1 shows how, during the "postbellum, pre-Harlem" period, a group of immensely ambitious figures—composer Harry Lawrence Freeman, impresario Theodore Drury, and critic Sylvester Russell—shared a conviction that they were on the threshold of a new era in Black musical life, in which opera would play an integral part. Freeman's first opera *The Martyr* (1893), Drury's opera company (est. 1900), and Russell's criticism were theoretically grand projects; each was also a social act, made possible by the ensembles that realized their ideas. Chapter 2 explores how practitioners established a place for opera within the Black public sphere during the 1910s and 1920s. Vocalists and pedagogues fostered connections between the Black operatic voice and the project of self-making. Critics, including Lester Walton and Nora Douglas Holt, introduced their readers to opera in the pages of the Black press, while educators such as E. Azalia Hackley trained vast ensembles of amateur singers. Their efforts remade opera's experiential meanings, expanding both the cultural significance of operatic sound and the institutional landscape in which it could be heard.

The next three chapters focus on developments that took place beginning in the 1920s, when the cultural conditions of the Harlem Renaissance—characterized by both a flowering of activity among Black artists and intellectuals, and a vogue of white interest in Black performance—presented African Americans with opportunities to engage with opera in previously impossible ways: as guest artists with white companies, for instance. In some ways, these years marked a new stage of Black operatic counterculture. Black artists made more concerted efforts to challenge the art form's history of white supremacist exclusion, both by claiming space within its central institutions and by creating expansive, conceptually ambitious new works about Black life. But important similarities linked this era to earlier ones. Chapter 3 emphasizes these continuities by focusing on the Black operagoers, workers,

and supernumeraries whose presence in the mainstream opera house dated back to the late nineteenth century. These figures crucially shaped the racial politics of operatic institutions, and if their relationship to opera was not always explicitly oppositional—they tended not to make overt calls for systemic change, or to challenge the genre's representational norms—they nonetheless found creative ways to engage with the art form as listeners and laborers. In Chapter 4, singers take center stage: in particular, Black women including Florence Cole-Talbert and Caterina Jarboro, who sang principal roles in mainstream opera houses during the late 1920s and early 1930s. Appearing in the racialized title role of *Aida* in both Europe and the United States, they used a combination of sonic, visual, and narrative strategies to reimagine Verdi's opera in relation to contemporary racial politics, and to highlight their own position as advocates for social change. Chapter 5 explores how composers repurposed opera as a genre through which to make historical claims about the African American past. As popular new white-authored operas put forth stale tropes about Blackness, Black composers insisted on the art form's capacity to serve as a vehicle for sociopolitical world-making. Most notable among them was Shirley Graham, whose opera *Tom-Tom,* a revolutionary Afrodiasporic epic, premiered before an audience of thousands in a Cleveland baseball stadium in 1932.

The final chapters of the book turn to what is typically considered to be an era of "firsts," bookended by the 1935 premiere of George Gershwin's *Porgy and Bess* and Marian Anderson's 1955 debut at the Metropolitan Opera. During years shaped by the gathering speed of the long civil rights movement and World War II, desegregation of the operatic mainstream became a priority. Chapter 6 details how this new focus played out across the realms of composition, institution-building, and performance. Even as institutions like the National Negro Opera Company (est. 1941) and events like soprano Camilla Williams's debut with New York City Opera (1946) emphasized the democratic potential of interracial music-making in the public sphere, individual artists took care to honor the marginal roots of their work. Chapter 7 retells the well-known story of Anderson's Met debut by foregrounding the role of Black women artist-activists—including the sopranos Muriel Rahn and Ellabelle Davis, as well as the vocal coach Sylvia Olden Lee—in making such an occasion possible. It locates this triumphant event alongside two other strains of Black operatic activity: the continued struggles of Black composers to have their work produced, on the one hand, and the commemorative and archival work of artists who sought to document Black operatic history, on the other. As these intertwined

narratives show, Black opera's countercultural impulse persisted even as individuals reached the art form's centers of power.

It is easy to lose sight of how profoundly imaginative Black operatic counterculture was in its time. The fact that Black music has taken so many other deeply innovative, more popular forms over the past century means that other genres and traditions continue to take precedence in both the scholarly literature and the public imagination. More broadly, opera's contemporary reputation—as white, elite, stodgy, conservative—is so entrenched that it can be difficult to conceive of the art form as a site of radical critique or minoritarian dissent. Yet these dispiriting conditions only raise the stakes of an alternative history. Through their aesthetic and political labor, Black operatic artists redefined opera to transformative effect, embracing the art form's inventive and even liberatory possibilities.

❧ 1 ❧

The Dawning of Black Operatic Counterculture

"'Tis the hour before dawn" at the royal courtyard of Thebes, writes Harry Lawrence Freeman, and the Wailers are awash in grief. As the curtain rises on act 1 of Freeman's opera *The Martyr* after a lush orchestral overture, the six women of the chorus sing of their "pain" and "anguish" upon witnessing the suffering of Platonus, the opera's titular character.[1] Platonus, condemned to death due to his belief in Jehovah, mourns his imminent demise. His somber opening aria begins with a sorrowful lament, sung above an unyielding ostinato pattern evoking the "chains" that confine him. Then it moves into a martial, triplet-driven fanfare, a boldly stated declaration that he "fear[s] naught," because he will soon find himself in the Holy City. In the aria's concluding section, an *andante* with a waltz-like lilt, he accepts his fate with serene tranquility.[2] Despite the challenges that await him, he maintains a steadfast faith.

As day broke in onstage Egypt—in a sumptuously decorated scene "adorned by lofty pillars, resplendent with multi-colored hieroglyphics"— it was a summer evening in Denver, Colorado, where the premiere of *The Martyr* took place on August 16, 1893.[3] Freeman, a recent migrant to the city, was in his early twenties, young, confident, and ambitious. He had assembled an amateur cast of friends and peers, all newcomers to opera. The score had been completed just two weeks earlier, leaving little time for rehearsal. But if the premiere was modest in scale, the composer's aspirations were vast. Over the next six decades, Freeman would go on to compose more than twenty operas exploring the African diasporic past in epic registers.

The Denver press hailed Freeman as "the first colored man to ever compose and produce an opera."[4] This was false. The first opera by an African American composer is generally considered to be John Thomas Douglass's *Virginia's Ball*, which premiered in New York in 1868; another early composer, Louisa Melvin Delos Mars, wrote five operettas staged in Providence or Boston between 1880 and 1896.[5] Beyond the narrow question of veracity, this claim to primacy had ambivalent implications. If describing Freeman as a "first" emphasized the magnitude of his achievement, it concomitantly cast his work as a racialized novelty, reinscribing the notion that Blackness and opera were fundamentally at odds. The descriptor might be interpreted as evidence of a desire for assimilation into a historically segregated art form, or an attempt to prove cultural parity. More subversively, though, to be a "first" could also be, as George Lewis has argued, an "oppositional stance," from which the Black composer could decline to play by the established rules and instead rework a musical tradition toward distinct aesthetic and intellectual ends.[6] Such a reworking was at the heart of Freeman's operatic endeavors, in *The Martyr* and throughout his career. The opera was the first major work in a lifelong project that Freeman would, in a manifesto-like 1898 article, describe as "an entirely new attraction, in the shape of negro grand opera."[7] This subtle but significant rhetorical difference—the "first . . . ever" versus the "entirely new"—elucidates the ambitious conceptual parameters of Freeman's work. From his perspective, a new day was dawning both on and off stage for Black opera, an art form he yearned to cultivate and bring to fruition.

The 1893 premiere of *The Martyr* marks an inaugural moment in Freeman's career and for Black operatic counterculture writ large. In its earliest stages, this new creative phenomenon was concerned primarily with definitional work: the creation of a set of aesthetic, social, and intellectual parameters for Black opera, theorized and enacted across the fields of composition, performance, and criticism. In contravention to cultural-racial hierarchies that presumed an unbridgeable divide between Blackness and opera, Black operatic counterculture positioned itself against and in conversation with multiple hegemonic systems. Rather than imagining a Du Boisian ideal in which Black operatic artists were "co-workers in the kingdom of culture," it staked out a deliberately marginal relationship to the art form.[8] It shared in the Black intelligentsia's investment in racial uplift ideology to some extent, but it never reduced opera to a signifier of class status or cultural capital. It asserted African Americans' right to engage with the canon of opera (the meaning of which, James Parakilas argues, extends beyond a standard repertory and toward an entire "system of

cultural upbringing"), but it declined to accept the exclusionary premises of that canon outright.[9] It aspired to become part of modern Black expressive culture, but it contested the commodification and homogenization of that culture.

A constellation of endeavors exemplify the inaugural contours of this new cultural formation. Freeman put forth an immensely ambitious vision for Black opera and created foundational works in the genre, including *The Martyr*. His work was shaped by the scale of his aspirations, the marginal position from which he aimed to realize them, and his use of the print archive to write himself into history regardless. Whereas Freeman maintained that "negro grand opera" required newly composed works, others used canonical operas to showcase Black ensembles' talents. Baritone and impresario Theodore Drury founded a grand opera company in New York City in 1900, the first organized by and comprised of African Americans. As he trained an ensemble of singers with little operatic experience, Drury used performance to both embrace and critique the canon, sidestepping the elite social practices increasingly associated with opera in favor of what Saidiya Hartman might call a more "wayward" approach to performance and pedagogy.[10] The singer-turned-theater-critic Sylvester Russell, who actively supported both Freeman's and Drury's projects, sketched out a vision of opera's centrality within the emerging field of modern Black culture. Reaching a vast audience through his national critical platform, Russell reoriented prominent models of cultural hierarchy toward liberatory ends. Although Freeman, Drury, and Russell worked independently from one another, they were exceptionally influential figures within their respective spheres of composition, performance, and criticism. Their work collectively advanced a theoretical claim about opera's aesthetic and social suitability to become an apex of Black cultural production.

These figures' ambitions often exceeded the material opportunities available to them—a circumstance that, paradoxically, allowed for the exploration of expansive creative possibilities. Like many Talented Tenth intellectuals, Freeman, Drury, and Russell were charismatic male leaders whose notion of racial uplift walked a fine line between a broadly conceived commitment to collective progress and a narrower, class-based attitude that equated racial progress with the success of elite men.[11] They worked in a curious space shaped by the collision between the totality of an artistic vision and its incomplete realization. But it would be an oversimplification to understand these men as unfulfilled visionaries—martyrs, perhaps, for the Black operatic cause. In practice, these operatic endeavors were made possible not by individual "great men," but rather by ensem-

bles of historical actors: chorus members, soloists, students, writers, editors, audiences, listeners. These collectives functioned as a nexus between aspirations and realities, a mutually constituted space between grand theoretical vision and embodied social practice. Their work ultimately produced Black operatic counterculture's meanings, even more so than (or at least, in conjunction with) the idealistic theorists who imagined a future beyond what contemporaneous conditions made possible.

Decentering the presumed leader and recognizing the ensemble as cocreators of cultural meaning brings into view how early participants in Black operatic counterculture unsettled the art form's relationship to the notion of "high culture" and complicated dominant conceptions of racial uplift. Fred Moten observes that opera is "born in and by the vernacular, delivered gesturally, by bodies more likely than not to be out of all compass, hyperbolic, hyperphysical, nonsensical. Opera always threatens, in the delivery of its material, to deliver nothing more."[12] The material facts of who is onstage and what they are doing—the embodied act of performance—can problematize or even supersede the art form's presumed cultural meanings. As scholars of opera and identity in the early twentieth-century United States have observed, marginalized groups—including Jews, Italian Americans, and women—actively contested the art form's sacralization through their acts of interpretation and listening.[13] It proved similarly rich interpretive terrain for Black performers and listeners, who rejected reductive notions of opera as a proxy for respectability or assimilation. Instead, operatic ensembles became focal points of what Imani Perry calls "black formalism": class-crossing facets of Black public culture that, instead of presuming the attention of a white audience, existed alongside rather than in competition with vernacular practices, making space for "an articulation and expression of grace and identity that existed in refuge from the violence of white supremacy."[14]

Early Black operatic counterculture also had a mutually constitutive relationship with the African American cultural mainstream. As Freeman, Drury, Russell, and their ensembles entered the historically white space of opera, they were immersed in the richly heterogeneous Black cultural scene of the "postbellum, pre-Harlem" moment. Even as they set themselves apart from popular forms such as ragtime and vaudeville, they evoked the collective artistry developed by all-Black groups, from Sissieretta Jones's Black Patti Troubadours to the burst of theatrical productions with all-Black casts in 1890s New York City. They worked during what Perry characterizes as a heyday of "Black associational life," in which communities established institutions—schools, churches, newspapers, clubs, literary societies,

mutual aid organizations—through which to strengthen cultural and social identity.[15] Black formalist operatic associations—from the hodgepodge cast of friends that Freeman assembled for *The Martyr* to more deliberately organized institutions—counter-institutionalized opera in a manner that was deeply indebted to models from within African American artistic life. Often working outside major urban centers, and beyond the institutional confines of the opera house, they aimed neither to enter nor to create an autonomous "shadow" of the operatic mainstream, but rather to reinvent it—a goal made evident in the aspirational, often imaginative quality of their collective work.

"Grand Opera in Every Sense of the Word"

The fairgrounds of the World's Columbian Exposition in Chicago opened to the public on May 1, 1893. Designed to commemorate the four-hundred-year anniversary of Columbus's arrival in the New World and make a case for US global power on the cusp of the twentieth century, the event was monumental in scale. More than twenty million visitors strolled through the palatial exhibition buildings known as the White City, and cavorted along the Midway Plaisance, which combined amusements like the Ferris wheel with pseudoscientific ethnographic displays of "primitive" peoples from around the world. In a fast-growing city where most of the population comprised either immigrants or the children of immigrants, the World's Fair offered an assertive display of national pride—one that all but erased the presence of African Americans. The organizers' refusal to include Black Americans famously prompted protests led by Ida B. Wells and Frederick Douglass, and many interpreted the subsequent establishment of a "Colored American Day," on August 25, 1893, as a token gesture of appeasement.[16] Despite these exclusionary conditions, an illustrious gathering emerged. A concert held that day featured Desseria Plato and Sidney Woodward, two young stars of the Black classical stage, as well as a reading by Paul Laurence Dunbar and a speech by Douglass. Yet what did not occur was equally noteworthy. The composer and violinist Will Marion Cook had begun work the previous year on an opera based on *Uncle Tom's Cabin*, which he envisioned being performed at the fair by such luminaries as Sissieretta Jones and Harry T. Burleigh. The proposed opera had garnered financial support from Douglass and extensive promotion in the Black press, which promised a "great scheme" with a cast featuring "only members of the race"; Jones declared that it would include "the most beautiful music she'd ever heard."[17] But for reasons that remain unclear, when the day ar-

rived, both Jones and Cook failed to appear, and only a brief duet from Cook's opera was sung. Instead, the program featured a selection of arias by Verdi, Meyerbeer, and Bizet.[18] One could hardly ask for a neater exemplification of the struggles that Black composers faced at this early stage: their work was ambitiously imagined but precarious in a cultural landscape hostile to their very existence.

Also present at the Columbian Exposition was the Czech composer Antonín Dvořák. Earlier that year, in conjunction with the premiere of his *New World Symphony,* Dvořák had proclaimed in the pages of the *New York Herald* that "Negro melodies" should be the "true basis for a distinctively American school of music," which "must strike its roots deeply into its own soil."[19] Dvořák's statement garnered ample critical and popular attention, including praise from African American critics. But it was neither a new idea nor a radical one. Dvořák emphasized the potential overlap between Black musical material and white authorship over the contributions of Black composers themselves—an extractive way of thinking more closely aligned with the "love and theft" paradigm of blackface minstrelsy than with the liberal cultural pluralism it is often assumed to evoke.[20] "Who is to write us oratorios, symphonies, sonatas, operas, &c. in the African style?" asked a commentator in the *Baltimore Sun* in response to Dvořák's pronouncement. He answered his own question by falling back on nationalist and racialized frameworks: "We shall unquestionably have to ask our colored musicians, by study and application, to develop the principles of negro melody and give us a true negro opera . . . The world will readily welcome the appearance of a composer who will combine the hilarity of the African with the grace of the Frenchman and the sentiment of the Italian."[21] Though the writer failed to acknowledge it, a composer working toward "true negro opera" already existed: Harry Lawrence Freeman. But Freeman declined to ground his work in the "principles of negro melody" described here, rejecting the very notion of Black music that undergirded Dvořák's project and, by extension, other essentialist notions of musical and racial difference. Such a constrained vision simply could not encompass the magnitude of his aspirations.

A maximalist artist with a sweeping vision of opera's role within Black cultural production, Freeman embraced the aesthetic plenitude of grand opera in multiple senses. In an approach to self-fashioning that evoked both the image of the revered, solitary classical composer and the masculinist trope of the Talented Tenth "race man," he styled himself a grand figure, even a genius.[22] He also used opera to put forth an expansive vision of Blackness that was intentionally international in scope. His work suggested that

opera's grandeur equipped it to tell the grand stories of a global people; it was therefore an apt artistic site for the creation of Afrodiasporic solidarity. He offered a notion of opera's cumulative aesthetic, racial, and historical potential that remade Blackness—which had customarily been absent from narratives of opera's past and present—into the central standpoint from which the art form could and should develop.

Freeman was born in Cleveland, Ohio on October 9, 1869. His father, Sylvester Lemuel Freeman, was a carpenter from a family of free Black landholders. His mother, Agnes Sims Freeman, was known for her lovely soprano voice. She died while Freeman was an infant, and he was raised mostly by his grandmother, Mary Louise Sims, who had been enslaved as a child. In Cleveland, the family lived in a home that Freeman's paternal grandfather had built in the 1840s, and they enjoyed a measure of class privilege: Freeman's son, Valdo, would later recall that his father's family was "very well off," and that "as a child he was spoiled."[23] During his youth, Freeman played the piano and sang in a quartet; from age twelve, he served as organist at Mount Zion Congregational Church. Educated at Cleveland's Central High School, he never obtained a college education and remained a proud autodidact throughout his life.

Many biographical details about Freeman's early years derive from his published and unpublished writings, including a four-hundred-page manuscript titled *The Negro in Music and Drama*—a monumentally detailed cultural history that doubles as a work of proud self-representation. By his own account, Freeman's "early environment was a happy one," and he moved in elite cultural circles from a young age.[24] In contrast to the prevailing view that New York and Chicago were the primary hubs of African American culture, he maintained that Cleveland, "as early as the late 80's, had become the focal point—the Half-Way-Rendezvous of the sepian artistic nomad."[25] Among his childhood schoolmates was the singer Rachel Walker, later known as the "Creole Nightingale," whom he accompanied at local concerts.[26] The celebrated coloratura soprano Madame Marie Selika, a regular guest at a neighbor's home, would listen to a teenage Freeman play the piano; another visitor was the poet Paul Laurence Dunbar, whom Freeman first met in 1887.[27]

Freeman, his father, and his stepmother moved to Denver around 1889, joining a small but fast-growing African American population.[28] He taught piano and voice lessons; took up a position directing music at the city's Central Baptist Church; and attended social functions like masquerade balls and variety shows.[29] Denver's rich musical scene encompassed touring English-language troupes, local amateur productions, and

genre-crossing offerings by itinerant musicians.[30] Although performances by African American musicians were rarer, the California-based Hyers Sisters, highly successful concert artists, had appeared multiple times, offering a double bill of *Out of Bondage,* a sympathetic depiction of life under slavery, and the "operatic bouffe extravaganza" *Urlina, the African Princess.*[31] Minstrel troupes also appeared regularly on local stages. Just weeks before the premiere of *The Martyr,* the Tabor Opera House featured blackface performer George Thatcher's *Africa,* a comic opera in six scenes.[32]

On the evening of March 9, 1891, a friend invited Freeman to attend a performance of Wagner's *Tannhäuser* by the Emma Juch Grand Opera Company. Although most of the era's traveling opera troupes focused on French and Italian repertoire, Juch's troupe had a penchant for Wagner, whose operas were becoming an object of national cultural fascination.[33] As Freeman later recounted, he was initially "very reluctant . . . never having attended an opera, and having been reared with the idea that they were everything that was low and degrading." But he "soon discovered [his] error."[34] The performance changed his life: "When I retired that night I could not sleep as the music was a revelation to me and I was stirred by strange emotions. At five o'clock in the morning I arose, and seating myself at the piano, composed my first piece—a waltz song of the dimensions of Arditi's 'Ecstasy.' Every day thereafter for two hundred days I composed a new song. None of them, however, had words. It was some months later that I discovered I could write verses as well as music. These songs were all composed before I had ever had one lesson in theory or composition."[35] After this epiphany, Freeman moved fast. Just over two years later, *The Martyr* was complete.

A tale of love, faith, death, and power set in ancient Egypt, *The Martyr* exemplifies the spectacle and excess of nineteenth-century European grand opera while also displaying a strikingly modern originality. As David Gutkin observes, the work's "exotic subject matter [and] romantic score would in many respects set the mold for his output over the next fifty years," serving as the foundation for an ambitious operatic vision.[36] A synopsis written by Freeman articulates the plot in his characteristically elaborate rhetorical style:

> Act I. Platonus, an Egyptian nobleman, having forsaken the faith of his forefathers and accepted the Lord Jehovah as his deity, has been cast into prison. He is subsequently brought to trial by Rei, the High Priest of the land, in the presence of the King and Queen, flanked

by the royal retinue, as well as the vast assemblage of courtiers and their ladies.

He remained steadfast to his new allegiance, even casting aside the importunities of the beautiful Shirah, his betrothed, who has come to the court seeking to cause him to renounce his alien creed. When all else has failed to move Platonus, Rei prevails upon him to give some great manifestation of the power of his vaunted God, whereupon the prisoner approaches the colossal statue of Osiris and hurls it from its base. Consternation prevails, and amid the flashing of livid flames of lightning and mighty crashes of thunder, the entire assemblage rushes forth—terror-stricken. All except Shirah who falls prone at the foot of the dais—apparently lifeless—as the curtain falls.

Act 2. As the curtain rises upon this act, Shirah is discovered in the same inert condition; but soon afterwards consciousness returns, and kneeling before the shrine she implores the aid of Mother Isus on behalf of her condemned beloved. Pharaoh enters and beseeches her to grant him her favor, whereupon the Queen suddenly enters, accompanied by Rei, denounces the unfortunate maiden and decrees the death of the Martyr. Later Platonus is heard proclaiming the glories of Jehovah as the flames envelop him.

Note: there is no dancing in this opera.[37]

The synopsis illuminates *The Martyr*'s indebtedness to multiple conventions of nineteenth-century European grand opera. Although the term grand opera eventually came to encompass a variety of large-scale works, it originally referred to works by French composers performed at the Paris Opéra beginning in the 1840s. Grand operas had no spoken dialogue, consisted of four or five acts, and required an army of performers, including stellar soloists, large choruses and orchestras, dancers, and supernumeraries. Plots merged interpersonal narratives with broader historical backdrops taken from various eras, often with contemporary political overtones. Scenery and costumes were decadent and technologically spectacular.[38] *The Martyr*, which Celia Davidson vividly describes as "a collage—a scrapbook of ideas, and the use of those ideas within Freeman's concept of the musical techniques of the latter half of the nineteenth century," lies firmly within this tradition.[39] It calls for six principal singers (four men and two women); a mixed chorus; and a large orchestra of strings, doubled winds, two saxophones, four horns, three trombones, tuba, timpani, bass drum, celesta, and harp. Easy lilting melodies alternate with virtuosic passages full

of wide skips over extensive ranges; long, lush orchestral interludes create an atmosphere of extravagance. Set in an ancient and putatively exotic locale, it features a "vast assemblage" of choristers and supernumeraries, and the drama is heightened by "livid flames of lightning and mighty crashes of thunder." The sole departure from grand opera's conventions—the exclusion of dance, flagged in the final sentence of the synopsis—serves to distance Freeman's work from the song-and-dance format common to minstrelsy and Black musical comedy.

Ancient Egypt might seem an unlikely setting for an inaugural work in Black operatic counterculture, but in fact, this milieu gestured toward multiple artistic legacies. It recalled the specific antecedent of Verdi's *Aida;* both operas feature a love triangle, characters who challenge national loyalty, and a chorus of slaves. More broadly, it facilitated what David Charlton identifies as grand opera's thematization of "political imperatives refracted from the distant past towards the composer's present."[40] As Scott Trafton has shown, ancient Egypt was a ubiquitous and contradictory symbol in the nineteenth-century United States, eliciting notions of both "secular empire" and "religious despotism," both the tyranny of slaveholding and the miracle of escape from bondage.[41] From the hieroglyphic-inscribed obelisks featured at the 1893 World's Fair as a symbol of US imperial power, to the invocation of a liberated "Egypt land" in the spiritual "Go Down, Moses," symbols of Egypt abounded in the cultural imaginary. Claiming space in this discursive landscape, *The Martyr* marshalled the idea of ancient Egypt to invoke the grandeur of Italian opera and the pathos of the spirituals in equal measure, repurposing a fluid cultural symbol as a locus of Black operatic counterculture.

The Martyr also joined a tradition by which nineteenth-century African American intellectuals linked ancient Egypt to Ethiopia, positing that Ethiopia was an unacknowledged source of Egyptian greatness (and, thus, of what white scholars imagined as a birthplace of "civilization").[42] Freeman reiterated these associations in his book manuscript *The Negro in Music and Drama,* which bears the epigraph "Ethiopia shall stretch forth her hand unto God in song" and is dedicated to "those forbears [*sic*] of our own who suffered, bled and died in martyrdom that we, their beloved progeny, might thrive and evolve."[43] By placing Ethiopia, Egypt, and martyrdom at the literal forefront of his work, Freeman amalgamated his opera, the whole of Black musical history, and the figure of the martyr: a hero who breaks from tradition, bears witness, and sacrifices himself for the sake of his people. He left unspecified the identity of the forebears—perhaps they were his enslaved ancestors, Black musicians of earlier eras, or even the composer

himself—in a manner that emphasized the interplay between old and new at the heart of Egyptian symbolism.

A series of ensembles—social formations remixed and reassembled for the stage—realized *The Martyr*. For its first performance, which took place at Denver's Turner Hall in August 1893, the composer recruited a cast of African American amateurs. The principals included his friend and roommate Abram Williamson, a cook, as Pharaoh, and the schoolteacher Adah Roberts as Pharaoh's wife, Meriamum. William Carey, a waiter, played the heroic title character Platonus, and Ida Williamson was his beloved, Shirah. Edward Bennett, a pharmacy clerk, appeared as the high priest Rei, and several members of the church where Freeman served as music director sang in the chorus.[44] (The composer's son, Valdo, would later recall that throughout his career, Freeman "had to train his own singers. He had to train people that were domestics—maids, cooks, chauffeurs—he had to teach them to sing."[45]) Freeman likely played the score from the piano rather than assembling an orchestra. If it is difficult to imagine how a group of newly trained amateurs and a single pianist might fully convey the opera's musical and dramatic grandeur, these conditions may also have emphasized the sheer potential of the Black operatic tradition—how, under more hospitable circumstances, it would ultimately flourish.

In October 1893, the composer traveled to Chicago, where he attended the Columbian Exposition and staged *The Martyr* at the city's Bethel AME Church. After moving back to Cleveland in the mid-1890s, he staged the opera twice more, in 1895 and again in 1900. From 1902 until 1904, he taught at Wilberforce University in Xenia, Ohio, where he revived *The Martyr* with a cast of student performers; his wife, Carlotta, a talented singer and actress whom he had met in 1898, took the role of Shirah. Freeman also incorporated his operatic expertise into his work as a musical director for Black traveling shows: a quintet from act 2 of *The Martyr* appeared in Ernest Hogan's *Rufus Rastus* (1906–1907), alongside other operatic music he composed especially for the show.[46] Critical responses reflect the distance between Freeman's aspirations and the circumstances under which his work was performed. Reviewers foregrounded Freeman's innate skill: one, for instance, lauded him as "one of the greatest musical geniuses and composers, belonging to the Afro-American race, in this or many other country [*sic*]," and called *The Martyr* "his masterpiece."[47] Yet accounts of the performances themselves tended to be less complimentary. One reviewer marveled that the music in *Rufus Rastus* "was simply grand opera . . . capably handled by a chorus unexcelled in training and knowledge of higher

musical art."[48] The pseudonymous S. A. Tan offered a tongue-in-cheek account of a Cleveland performance of *The Martyr:* "The music started off gently, then there was a biff! Bang! Br-r-r-du-lurn-dum! And a rolling sound for all the world like a flat car loaded with railroad iron and broken bottles running off down the hill."[49] A persistent dissonance between Freeman's ambitions and the conditions of their realization emerged, reflecting the marginal status of Black operatic counterculture within the broader cultural landscape.

In parallel with his efforts to stage *The Martyr,* Freeman continued to develop an aspirational vision for Black opera throughout and beyond his compositions. Like other Black artists and intellectuals of his era, he repurposed the evolutionist rhetoric of "cultural development" to antiracist ends.[50] A faith in Black culture's potential pervades *The Negro in Music and Drama,* in which Freeman describes the early years of his own career as an "embryonic period" and characterizes other promising Black artists as "embryonic aspirants."[51] The leader of that effort would be none other than Freeman himself. Early in his career, the Cleveland press characterized him as a "professional musical genius," "real genius," and "great genius." One article breathlessly reported, "Freeman can conceive, musically, great emotions and passions of the human soul; then it only remains for him to write down his conceptions."[52] Another praised Freeman's "divine gift," noting that he "was on the threshold of his career and has unconquered worlds before him."[53] This emphasis on Freeman's genius worked against the white compositional vogue for Black music exemplified by Dvořák's statement: by casting Freeman as uniquely gifted, it foreclosed the appropriation or cooptation of his musical ideas.

Freeman was often linked to one particular operatic genius: Richard Wagner. *The Martyr* makes use of Wagnerian leitmotifs (for instance, a bombastic, martial triplet rhythm that typically precedes Pharaoh's entrance) and features a subtle but unmistakable "Tristan" chord in Platonus's opening aria.[54] "Wagner was his big man," his son Valdo recalled.[55] Freeman kept a bust of the composer on display in his studio and pored over the scores for *Rienzi, Der Fliegende Holländer, Tannhäuser, Tristan und Isolde, Die Meistersinger von Nürnberg,* and the Ring Cycle to make "an exhaustive study, dissecting them bar by bar, balancing every phrase."[56] He embraced his status as the "colored Wagner," placing the term at the top of his resume.[57] But as Kira Thurman points out, although the sobriquet emphasized affinities between the two composers, "*the* difference between Freeman and Wagner accounts for the particular hardships Freeman experienced throughout his career: Freeman was Black."[58]

Yet race was never only a limitation on Freeman's success; it was also a constitutive component of his aesthetic vision. He made the audacious argument that grand opera, which he described as "the conception, evolution and final development of all the aesthetic arts—the fusion of the vital elements of music, drama and the dance," represented the desirable and inevitable culmination of *all* Black cultural production.[59] "When we say Grand Opera, it doesn't mean musical operetta, but Grand Opera in every sense of the word," he elaborated. "Speaking of Negro originality, here is the greatest field in which to prove it. It goes without saying that such a venture would mark for the Negro the most wonderful of any undertaking."[60] Freeman wrote this idea into being in his operas, through-composed works in multiple acts that called for large casts and orchestras, elaborate sets, and lavish costumes. The plots were fantastical and convoluted; the libretti, all of which he wrote himself, made use of high-flown, archaic language far removed from vernacular speech. Such grandeur attracted both admiration and exasperation. Recalling an occasion when Freeman replaced "bright" with "effulgence" in a libretto, for instance, his son, Valdo, remembered that Freeman often "had a dictionary open near him, and I think he looked up these different things . . . putting those words in there was, to my mind, terrible."[61] Valdo's assessment coheres with that of Celia Davidson and Elise Kirk, who posit that Freeman's stilted language and over-the-top plots hindered his success.[62]

By calling his work "grand opera," Freeman both distinguished his work from other types of music theater prevalent in the turn-of-the-century United States and aligned himself with a historical tradition. He claimed a place within a Eurocentric artistic genealogy and showed how "negro grand opera" required a wholesale revision of that genealogy. As he explained, "There are those of narrow minds who would say that Grand Opera does not belong to the Negro, and for that reason this field has been passed over. But they are wrong entirely. Grand Opera belongs to all; that is, the themes first for the story are among the race, or can be taken from our foreparents."[63] In light of opera's long history of exoticist misrepresentations of racialized subjects, entrenched associations with European high culture, and distance from the Black popular-culture mainstream, the claim that grand opera *belonged* to Black people was a radical one. To assert that Black people could write their own history through opera, rather than serving as the symbolic stuff of the white composer's imagination, demanded nothing less than to reimagine the art form's history and future.

An abiding interest in Africa and African music undergirded Freeman's operatic vision. An 1898 article in the *Cleveland Press* noted his plan to

"plunge into the heart of Africa . . . He wants to meet the Zulus [and] the Abyssinians and other nationalities and study their legends, mythology and native music. He believes that he can construct truly grand and noble operas on these foundations."[64] Valdo later remembered, "That haunted him all his life, African music. He always loved to do it. He wanted to get to Africa . . . Anything African he went for it. He was crazy about it."[65] This interest aligned Freeman with various endeavors within transatlantic Black performance culture, including popular "Back-to-Africa" Williams and Walker musical comedies like *In Dahomey* (1903) and *Abyssinia* (1906).[66] But he downplayed such genre-crossing thematic convergences, arguing instead that Black life in Africa and throughout the diaspora was material ripe for, and ideally suited to, the operatic stage. Although Freeman never left the United States—like so many of his ambitions, this one went unrealized—he wrote several operas on African themes. In addition to *The Martyr*, two other early operas, *Nada* (also known as *Zuluki*) and *An African Kraal*, were set on the continent. At Wilberforce, he invited African students to join the 1904 cast of *The Martyr* (later recalling his delight at hearing them sing African "melodies, akin to those of the American Negro").[67] The encounter evokes what Tsitsi Jaji theorizes as Africa's constitutive role in Black diasporic cultural production, wherein "music has quite literally *rehearsed* transnational Black solidarity" through artistic collaboration.[68] The students' presence dramatized Freeman's conception of grand opera as a site for transnational connection, while the opera's plot simultaneously demonstrated a historical link between the Egyptian past and the African diasporic present.

A subtle radicalism underscored Freeman's dedication to opera, and that of early Black operatic counterculture writ large. He declined the straightforward conflation of new cultural forms with new sociopolitical arrangements. Nor did he look backward to a romanticized version of the Black musical past via genres like concert spirituals. He further distanced himself from nationalist notions of Black music by imagining the relationship between opera and race as international and diasporic. Freeman characterized his work as "grand operas based upon subjects peculiar to the darker races of the world in general—the Negro and native African races in particular," and noted that Black operatic composers had "the right to depict certain episodes of the other dark skinned races, such as the Indian, Mexican, Mongolian and other oriental peoples, especially those who have made their abode in Africa from time immemorial, such as the Egyptian and the Arab."[69] Positing a natural fit between musical form and racial substance, he argued that opera was the ideal vehicle for the telling of African diasporic

history. Its grandeur equipped it to articulate so grand a vision as global racial solidarity—a formulation that reconciled the art form's origins with contemporary political concerns.

The expansiveness of Freeman's notion of Blackness meant that his work was not always legible as African American music. *The Martyr*, for instance, was variously defined in the press and in Freeman's own writings as a "Negro opera," "sacred opera," "Egyptian opera," "racial opera," "original grand opera," and "Egyptian grand opera."[70] When excerpts from the opera were included at a 1930 concert titled "The Story of Negro Music," a note in the program clarified, "While 'The Martyr' is not Negroid in character, it is herein appended because it is the first opera ever written by a Negro."[71] This complicated caveat demonstrates the challenge of disentangling *The Martyr* from its composer's racial identity, and it troubles the assumption that Black composers necessarily wrote "Black music." Indeed, Freeman's other early operas were about people of color worldwide rather than African American subjects: *Valdo* was set in rural Mexico, for instance, and *The Tryst* among Native Americans in Michigan. To compose opera was already to be on the margins of Black cultural production, but to compose operas that were not about African Americans, or even the African diaspora, was a true departure from its norms.

In a remarkable anecdote from *The Negro in Music and Drama*, Freeman recounts how Paul Laurence Dunbar took issue with his choice of subject matter. Following the composition of *The Martyr* and *Valdo*, Dunbar told Freeman that he was "devoting valuable time and talent to the creation of two foreign works—one Egyptian and the other Mexican." Dunbar complained, "I can't see why you don't base your works upon Negro themes—the folk, work or camp-meeting songs of the South. There is nothing at all Negroid in any of your compositions." Freeman replied angrily: "'I didn't intend that there should be. What do I know about those things?' (I was insulted—outraged—exasperated.) 'Let somebody else do it; for it is all totally *foreign* to me.'"[72] In his pointed echo of Dunbar's term "foreign," Freeman claimed diasporic cultural citizenship rather than identifying with the Black southern vernacular. A few years later, after Freeman wrote *Zuluki*, an opera based on African themes, Dunbar gave it his "heartiest approbation." With a "whimsical smile," he mused that he had been "reveling in a fool's paradise; since it now appears that practically all the acclaim I, myself, have received, is entirely due to my poems that are characteristic of Negro life—those couched in illiterate dialogue. My more serious, deeper moods are set aside, gingerly, or merely given a cursory perusal—out of curiosity, probably. Well, we can't have everything! But do not follow my

example, Harry—write as your muse dictates. Mix them up!"[73] The exchange articulates the double bind that constrained African American artists. Neither Freeman's rejection of idiomatically African American material nor Dunbar's embrace of the same was a foolproof strategy. Moreover, Dunbar's response suggests that (white) public opinion would seize on whichever elements of a Black artist's work it found racially representative, often against that artist's wishes. So long as race and genre remained representationally linked, and cultural and racial hierarchies intertwined, there was no way to evade them entirely, no matter how much one sought to "mix them up."

Under such constrictive circumstances, Freeman turned to creative practices that sidestepped and, ultimately, exceeded the possibilities of public performance. If the production and reception history of *The Martyr* tells a rather haphazard tale, then the opera's visual archive offers alternative evidence. The score of the opera vividly renders Freeman's commitment to aesthetic grandeur. The letters of the title stretch across the entire width of the first page. They are inscribed in Freeman's distinctive, calligraphy-like script, which is inky and bold, full of curlicues and flourishes. Pinwheels adorn the corners, and a dedication to Freeman's "sainted grandmother" lies at the top. Turn the page, and the opera's overture is boldly marked. Instructions to the performers abound: hairpin crescendos and diminuendos, fermatas, sforzandos, accelerandos, fortissimos and fortississimos. Heavily drawn slurs swoop assertively across the notes. Measure after measure, atypically thick bar lines literally fill each of the score's nearly two hundred pages with Blackness.[74] This score is weighty and sturdy, meant to be taken seriously. One might imagine Freeman lugging the material object from Denver to Chicago to Cleveland, packing it away as he boarded trains from city to city. It is a powerful visual manifestation of Naomi André's assertion that opera is "a space where Black people are writing themselves into history," making their presence known.[75]

Equally spectacular is a series of watercolor costume designs for *The Martyr*, created by the Harlem Renaissance artist Amos Dickson. Generously sized at eleven by fourteen inches, and colored in vibrant shades of purple, magenta, and metallic gold against a dark background, they depict beautiful figures adorned in exquisitely ornamented clothing. In one, Shirah is clad in a glamorous purple gown, dotted with red flowers, and a tasseled silver cape. One hand rests on her head, while the other is outstretched, perhaps reaching out to her beloved Platonus. With curly hair, light skin, dramatically lined eyes, and a downcast glance, she is beautiful and facially ambiguous—a quality that aligns her with the "iconography of the

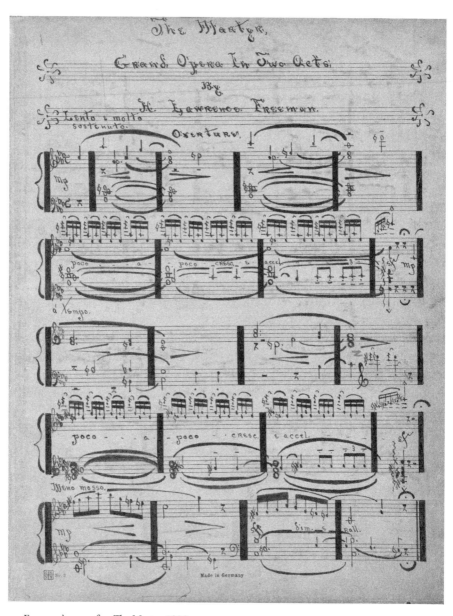

Freeman's score for *The Martyr,* 1893.

sexualized Creole woman," which Jayna Brown identifies as a mainstay of the late-nineteenth-century stage, while also offering a visual reminder of the opera's ambivalent relationship to the racialized category of "Black music."[76] A similarly depicted figure anchors a rendering of the scene in which Shirah pleads with Pharaoh to spare Platonus's life. Painted by the artist Edward Elcha, the scene became a visual hallmark for the Negro

Costume design for Shirah in *The Martyr,* by Amos Dickson, ca. 1920.

Grand Opera Company, which Freeman established in 1920, appearing on the company's stationery, programs, and business cards. It is a meticulously detailed parallel to Freeman's written portrayal of the opera's setting, perfectly matching his descriptions of "lofty pillars," Pharaoh's throne, and the Nile snaking through the background.[77]

The magnificent visual record of *The Martyr* that emerges via manuscript scores, costume designs, and paintings offers a compelling counterweight

A scene from *The Martyr,* painted by Edward Elcha. Throughout his career, Freeman used this image in materials related to his Negro Grand Opera Company.

to its checkered production and reception history. Crafted not only in conjunction with the opera's initial creation, but also in subsequently produced materials that reflect the trajectory of Freeman's career, these images inscribe Freeman's aspirations into the archive, insisting that a record of partially realized performance would not be the only documentation of his work. Their patent excesses suggest that Freeman's obsession with grandeur was not so much quixotic as it was compensatory—a way of crafting an operatic universe, regardless of the structural racism that would likely prevent that universe from coming into being.

The "Bronze-Colored Impresario" and His Ensemble

In May 1902, Freeman visited New York City to hear a production of *Faust* helmed by Theodore Drury, a "bronze-colored impresario" of growing renown.[78] Drury had founded an opera company comprised of African American artists in 1900.[79] He shared Freeman's passion for the creation of a Black operatic tradition, but evinced an even stronger commitment to opera as a social practice. Like Freeman, he worked from a posture of admiration

for the European canon and enthusiasm about claiming space within it. Rather than seeking to create new musical works, however, Drury aimed to remake existing ones. The company took a countercultural approach to the performance of operas by Gounod, Verdi, Bizet, and others, departing from some of the normative social associations that coalesced around this conventional repertoire. Whereas the amateur ensembles that performed Freeman's music had laid bare a tension between compositional grandeur and material constraint, Drury's ensemble was vital to the implementation of his ideas. The company became a site of collective Black sociality that challenged the homogenization and commodification of musical-racial difference, using opera to create an alternative public sphere in the musical world.

In preparation for each yearly production, Drury organized, trained, and rehearsed an ensemble of dozens of singers, most of whom had never before sung opera. This chorus of subjects—and the slow, laborious work that they completed during the historically undervalued processes of learning and rehearsal—collectively shaped the company's cultural and social meaning.[80] Although these singers have a fleeting presence in the archive as individuals, they might be likened to someone like Mabel Hampton, a twentieth-century queer Black singer and dancer, aspiring concert artist, and opera devotee. Saidiya Hartman, in her profound *Wayward Lives, Beautiful Experiments,* describes Hampton's love of opera as vibrantly personal, a manifestation of the radically intimate ways in which young Black women made meaning out of their lives: "To Mabel's ears, it conveyed the anguish of the blues and shared its chronicle of catastrophe; it simply spoke to her more deeply," and thus facilitated "slipping into another arrangement of the possible."[81] Like Hampton, members of the Drury Company generally have not entered the historical record as "opera singers" per se. It is not despite, but because of this position that their efforts are so illuminating. Their collaborative artistry necessarily destabilizes an exceptionalist narrative of Black operatic achievement that privileges only those who "succeeded" in the art form according to putatively meritocratic logics.

By establishing his own opera company, Drury joined a growing movement among Black performers to set the terms of their appearances on the stage. This shift was concentrated in New York City, where more than thirty shows with all-Black casts were produced between 1890 and 1915, an era that Thomas Riis has called the heyday of Black musical theater.[82] Yet many remained under the control of white managers who were beholden to minstrel stereotypes and mistreated Black performers. The actor and composer Bob Cole demanded Black artistic self-determination in his "Colored

Actors' Declaration of Independence of 1898": "We are going to have our own shows. We are going to write them ourselves, we are going to have our own stage manager, our own orchestra leader and our own manager out front to count up. No divided houses—our race must be seated from the boxes back."[83] A similar ethos guided Drury's work. Revising the racially exclusionary concept of the "opera house," the company articulated a different version of communal musical-civic space predicated on not only the shared identity of its participants, but also a commitment to pedagogy, sociality, and collective artistry.

Like many other musicians on the New York cultural scene, Theodore Drury migrated to the city in search of opportunity. Born in Shelby County, Kentucky, in 1867, he "absorbed the sunshine of his early life in the Blue Grass region" before moving east in the mid-1880s.[84] He studied voice and piano, learned French and German, and established himself as "New York's Premier Thespian and Barytone."[85] Early singing engagements placed him alongside a genre-defying array of popular entertainments: cakewalks, vaudeville, oratory. He became part of the network of Black performers and artists centered at the Hotel Marshall in midtown Manhattan, a gathering place that James Weldon Johnson memorialized as a hub of activity for "the actors, the musicians, the composers, the writers, and the better-paid vaudevillians."[86] Drury toured the United States as a soloist, gaining praise for his rich timbre, clear diction, and interpretive precision. One critic raved, "His notes possess all the liquid, melting tones of the true tenor and his lower register is of grand power and resonance, vibrating with intensified, passionate emotion which thrills the hearer."[87] He developed an interest in organizing musical groups. In 1887, a Theodore Drury Concert Company appeared at the AME Zion Church in Yonkers, New York, and similarly named groups appeared across the state throughout the 1890s.[88]

Such short-lived endeavors laid the groundwork for Drury's opera company, which produced one or two operas per year beginning in May 1900. With the exception of a 1901 production of *Il Guarany*, by Brazilian composer Antônio Carlos Gomes, the company performed exclusively well-known operas by white male European composers: *Carmen* in 1900, *Faust* in 1902, *Aida* in 1903, *Cavalleria Rusticana* and *Pagliacci* in 1904, *Carmen* again in 1905, and both *Aida* and *Carmen* in 1906. This reportorial focus inaugurated and anticipated a trend of Black-cast performances of canonical opera that would become central to Black operatic counterculture in the years to come. Unlike Freeman's operas, which foregrounded the global experiences of people of color, Drury's company offered Black artists the opportunity to act as what Marvin McAllister calls "stage Europeans," a

theatrical practice wherein Black performers "trespassed on representational terrain long thought to be the exclusive domain of white performers."[89] Far from representing an assimilationist desire to gain entry to that terrain, McAllister argues, such performances threw racial hierarchies into question to subversive effect.

As a performing ensemble that was also a pedagogical project, the Drury Company stood in contrast to the prevailing trend of haphazardly assembled, hastily rehearsed popular productions on the turn-of-the-century New York stage. Both its focus on nineteenth-century European grand opera and its sustained, detailed training practices were at odds with, if not entirely divorced from, the commercialized mainstream of modern urban Black performance. In both repertoire and rehearsal, the company departed from representational norms, evoking neither the frenetic syncopations of ragtime nor the ostensible timelessness of the southern Black pastoral. Yet even if they did not fall within the narrowly conceived parameters of the burgeoning entertainment industry, the company's efforts were also forms of labor through which artists might "disturb the conditions of their own commodification," as Daphne Brooks writes of Black popular musicians.[90] As the ensemble sang opera, they engaged in learning *as* labor, a gradual, experiential process that Hartman might call a "beautiful experiment."[91]

Press reports described Drury as a teacher who engaged in "the work of training" as he "labored for some time with about forty singers of his own race, drilling them in the music of Bizet's opera."[92] In interviews, he tended to couch his efforts in the hierarchical rhetoric of racial uplift. He told one journalist that the singers were "as a rule ignorant of music, and the work of teaching them is very laborious."[93] Elsewhere, he described his leadership as "missionary work," representing himself as a "race man" guiding the unenlightened masses toward refinement.[94] But this was misleading. Like the ensembles who realized Freeman's productions of *The Martyr,* most members of the Drury Company were new to opera, yet many arrived with substantial experience in other musical and theatrical genres. Several choristers had studied with Drury prior to joining the company, while others may have been recruited from other corners of the New York musical theater stage via his network at the Hotel Marshall.[95] In this sense, the composition of the chorus reveals the Drury Company's closeness to other facets of Black expressive culture, as well as its difference from contemporaneous white opera companies. Comprised of those singers who might, on another night, be found on the popular stage, it constituted a sort of aesthetic contact zone, filled with Black artists who moved across cultural spheres.

In fact, the upsurge of commercialized mass entertainment, coupled with the newfound visibility of Black performers, threatened to squeeze out the Drury Company altogether. "The services of negro singers are so much in demand now," the *New York Sun* noted in 1905, "that it is not always easy to get them for opera, as they make money easier in the variety theaters" or the "vaudeville companies, of which there are several on the road."[96] To that end, Drury declared his intention "to create a place and condition among my people so that classical students can get employment as easily as those whose time and talent is devoted to ragtime."[97] That aspiration was, of course, restricted by the fact that all other opera companies were open only to white performers. At the same time, to join the Drury Company was to *not* participate in the popular culture industry as a worker and artist, to opt out—at least temporarily—of that industry's commodification of musical and racial difference. Put simply, those weeks spent learning *Carmen* were weeks spent away from the variety stage or vaudeville company. They were also weeks spent away from the artistic and administrative control of white managers: echoing Cole's "Declaration of Independence," one reviewer of the Drury Company noted, "This the Negro is doing for himself, unaided."[98] To be sure, this choice necessitated a degree of economic privilege. The company offered only one or two productions per year, and pay was low; singers often were not paid at all during the rehearsal period.[99] "Most of the chorus men and women have employment from which they live," Drury explained, "and take up this work merely for the pleasure of it."[100] Even if the company aimed to offer a stable institutional structure and an alternative sphere for Black musical performance, its status remained precarious.

The company's inaugural production of *Carmen* took place on May 14, 1900. Drury led the cast as Don José, pushing his baritone voice to its upper limits. Other principals included Desseria Plato as Carmen, Emma de Lyon as Micaela, and Frederic Sheldon as Escamillo. Some reports suggested that the eminent Harry T. Burleigh conducted, while others indicated a conductor named Frank Paret. In later years, the company engaged several principals who were members of well-known Black families—the Ruffins of Boston, the Terrells of Washington, DC—while chorus members tended to be from less elite backgrounds.[101] Drury's goal was to cast only Black singers, but a lack of available personnel meant that he often hired white choristers (and occasionally white soloists) as well.[102] The chorus, which rehearsed for several weeks prior to the premiere, included "Miss Annie Hawkins, Mrs. Emma Wheeler, Miss Daisy LaTunner, Miss DeLina Browne, Mrs. Lighton, Mrs. Theresa N. Fields, Miss Marie Jackson, Miss Clarissa

E. Scott, Mrs. Ida B. Clay, Miss Emma Tolliver, Mrs. F. Sheldon, Miss Maud Barnes, Mrs. H. Boone, Miss Lucy Ross, Miss Georgie Smith, Miss Lillian Vrooman, James Rasin, D. P. Pendergrass, Thomas F. Doyle, Jean DeFischer, T. Fletcher Hurlong, J. E. Robinson, Rufus Johnson, Charles M. Baker, William Petters, Francis Van Arsdale, Albert DeAncy and Harry B. Garden."[103] Although not anonymous, these singers retain a certain opacity. As Katherine Preston observes, opera choruses tend to be "vexing" archival subjects whose reception is riddled with "contradictory assessments, frequent lack of comment, [and] generally vague observations," and for the Drury Company, this critical marginalization is compounded by a lack of archival material.[104] Yet these singers' sustained engagement with opera—week after week, rehearsal after rehearsal, performance after performance—meant that in practice, they were the primary agents of Drury's contributions to Black operatic counterculture.

Carmen prompted the same double-edged rhetoric of newness that had accompanied *The Martyr.* Drury himself promoted it as "the first time in the history of the world that the negro has ever given a complete performance of grand opera," and both Black and white reviewers emphasized its unprecedented nature: "the only Negro opera company in the world" was "a novelty" and "a notable departure in the field of music," marking "the first time in this country," and "probably . . . the first time in the world," that opera was "sung on the ebon keys of the human scale."[105] In the Boston-based *Colored American Magazine,* Robert W. Carter located the company within the context of racial uplift, contending that Drury's "extraordinary undertaking is the evidence of a superior mind and of a greater ambition to fill more important positions in life." By offering an alternative to minstrelsy's noxious stereotypes of African Americans "convulsing their audience with ludicrous songs," the company was "clearly proving that we, as a race, are something more than the 'hewers of wood and the drawers of water.'"[106]

Notably absent from most reviews was any sustained discussion of *Carmen*'s fraught politics of race, gender, and class. Bizet's representation of Spain, steeped in notions of extreme primitivism and uncontrolled passion, bespeaks the exoticism that coursed through nineteenth-century European opera.[107] Carmen is a dangerously seductive woman, whose status as a laborer in a cigarette factory only enhances the threat she poses to the hapless soldier Don José. Frederic Nietzsche praised the opera's music as evincing an "African" "cheerfulness"; Carl Van Vechten echoed this sentiment in his book *The Music of Spain* (1920), which posited an "elemental" linkage between African American and Spanish music.[108] Such discussions are

effectively missing from most press coverage of the Drury Company's production, which instead equated *Carmen* with "grand opera" more generally. At this early stage, the notion of a Black opera company was so atypical that it seemed to supersede in-depth critical consideration of the particular opera in which they appeared. Yet for the production's participants, the slippage may have facilitated an opportunity to experiment with Bizet's opera, reimagining a representationally restrictive work as an open text.

On opening night, Emma Wheeler, Annie Hawkins, Daisy LaTunner, and the ensemble's dozens of other members huddled backstage at the Lexington Avenue Opera House, dressed in costumes of the "most brilliant colors."[109] As the overture played, they took their places onstage, the men dressed as soldiers and the women as factory workers. In act 1, they echoed the sensuous melody of Carmen's Habanera. Throughout the opera they would reappear as "dragoons, gypsies, smugglers, cigarette girls and street boys," shifting into new roles as the score demanded.[110] As they sang, these artists enacted a collective social formation with distinct aesthetic and political ramifications: the opera chorus. James Parakilas has written that "the chorus puts the 'grand' into grand opera," and other musicologists have explored the social implications of its centrality in nineteenth-century European repertoire, noting that in the many grand operas that functioned as political allegory, the chorus took on new expressive power as the "voice of the people."[111] Ryan Minor, for example, argues that the chorus constituted a "new character," imbued with "a moral and sonic authority it had never before possessed."[112] Strikingly resonant with characterizations of Black vernacular musicking as a vehicle for social representation and moral force, these descriptors suggest that in Drury's productions, the symbolic power of the chorus was amplified by its racial composition, recalling both operatic associations and those linked to other forms of Black collective singing.

Critical assessments of the ensemble varied. Although Black and white reviewers were largely unanimous in their praise of the company's principal singers, their evaluations of the chorus were tellingly diverse. In "Grand Opera as We See It" (June 1900), *Colored American Magazine*'s musical editor, H. S. Fortune, proclaimed that "Grand Opera by colored singers, both principal and chorus, is progress worth mentioning" and praised the entire company for not only their "high degree of suavity," but also their "very high degree of attainment, study, and devout application."[113] Many members of the white musical press, however, implied that Black musicians were untutored, naturally musical, even recalcitrant. The *New York Dramatic Mirror* noted simply that the "chorus seemed to enjoy their work

hugely and sang with enthusiasm," obscuring the labor and training that underscored their artistry.[114] Another critic, seemingly unable to see Black bodies in opera as anything other than an irresolvable dissonance, wrote that "the chorus, in its ideas of dancing, had a tendency to tread measures more popular with the colored race than are the studied graces of the ballet master."[115] Still another rendered them unruly, childlike subjects: "the chorus comes in for criticism on a charge of musical rebellion. The baton beats in vain for them; they go their own sweet way."[116]

Similar critiques were levied against the opera's audiences, whom reviews described in vivid, somewhat unserious terms: "exceedingly attractive" listeners who arrived "in carriages, automobiles, and stages," the men in "conventional evening dress" and the women "handsomely gowned."[117] Then they took the stage themselves, as "after the opera the floor was cleared and dancing was indulged in," late into the "scorchingly hot" night.[118] Even Drury himself was not exempt from ridicule: Ernest Hogan's musical comedy *Rufus Rastus* featured the tenor Frank Fowler Brown, who sang leading roles in Drury's productions, as an obviously parodic "Signor Brury, with operatic aspirations."[119] James Weldon Johnson, who knew Drury via the Hotel Marshall network, recalled in his 1933 memoir *Along This Way* that Drury was "the picturesque one" who "cultivated a foreign air." "As for the operas," he reminisced, "none of us took them too seriously— that statement possibly includes Drury himself."[120] The dissonance among these interpretations—familiarity and novelty, serious uplift and frothy entertainment—speaks to opera's multi-signifying potential, the different affective and political meanings that a single production could hold for its various listeners and participants.

But in illuminating what Hartman might call the "wayward" nature of the Drury Company's performances, these critiques foreground the ensemble's experiential engagements with opera: the pleasure they took in singing Bizet's music, the way their bodies inhabited the stage, their sly revisions of the grand opera tradition. Even more intriguing are characterizations of the chorus as transgressive and rebellious, refusing the dictates of the "ballet master" or the conductor's baton. In apparent contrast to Drury's aspirational directorial vision, this chorus exercised a measure of artistic control by dancing and singing in "their own sweet way"—a way that, significantly, aligned them with popular styles and embodied Blackness as well as European opera. In doing so, they made a cultural and political claim rooted in what Minor calls the chorus's "moral and sonic authority." Asserting as a collective that Black operatic counterculture was not a narrow, uplifting project divorced from other arenas of Black cultural production, they

claimed the ability to speak back to Drury's "drilling," contest the culture industry's homogenizing notions of musical-racial difference, and perform opera on their own terms.[121]

It was through the chorus that the Drury Company was able to generate artistic self-determination out of a canonical repertoire. This may seem paradoxical, given that operas like *Carmen* and *Faust* were not only impractically difficult and expensive to produce, but also failed to fulfill Bob Cole's demand for shows that "we write . . . ourselves." Yet in lieu of the multidisciplinary group of Black artists that Cole imagined—performers, composers, managers, conductors—the group's collective singing offered visible and sonic evidence of a new social arrangement sung into being. Hartman theorizes "the beauty of the chorus" by analogizing the collectives who appeared onstage in musical revues to the "common folk" whose everyday lives made them "anonymous members of the ensemble" of Harlem.[122] She writes: "The chorus is the vehicle for another kind of story, not of the great man or the tragic hero, but one in which all modalities play a part, where the headless group incites change, where mutual aid provides the resource for collective action, not leader and mass, where the untranslatable songs and seeming nonsense make good the promise of revolution. The chorus propels transformation."[123] The forty-some singers who appeared in *Carmen,* and those who joined the company in the years that followed, embraced the possibilities of reinvention that resonated in opera's aesthetic and embodied details. They sang "another kind of story," finding within grand opera the potential for "musical rebellion" and collective transformation.

"A National Hearing by Criticism"

As Black operatic counterculture took shape on stages from Denver to Cleveland to New York, it also came to life within the pages of the newspaper. Its early days coincided with the meteoric rise of the Black press. Fundamental to the post-Reconstruction Black public sphere, the press became a vital outlet for discourse and community formation in a period marked by the repressive constraints of Jim Crow and the diminishment of Black political power. In 1890, there were roughly one hundred Black newspapers in the United States. By 1911, there were over three hundred; many had a national reach, and their combined circulation exceeded half a million.[124] Elizabeth McHenry has argued that a defining feature of the early Black press was its "social model of knowledge," wherein journalists reported on cultural events such that readers might approximate the expe-

rience of participation.[125] Further, as scholars of Black print culture have noted, nineteenth- and early twentieth-century periodicals were "often the best and sometimes the *only* possible publication venue for many African American writers."[126] This was certainly the case for African American opera critics. Although opera criticism is often considered the exclusive domain of white men, a number of Black writers took up the subject, combining straightforward reportage with more essayistic writings to create a body of knowledge around the art from for their readership.[127] Opera was rarely front-page news (nor was other arts criticism), but periodicals were the primary medium through which Black critics published their ideas about opera. In other words, if opera criticism was not central to the Black press, the Black press was central to opera criticism's creation and circulation.

Although Black opera criticism has received minimal scholarly attention, scholars of African American studies have emphasized the value of arts criticism more generally as a social force. Anna Everett notes that early Black film critics were well attuned to the "sociopolitical pragmatics" of cultural production; they understood that ostensibly esoteric debates—about high versus low culture, for instance—had serious ramifications.[128] Jennifer Stoever argues that nineteenth-century concert reviews and other forms of print culture "perform[ed] race," contributing to the racialization of sound on the level of ideology. While white critics naturalized racist ideas about sonic difference, Stoever argues, Black critics employed the format to opposite effect, using criticism to contextualize or even evade the color line.[129] In a different context, Daphne Brooks has emphasized the disruptive potential of music criticism that refuses narrow notions of tastemaking, "the kinds of criticism and performance practice produced by people of color and women that generate their own alternative, world-making ideas that amount to thrilling forms of epistemological intervention."[130] As vital architects of Black operatic counterculture, opera critics did not just reflect, but also imaginatively remade, the art form's cultural meanings.

Among the most provocative and prolific voices in the Black press was Sylvester Russell, a supremely ambitious thinker who aspired to shape the development of African American culture. Russell was ideologically aligned with Freeman and Drury in their shared devotion to envisioning opera as a zenith of Black cultural achievement. Yet if the audiences for Freeman's and Drury's work were limited to residents of the urban centers where their operas were staged, Russell had a far broader reach. From 1901 to 1916, he wrote regularly for the *Indianapolis Freeman*, his reviews and essays also appeared in the *Chicago Defender, New York Age,* and *Pittsburgh Courier.* The

Freeman, which one scholar has described as the "circulatory system of Black show business," featured copious criticism, advertisements, and even a message board for stage performers.[131] Though based in the Midwest, it had a national scope: agents across the country circulated the paper at a price of $1.50 per year, and editors solicited and published news from local correspondents. Russell's contributions therein exuded self-confidence. Outspokenly interventionist, he took pride in standing apart from and, indeed, ahead of the crowd: he was a self-styled prophetic voice who would lead Black music and drama out of the dark past of minstrelsy and into a promising modern future. In nuanced, opinionated prose, he put his expertise on full display. Unlike most Black arts critics of the era, who tended to lavish praise upon performers, Russell could be hard-hitting, unafraid to tell artists what was wrong with their work and what they should do differently.

Russell's path to the critical profession was peripatetic. Born in East Orange, New Jersey, in the late 1860s, he attended elementary school in Newark before moving to New York City as a teenager. There, according to a biographical article, he received "a free grand opera vocal education" from Harry Bragaw, a retired white singer who had toured with traveling opera troupes. As Bragaw's student, Russell received free tickets to various musical and theatrical performances in New York, as well as the opportunity to learn from and interact with other pupils.[132] Around 1887, he moved to Providence, Rhode Island to work as a servant for two young white men, Arthur Hutchins Colby and George Walker. Both Brown University students, Colby and Walker asked much of Russell: he served as their "copyist and private secretary," cut their hair, took care of Colby's dog, assisted with their performances as members of Brown's amateur minstrel society, and because Walker was a lackluster student who suffered from "relaxation of memory," read and studied on his behalf.[133] Russell's professional musical career also began in Providence, which had a robust Black musical community rooted in its churches. For the next decade, he worked as a singer. He traversed the northeast as a solo recitalist and with various companies, and even sang the role of Eva in a production of *Uncle Tom's Cabin.*[134]

Around 1900, Russell ceased performing and began working as a critic. His first byline in the *Freeman* appeared on December 28, 1901. He soon appointed himself the "foremost dramatic critic," with that phrase appearing below his byline alongside a picture of him in suit and tie, his chin resting on his hand in a cerebral pose.[135] These visual and textual acts of self-fashioning positioned Russell as an elite male intellectual whose critical authority was entwined with his name, mind, and body. Opera emerged as

a central focus of his criticism. He discussed the art form in more than one hundred articles and essays ranging from individual reviews to expansive pronouncements about its significance. His ambition, he wrote, was to facilitate "a national hearing by criticism from a critic in whom the public believes and recognizes, and through the medium of The Freeman, which reaches the English-speaking world."[136]

Russell's criticism espoused an idealistic vision of what Black culture should be, documented its current iterations, and offered advice on how to bridge the gap between the two. His work was rife with tension and ambivalence. Some aspects of his thought align him with the conservative tradition of "race men" who embraced the moral and aesthetic precepts of Victorian respectability and attempted to manage the behavior of the Black masses: he promoted strict cultural hierarchies, lamented the "decline" of great art, and valorized the critic as an arbiter of cultural taste.[137] Yet other elements of his criticism subverted those same ideas. Despite his stated preferences for certain types of art, in practice Russell's musical tastes were broad and did not adhere to the classificatory logics that he claimed to endorse. His prescriptive statements about art and his descriptive accounts of particular performances diverge. In short, his critical voice (described by other scholars in such outsized terms as "grandiloquent," "tetchy," "mildly ludicrous") was a *doubled* voice, in which affect and substance could be at odds.[138] As such, it evokes Du Boisian double-consciousness—in which the subject is already a critic of sorts, "always looking at one's self through the eyes of others," "measuring one's soul by the tape of a world that looks on in amused contempt and pity. One ever feels his two-ness, an American, a Negro; two souls, two thoughts, two unreconciled strivings; two warring ideals in one dark body, whose dogged strength alone keeps it from being torn asunder."[139] But doubling has, as it were, a double meaning here: before becoming a critic, Russell worked as a "double-voiced singer," a popular type of stage performer, usually male, with an uncanny ability to switch seamlessly between high and low vocal registers.[140] The correlation offers an intriguing point of entry from which to consider how performance and criticism were mutually constitutive in his work, and how he blurred the line between them.

One of Russell's interventionist priorities was to classify artistic forms and establish clear performance conventions for each. As Paige McGinley has written, Russell understood the evolution of Black performing arts in "strictly teleological" terms and viewed himself as "an architect of a new industry" that would leave behind the caricatures of minstrelsy and burlesque, moving toward more artistically "legitimate" forms.[141] In 1902, he

wrote that the question of how to categorize forms like "farce comedies, musical comedies, [and] comedy dramas" was "lying heavily on our minds," and that it represented "a problem for the musical critics, alone, to decide."[142] Offering the example of Will Marion Cook and Paul Laurence Dunbar's *Clorindy* (1898), which was "simply a good, first-class, rag-time, musical cakewalk," he clarified that "there is no such thing as a rag-time opera; no opera can be written all in rag-time."[143] It was thus imperative that African American performers follow modern artistic rules and eliminate potential sources of genre confusion. Warning that he had "no particular respect for performers who happen to fall in the footpath of my criticism," Russell admonished performers who broke the rules of the stage as he defined them—for instance, calling out "the impropriety of talking to an audience . . . in a so-called legitimate show" because it ran counter to the "intelligent conception of modern comedy."[144]

He fashioned himself a benevolent guide who would teach uninformed performers, whom he once referred to as "the infant race of actors," to become great. Paternalistically, he declared that "they know not [how to perform], some of them, but I will tell them."[145] In line with the patriarchal orientation of racial uplift ideology, his critiques of female artists often veered away from aesthetic evaluation and toward intrusive moralistic disciplining. In "Should Respectable Girls Adopt the Stage?" he argued that women could pursue careers in the arts only if they maintained strictly moral conduct.[146] Further, he idealized masculinity as a proxy for artistic quality: one of his quirkier columns linked vocal excellence to gender to poultry, comparing the "force and power" of the crowing gamecock to the "grand opera singer" while mocking the "coward rooster" who "sings like a hen."[147] He rejected the assumed authority of white critics—"the white press will not direct our individual or collective fortunes"—but also departed from the example set by earlier Black critics who relied on "flattery" and failed to "criticize a colored man on his merits or demerits." "They encourage," Russell scoffed. "I construct."[148]

Russell's conceptual contribution to Black operatic counterculture was to decree that grand opera composed, performed, and heard by African Americans would represent the apex of modern musical progress. This teleology was a reformulation of cultural hierarchy that rejected the logic of white supremacy. As Stoever explains, opera's preeminence in nineteenth-century cultural hierarchies was linked to its putative whiteness, such that "the sound of opera signified the Other's fixed position at the bottom of the 'Great Chain of Being' and on one side of the sonic color line."[149] Russell's argument that opera was the natural endpoint of a modernizing *Black*

cultural sphere revised that conceit, embracing the idea of opera as a cultural zenith but rejecting the idea of that zenith as exclusively white. As evidence, he argued that "the real admirers who attend the performances [of opera] are immigrants and colored people," dismissed "white grand opera in America" as "little short of failure," and envisioned a future in which Black composers would lead the art form's development.[150] "The new advent in classical music which is to come must come from a Negro composer," Russell wrote, and the "future American composed grand opera" would constitute his most important work.[151]

He imagined that Harry Lawrence Freeman would assume that role. Russell energetically bolstered Freeman's reputation as a composer (unusually, given his typically harsh critical proclivities), deeming Freeman the "greatest heavy composer of his race now living," in fact "easily entitled to a rank equal to any of the best of any race born in America."[152] Freeman was "the most prolific writer of music in America. He can compose an aria in the classics quicker than any two white composers and write music with more speed than an expert stenographer. There can be no disputing of these facts which I have seen of his genius."[153] Yet Russell also lamented the persistent gap between the ambitious nature of Freeman's work and its ability to be fully realized in performance. "Some of his classical music as I have heard is simply unsingable—that is, if we are to apply its registration to the capacities of ordinary singers," he observed. "But his vocal written art is excellence itself . . . [I note] how hard his music is to sing and how, like Wagner, great vocalists are needed to master his songs. If, then, vocal music is to be a future specialty in Prof. Freeman's compositions, let us remind him to please bring his music down—down to the level of a weaker and wiser generation of warblers."[154] While composer and critic were ideologically aligned in their vision of a Black operatic future, Russell worried that the present material conditions of Black stage performance thwarted the realization of that vision.

Russell's observations of the Drury Company reflect similar preoccupations. Like Drury, Russell revered the grand opera canon, and he applauded the Drury Company for producing *Aida,* "the most tuneful opera that Verdi ever wrote," and *Carmen,* "a tragic drama of a musical sort."[155] In a review of the company's 1902 performance of *Faust,* he praised Drury for assuming the dual role of "star and instigator," for being a talented singer who crafted a grand "gala occasion" for the audience. Yet as in his commentary on Freeman, he cast doubt on the pragmatic value of Black grand opera: he observed that Drury "is the greatest male opera singer, of his race, but not the greatest male singer of his race by odds," and thus might be more

conventionally successful in another genre.[156] "Mr. Drury has started at the top of the ladder and must come down to a musical level that will suit the general public, that is if he desires to make money," he scolded.[157] Although by 1906 Russell was admitting that the company had improved, and that their *Aida* was "the most perfect performance of grand opera I have ever seen presented by Theodore Drury," he maintained an ambivalent perspective that celebrated grand opera as a point of aspiration while characterizing actual performances of grand opera in ways that undercut that notion.[158]

If Russell was eager to modernize African American culture, he also waxed nostalgic. As his career progressed, opera became a touchstone in his laments for the good old days; he mourned the loss of the critic's "primary authority" in determining standards and genre distinctions, and the consequence, that "grand opera has been reduced."[159] In "Decline of Art and Lack of Appreciation for Real Artists" (1913), he decried "immoral scenes" and audiences who wished to "laugh instead of to learn," and he connected moral failure to aesthetic decline: "Much of the new style of music lacks in tonal beauty," and audiences no longer wished to hear "standard opera and the classics." In "Lack of Appreciation for the Classics" (1915), he grumbled, "I would give one hundred dollars if the young rising generation could see art as I saw it and heard it explained twenty-five years ago. Those were the balmy days when real art was appreciated."[160] That "real art" included grand opera, which he felt to be losing its cultural distinctiveness amid the fragmenting cultural landscape of the early twentieth century: in 1925, he lamented that "Grand opera, classic drama, musical comedy, vaudeville and cabaret attractions are unfortunately too closely associated in these days."[161]

To Russell, the success of modern African American culture was bound up with the success of the critic, and there was not so much a bright line between criticism and performance as there was an opportunity for productive intermixing. His explicit interest in classification extended to an implicit understanding of his own role: one in which certain genres surpassed others, critics surpassed performers, and Russell himself emerged as an authority figure par excellence. But that authority once again recalls Russell's origins as a "double-voiced" performer. In his work, ideological conservatism collided with liberatory aspirations: to detach cultural hierarchies from white supremacy, empower performers to reject the racialized strictures that limited their work, and usher into being a vibrant artistic future. In her foundational work on race as metalanguage, Evelyn Brooks Higginbotham, citing Bakhtin, describes race itself as a "double-voiced

discourse," originally intended to justify Black oppression but repurposed in service of Black liberation.[162] Higginbotham's formulation gestures toward a central conundrum of early Black operatic counterculture: could a Eurocentric art form saddled by a history of racist misrepresentation and white supremacist exclusion ever become an emancipatory tool for African Americans? Or would it end up reproducing the hierarchical structures it sought to dismantle?

Freeman, Drury, and Russell answered these questions by means of their powerfully articulated vision for opera's role within Black life. Working across the fields of composition, performance, and criticism, each positioned himself as a solitary figure; yet Freeman and Drury both relied on ensembles to realize their operatic ideas, and Russell engaged in criticism as a social practice. Furthermore, their ideas about opera were so closely aligned that these three putatively singular figures might be considered an ensemble in their own right. From Freeman's portrayal of the grandeur of Egyptian antiquity in *The Martyr* to Drury's subversively joyous revision of *Carmen,* they collectively reimagined the art form as central to what Russell once called "the futurity of American music": a horizon on which "some spark of hidden genius suddenly alarms the universe," where Black opera would become a grand resource for artistic imagination.[163]

Yet that hopeful outlook would soon be challenged. Although *The Martyr* was performed several times after its 1893 premiere, it vanished from the stage around 1905. For the next several years, Freeman and his wife, Carlotta, worked as itinerant musicians. It was a precarious life. Valdo recalled that his parents sometimes left him with friends while on the road, and that "they didn't get paid half the time."[164] Traveling shows also required venturing through the Jim Crow South, where Freeman felt both unsafe and humiliated by everyday indignities: for instance, when conducting pit orchestras that included white musicians, he was required to conduct sitting down rather than standing up. "They went through parts of the South they'd never been in, where they saw this terrible prejudice," Valdo explained. "My mother came in and she was a nervous wreck because she was worried about my father. He walked around with his walking cane all the time. He held his head up, and you weren't supposed to do that down there."[165] The Drury Company offered its final yearly production in 1906. Later that year, while traveling by train in Vermont, the company was involved in a terrible crash. Seven people were killed, including one member of the company, chorister Rosetta Faulk. Drury fractured his hip, and nearly twenty other company members were injured.[166] In 1907, Drury moved from New York to Boston,

where his productions became smaller in scale and more sporadic. Although Russell continued to work prolifically as a critic, the tenor of his work grew more pessimistic, perhaps due to his experience witnessing the structures of segregation harden and the aesthetic possibilities he had once envisioned fail to materialize. The bright modern future all three had hoped for seemed dim and distant.

∽ 2 ∾

New Selves, New Spheres

In November 1909, a notice appeared in the *Indianapolis Freeman* that "Mr. Scott Joplin, the composer of the Maple Leaf Rag, has got a new opera," complete with an overture "great as anything ever written by Mr. Wagner."[1] Joplin enjoyed unparalleled acclaim as a ragtime songwriter and pianist, composing some of the genre's best-known songs. Since childhood, he had also been interested in composing opera.[2] His first opera, *A Guest of Honor* (1903), which dramatized the historic 1901 meeting at the White House between Theodore Roosevelt and Booker T. Washington, had a handful of well-regarded performances, and when he moved to New York City with the intent of composing and producing a second opera, *Treemonisha,* further success appeared imminent.[3] Joplin was one of many "colored writers busily engaged even now in writing operas," one critic wrote, and although "from ragtime to grand opera is certainly a big jump . . . we believe that the time is not far off when America will produce several S. Coleridge Taylors who will prove to the public that the black man can compose other than ragtime music."[4] But this confidence proved premature. When Joplin completed *Treemonisha* in 1910, he was unable to find a publisher and instead released a piano-vocal score at his own expense. Despite reports that he had "signed several contracts, iron-clad," a production never reached the stage; the only performance was a modest reading with the composer at the piano.[5] When he died tragically in 1917, at age forty-eight, it was speculated that a "burning desire" to have *Treemonisha* produced "was responsible for the composer's death."[6]

Much as this rather sensationalist account equates the opera's failure to Joplin's demise, *Treemonisha* is often described by scholars of African American cultural history as "ill suited for its age," and so emblematic of the difficult—even tragic—status of Black opera at this historical juncture.[7] There is some truth to this claim. Although the work is, paradoxically, now lauded as a signature achievement among early twentieth-century African American composers, Joplin's struggles mirror a broader transition in Black operatic counterculture. The fully staged productions of Harry Lawrence Freeman and Theodore Drury, which had augured the dawn of a new era, began to fall out of favor in the first decade of the twentieth century among both Black and white audiences. Indeed, Black music theater was in flux across the board. In vaudeville, the deaths of Ernest Hogan and Bob Cole in 1909, and George Walker in 1911—as well as the disbanding of the Black Patti Troubadours in 1914—marked the end of an era. Cole's death, one observer noted, "cause[d] a state of lethargy to fall over the Negro in the theatre world."[8] Among Black classical musicians, the untimely passing of Afro-British composer Samuel Coleridge-Taylor in 1912 had a similar effect, prompting lamentations that "never before, and perhaps never again, will an individual of Negro extraction be so glorified."[9] A vogue for operetta displaced numerous Black shows onto subpar touring circuits, while the rise of movies and legitimate theater pulled audiences in new directions. The explosive success of Tin Pan Alley music publishing, coupled with the growth of the nascent recording industry, meant that ragtime and other popular genres circulated more widely and speedily than ever before—even as artists working within these industries remained vulnerable to exploitation.[10]

As the Great Migration propelled huge numbers of rural African Americans northward, the culture of Black entertainment moved with them. Across the nation, cities swelled in size as rural migrants and European immigrants arrived. New technologies transformed the built environment: teetering skyscrapers, electric lights, rumbling subways. Commercialized mass entertainment flourished, with dance halls, movie palaces, and vaudeville theaters dotting the landscape. From New York to Philadelphia to Chicago, cabarets and nightclubs offered a respite from Jim Crow and a space in which Black popular culture could thrive (even as white reformers vilified these same venues as spaces of vice and immorality, and as white voyeurs flocked to them). In cities, Black newcomers found both opportunity and danger. In the South, they had lacked economic and political rights and faced the constant threats of racial violence and white supremacist

terror. Yet upon arrival in the North, they faced harsh conditions, including poor-quality jobs and housing, class-based derision from established Black elites, and tensions with white immigrants that often turned violent.[11]

Beginning around 1910, African Americans remade opera's cultural meanings in tandem with these shifting dynamics. Freeman, Drury, and Russell, intent on asserting opera's potential to stand as a pinnacle of Black creative achievement, had foregrounded the composition and performance of large-scale works. But in the context of an increasingly segregated cultural landscape tilted toward mass entertainment and popular music, other types of engagement with opera came to the fore. Building on the conceptual foundations established by an earlier generation of charismatic theorists—as well as the artistic and social experiences that those theorists had enabled—new practitioners offered a different perspective on how opera might circulate within and contribute to Black artistic and social life writ large. Vocalists might forgo the stage in favor of the studio, offering private lessons to interested students. Educators might establish musical clubs or companies in which amateur singers could develop their voices. Critics might use their journalistic platform to educate a general readership, while listeners might purchase recordings of arias by professional singers.

While these activities may seem scattered or diffuse, they collectively furthered the development of Black operatic counterculture along two distinct paths. First, singers and pedagogues fostered connections between operatic aesthetics, Black vocality, and the affective project of self-making, particularly for Black women. And second, teachers, students, and critics established a place for opera within the Black public sphere, making schools, newspapers, and other social institutions into hubs of collaborative operatic activity. These endeavors proceeded from a shared countercultural standpoint in that they foregrounded Black artists' marginal relationship to the art form's mainstream. Yet their ideological connotations varied; marginality did not necessarily lead to radical or resistant political stances. To illustrate these ambivalences, I will offer a case study of the singer-turned-educator E. Azalia Hackley, whose operatic training shaped her diverse professional investments in Black folk music, racial uplift, and gendered respectability politics—sometimes to reactionary effect.

Sustained attention to this disparate set of operatic activities complicates the narrative that opera's cultural meanings consolidated as the art form became sacralized—confined to the opera house, and increasingly associated with whiteness and elitism—in the early twentieth century. As Kristen M. Turner, Larry Hamberlin, and others have shown, opera continued to

proliferate across various cultural locales, from phonograph records to vaudeville shows to concert programs.[12] Yet although African Americans were not the only practitioners to challenge the art form's popular-to-elite trajectory, they employed distinct strategies to connect their operatic activities to broader theorizations of race, culture, and identity. They circumvented the sonic color line that racialized opera as white by displacing the nineteenth-century European canon as a primary point of reference; in turn, they expanded Black operatic counterculture's aesthetic dimensions by emphasizing both opera's relationship to other musical genres and the potential utility of an operatically trained voice in settings beyond the operatic stage. More broadly, they recognized that though ample historical precedents existed, there was no settled or inevitable relationship between opera and Blackness; in addition, the equally unstable relationship between whiteness and opera was not determinative of the relationship between Blackness and opera. While Black artists certainly took note of the art form's mainstream iterations, they understood that cultural scene as a frame of reference rather than a point of aspiration as they worked out opera's relationship to Blackness across various contexts.

Foregrounding the efforts of students, amateurs, and women enables a feminist and anti-exceptionalist approach to the question of who counts as a historical actor within Black operatic counterculture. To build on Naomi André's formulation, the iterations of "shadow culture" addressed here took place more in the shadows, farther from mainstream attention. Few of its central figures went on to illustrious professional careers; many engaged with opera only intermittently within their rich creative lives. Their work, which was directed primarily toward African American audiences and listeners, reorients our attention away from figures understood to be exceptional, or even just "successful," under the meritocratic logics often associated with the history of Black opera. Those rationales are often determined by the critical attention bestowed on Black artists by white tastemakers, a phenomenon that can lead to misleadingly narrow accounts of Black cultural practices.[13] Like other scholars of Black classical music, including Samantha Ege and A. Kori Hill, I focus instead on the institutional and interpersonal networks in which Black operatic activity flourished.[14] Within these contexts, and via the intimate and affective engagements with the art form that they facilitated, opera became something other than a distant endpoint toward which Black artists might aspire. Rather, the everyday and ephemeral making of opera was meaningful in its own right.

Operatic Vocality and Self-Making

To train one's voice to sing opera was, fundamentally, to imagine the embodied self anew. The relationship between singing and self-making in contemporaneous genres of Black music is well established; Angela Davis, for instance, argues that the postbellum emergence of the blues "articulated a new valuation of individual emotional needs and desires" for Black women.[15] But the association of opera with self-making may seem counterintuitive or surprising, given that classical vocal pedagogy is often described in terms of its disciplinary function. For example, Nina Sun Eidsheim has detailed the process of vocal "entrainment," explaining how classical vocal teachers in conservatory settings presume an unmediated connection between a student's voice and their racial identity that essentializes what is actually a socially constructed relationship.[16] More broadly, studies of Black music often use the phrase "classically trained" as shorthand for aesthetic conformity or interpret it as a proxy for the "training" implicit in racial uplift, an encapsulation of an assimilationist model that aspires toward Eurocentric artistic standards.[17] In other instances, classical training is described a position from which musicians working in other genres—from Will Marion Cook to Nina Simone to Miles Davis—ultimately departed in favor of more adventurous creative pursuits. Yet this perspective occludes the ways in which operatic vocal training could be an opportunity for capacious aesthetic and social experimentation, particularly within the countercultural context of Black institutions and organizations. African American women, in particular, found within opera the opportunity to fashion a self beyond the confines of anti-Black stereotype and gendered respectability politics.

Opportunities to pursue individualized vocal training were abundant. In the pages of periodicals like the *Crisis,* voice teachers advertised their availability for private lessons, which were typically held in home-based studios. Under their guidance, operatic pedagogy became a countercultural practice of intergenerational creation. Masi Asare has argued that early twentieth-century vocal pedagogy crossed the lines of genre and style, such that blueswomen—often assumed to have "untrained" voices—engaged in a citational practice that drew on the work of their own voice teachers, who were most often other Black women.[18] Similar lineages arose in opera. When Harry Lawrence Freeman moved to New York City in 1910, he began to teach voice, theory, and composition, at one point working with more than 150 students weekly.[19] As Freeman perceptively noted, this was a common trajectory following the downturn in Black musical comedy: the "great

Negro road shows disbanded in 1910–11, thereby flooding [New York] city with a preponderance of vocal artists."[20] Other luminaries of Black operatic counterculture's inaugural period also moved from the stage to the studio. Estelle Pinckney Clough, who starred in some of Theodore Drury's productions, opened a voice studio in her hometown of Worcester, Massachusetts.[21] The promising tenor Sidney Woodward also turned to teaching, abdicating what he described as a career spent "along a path brilliant with the light that shines from the footlights of the public singer's life" in favor of "seeing hundreds of young women and men pass under [his] instruction."[22] Unable or unwilling to sustain careers based on performance alone, these artists turned to pedagogy and, in doing so, created new opportunities for African Americans to pursue operatic training.

A smaller coterie of Black singers attended predominantly white conservatories. Hermann DeVriès, a French-trained voice teacher who performed with the Paris Opéra before emigrating to the United States and taking up an appointment at the Chicago Musical College, provided training to numerous African American singers. Among his students were Bertha Dickerson Tyree (praised in the *Chicago Defender* for her "voice of remarkable range, of a quality sweet and thrillingly dramatic, with great carrying power") and Maude Roberts George (whose "well-balanced soprano voice is matched by a range of interpretation").[23] Some singers traveled to Europe to pursue further training. The Parisian Jean de Reszke, a celebrated tenor, was an especially well-regarded teacher of African American students. Attending performances in Europe was another key social ritual. The teacher and activist Mary Church Terrell, for example, reportedly attended the opera several times a week while living in Berlin. As Kira Thurman writes, the opera house became an "international meeting ground" where Terrell and other African Americans could meet fellow students from across the globe.[24]

The popularity of vocal training grew out of the "vocal culture" (or "voice culture") movement, a turn-of-the-century cultural phenomenon. More than 150 manuals for amateur singers were published between 1880 and 1920, collectively aimed at producing a standardized American voice, and the National Association of Teachers of Singing was founded in 1906. Centered in New York City, amid the cacophony of an urban soundscape noisy with new technologies and sonically diversified by the racialized voices of European immigrants and southern Black migrants, the vocal culture movement has been described as a strategy of racial subject formation and a means of creating ideal sonic citizens.[25] At times, its entanglements with discourses of racial science were explicit. An earlier generation

of European thinkers had located the fundamental racial difference between European and African peoples in the voice, and eminent figures in early twentieth-century American music did so as well. In 1910, for example, music historian Louis Elson made the groundless assertion that "the voice of the American Negro is distinguishable from that of the white singer . . . thick lips and a flat nose must influence the tone-production in a certain degree, and many, though by no means all, of our colored population have these anatomical peculiarities."[26] Other pedagogues argued more insidiously for the aesthetic supremacy of European vocal technique: pure, clean, effortless, and emanating from a restrained and properly comported (white) body.[27]

Yet focusing exclusively on the racist ideologies of vocal culture's most visible proponents risks eliding the ways in which these pedagogical techniques were repurposed and reimagined by the very voices they sought to suppress. Black vocal pedagogues' guidance for amateur singers offered a distinct perspective on the relationship among body, voice, and race. Some teachers linked music with diligent self-application: Harry A. Williams proclaimed that "he who would sing well must first learn the lesson of patience, perseverance, 'stick-to-itiveness' and self-denial," engaging in "indefatigable plodding and struggling to the end that victory may be the reward."[28] Such zealous rhetoric yoked vocal culture to racial uplift ideology, effectively democratizing *and* stratifying beautiful singing as universally attainable in theory, but reached by only a few in practice. The choral director Pedro T. Tinsley's 1912 manual *Tone-Placing and Voice Development* promised to demystify "the technical side of the vocal art" by way of "a course in the art of breathing, structure of the vocal apparatus, hearing the voice."[29] In line with the era's dominant aesthetic ideals, Tinsley prized voices that sounded effortless and technically poised, yet still artistically individuated: he maintained that singers "of the race" "may be compared to flowers," each with a unique profile.[30] A satisfied reader from Washington, DC praised Tinsley's guidance as transformative: "It seems to me that I am getting a new voice."[31]

Hallmarks of the well-trained Black operatic voice included strength, effortlessness, range, and interpretive versatility. These descriptors differ from qualities admired in African American singers not trained in opera: the contemporaneous vaudeville and Broadway star Florence Mills, for instance, was often described as sounding sweet, pure, and delicate.[32] They also differ from white critics' racially essentialist characterizations. A 1918 *New York Times* review of a Black soprano's performance of French and Italian arias highlighted her "refined natural charm, not without racial

touches of deep feeling and of humor"—language exemplifying what Nina Sun Eidsheim describes as the "phantom genealogy" haunting Black operatic singing, in which white listeners invariably perceive Black voices as dark, dusky, or rich, regardless of their timbral quality.[33] By contrast, a review of the same artist in the *Defender* noted her "resonant and appealing voice" and effective use of the "coloratura style," both evidence of her "training" and "continued studies."[34] A vivid review of the "strong" and "vibrant" singing of Mayme Calloway-Byron praised her French diction and ability to sing with "beautiful nuances" that "flowed like a limpid stream," marveling that there seemed to be "not a whit" of effort in her performance. In a moving conclusion, the critic noted that Calloway-Byron was not to be considered the "colored" or "Black" Patti or Galli-Curci (an allusion to the common pattern by which Black singers were described in relation to white counterparts). No: "She is herself; beautiful, sufficient and superb."[35] Unconstrained by reductive essentialism, the Black operatic voice became a conduit for individuality and artistic self-invention.

Such questions of selfhood were bound up with issues of repertoire and subjectivity. An illustrative example comes from the career of the Chicago-based soprano Anita Patti Brown. Born Patsy Dean in Georgia, Brown was a talented singer who was uninspired by the popular stage. Instead, she nurtured what one writer called an "ambition to become an opera star," bolstered by "a self-conviction that she had been endowed with a voice." Alas, "instructors and audiences alike wanted only to hear her sing the spirituals. 'You can never hope to become an opera star,' they told her, 'your color is against you. True, you have a voice but unfortunately you are handicapped.' Anita was soon to learn that Negro, handicap, and barrier were all synonymous. Who for instance could better interpret the spirituals than a Negro? . . . Any Negro with a voice at all, *devoid of training*[,] could sing with all the pathos capable of wringing from the audience the sympathy and understanding of a persecuted race."[36] In its tight conflation of voice, repertoire, and affect, this framing not only naturalized the Black voice as untrained, but also suggested that Black singers should limit themselves to the spirituals. It filtered Brown's voice through the lens of what Jon Cruz calls "ethnosympathy," a mode of listening that prioritized white liberal audiences' emotional response over singers' own artistry and subjective experiences.[37] Despite these frustrations, the writer maintained a belief that operatic singing might "[reveal] to an unbiased world the arrant injustice suffered by a people."[38] If this optimism might seem overstated, given the racialized perceptual filters that continued to haunt Black opera singers, it nonetheless illuminates a fundamental aspect of these artists' self-

perception and the hopes they invested in opera. The art form promised an opportunity for artistic and social success (note the repeated use of the term "opera star"); disentangled the Black classical voice from the historical suffering associated with the spirituals; and offered a pathway toward a more just world.

The vast majority of Black operatic singing went unrecorded. Yet those artists who did reach the recording studio created a small but significant body of arias and art songs, working against the industry's segregated norms.[39] Black Swan Records (named after the nineteenth-century concert singer Elizabeth Taylor Greenfield, known as the "Black Swan") was the primary studio to record and produce Black operatic singing. Launched in 1921 by Harry Pace, Black Swan distinguished itself as the first major Black-owned and -operated recording company. Its musical purview was eclectic: blues, opera, spirituals, ragtime, comedy, and more, intended to represent "every type of race music," including "the high-class ballads and operatic selections."[40] In one striking advertisement, the company took on the presumption that African American audiences would prefer popular music. Sardonically titled "Colored People Don't Want Classic Music!," it urged the reader to "go to your Record Dealer and ask for the Better Class of Records by Colored Artists. If there is a Demand he will keep Them." At the top of a list of "better class" records were arias from *Rigoletto, La Traviata,* and *Lakmé.* The advertisement relied on a fairly reductive linkage between musical genre and racial uplift, but it was also indicative of an interest in listening to opera among Black consumers.

Black Swan's commitment to recording opera proved unsustainable: the company disbanded in 1923, and during its brief existence, most of its revenue was derived from blues and jazz records. Its few extant recordings of opera, shaped by the specific conditions of the recording studio, cannot be taken as wholly representative of how these singers sounded in the context of a staged production or a recital. But to "listen in detail" to these recordings, to use a term theorized by Alexandra Vazquez, is to directly access the sounds of early Black operatic counterculture.[41] Take, for example, the singing of Antoinette Garnes, who is credited as having made some of "the first opera records using the Negro voice" for Black Swan.[42] Known as the "nightingale of the race," Garnes grew up in Detroit and studied at Howard University before moving to Chicago.[43] Upon graduating from the Chicago Musical College in 1919, she was awarded a prize for her vocal skill, along with the opportunity to perform the aria "Caro nome," from Verdi's *Rigoletto,* during commencement exercises.[44] She became the only African American to sing in the chorus of the Chicago Grand Opera

Company, which she did for several years. She was reputed to have sixty-five operas in her repertoire, as well as knowledge of Spanish, French, Italian, and German.[45] One reviewer likened Garnes's voice to that of the English soprano Maggie Teyte, a specialist in French art song (notably, a far more nuanced comparison than sobriquets like the "Black Patti," which foregrounded shared celebrity rather than shared vocal characteristics).[46] The *Defender*'s critic described Garnes's voice in vibrant detail as a "cerise voice, warm, highly pathetic, tender, passionless," qualities engendered by her "breath control, melodic flow and poetic content."[47]

In 1922, Garnes recorded "Caro nome" for Black Swan Records. The record is simple and elegant in its visual design. Below the company's logo, an image of a swan in rippling waters, the work is identified as "GRAND OPERA (Rigoletto) Verdi"; the name of the aria and the respectable moniker "Mrs. Antoinette Garnes" also appear. The aria would have been familiar to many listeners: it was (and remains) a popular showpiece for sopranos, and it figured prominently in the repertory of an earlier generation of Black concert singers, including Sissieretta Jones.[48] Virtuosic and technically demanding, it offers the soprano the opportunity to showcase her dexterity, vocal control, and ability to portray an emotional metamorphosis. The opera's heroine, Gilda, is a teenage girl, smitten with her beloved and happily overcome by her emotions. Although she will later learn that the object of her affections—of whose "caro nome," or "dear name," she sings—is not who he claims to be, at this moment she is filled with hopeful wonder, even naïveté. Perched above a shimmering tapestry of woodwinds and muted strings, the singer must first unspool a tricky, highly embellished vocal line with a swanlike ease, conveying her sense of innocence and tranquility. As the aria goes on, its emotional and technical demands intensify, requiring the singer to access new dimensions of her dramatic palette. Stepwise descending melodies, whose notes are separated by eighth-note rests, demand a façade of sustained lyricism punctuated by a heartbeat-like undercurrent that conveys the physicality of the heroine's romantic awakening. Bravura flights of fancy, rife with challenging skips and leaps, evoke the quickening of her sentiments.

Garnes takes the aria at a relatively brisk tempo. The matter-of-fact pacing complicates the simplicity of the melodic line, adding a dimension of maturity and sophistication to a character more often portrayed as an utter innocent. She moves deftly through moments of technical complexity, as if eager to reach high, sustained notes, which she gives ample space to bloom. In a final cadenza, she displays a flawless staccato, seeming to revel in her own virtuosity. There is a potent convergence of vivacity and dignity

in the performance. Both the joyful innocence of Verdi's music and the brilliance of Garnes's technique create affective distance from the melancholic sorrow often associated with the spirituals and, by extension, Black concert singing writ large. These qualities must have accrued additional significance when Garnes first performed "Caro nome" in 1919, at a commencement ceremony, at what she may have hoped would be the outset of a long career in opera. If, in the context of a full production, "Caro nome" is tinged with anticipation of the tragedies that will later befall its heroine, as a standalone piece it brims with uncomplicated potential. It is even possible to imagine Garnes singing the aria not to a lover, but to opera itself, as a youthful expression of the hope and possibility she invested in the art form. The racist policies of mainstream operatic companies meant that Garnes was never able to perform a full operatic role.[49] Yet even as she—like so many other aspiring singers—was denied this opportunity, Garnes repurposed Verdi's music as a means of individualized self-fashioning, a venue for her own virtuosity to flourish.

Opera in the Black Public Sphere

Just as opera created opportunities to forge a new relationship to one's own self, it also facilitated new forms of sociality and interpersonal encounter in the public sphere. The institutional contexts of churches, schools, political organizations, and social clubs offered myriad opportunities to engage with opera, ranging from the ephemeral—say, an aria sung before a speech—to sustained endeavors, such as the creation of a school dedicated to operatic pedagogy and performance. While such activities certainly offered opportunities for the transmission of existing information about opera, they were also arenas in which new ideas about the art form could be created. Collectively, they formed a foundational social infrastructure for Black operatic counterculture.

Musical organizations became a mainstay of Black institutional life. As Lynn Abbott and Doug Seroff have argued, the "variety and abundance of black vocal music training available early in the twentieth century suggests a bold socio-cultural experiment."[50] While many pedagogical initiatives were dedicated to spirituals, gospel, and other sacred traditions, others explored Western classical repertoire. Black choral societies, often affiliated with churches, proliferated, especially in cities with substantial middle-class populations. A singer in Washington, DC might join the Amphion Glee Club (est. 1891), Treble Clef Club (1897), Washington Permanent Chorus (1899), Coleridge-Taylor Choral Society (1901), or Burleigh Choral Society

(1903); one in Chicago might seek out the Choral Study Club (1900) or Umbrian Glee Club (1908), among many others.[51] In addition to their function as venues for collective singing, choral societies also provided a training ground for aspiring opera singers. Marian Anderson soloed with Chicago's Umbrian Glee Club in 1922 and 1923, long before white institutions opened their doors. Although these groups performed mostly oratorios and other concert repertoire—Coleridge-Taylor's *Hiawatha* and Mendelssohn's *Elijah* were popular choices—they made occasional forays into opera. For instance, in 1925, a choral group in Portsmouth, Virginia presented Saint-Saëns's *Samson et Dalila,* an ambitious selection for an amateur organization, at the Zion Baptist Church.[52]

African American students might also encounter opera within the context of their general education. In the late 1920s, under the tutelage of the African American conductor and educator W. Llewelyn Wilson, students at Baltimore's Frederick Douglass High School presented full operatic productions, including Viktor Nessler's *The Pied Piper of Hamelin* and Wagner's *The Flying Dutchman*—a work that, as one critic noted, "taxes the abilities of veteran Wagnerian singers."[53] (When Wilson met the composer's son, Siegfried, at a Baltimore Symphony concert in 1925, the younger Wagner, though "surprised," was encouraging about the "daring undertaking."[54]) These were yearlong projects in which Wilson trained a chorus of hundreds of singers, and "various departments of the school and the entire faculty collaborated with the music department in contributing to the costumes, scenery, dramatic direction, etc."[55] Most of those involved did not pursue opera further, but student Avon Long, who offered "a most convincing performance" of Wagner's title role, became a well-regarded singer and actor who sang the role of Sportin' Life in the 1942 revival of *Porgy and Bess.*[56] Soprano Anne Wiggins Brown, who created the role of Bess in 1935, also attended Douglass High School, and she later recalled that the "nearly professional" productions offered her "a good deal of training."[57] Long and Brown's trajectories illuminate a counterhistory of Black operatic singing by showing how their knowledge of canonical opera was formulated in Black collective spaces.

By contrast, although many historically Black colleges and universities featured extensive classical music curricula, their vocal programs tended to foreground Austro-German choral music rather than opera. Fisk University's Mozart Society, for instance, performed works by Handel, Mendelssohn, and Brahms, as well as its namesake composer.[58] The comparative lack of attention to opera frustrated some students. At Howard University, the student journalist R. G. Doggett praised his peer, Perle Alexander, as a

stupendously gifted soprano, an "undeveloped genius" who was qualified to join "the front rank of grand opera prima donnas," yet lacked the "necessary attention for the cultivation of her wonderful gifts" under the tutelage of Howard's "two over worked music teachers."[59] Absent sustained institutional support, pursuing an in-depth education in opera remained a challenge.

A burgeoning national network of Black musical institutions offered additional opportunities. The National Association of Negro Musicians (NANM), founded in 1919, assumed what A. Kori Hill has described as a "self-determinist mission," facilitating collaboration and connection among Black classical musicians via a network of local chapters.[60] The Chicago Musical Association, a NANM affiliate, presented a series of "Opera Nights" in 1920, wherein "On Monday night, Feb. 2, Mrs. Martha Mitchell gave a paper on the Origin of Opera; Mrs. Mayme Marshall sang an aria from Salome; Mrs. Clara Hutchinson gave the story of Mozart's Magic Flute; T. Theo. Taylor gave excerpts from the Bohemian Girl and Miss Nannie Strayhorn played the left hand arrangement of the sextette from Lucia. Feb. 16 Mrs. Maudelle Bous-Wagner, and Mrs. Antoinette Garnes read a paper on The Ring [and] gave the story of DeKoven's Rip Van winkle with vocal illustrations."[61] These details evoke an intriguing scene, a gathering of like-minded Black Chicagoans learning about opera as they crafted a self-sustaining alternative to the art form's exclusionary mainstream institutions.

This account on "Opera Nights" appeared in the *Chicago Defender*, one of several Black newspapers that functioned as vital venues for the circulation and creation of operatic knowledge. Building on the groundbreaking work of Sylvester Russell, a new cohort of critics used the press as a creative terrain on which to work out the relationship between opera and Blackness in public. Given that the Black press was, as Anna Everett has written, "the only dedicated forum for the mass cultivation, appreciation, and dissemination of African American ideas, culture, values, talent, literature, thought, and analysis," these critics' work became a primary site of African Americans' ideas about what opera sounded like, who it was for, and why it mattered.[62] The press also provided an opportunity to counteract white journalists' tendencies to ignore, misrepresent, or spectacularize Black cultural life.[63] African American opera critics strove for breadth and quantity, less interested in filtering out impressive "firsts" than in portraying the full sweep of Black participation in the art form. This approach might be understood as the democratizing flipside of the politics of respectability: eager to present African Americans in a positive light, journalists had an

ideological investment in describing Black achievement in abundant detail, refuting racist stereotypes with a deluge of counterexamples.[64]

Black newspapers both documented and shaped perceptions of opera within African American communities. They contributed to the ongoing evolution of the art form's class-based associations, a debate that took on particular significance as the arrival of rural Black migrants exacerbated intraracial class tensions in northern cities. When the esteemed Abbotts of Chicago rang in the new year at a production of Strauss's *Die Fledermaus,* the *Defender* detailed their luxurious outfits and decadent afterparty, reiterating a connection between opera and elite society. Yet the newspaper also reported on middle-class opera enthusiasts like the "20 barbers" who took to attending the Chicago Grand Opera "almost nightly," as well as a recent migrant from Mississippi who worked as a shoe shiner and was a frequent attendee.[65] (Such reports also disproved the pervasive assumption that Black audiences were unfamiliar with opera. In 1923, the *Defender* reported on the white, Arkansas-born singer Mary McCormic's vexing decision to exclude arias during a South Side recital, due to what a reporter surmised may have been "a fear that the audience would not understand"—even though "everyone in the audience would have welcomed 'One Fine Day,' from 'Madame Butterfly,' or the 'Bell Song' from 'Lakme,' both well known and giving every opportunity for a glorious display of the voice."[66])

Critics embraced the participatory sociality that the Black press made possible. In 1913, the *New York Age* published reviews by R. G. Doggett of two student productions: *The Mikado,* performed by the Washington Conservatory of Music's Choral Society, and *The Lady of Lyons,* presented by the College Dramatic Club of Howard University.[67] Doggett's uncomplimentary reviews elicited angry responses from readers, which appeared in a follow-up piece, "The Critic Criticised." Some respondents took issue with Doggett's harshness toward student performers, but others took a more expansive tack, opining that the "columns of The Age should be used to encourage rather than to dampen the ardor of the members of the race in their efforts making for the uplift of the race."[68] The debate's narrow subject matter had broad implications, raising questions about whether there was value in artistic criticism that did not advance racial progress; whether genuine but negative criticism was antithetical to racial uplift; and whether uncritical celebration did more harm than good.

One especially incisive critical voice was Lester Walton, who, as a writer and editor for the *Age* beginning in 1908, contextualized the New York opera scene in relation to US racial politics. Born in St. Louis in 1882, Walton led a varied career as a journalist, theater manager, composer, lyri-

cist, activist, and diplomat.[69] He used his platform as a critic to argue for opera's political urgency, making evident its complicity with extant social structures and potential to compel those structures to change. His ideas about opera, in other words, were not an inevitable consequence of his status as a Black opera critic in a racist nation; they were an original theoretical contribution to opera criticism through which he re-envisioned the form and its political possibilities. His criticism revealed a disturbingly cozy relationship between opera in New York and the climate of white supremacist terror and extrajudicial violence across the Jim Crow United States. In 1919, he reported on a campaign led by US Navy sailors to stop the performance of German opera and operetta at the Lexington Opera House in New York during World War I. At first, the mayor's office defended the opera house's right to stage this repertoire, but popular protests—rotten eggs tossed at the stage, bricks hurled into the orchestra pit—ultimately led to cancellations. Walton compared the hullabaloo to that which had surrounded the release of D. W. Griffith's notorious *The Birth of a Nation* in 1915, a few years prior; despite immense effort, Black activists had been unable to prevent the film's release in New York. Outraged by this double standard with respect to cultural production, racial violence, and censorship, Walton called out the city government for paying more attention to "two thousand sailors" than to "many thousands of colored taxpayers." He identified a fundamental hypocrisy: "Aversion against German opera is a mere matter of sentiment; the anti-Negro propaganda strikes at the very roots of the fundamental principles of democracy." Perhaps most damning was the article's final sentence, which suggested that the protesting sailors "would just as soon take an active part in lynchings in the South and elsewhere."[70] The sailors' ostensibly patriotic opposition to German opera could not hide the fact that, if given the chance, they would likely commit racist violence against fellow Americans.

While Walton used opera criticism as a vehicle for contemporary social critique, the critic Nora Douglas Holt articulated a sophisticated conceptual revision of opera's past and present. Holt became the *Defender*'s classical music critic in 1917; her column, which ran for six years, was the first dedicated exclusively to opera and classical music in an African American newspaper. An extraordinary pianist and composer, Holt was the first African American in the United States to earn a master's degree in music. The *Defender* reported that her master's thesis consisted of a "symphonic rhapsody of forty-two pages for a hundred-piece symphony orchestra," but this and most of her other composition manuscripts were stolen from her during her travels in Europe—an event she would later mourn as "the tragedy of

my life."[71] Devoted to creating a strong infrastructure for Black musical life, Holt was a co-founder of NANM.[72] In January 1921, she also established a magazine, *Music and Poetry,* that featured editorials, essays, and sheet music by a distinguished roster of primarily African American contributors, including composer Clarence Cameron White, violinist Kemper Harreld, pianist Helen Hagan, and musicologist Maud Cuney Hare.[73]

On the level of form, Holt declined to organize her *Defender* column, "News of the Music World," according to what segregation demanded. Instead, the "Music World" became an aspirational evocation of W. E. B. Du Bois's vision of Black and white artists as "co-worker[s] in the kingdom of culture."[74] Her criticism traversed local, national, and international borders, sometimes within the space of a single column. A representative dispatch from October 22, 1921 covered a recital by German-British pianist Harold Bauer; opening night at the Chicago Symphony; and an "autumn songfest" at Olivet Baptist Church, the city's largest Black congregation.[75] Another recounted an April 1918 recital at Walters AME Zion Church: "Gloria in Excelsio Mass in B Flat, a beautiful blended theme of tender airs, was rendered by the choir, along with the renditions of Miss Ruth Woolen, Mrs. T. Howell and N. Komo, who gave the affair a foreign touch of songs in Zulu language. The designed dedication of Von Suppe's 'Poet and Peasant' was produced in a duet played by the Misses Thelma and Annie Pierce. Rev. Dr. B. Solin, Jew, pastor of the 12 street Hebrew Presbyterian Mission, lectured, giving a wonderful description of Jewish destiny and Christianity, which was followed by sentimental selections by Mrs. S. Mackler (white), soprano, and Hardy B. Woodfolk, tenor."[76] The remarkable heterogeneity of this program offered tangible evidence of how people, sounds, and ideas traveled across the borders that Jim Crow attempted to enforce.

Holt's *Defender* columns regularly featured synopses of canonical operas, including *Tosca, Madama Butterfly,* and *Aida.* In one column, she addressed the question of why Black audiences should care about an art form created and performed mostly by white people. "One might ask, 'What have these affairs to do with the Negro?' she wrote. "To the torpid mind, nothing; to the discerning mind, much." As she explained, "An impresario has not successfully culminated his opera season without a performance of 'Aida,' the story of an Ethiopian princess, or 'L'Africaine,' of an African queen; 'Lakme,' 'Othello,' and others."[77] With this observation, Holt put forth a narrative of opera's history in which Blackness had always been central, disentangling the music itself from the white-dominated institutional settings in which it was most often performed. And she articulated an urgent need for Black

composers to contribute to the art form's development: "Personally, I am skeptical of American whites writing Negro music . . . The Negro and the Indian are being sacrificed on the altar of popularity by ambitious composers," resulting in distortions "so exotic as to be wholly unrecognizable by the Race." Holt instead advocated for a sort of musical-racial self-determination, arguing that nonwhite composers should "guard [their music] jealously . . . I predict that within the next twenty years the music world will hail a Black Wagner and call him master."[78] The critique inverted and reclaimed the linguistic tropes of white supremacy; in her imagining of the musical future, white-authored music is "exotic" and the Black composer reigns as "master."

By writing about opera in the Black press, critics like Walton and Holt enabled the art form to become part of their readers' daily lives. Embracing the variety that was an inherent characteristic of the weekly newspaper, they de-exceptionalized and even democratized opera, rejecting its typical associations with whiteness and elitism by placing it on the page alongside other aspects of Black culture and the broader sociopolitical landscape. If, as Karl Hagstrom Miller has argued, the emerging music industry was involved in the work of "segregating sound" during this era, then critics used the Black press to desegregate operatic sound.[79] Walton did not look to operatic institutions as aspirational models or potential sites of desegregation, but rather illuminated their complicity in racial injustice. Holt, in contrast, prioritized the broad dissemination of musical knowledge and illuminated opera's multifaceted relationship to Blackness. The breadth of their respective engagements with the art form indicates just how interwoven opera was with other facets of Black associational and public life. It also demonstrates how Black operatic counterculture was never exclusively, or even primarily, about a desire for the desegregation of existing spaces and systems. Rather, these critics thought about opera's relationship to white supremacy and to Black cultural production in far more capacious ways.

Not only was operatic knowledge embedded within schools, universities, musical associations, and newspapers, but it also prompted the creation of new institutions. The South Side School of Grand Opera was founded in 1920 by James Ahlyn Mundy, a storied member of Chicago's Black musical community. Born in 1886 in Maysville, Kentucky, Mundy moved to Chicago in 1906 to work as a post office clerk and study at a conservatory. After organizing his fellow postal workers into a group called the Federal Glee Club in 1910, he became one of the city's most renowned choral directors; by 1916 "more than a thousand singers [had] come within the inspired sway of his baton."[80] Mundy's own operatic singing was perhaps

underwhelming (an early review noted that although he directed the Glee Club in a "calm, dignified manner," his rendition of the Toreador Song from *Carmen* revealed that his voice was "in bad condition and the pity is Mr. Mundy does not seem cognizant of that fact"), but his investment in the art form was longstanding.[81] In 1913, he conducted the chorus "Hail, Bright Abode" from Wagner's *Tannhäuser* as part of an Emancipation Celebration organized by Ida B. Wells.[82] At a 1918 YWCA festival, he appeared in scenes from Gounod's *Faust*.[83] Mundy coached private students in arias from *Aida* and other canonical repertoire, promoting himself in advertisements as an "opera coach."[84] These diffuse efforts coalesced on November 6, 1920, when he announced the opening of the South Side School of Grand Opera. "Mr. Mundy believes that there are enough serious minded male and female singers in Chicago," the announcement read, "to support a school for the study and performance of grand opera."[85]

Like the Drury Company before it, the group was predicated on an ethos of self-determination. But while Drury had recruited performers from across the professional musical and theatrical landscape of turn-of-the-century New York in an effort to demonstrate opera's potential to serve as a locus of Black cultural achievement, Mundy sought out amateur musicians interested in studying the art form for their own edification. Meeting weekly on Tuesday evenings at the Raymond Public School, they began an intensive study of Friedrich von Flotow's *Martha,* a hallmark of the nineteenth-century repertory that tells a lighthearted story set in provincial England. Ninety students joined the first rehearsal, scores in hand, and by January 1921, the ranks had swelled to more than one hundred. It was, the *Defender* reported, "a beehive of musical activity every Tuesday night," in which "the technique of opera is taking hold upon the interested students and much improvement is being shown."[86] Munday also recruited a handful of experienced soloists. James A. Lillard, a tenor who had appeared in vaudeville but specialized in Russian art music, joined the company in a principal role, as did soprano Nellie Dobson and mezzo-soprano Lillian Hawkins Jones. After rehearsing for more than a year, the company gave two sold-out performances at the Aryan Grotto Theater in December 1921. Their success prompted an additional performance—at a larger venue, Auditorium Hall, with an expanded orchestra and chorus—in February 1922.

Mundy's school enacted new forms of sociality that fostered intraracial collaboration and eschewed the desegregationist burden of breaking new ground. Performance was in some ways subordinate to the group's core educational mission—a focus borne out by the intensity of the rehearsal process, which required a sustained, months-long commitment throughout

the cold Chicago winter. Extramusical activities reinforced the group's communal ethos. Within months of its founding, the school had amassed nearly two thousand dollars in donations from fifty individual donors, in amounts ranging from five to one hundred dollars.[87] Tickets for performances were sold at neighborhood barbershops and the YMCA. Prior to the planned performances, a newspaper preview urged the "average citizen" to attend, offering both a plot synopsis of *Martha* and a rationale: "Opera, after all, is a first-class musical show . . . many prominent people [plan to attend, and] it is expected that You will follow."[88]

Other experiential details are more difficult to parse. Archival evidence scarcely captures what happened as a student who had scrounged together the funds to purchase a score trekked to rehearsal each Tuesday after work and practiced her part at home in the interim, squeezing in time to go over tricky passages between rehearsals. The particulars of Mundy's pedagogical strategies remain opaque, although one reporter approvingly noted that— in contrast to the "many poorly trained and equipped teachers of music loose in the land"—Mundy offered "splendid training . . . [The ensemble's] teamwork is admirable and their attention to the details of absolute correctness in the matter of notes, good attack, and release, combined with interpretation of a high order, forcast [*sic*] for their first real opera, 'Martha' a real success."[89] While the production was lauded as a landmark event (the first performance of opera by an all-Black group in Chicago, one critic noted, since Freeman's *The Martyr*), critical assessments of its musical quality were minimal, particularly with respect to the ensemble. "The chorus was sufficiently acquainted with the score, kept in time and tune, and admirably acted their minor parts," wrote one reviewer; the performance "gave ample evidence of the careful training of the members of the company, their intelligent grasp of the thought and material of the opera," wrote another.[90] Such comments echoed Mundy's pedagogical priorities by decentering the performance itself, instead drawing attention to the long-term training that members of the ensemble had undertaken.

In their yearlong commitment to a collective study of *Martha,* Mundy's company offered neither straightforward resistance to the segregation of the operatic mainstream nor unassailable evidence of Black cultural uniqueness. The production was instead distinct because of the institutional structure that emerged to support it, as well as the school's explicit prioritization of pedagogy and process. As Jarvis Givens has explained with respect to early twentieth-century Black educational endeavors, "Antiblack exclusion partly triggered the formation of these institutions, but to assume that this is the sole reason for their emergence or that they mimicked the aims and ideals

of the white public sphere, where black inclusion hinged on domination, would be a mistake."[91] Accordingly, teachers and students engaged in what Givens called "fugitive pedagogy," a practice by which they were able to covertly critique white supremacist norms. To create a Black institutional space in which to study and perform canonical European opera (rather than, say, newly composed opera by Black composers) was to forge a fugitive pathway toward artistic self-determination. The group's embrace of *Martha*—its canonicity, its virtuosity, its popularity—might even be understood retrospectively in Afrofuturist terms, as an endeavor that revisited and revised the European musical past so as to conceptualize a different future for Black culture.

The South Side School of Grand Opera was, in many respects, short-lived. *Martha* was its only full production, though on multiple subsequent occasions, members of the ensemble appeared in programs featuring excerpts from *Rigoletto, Les Huguenots,* and *Il trovatore.*[92] Mundy continued to conduct choirs until the age of ninety, but he never again staged a full opera.[93] Yet despite the brevity of its existence and the atypicality of its organizational structure, the group laid an important foundation for later endeavors within the diffuse, sprawling, and perpetually evolving institution of Black operatic counterculture. Much like the Baltimore high-school students who sang Wagner before becoming key figures in *Porgy and Bess,* several participants went on to perform with other operatic ensembles in the 1930s and 1940s. The experience of singing with the company also shaped the lives of participants who did not pursue the art form further. Hyman Mills, who sang a principal role in *Martha,* was a Mississippi-born insurance clerk who later became a minister. After joining the company, he went on to sing with several local church choirs, and even organized a choir of his own to help his church pay off a mortgage. In 1959, he officiated the funeral of Cleo Dickerson, the group's accompanist; at Mills's own funeral, in 1961, Mundy led a choral performance. This web of connections suggests that for those who trained their voices at the South Side School of Grand Opera, the experience of being part of the company was anything but ephemeral. Rather, singing opera became one facet of a rich Black public sphere in which enduring relationships might be formed.

Deep Breathing

As the cultural uses of opera changed throughout the 1910s and 1920s, so did the meaning of opera itself. The art form's newfound potential as a locus of Black artists' self-making meant that not only operatic music, but also

operatically trained voices, could now be repurposed across a variety of settings, allowing classical vocal training to permeate other musical and social activities. And as opera collided with other creative endeavors in classrooms, newspaper columns, and choral societies, its parameters became more capacious, creating conditions ripe for experimental revisions of the art form that might unsettle extant racialized cultural hierarchies. Unmoored from its culturally sanctioned place in the (white) opera house, it could be attached to a variety of political and social standpoints. In the 1910s, the soprano-turned-pedagogue E. Azalia Hackley reoriented her own operatic training to develop a formalized program of vocal pedagogy for Black amateur singers across the country, as well as a more wide-ranging program of respectable behavior for Black women and girls. Hackley's efforts exemplify the conceptual mutability that opera took on within African American culture, as well as its imbrication in broader discourses of race, gender, and sexuality.

Hackley, born Emma Azalia Smith in Tennessee in 1867, had a tumultuous early life. When she was a child, her family fled racial violence and the rising prominence of the KKK and moved to Detroit. She taught elementary school before moving to Denver in 1894 to marry the lawyer and activist Edwin Hackley, whom she had met backstage at a recital given by Sissieretta Jones. Arriving in the city just months after the premiere of Freeman's *The Martyr,* she studied voice at the University of Denver and became the school's first African American graduate in 1900.[94] She gained accolades for her interpretive acumen as well as the "agility" and "tallishness" of her voice.[95] Predisposed toward mobility—she once reminisced that even when she was a "tiny girl," the "faint sound of a locomotive bell" prompted "a strange yearning to jump on the train and go with it—to see the world"—Hackley traveled extensively within and beyond the United States.[96] (As her biographer, Juanita Karpf, notes, her light complexion may have enabled her to pass as white during her journeys, insulating her from some of the racism that Black travelers encountered.[97]) She ventured to Europe to augment her training, studying with the esteemed operatic tenor Jean de Reszke in Paris and the English oratorio singer William Shakespeare in London. But in 1910, at age forty-three, Hackley announced that she would retire from the stage.[98] Having established herself as "the latest star in the musical firmament," she began to find that status unfulfilling.[99] Offstage, she finalized her separation from Edwin Hackley, whom she had married sixteen years prior. She embarked on a nationwide tour that included appearances in Denver, Chicago, Pittsburgh, and New York, as well as a six-month period spent visiting Black high schools and colleges in the South.

Within a few short years, Hackley reinvented herself as a modern, mobile educator, the "vocal teacher of ten thousand" who would travel the nation teaching African Americans how to sing beautifully—and how to transform themselves in the process.[100]

Hackley's transition from recitalist to pedagogue was documented by Sylvester Russell, a longtime admirer of her artistry. In a review of a performance she gave at Chicago's Orchestra Hall in 1911, he deemed Hackley the "prothonotary administrator of musical science and the queen of extemporaneous bewitchery."[101] The program mixed arias from *Mignon* and *The Barber of Seville* with English and Scottish folk songs, then concluded with three spirituals. Interspersed with the musical selections were spoken demonstrations during which Hackley expounded on such topics as the "racial characteristics" that made Black people natural singers; the technical requirements for strong "exclamation and breathing"; and the combined importance of "brains, breath, and voice." Though Russell acknowledged the usefulness of Hackley's lectures and commended her singing, he found the format unsatisfying, asserting that to merge excellent singing with pedagogy was "beneath her position, dignity and standard as an artist."[102] The critique exemplifies the difference between Russell's understanding of opera, which was premised on the art form's singular and aspirational status, and Hackley's, which concretely demonstrated how operatic singing could be repurposed as a means of education.

"As I sang, season after season, I could see that no community was materially benefitted from my singing," Hackley wrote, "[so] I decided to give the best years of my life to my race for their musical uplift."[103] Her turn from the concert stage to the teaching studio aligned her with other Black female vocalists such as Anita Patti Brown and Antoinette Garnes, who also became teachers later in their careers. But Hackley was not content simply to take on private students. Instead, to promulgate her ideas, she both engaged with existing institutional contexts and created new ones. While living in Philadelphia, she founded a community choral ensemble called the People's Chorus, one hundred voices strong. Like Baltimore's Douglass High School and Chicago's South Side School of Grand Opera, the group cultivated a new generation of singers (among its members was a preteen Marian Anderson, who stood on a chair while singing solos so that she could be seen by the audience).[104] Hackley's pedagogical project reached its zenith over the course of the 1910s when she launched a series of multi-day choral workshops offered in communities across the country. She traveled from city to city and school to school, sometimes working with individuals or small groups, sometimes leading an ensemble of hundreds. In 1912

alone, she reached more than 64,000 students, from schoolchildren to adult enthusiasts, once teaching three thousand people in a single day.[105] In addition to her work as an itinerant teacher, Hackley also established the Normal Vocal Institute in Chicago, which promised to train young Black musicians as concert singers and vocal teachers. Over the course of its four-year existence, it attracted more than one hundred pupils and offered free or inexpensive training in Hackley's methods of vocal culture.

These ambitious projects built on Hackley's own training in opera. Karpf argues persuasively that Hackley "had to assemble her own pedagogical approach" as she developed a method that "explored areas of commonality between classical repertoire and music education, [and] presented to her public an empowering compromise between these two seemingly disparate worlds."[106] Her European instructors influenced her pedagogy: de Reszke was known for his spectacular approach to teaching, in which individual vocal lessons took place in a private theater in front of other members of his studio, while her London-based instructor, Shakespeare, was a dedicated teacher of large groups who instructed audiences in the fundamentals of singing. Yet even as Hackley incorporated these approaches, she also theorized an original relationship between Blackness and vocality. As Nina Sun Eidsheim has shown, classical voice teachers often "train and pair timbre profiles with conceptual areas such as identity and authenticity," relying on the epistemologically incoherent idea that operatic voices should be classified in terms of racial or national schools (a "German tone," a "French sound").[107] For Hackley, however, the notion of an essential, embodied link between race and voice was a compelling means of retheorizing a culturally constituted notion of the Black voice as unserious, comedic, and debased. Perhaps surprisingly, she critiqued her European instructors for disregarding racial particularity—for failing to "tell [her] anything about the characteristics of the voice of the Negro. All the Negroes that they had heard sing sang exactly like other people if they sang correctly." She took matters into her own hands, conducting what she called "investigations," "observations," and "experiments" to "discover what characteristics the Negro possesses, and what he lacks."[108]

This quasi-scientific inquiry eventually led Hackley away from opera and toward a repertoire comprised primarily of folk songs and spirituals.[109] To reconcile her investment in classical vocal training with her commitment to "musical uplift," she separated the Black operatic voice from the operatic repertoire, reimagining that voice in relation to genres already racialized as Black. By 1915, her mass choral trainings had evolved into events that she termed "folk song festivals," at which she conducted large choruses,

Azalia Hackley (*front row, fifth from left*) with one of her choruses.

numbering in the hundreds, in communal renditions of spirituals. Held in Atlanta, Baltimore, Chicago, Dallas, and many other cities, these were festive affairs, with spectacular performances preceded by rehearsals at which Hackley trained the assembled singers in vocal technique. A photograph of a chorus from an event in Harlem, in November 1917, depicts Hackley seated in the front row of a group of young singers. They are dressed formally in white gowns and dark suits, crowded together in an auditorium. Rather than lecturing from a podium or appearing alone onstage, Hackley sits among the singers, hands demurely in her lap, as if to visually demonstrate what she called the "absolutely democratic" structure of the community chorus and the potential for collective uplift it portended.[110]

In reimagining classical vocal training as foundational to Black collective folk singing, Hackley both expanded and constricted opera's aesthetic parameters. If her work invoked the nineteenth-century genre of the concert spiritual, it also disrupted a "folk song to opera" paradigm that imagined Black musical material as a catalyst for the development of classical compositions. Hackley theorized that relationship as multidirectional rather than evolutionary: operatic pedagogy made beautiful performances of the spirituals possible; in turn, the spirituals played a critical role in expanding what "opera," as a category of vocal art, might sound like. Yet in contradistinction to other Black opera singers (such as Anita Patti Brown, who resented the assumption that she would sing only spirituals), Hackley's

DREAMING IN ENSEMBLE

operatic training paradoxically led her to draw ever-stricter associations between race and genre, undermining the emphasis on artistic freedom and creative versatility on which other practitioners insisted.

The conceptual slipperiness implicit within Hackley's shift in repertoire extended to her citation of vocal pedagogy in non-musical contexts. A believer in what she called "musical social uplift"—or the idea that "a solution of the race question" was "in the depths of the throat where the musical notes are shaped"—she was also a fervent proponent of respectable self-improvement, particularly for African American women.[111] Her advice column, "Hints to Young Colored Artists," which appeared in the *New York Age* alongside Lester Walton's criticism in 1914 and 1915, emphasized the importance of individual excellence to professional and personal success. In 1916, Hackley published *The Colored Girl Beautiful,* an expansive treatise on beauty, race, and womanhood. Compiled from "talks given to girls in colored boarding schools" during Hackley's years as a touring recitalist, it is a fascinating—and often profoundly disquieting—assessment of how young Black women should act in a world hostile to their existence.[112] It covers such quintessential domestic topics as childhood, marriage, motherhood, religion, school, and the home, urging the reader to conduct herself with dignity, grace, and poise. It suggests that personal conduct and self-confidence can offset the ill effects of racism, imploring individual readers to "act upon the minds of others" and "send out strong thoughts of peace and love to counteract the overwhelming tide of thought against us."[113] Frequently cited as an exemplar of Hackley's investments in respectability politics and uplift ideology, the book also drew on eugenicist rhetoric, especially in its call for Black women to bring forth "a better breed of babies."[114] Hackley's faith in the Black woman's body as a conduit for social transformation is striking given her own status as a light-skinned, potentially white-passing woman, whose own physical appearance undoubtedly facilitated some of her own social mobility.

Within Hackley's writings, operatic vocal pedagogy takes a sharp ideological turn. She harnessed the same concepts that she had once used to destabilize opera's putative place at the top of a cultural hierarchy in support of biological essentialism and class-based elitism. In her advice column, she posited that God "gave [the Black singer] a large mouth with a high roof and large, fine hard teeth to hold the tones. He gave him a large nose with big nostrils to take in plenty fresh air that he might be able to do big things."[115] In *The Colored Girl Beautiful,* she extended this rhetoric to social conduct, fretting that the "leaking mouth with the hanging under jaw causes a tendency to 'leak' along other lines. One's business and personal

affairs 'leak' in street cars, public places, and on the streets to the detriment of the race"; moreover, "grinning widens the nose and prevents its upward building, so grinning must cease."[116] Seemingly drawn straight from the visual playbook of blackface minstrelsy, this was self-making taken to a troubling extreme, using noxious ideas about race and physiognomy under the banner of ostensible progress.

A chapter entitled "Deep Breathing" linked Hackley's pedagogical emphasis on bodily control to Black women's ability to protect their bodies from sexual transgression. As a vocal pedagogue, Hackley taught her students how to strengthen the diaphragm muscles and solar plexus, providing them with exercises by which they could learn how to engage these muscles properly and breathe deeply to produce a strong, precise tone. In *The Colored Girl Beautiful,* she asserted, "Deep breathers are seldom mentally weak because deep breathing develops Will power," and "the habit of deep breathing cultivates Personality and Personal Magnetism and thus makes one attractive."[117] Marking the body as fundamental to both self-transformation and social transformation, she conflated physical strength, social status, and vocal training in a manner as powerful as it was seductive. In another chapter, "Love," Hackley extolled the virtues of womanly purity and offered veiled guidance on how young women might protect themselves from sexual violation:

> When boys and men desire caresses and kisses, a girl should send a message to her Solar Plexus—her reflex nerve—to help her to say, "No." . . . In order to resist temptation, girls should be taught deep breathing, that the diaphragm and educated nerves may obey emergency orders. The practice of deep breathing is invaluable in the matter of resistance, and will back up the "I won't", "I won't", "I won't", "Hands off", "Hands off". A girl must hold her fists tightly and resist.
>
> She must psychologize the mind with thoughts of resistance by practicing simple breathing movements, so that when temptation is imminent the holding of a deep breath will be her salvation. The action of her diaphragm and Solar Plexus will prevent any wavering.[118]

Ostensibly directed toward young women who wished to ward off amorous suitors, the passage also invokes the pervasive threat of sexual violence. Yet in this context, the galvanizing notion that women can fashion their voices and bodies into instruments of musical beauty transmutes into the dangerous suggestion that they are ultimately responsible for preventing harm to those same bodies.

By the time Hackley died of an illness in 1922, her career had moved far from opera—at least superficially. The work of instructing choruses on how to sing spirituals, and young women on how to comport themselves, seemed distant from the Parisian studio where she had once sung arias. Yet as one obituary noted, it was knowledge of opera that had made Hackley "eminently fitted for the work which she later took up—that of carrying to the masses a fundamental knowledge of correct principles in the art of singing, together, with plain, simple rules by which health may be conserved."[119] If her vocal pedagogy ultimately veered in reactionary directions as a disciplinary framework for Black women's behavior, it took on a more radical cast as a theoretical intervention into the meaning of opera itself. She insisted that operatic knowledge was broadly applicable for African Americans, including those who had no intention of becoming singers or composers of opera themselves. As she brought opera into new contexts, its definitional parameters wobbled. Repurposed as pedagogy, it became more method than form, more process than object.

A similar shift characterized many endeavors within Black operatic counterculture during this period. Whereas one effect of opera's mainstream sacralization was to constrict the art form's possibilities, ossifying its repertory and attendant social rituals within the opera house, Black countercultural engagements with opera remained markedly flexible. Nor were these activities oriented toward the goal of inclusion within that mainstream. In what Nathaniel Mackey might describe as a fugitive move "from noun to verb," the art form became nothing more, and nothing less, than a way of being for its practitioners.[120] For these singers, students, critics, and pedagogues, opera was not so much an aspirational endpoint as an impetus for creative action: a means of aesthetic self-fashioning, an occasion for social commentary, a reason for gathering together with others. Such activities are not necessarily easily identifiable as "opera" per se. Yet they are reflective of how, even as the sonic color line and white supremacist norms largely restricted their access to performance and composition, Black artists continued to generate new meaning from the art form's collaborative aesthetic characteristics and peripheral cultural position. Samuel Delany has written that, given opera's exclusionary racial politics, its Black subjects typically "have been opera-ed, have been operated upon, have been operationalized."[121] But as these artists remade opera's cultural meanings beyond the opera house, they flipped that script to become agents of their own actions, tellers of their own story.

❧ 3 ❧

"The Forgotten Man of the Opera"

A few years after he began directing operas at Douglass High School, W. Llewelyn Wilson appeared in an opera himself. In April 1932, during the closing performance of the Metropolitan Opera Company's annual visit to Baltimore, he hoisted up the "throne chair" on which the princess Selika makes her "triumphal entrance" in act 4 of Meyerbeer's opera *L'Africaine*. Silent but visible, Wilson appeared on the stage in the non-singing part of a "native" on an unnamed exotic island, joining a crowd of "dancing girls, warriors, and temple vestals" who provided a spectacular backdrop for the production's stars, the "supremely gifted" Rosa Ponselle and Beniamino Gigli.[1] In his capacity as an educator, Wilson had once explained that he taught opera to high-school students because "white audiences, by and large, consider colored artists chiefly as entertainers in the sense of affording amusements." He wished to show his students that alternatives were possible, insisting that "we must continue to create a place for artists of different types."[2] His appearance in *L'Africaine* seemed to blur the line between these options: Wilson may have challenged white audiences' preconception that Black artists were mere "entertainers" by appearing onstage alongside some of the era's most esteemed opera singers, yet the aesthetic and institutional context in which he did so—a racialized, silent part in a European grand opera, presented by the nation's best-known opera company—was distinctly not of his own making.

Wilson's experiences speak to the evolving relationship between Black operatic activity and the art form's mainstream during the 1920s. The first phase of Black operatic counterculture had been concerned primarily with

the theory and practice of opera within the Black public sphere: the creation of new musical works and institutional settings in which the relationship between Blackness and opera could be defined and enacted. Under such circumstances, Black artists maintained a marginal relationship to the white opera scene in the United States. They envisioned "Negro grand opera" as a discrete artistic phenomenon that might represent the pinnacle of Black culture, and they made it possible for African Americans to become practitioners and students of the art form within their own communities. But beginning in the mid-1920s, African Americans increasingly sought out opportunities to challenge opera's historical practices of white supremacist exclusion. The Harlem Renaissance, sparked by the mass demographic shifts of the Great Migration, brought on a flowering of activity among Black writers and intellectuals, a double-edged development that both created new opportunities for Black artists to appear in previously closed venues and intensified voyeuristic white interest in Black performance cultures. And as the long civil rights movement gathered steam, opera became one among many battlegrounds on which the fight to desegregate public space and cultural life might play out. Even as many activities that had characterized earlier iterations—including private study, self-organized companies, criticism, and composition—continued apace, new opportunities arose for Black artists to engage with opera under previously impossible circumstances. For the first time, all-white companies engaged African American singers in principal roles and commissioned the work of African American composers. Although such opportunities remained few and far between, they marked a significant departure from previous norms.

Yet even as shifts in the cultural landscape portended new opportunities for some exceptional Black operatic artists, there were important continuities between this era and the one that preceded it. Longstanding modes of racialized listening, labor, and performance persisted and evolved among African American audience members, house staff, and artists whose physical presence in the opera house first preceded, and later coexisted with, iconic moments of desegregation in mainstream institutional spaces. These figures had worked in American opera houses since the earliest years of Black operatic counterculture, contributing in subtle but pervasive ways to the visual, sonic, and social spectacle of grand opera. Some worked in offstage capacities, while others made creative contributions to mainstream operatic productions: the translator who crafted an English-language libretto with only minimal credit, or the supernumeraries who, like Wilson, appeared onstage, silent but vital, in spectacular productions. Their work was formative to the racial politics of the mainstream operatic institutions into which other African American

singers and composers eventually entered. It was also meaningful in its own right, enabling them to develop personal relationships to the art form as laborers and listeners. Although these individuals are not typically centered—or even acknowledged—in narratives of opera's history and cultural import, they both shaped opera's racial meanings in the United States and embraced the art form's creative, affective potential. Their stories gesture toward the subterranean presence of African Americans throughout the art form's institutional history and form a crucial backdrop for understanding the long sweep of Black operatic history, including those temporal periods and experiential capacities that lie beyond the domain of integrationist narratives.

Unlike many of their counterparts in other facets of Black operatic counterculture, these individuals generally did not make grand pronouncements about opera's significance in relation to the present and future of African American cultural production; nor did they engage in unambiguous acts of artistic self-determination. Their presence within operatic institutions was not explicitly marginal or oppositional—indeed, it could sometimes even seem to reinforce racial hierarchies rather than challenging them. As such, understanding their contribution requires a different way of thinking about the relationship between opera, race, and counterculture. As scholars from Robin Kelley to Saidiya Hartman have argued, Black quests for freedom have employed almost infinitely varied strategies, particularly in settings that do not involve formal political action; interpreting their significance in relation to more forthright acts of activism requires close attention to the quotidian practices of refusal and imagination that surfaced in ordinary people's daily lives.[3] Such practices were essential to Black listeners and laborers in the opera house, who took a subtle, elusive approach to political expression: a moment spent listening rather than working, a refusal to leave the building as soon as their labor was no longer needed. They claimed the right to cross the sonic color line as listeners, participating fully in the affective experiences that the art form offered. In other words, they forged a countercultural relationship not so much to opera itself, but to the social and cultural practices that occurred within the institutional space of the opera house.

Consideration of this expansive cast of characters, and the more oblique forms of countercultural action that they pursued, unsettles a perception of this era as a moment of straightforward desegregation led by exceptional performers. In fact, African Americans had a longstanding representational *and* lived presence within opera houses, which made these cultural institutions into spaces of contested, unstable racial meaning. This perspective not only emphasizes the gradual, uneven progress of desegregation in opera, but

also helps to disentangle inclusion from antiracism: that is, the very presence of African Americans within operatic spaces did not guarantee that the racial politics of those spaces would be transformed. Moreover, locating representation (the appearance of Black performers in operatic roles onstage) alongside spectatorship and employment (listening or working at the opera house) illuminates how the opera house was a place where labor and artistry overlapped and even blurred into one another. Yet even as African Americans faced constrictive circumstances within the opera house, they were intellectually aligned with earlier participants in Black operatic counterculture in their commitment to making sense of their own involvement with opera. Even under potentially disempowering structural conditions, they continued to reimagine the art form for inventive and liberatory purposes.

Jim Crow Listening

The opera house is a place to see and be seen. Spectatorship and performance are multidirectional and pervasive as soloists, dancers, and choristers look out from the stage; operagoers observe performers and one another; ushers, door attendants, and other staff ensure the space's smooth functioning; and critics prepare to translate their experience into words to be read by a wider audience. At the turn of the twentieth century, the opera house was depicted as a microcosm of democratic social admixture. As Henry James described it in 1904: "the *whole* social consciousness thus clamber[s] into it, under stress, as the whole community crams into the other public receptacles, the desperate cars of the Subway or the vast elevators of the tall buildings."[4] But a few decades later, it had come to be known as a pinnacle of elite society. In 1920, Edith Wharton would write that it was a "world of fashion" where "carefully-brushed, white-waistcoated, buttonhole-flowered gentlemen" mingled in the expensive box seats."[5] More recent scholarship theorizes the opera house as a focal site for the performance of power, interrogating its material and spatial elements alongside the aesthetic and representational qualities of the operas produced within—an approach that clarifies the many simultaneous levels on which racialized expressions of power might occur within this space.[6]

In the postbellum era, the opera house had been a flashpoint in struggles over the desegregation of public space. One of the five cases grouped together under the US Supreme Court's Civil Rights Cases of 1883 was that of a formerly enslaved man named William R. Davis who, in 1879, was refused entry to a matinee performance at the Grand Opera House in New

York. The Court ruled that the Civil Rights Act of 1875 was unconstitutional, paving the way for the legal codification of Jim Crow. In 1894, a Black man named Andrew Johnson successfully sued the manager of the Chicago Opera House, David Henderson, for denying him entrance to the theater; four years later, Henry T. Richardson sued Henderson on similar grounds and achieved the same result.[7] But by the 1910s, such legal challenges were regularly struck down amid a social climate of resegregation. As Lester Walton wrote in 1912, "the unnecessary segregating of colored people in the theatres of New York City" was "getting worse instead of better."[8] When James Weldon Johnson wrote a letter of complaint regarding discriminatory seating practices at Harlem's Victoria Theater in 1921, he received a response that confirmed awareness of the law but lacked a plan for compliance.[9] Change was nonexistent: eight years later, the NAACP's Jacob Brigman informed the same theater's management that "it would be more honest to Colored people to place a sign in the box office with lettering (merely as a suggestion) words 'NO COLORED PEOPLE ALLOWED IN THE ORCHESTRA OF THIS THEATRE' with such a sign the Colored people would feel less embarrassed."[10]

In the age of Jim Crow, listening to opera, like virtually all other public activities, remained separate and unequal.[11] Some southern venues barred Black audiences outright: when the Metropolitan Opera toured Atlanta in 1921, African Americans waited in line overnight to purchase tickets on behalf of their white employers, but were prevented from attending performances themselves.[12] Others instituted discriminatory systems: when the Chicago Grand Opera Company toured New Orleans, Black operagoers were permitted to attend but forced to pay higher prices for inferior tickets.[13] Despite the existence of state antidiscrimination laws, white-owned venues in the North regularly refused to sell tickets to Black patrons, charged them higher prices, or confined them to certain sections of the theater. One unofficial policy at the Metropolitan Opera House, for example, prescribed that African Americans should sit only in the Family Circle, the section of the house farthest from the stage.[14] The Met was also reputed to maintain a covert practice of seating Black patrons in aisle seats and "tear[ing] up the ticket for the neighboring seat, so that no white patron will have to rub shoulders with a Negro."[15]

The effect of such policies was psychological as well as material. Jacqueline Stewart notes that for African American moviegoers, "the practice of segregated seating complicated the process of forgetting one's social self and becoming completely absorbed into an increasingly self-enclosed narrative"; a similar process no doubt affected operagoers as well.[16] Kristin Mo-

riah takes up a similar quandary in a study of Black audiences in early twentieth-century concert halls, asking: "What did it mean for African American audience members to have to go to the top galleries and experience compromised forms of listening? How did these compromised listening experiences shape the way African American performers were received domestically? How did they influence the ways African American performers framed themselves?"[17] Such inquiries productively center the question of how Jim Crow affected African American listeners' aesthetic and social experiences, perniciously shaping the relationship between art and audience.

Accounts of African American operagoers during this era, particularly those who attended performances in predominantly white spaces, are frustratingly scant. White-authored accounts tend to frame Black operagoers as disruptive, unwelcome, or simply novel, further obscuring the particularities of their experience. Members of the Black elite also produced limited representations of operagoing, framing the activity (along with attendance at other types of classical music performances) as a proxy for social standing. For example, Robert Abbott, editor of the *Defender*, stuffily opined that "Jazz music, dance halls, cabarets and underground taverns have conspired to scandalize the morals of our young people," so "we must train ourselves to enjoy formal music, symphony concerts and chamber music, [which] tends to purify the senses and edify the imagination."[18] These discursive patterns make it difficult to determine the substantive contours of listeners' experiences in the opera house: how Black audiences responded to what they saw onstage, identified with the performers they heard, or evaluated fellow operagoers.

A richer narrative emerges in the criticism of Nora Douglas Holt. While most of Holt's columns focused on the achievements of Black musicians and representations of Blackness onstage, she also conveyed her own embodied experiences at venues that were nominally open to Black audiences but had few Black attendees in practice. In one remarkable review, published in the *Defender* in 1917, Holt transformed an account of her experience at the Chicago Opera Association into an opportunity for trenchant commentary. Using atmospheric details to convey her affective experience, she invited her readers to become, in effect, vicarious operagoers. The review begins with Holt's characteristic vivacity: "First night at the opera! Amber lights, accentuated by gold settings; greens and blues of peacocks, listless, tip-tilted and defiant; murmuring voices, Schonbergerian [*sic*] in nuances and dissonances; stately ladies, warm velvets and luxurious furs; a raised baton and Maestro Campanini has launched the Chicago Opera

company into history as the most remarkable in the world."[19] With these lines, which preceded a review of the performance itself, Holt used her embodied subjectivity to invite other African American readers into the predominantly white institutional space of the opera house, creating a discursive space in which music could create powerful affective bonds. Come with me, she seemed to say; imagine yourself basking in the glow of the amber lights. Moreover, by characterizing her fellow audience members' voices as "Schonbergerian," Holt emphasized her ability to critique both performance *and* audience. She was observing her fellow operagoers just as they were likely surveilling her, a Black woman in a white space. With this characterization, Holt taught her readers how to listen to the voices that pervaded the terrain of the opera house, both onstage and off. Her further description of those voices as "dissonances" subtly spoke back to how white operagoers might consider her and others' racialized presence socially dissonant, implying that white listeners' voices, not Black ones, held disruptive potential.

Holt also showed how listening could serve a social function, shaping Black audiences' sense of community. She encouraged her readers to join her in attending performances, noting that she was "always fascinated and sometimes influenced by intelligent audiences."[20] When previewing upcoming Chicago Symphony Orchestra concerts, she announced that "students attending Saturday evening programs will find the musical critic in the lobby of the first balcony during the ten minutes' intermission, where she will be pleased to discuss various symphonic works with interested persons."[21] The image compels speculation about what might have happened when a group of Black listeners congregated in the Orchestra Hall lobby, carving out physical space within a white-dominated institution in what amounted to a sort of symbolic sit-in, engaging with the music therein on their own terms. Their very presence and the sound of their voices joining in discussion—the colors and fabrics of their clothing, the murmuring expression of their ideas—would become part of the sensory ambience that Holt would evoke in her writing; their conversation about "various symphonic works" would constitute an instance of music criticism in its own right. Readers' heretofore vicarious experience of reading about music would become an opportunity to forge a tangible, if ephemeral, Black musical community.

Such fleeting accounts gesture toward opera's potential as a site of what Stewart calls "reconstructive spectatorship," in which African Americans could engage in cultural activities "to rebuild their individual and collec-

tive identities in a modern, urban environment."[22] The realities of white supremacy meant that attending performances put one at risk for racist treatment (and offered a stark reminder that, despite its proponents' claims to the contrary, Western art music did not, in fact, guarantee transcendent or universal experiences for its listeners). Listening to opera under Jim Crow certainly entailed contending with the everyday indignities of segregation. Yet it was also an opportunity to engage in aesthetic experiences inaccessible in other contexts, to appreciate the beauty and grandeur of the art form and forge an identity in which opera played a meaningful part.

The Operatic Workplace

While for audiences the opera house was a site of spectatorship, for others it was a workplace. A small number of African Americans staffed opera houses across the country, completing duties that ranged from welcoming arriving boxholders to managing other employees to attending to the needs of visiting artists. These workers' very presence complicates the perception that American opera houses were entirely segregated prior to the arrival of highly visible Black performers onstage, showing instead how Black labor was crucial to these institutions' functioning. But employment at an opera house also created conditions under which workers might take part in sustained aesthetic engagement with opera, carving out opportunities for critical listening and interpersonal interaction within the context of their labor.

At the Metropolitan Opera, a man named Edward Johnson served as the house's door attendant and head carriage manager for more than twenty-five years. Born around 1870 and raised in Kansas, where he worked briefly for a regional opera impresario, Johnson toured on the Black vaudeville circuit as a magician. Lauded as an impressive "prestidigitator" who "kept his audience in a state of wonderment over his exhibitions of sleight-of-hand," he adopted the name "Black Carl," an allusion to the famed magician Carl Dante.[23] As a performer, Johnson toured Australia and New Zealand with Ernest Hogan, appeared on vaudeville bills with Bert Williams and George Walker, and brushed shoulders with classical and concert musicians; in 1905, for example, he appeared on a dramatic program alongside Harry Burleigh and Theodore Drury. He also pursued stage management and theater administration. A leader of the Colored Vaudeville Benevolent Association (a group that advocated for Black performers on the vaudeville stage), he managed Hogan's touring show for years, served as stage manager

for a 1913 New York production of *H.M.S. Pinafore,* and joined the backstage staff of *Shuffle Along* in 1921. Indeed, Johnson was so well-regarded as a stage manager that in 1924 he was described as "probably the highest paid and most important Negro executive in the show business."[24]

To mitigate the precarity of a career in popular entertainment, Johnson took on an additional job at the Metropolitan Opera House in 1904. There, dressed in an elegant maroon coat, he greeted prominent operagoers by name, opened the doors of the vehicles in which subscribers arrived, and supervised a staff of eleven, including several other Black workers. According to Harry Lawrence Freeman, who profiled Johnson in *The Negro in Music and Drama,* his "courteous demeanor and affable nature" enabled him to become a "set fixture—a human land-mark at that celebrated institution."[25] He became friendly with many of the opera singers who appeared regularly at the house, and he listened enthusiastically to their performances. In a profile commemorating Johnson's twenty-fifth year at the Met, Lester Walton detailed his artistic preferences: "'Black Carl' is a particular admirer of 'Aida' because of its gorgeous set . . . 'Tosca,' because the singing and acting of Scotti; and 'Martha,' with Caruso and Sembrich in the principal roles."[26] Walton characterized Johnson as a simultaneous laborer *and* listener who, in the course of his employment, not only facilitated the house's offstage operations, but also became a connoisseur of its onstage productions.

When Johnson suffered a stroke in 1928, a Metropolitan representative collected five hundred dollars in assistance, and the opera's house doctor visited him in the hospital. He died the following year. Memorial notices published after his death indicate how his role within the opera house was perceived in racialized terms. An obituary in the *Herald Tribune,* a white newspaper, paternalistically portrayed an "opera doorman" who "made his work his life, managing by any possible means to learn the names of the regular patrons and finding his greatest delight in having one of the boxholders acknowledge his greetings with a 'Hello, Black Carl.'"[27] Yet what white operagoers perceived as polite hospitality might also reflect a necessary savvy gained from years of experience living under Jim Crow. As the African American journalist J. A. Jackson once noted, a penchant for "quiet dignity" served Johnson well as a stage manager for Black traveling shows, making him "a great asset in handling the hotel and stopping place business for the whole show . . . a vital question with a Negro attraction fraught with possibilities of discomfort."[28]

The *Herald Tribune* also minimized Johnson's aesthetic investment in opera: "'Black Carl' never heard an opera from beginning to end. If this worried him he told no one, and his friends today have no idea whether

or not he enjoyed classical music. They say that at times he would stand at the back of the opera house for certain performances, but they do not recall what those operas were."[29] By contrast, a memorial notice for Johnson in the *Defender* centered the "opera he loved" rather than his putatively deferential demeanor. Describing Johnson's final moments, the paper reported that, after seeming to have recovered from his stroke, Johnson "read of the plans for the opening of the opera and suffered a relapse. From then until his death he talked continuously of the opera. His condition grew worse. During his last few hours he was delirious and called the names of opera singers he had known."[30] If one had "no idea" what he thought about the opera, it was because they had not asked—or had been simply unable to imagine that his relationship to opera entailed a deep love of the art form.

A few years after Johnson's passing, a young man named Julian Elihu Bagley began working at San Francisco's newly constructed War Memorial Opera House. Born in Jacksonville, Florida to a family of shipyard workers, Bagley had a predilection for poetry, writing, and art from an early age. While working toward a degree in agriculture at the Hampton Institute, he published short stories and poetry in Black literary journals; a since-lost story, intriguingly titled "Vagabonding in a City of Opera Seats," received a prize in a contest sponsored by the *Crisis*.[31] By 1932, Bagley was living in San Francisco and had learned that the construction of an opera house was under way. He later recounted that he "said to friends of mine that I was going to get a job in the opera house, and they said, opera house! They thought that was absolutely crazy . . . I went to see the man who was the manager of the opera house and he said, well, you can try it, if you want to. It's going to be very difficult to do it the way you want to do it, because I had an idea that I would work at performances and then in the daytime I would take visitors from all over the world through the opera house. And that's what I did and that's why I made so many friends."[32] Bagley's essentially self-invented position carried the title of "concierge" or "greeter," yet encompassed a vast array of responsibilities. In the words of one observer, "His job, which could have been nothing more than that of handy man and custodian . . . evolved to include guide, historian, critic-in-residence and interpreter for foreign stars and dignitaries."[33] He would go on to work at the opera house for more than four decades, becoming an indispensable figure within the institution.

Bagley recalled his career in a series of oral history interviews, which offer a remarkable narrative of how labor and listening intersected in his life. His position enabled him to become enmeshed in a national network of artists

and performers. When visitors arrived at the house, he guided them through the nooks and crannies of the space, drawing on his encyclopedic knowledge of the building. During rehearsals, he attended to elite performers backstage ("they all liked me because I approached them as human beings," he recalled).[34] He hosted dinner parties for visiting artists, and on occasion—for instance, when Katherine Dunham's dance troupe visited—they stayed at his home. Through his work, he came to know virtually all the major singers of the era, including such luminaries as Marian Anderson ("She wasn't too enthusiastic about meeting people. She was there to sing"), Roland Hayes ("a very wonderful man"), and Leontyne Price ("very gracious and a very wonderful singer"). He also met Duke Ellington and Nat King Cole, whom he found "very agreeable" even though their music was not exactly to his taste ("I don't care too much for that kind of music. Mine is opera and symphony").[35] While Bagley's reflections rarely centered race, he did note that he and Price once discussed "experiences [of discrimination] that she had had and that I had had and how things have changed. Both of us were very close to those things."[36] He also, when asked whether Dunham's troupe attracted a primarily Black audience, corrected the (white) interviewer's assumption that its "primitive, African-type" performance would appeal: "No. That doesn't especially appeal to the Negroes in this country. They are interested in art, more or less, and it doesn't make any difference whether it is white art or black art."[37] He refused the interviewer's entreaties to discuss race and racism in detail, instead electing in his narrative self-representation to focus on the artistic and social experiences that were most important to him.

Over the course of his career, Bagley developed a deeply personal relationship to opera. He found it uniquely moving: "When you get used to opera, nothing else would pleasure you in the way of singing . . . you don't find any of that in jazz singing and in ordinary singing. It isn't there. But it's all there in opera."[38] While *Aida* and *Il trovatore* were his favorites, he resolutely attended every performance—opera, jazz, ballet—that took place in the War Memorial Opera House. For nearly forty years, he did not miss a single event; he would remain standing while listening to ensure that he could absorb every detail of a performance. This combination of aesthetic expertise and consistent presence allowed Bagley to become an artistic adviser, serving as a conduit between audiences and administrators: "They [the audience] always tell me when they like a thing, and I am a sort of a runner to the different productions. If people like it, they don't fail to tell me, but if something is bad and they don't like it, they also tell me. Then I tell that to the right person so that they won't make that mistake again."[39]

Perhaps Bagley's most remarkable legacy, though, was as a de facto archivist. In a mode of record-keeping reminiscent of Harry Lawrence Freeman's creation of a grand archive for his operas, Bagley acted as custodian of the opera house's Signature Book: a multi-decade project in which he invited virtually every distinguished person who appeared on the opera house stage to sign their name in a "large time-browned guest book."[40] Featuring the signatures of individuals from Marian Anderson to Igor Stravinsky to Harry Truman, it became an irreplaceable record of artistic and creative life in San Francisco, mediated through these figures' relationship to Bagley, who personally solicited each signature in the volume and compiled a comprehensive index as he did so. This archival impulse, which complemented the completionist mindset that compelled him to go forty years without missing a performance, enabled Bagley to document the institution's history on his own terms, and in a way that corresponded with

Julian Bagley at his desk, ca. 1950.

Julian Bagley's Signature Book. Note the names of prominent figures in opera, including soprano Kirsten Flagstad, tenors Lauritz Melchior and Giovanni Martinelli, and Frederick Vajda (a conductor who would, in 1941, direct the National Negro Opera Company's inaugural production; see Chapter 6).

his own perspective on opera. In the Signature Book, Bagley aestheticized, even idealized, the politics of inclusion: each signer occupied an equal position on the page, and the matters of racial, cultural, and class-based hierarchy that typically structure the opera house faded away. The project enabled him not so much to write himself into the story of American opera as to *become* the writer of a wholly egalitarian version of that story, thus contributing to the revision of its narrative.

"A Problem as Well as a Necessity"

As opera house employees, Johnson and Bagley blurred the line between labor and spectatorship: their presence was predicated on the service that they provided, yet over the course of their long careers, they also became careful listeners whose identities were shaped by the operas they heard. Other African Americans entered the opera house as creative participants in the operas themselves. Their presence was concomitantly recognized as atypical and shoehorned into predictable patterns of racial representation

that served to reify the opera house's associations with whiteness and elitism. Even as they set the stage, so to speak, for a future era of fuller integration, they could also be perceived in ways that shored up the sonic color line rather than challenged it.

"The first time in the history of the Metropolitan that an opera was sung with which a Negro had anything to do," to use the tellingly convoluted phrasing of the *New York Age,* occurred when James Weldon Johnson translated the opera *Goyescas* from Spanish into English in 1915.[41] In addition to being a well-respected author, lyricist, and activist, Johnson was a devotee of opera who once heard "the whole Metropolitan repertory" by attending an entire season's worth of performances on a weekly basis.[42] Also fluent in Spanish, he received a commission to produce a translation of composer Enrique Granados and librettist Fernando Periquet's opera, which takes its inspiration from paintings by Francisco Goya and depicts the romantic dalliances of young men and women in nineteenth-century Madrid. For two months, Johnson immersed himself in the task, using "every minute of [his] time" toward the project of producing a "singable and sensible" libretto.[43] Although *Goyescas* was sung in the original Spanish, copies of Johnson's translation were made available for purchase in the lobby so that operagoers could follow along during the performance.[44]

Johnson's elite position within the Black intelligentsia no doubt facilitated his work as a translator, yet his achievement was dissociated from his race almost in real time. The trenchant critic R. G. Doggett noted that "all the New York papers gave James Weldon Johnson credit for his splendid work, but not one of them let the public know he was a Negro."[45] In doing so, Doggett argued, the press effectively negated the possibility that Johnson's accomplishment might be interpreted as representative of African American intellectual ability and creative potential. Doggett's own report, titled "'Goyescas' Brings Colored Man to Front in New Role," served as a pointed corrective. Other participants in Black operatic counterculture also recognized the magnitude of Johnson's achievement. When Azalia Hackley relayed his accomplishment to one of her choruses, "they cheered and were very proud."[46] But for his part, Johnson remained skeptical that his work might have what Doggett called a "racial effect," maintaining that while race was less likely to limit the "creative artist" who produced written work offstage, it might be a "handicap" to "the interpreter [or] the performer."[47] The distinction he drew was especially apt in an era when principal roles on mainstream operatic stages remained out of reach for Black performers.

Perhaps Johnson was also thinking about those Black performers who did appear in the operatic productions he had seen at the Met and elsewhere.[48]

Alongside the extravagant sets, ornate costumes, and gorgeous voices soaring over the orchestra, the operatic stage would often teem with enormous numbers of non-singing performers: supernumeraries, whose task was to represent crowds of villagers, slaves, warriors, and the like. Appearing as a supernumerary—"suping," in popular parlance—was the primary means by which Black performers appeared in opera houses in the first half of the twentieth century. Yet unlike the African American principal singers who would eventually be credited as agents of desegregation, supernumeraries were only minimally acknowledged as racialized subjects. Their presence, labor, and artistry were so fundamental as to be made invisible; they were hidden in plain sight.

Supers occupied—and occupy—a strange place in the opera house. They are visually foregrounded but sonically absent: as Wayne Koestenbaum has noted, supers cannot "pass onto radio or record." Marginal yet essential, "the super is like the fan: a backstage spy, an onlooker, not a participant in the vocal festivities."[49] In the pithy phrasing of music critic Howard Taubman, early twentieth-century supers were "a problem as well as a necessity."[50] Considered closer to workers than artists, many lacked professional dramatic or musical training; joining the rehearsal process at the eleventh hour, they could potentially throw a production off-balance. Yet supers also embodied and constituted the spectacle at the core of grand opera, forming the abundant crowds whose presence is fundamental to the genre's sense of scale. It is in their bodies that opera's visual grandiosity resides.

African American supers appeared most often in productions of Verdi's *Aida,* the most frequently performed opera in the early twentieth-century United States. It was both a repertoire staple for traveling opera troupes and a centerpiece for major institutions: the Met, for instance, presented *Aida* forty-seven times between 1885 and 1900, then 394 more times between 1900 and 1940.[51] As an opera that centers Black characters, *Aida* would eventually become a touchstone in campaigns for the desegregation of the art form, when Black sopranos sought to take on the titular role of an Ethiopian princess. But those efforts were preceded by several decades' worth of appearances by Black supernumeraries, who played the part of the Ethiopian slaves and prisoners who dominate the stage in act 2's Triumphal March.[52] In 1898, the Castle Square Opera Company employed "real negro supernumeraries" in *Aida,* a detail praised by a critic as "almost perfect."[53] As early as 1900, a reviewer of a Metropolitan production praised the "unusually good" quality of "the dance of the slaves in the second [act],

too often deputed to negro boys"—implying that this was a longstanding practice.[54] In San Francisco in 1921, the traveling Scotti Opera Company featured "real, dyed-in-the-wool Afro-Americans" in nonsinging roles; five years later, in Los Angeles, the soprano Rosa Raisa starred in the opera's title role alongside a group of "colored film actors" moonlighting as supers.[55]

African Americans continued to appear in *Aida* throughout the 1930s, in locales from Baltimore to Cleveland to Portland, Oregon. In 1939, *Opera News* published a detailed timeline of backstage goings-on at the Met, which noted the "group of stalwart Negro supers" who arrived at the house at precisely 1:35 p.m., twenty-five minutes before the matinee performance of *Aida* was to begin.[56] Black supernumeraries appeared occasionally in other exoticist operas as well, including *L'Africaine* (the opera in which Llewelyn Wilson appeared in Baltimore) and *Salome*. Indeed, when the Met commissioned the architect Joseph Urban to build a new opera house in 1927, *Musical America* reported that it would feature separate "dressing rooms for white and colored supers"—a striking indicator not only of how frequently Black supernumeraries appeared in opera productions, but also of how Jim Crow permeated the entire spatial world of the opera house.[57] As a norm, and perhaps because they were comparatively scarce, Black supernumeraries were paid at a higher rate than their white counterparts; during the 1920s and 1930s, they typically received two dollars per performance rather than one. They also commanded a degree of economic power: in San Francisco, "It was whispered around that [Black supernumeraries] went on strike for double the stipend agreed upon and got it."[58]

By the 1930s, African American supers appeared so regularly in *Aida* that their absence became worth noting. In San Francisco, when the "usual contingent of Negro supers" failed to appear and "in their place a group of white supers and a supply of black make-up were to be secured," "the effect was not so realistic."[59] A 1935 Met performance of *Aida* featured a "dance of the big black slaves," which one reviewer appreciated for its "suggestion of a primitive Africanism which made welcome variation from the stereotyped procedure, and belonged believably to the moment."[60] In addition to revealing the national scope of the practice (and the casual racism of white opera critics), these comments trace an important conceptual shift from early commentary that characterized Black supers as a novelty ("dyed-in-the-wool Afro-Americans") to later remarks that cast them as figures who were "believable" rather than "stereotyped." In line with a broader Harlem Renaissance–era fascination with putatively "authentic" Black

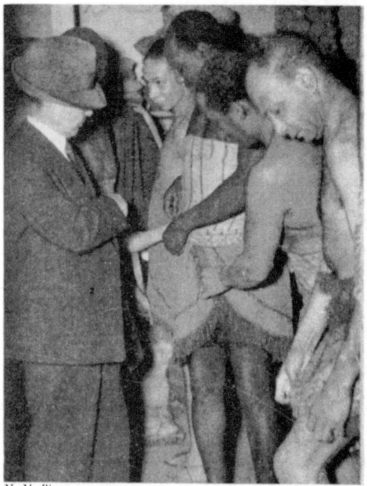

N. Y. Times Studio

Jules Judels inspects the Colored Supers

African American supernumeraries preparing to appear in a production of *Aida*.
In addition to the brief caption included in the image, the article included the
hyperbolic, mocking detail that the chair of the supers was "instructed to procure as
dark skins as may be found in the purlieus of Harlem or the gorges of Ethiopia."

artistry, these comments minimized the technique and craft of Black
performers in favor of the perception of realist authenticity they offered to
white audiences.

This newfound attention to supers' representational realism corresponded
with a shift in participants' demographics. In the first decades of the twen-

DREAMING IN ENSEMBLE

tieth century, suping was popular among white, elite opera aficionados. "It was a common practice among opera-smitten executives of big business, to hire themselves out as 'supers,' for the pleasure of going backstage, marching to music, and carrying an authentically operatic spear," one writer reminisced. "Lawyers, bankers, merchants, all used what influence they could muster up, to obtain a 'super's' assignment."[61] When the Metropolitan Opera toured Atlanta in 1912, the sons of "prominent citizens" relished the opportunity to share a stage with Enrico Caruso in the guise of "plumed knights" and "dusky slaves."[62] But by the mid-1920s, supernumeraries assumed a different profile. Students became a core constituency, even if the presence of "college boys" "awkwardly masquerading as Egyptian knights" onstage could be distractingly amateurish.[63] This motley crowd of "street sweepers, car conductors and college students" had diverse motivations: "To some it is one more way of picking up a dollar. To others it spells art, romance."[64] By 1938, Taubman could describe the super as "the forgotten man of the opera. More likely than not, he may also be the forgotten man of our social scheme—a down-and-outer earning a small piece of change."[65] In some instances, this class position was taken to be an artistic boon, as when the *New York Times* observed that "recruits from the Eighth Avenue lodging houses and park benches" were "very handy as slaves and prisoners of war."[66]

Both white and Black supers lacked access to conventional modes of operatic spectatorship and performance. Often selected more or less at random from a crowd that gathered outside the door just prior to the production, they were hustled out of the house before the performance even concluded. One cold evening in 1937, before a Metropolitan performance of *Aida,* prospective supernumeraries "huddled against the opera-house wall in two groups—one made up of poorly dressed Negroes who were to be Ethiopian slaves, the other a gang of ill-dressed white men who were to be the Pharaoh's soldiers." These "mercenaries" were "not allowed to hang around when they've done their bit; they turn in their accoutrements, sign for their dollar, and go right back to Flatbush or Hunts Point."[67] Supers "may have no voice in grand opera, but [they] help in no inconsiderable way in making the institution what it is," another reporter observed. "It is a strong lure that keeps men acting as supers in grand opera when they cannot even hear the finish of the productions in which they play a voiceless part."[68]

While supernumeraries had the potential to blur class distinctions in the opera house, their presence could also reify and strengthen racial divisions. For white participants, suping often entailed taking part in blackface performance. This was especially true in the ever-popular *Aida,* in which it

was the norm to don "eye shadow and grease paint [and] dark, coarse-haired wigs."[69] Supernumeraries thus became a conduit between the visual culture of minstrelsy and that of grand opera, often to a grotesque degree: Nora Holt wrote that the putatively Ethiopian supernumeraries she observed in Chicago "were so sooted one imagined them belched from a smoldering chimney, so profusely did they distribute the burnt cork."[70] Their presence not only naturalized the continued presence of blackface in American cultural life, but also served to define the opera house along the color line: a space in which predominantly white, elite audiences could hear music by white composers, and a space in which working-class white supernumeraries could shore up their racial self-identification through blackface performance.

Black supernumeraries assumed an equally complex visual role. Most were men and boys, whose onstage roles—abject slaves, fierce warriors—reiterated pervasive stereotypes about Black masculinity. Both male and female supers appeared in costumes that hypersexualized or dehumanized them: men in "loin cloths" and women in "skin tights" who "scurry on and crawl on the ground, as captives and slaves may be expected to do."[71] Given that so many aspiring Black opera performers lacked access to fully staged operatic productions and their corresponding visual grandeur, the retrogressive representations of Blackness offered to supernumeraries seem especially constrictive. They were also a far cry from the elegant, formal attire typically associated with Black concert singers, from the Fisk Jubilee Singers to Roland Hayes. Unlike other participants in Black operatic counterculture, who were largely from middle- and upper-class backgrounds, Black supers were unable to connect their work in opera to visual and sonic performances of respectability, and their experience of "high culture" did not align with the term's elite connotations. Given their lack of access to rehearsals or other facets of the creative process, they also lacked the opportunity to revise or contest the terms of their appearance on the stage.

Firsthand accounts by African American supernumeraries are scant, which makes it difficult to assess the practice's affective and conceptual significance for its participants. White-authored accounts are often filtered through paternalistic preconceptions about Black musicality, claiming, for instance, that "Negroes . . . make good supers. They are all music lovers and are especially fond of the operas of Verdi and such tuneful works as 'Pagliacci' and 'Cavalleria.'"[72] Supers also appear in the archival record in relation to moments of disruption or rule-breaking, in a manner that recalls the reception of Theodore Drury's wayward ensemble. In Chicago, two African American waiters-turned-supernumeraries in *Aida* "resumed street

clothes" after completing their part in the opera, but made a wrong turn, resulting in their "performing the astounding feat of walking across the river Nile in full view of the audience."[73] One critic noted Black supers' reluctance to leave the opera house immediately, as they were instructed to do: "In defiance of the rules they have been found crouching behind the scenes in the dark of the stage, intent on hearing the last note of the opera."[74] Like Edward Johnson and Julian Bagley, they sought an individualized aesthetic relationship to the art form, one that exceeded the limitations under which they had initially entered the opera house.

Other supers defied expectations by refusing to remain silent. In 1943, twenty-year-old Juanita Morrow planned to participate in a Cleveland production of *Aida*. Along with her mother and aunt, who also intended to appear as supernumeraries, she was refused entrance to the building by a door attendant who was unaware that Black supers were to take part. Once inside, she was excluded from backstage preparations by her white counterparts, many of whom were wearing blackface makeup. Morrow ultimately refused to appear onstage, instead taking a seat in the audience. She later recalled, "I felt quite triumphant when I recognized 'The March of the Priests' as the music I marched to when I graduated."[75] Flipping the script, she reframed *Aida* as integral to her education, and she repurposed the very language of the opera's design to describe her own achievements. Reclaiming the opera's "triumphal" march as her own, she superimposed a new plot on Verdi's opera. When she left the stage to become a listener instead, she seized the freedom of movement denied to the captive Ethiopians she had been intended to portray.

Morrow's refusal to participate and her subsequent written account of her decision exemplify the subtle, subterranean level on which suping might become a countercultural act. From the perspective of the (white) audience, the anonymized African Americans who appeared onstage served to reinscribe cultural images of Black unfreedom that evoked both the history of enslavement and the legacy of minstrelsy, thereby reinforcing the hierarchical racial politics of the opera house. Consigned into hackneyed roles, and largely excluded from the collaborative processes of rehearsal, they had little opportunity to exercise interpretive autonomy. They do not seem to have troubled what Saidiya Hartman calls "the fine line between witness and spectator": their appearance neglected to advance critiques of racial representation within the operas in which they appeared, make an uplift-oriented case for Black cultural parity, or otherwise generate audiences' empathy.[76] Unlike Black concert singers or participants in other art forms associated with "high culture," they did not embody or espouse

a politics of respectability; silent onstage, they were unable to engage in practices of self-making by way of operatic vocality. Such matters were beyond their purview.

These limitations do not suggest that supernumeraries were excluded from or unimportant to Black operatic counterculture. Rather, they underscore the importance of considering African Americans' experiences in the opera house beyond the narrow framework of representation. Supers themselves engaged with opera in ways that exceeded what audiences could perceive in their presence. Like Edward Johnson, who transformed his employment at the Met into an opportunity for careful listening, they focused primarily on what opera could offer them as individuals: a furtive lingering in the wings during *Aida*'s final act, for instance, was a chance to reengage with the production in which they had just appeared, and thereby a chance to unsettle the hierarchies of race and labor that had initially facilitated their entrance into the space.

Such quietly subversive listening practices were, in fact, what ultimately united the disparate ensemble of Black audience members, employees, and supernumeraries who entered the mainstream opera house in the early twentieth century. A diverse group that cut a wide swath across African American culture—from elite intellectuals like James Weldon Johnson, to workers like Julian Bagley, to erstwhile supernumeraries like Llewelyn Wilson and Juanita Morrow—they shared a common experience in which the private act of listening became an alternative to the public spectacles of labor and performance. If they did not necessarily disavow the potential of onstage representation as a political tool, they also declined to conflate representation with progress. Rather than calling for institutional change, they simply declined to participate in opera on the limited terms offered to them, wresting alternative meaning from their experiences. In the broader context of the Harlem Renaissance—characterized in part by an intense voyeurism for Black performance and a growing insistence that Black performers belonged exclusively on popular stages—this choice was oppositional in its own right. Transforming the public space of the opera house into an opportunity for private listening, these workers and artists created a place for themselves on the institution's lower frequencies.

≈ 4 ≈

"My Skin Was My Costume"

The final recital of the Ferrari Fontana Vocal Trials, held in the summer of 1925, was a celebratory affair. Having progressed through many rounds of auditions, the two dozen African American sopranos who reached the stage must have felt that they were on the brink of, as an advertisement for the contest put it, "break[ing] through the color barriers onto the operatic stage as a star."[1] Yet if the atmosphere in the concert hall that night was suffused with a sense of anticipation—one of these women, the advertisement promised, might sing at the Metropolitan Opera—it also relied on groundwork laid in earlier phases of Black operatic counterculture. The master of ceremonies for the evening was none other than Harry Lawrence Freeman.[2] Finalist Lillian Brown was accompanied at the piano by Emma de Lyon-Leonard, who, a quarter-century prior, had appeared in the Drury Grand Opera Company's inaugural production of *Carmen*. Marguerite Avery and Jessie Zackery, the contest's two winners, had developed their operatic expertise within the Black public sphere: Avery was a student of Harry A. Williams, a celebrated African American voice teacher who directed a Washington, DC choral society, while Zackery began her career singing recitals at Black churches and colleges across the Midwest.[3] Their appearance in this forum may have been unprecedented, but their investment in opera had deep roots.

Designed with the express purpose of identifying a Black soprano destined for operatic greatness, the Vocal Trials promised to catalyze singers' careers while concomitantly serving a gatekeeping function. The contest's

organizer, Edoardo Ferrari Fontana, insisted that in "no other race . . . will one find so many wonderful voices," a sentiment that mixed admiration with essentialism.[4] But he also proclaimed that "art, the true art, has neither nationality nor color," and mused, "It has always been a mystery to me why impresarios have not sought a Negro voice for an opera like 'Aida.'"[5] Fontana's aggressively naïve claim that such exclusion was a "mystery" rather than a manifestation of white supremacy highlighted his goodwill while eliding structural factors; his paradoxical statements articulate the limitations of a contest in which a white male sponsor preemptively determined what constituted the Black female winner's success. Some observers recognized and spoke back to this conundrum. An *Amsterdam News* editorial offered a trenchant critique of the contest model—"When a Negro achieves anything of distinction, he is immediately set up as the exception proving the rule that the Negro is inferior"—and instead urged readers to celebrate the collective talent, all "from our immediate community," on display.[6] The exhortation reimagined the contestants not simply as exceptional individuals who might fulfill a predetermined role, but as a musical collective—a countercultural ensemble akin to that formed by the Drury Company decades earlier.

The Vocal Trials exemplified both the peril and the promise of this historical juncture. The event's narrow focus on sopranos who might someday sing leading roles at the Metropolitan Opera House obfuscated the reality that by 1925, African Americans had for years been central to the production of opera in mainstream spaces as listeners, workers, and supernumeraries. It also foreclosed these sopranos' creative horizons by implying that singing canonical repertory at a white institution should constitute their ultimate ambition. Yet the very existence of the contest, coupled with the widespread attention it generated, suggested that change could be imminent. In the early years of Black operatic counterculture, the very idea of a Black woman performing a principal role with a major opera company was unthinkable. But by the mid-1930s, Black sopranos were landing such roles in both Europe and the United States. The Harlem Renaissance reshaped the relationship between Black culture and the white mainstream, enabling African American performers' access to some historically segregated cultural institutions. Black artists who escaped the constraints of Jim Crow by traveling to interwar Europe found both a ready audience among Europeans and a robust transnational network of African American performers and intellectuals.[7] It seemed a moment of immense possibility.

During the late 1920s and early 1930s, Black artists claimed unprecedented space within the operatic mainstream. Critics and listeners participated in robust debates regarding casting, representation, and the racial imagination. Transfiguring the observation that Black characters were central to the standard repertory into evidence that Black performers deserved a place on the operatic stage, they refuted a dominant paradigm in which representations of Blackness could substitute for the presence of Black people in the art form. Black sopranos enacted this shift by appearing in the title role of Verdi's *Aida* with major companies. Florence Cole-Talbert, who toured Europe in the late 1920s, reimagined the role as an opportunity for creative opposition to US white supremacy. Caterina Jarboro, whose 1933 appearance with a white New York company marked a turning point in Black operatic history, engaged in nuanced strategies of self-making that challenged facile assumptions about Black artists' rightful place on the operatic stage. Embracing the role's grandeur, glamour, and narrative complexity, these women crafted aesthetically expansive and politically urgent expressions of Black womanhood.

It is no coincidence that *Aida* was the central work through which these changes occurred. Not only was it the most frequently performed opera in the early twentieth-century United States, but it also loomed large in Black operatic counterculture: it was an inspiration for the Egyptian setting of *The Martyr*, a staple of the Drury Company's repertory, and the opera in which Black supernumeraries most often appeared. When Black sopranos sang its title role, assuming the part of an enslaved Ethiopian princess, their performances rested on the contradictory premise that Blackness was both a requirement for participation and a quality that might eventually become irrelevant—a type of "confined inclusion," to borrow a phrase from Jarvis Givens, that left room for the legitimation of racialized casting and the perpetuation of existing imbalances of power.[8] But rather than simply adhering to the opera's preconceived model of Blackness, these performers rewrote limited cultural scripts to become what Daphne Brooks calls "agents of their own liberation."[9] They particularized *Aida*'s dramatic narrative as commentary on contemporary racial politics, weaving their own experiences into the operatic canon. The effect of these interpretive shifts was to reimagine the Black opera singer, and particularly the Black female opera singer, as a conduit for social change. Departing from the masculinist model provided by the "race men" who had theorized Black operatic counterculture's inaugural contours, singers like Cole-Talbert and Jarboro showed how Black women could become its primary agents of change. They embraced

the hypervisibility of their position, willfully assuming a more populist role as the "voice of the people."

By emphasizing the intertwined aesthetic and political stakes of Black artists' appearances in canonical roles, African Americans generated new, potentially liberatory meanings from opera's essential texts—a transformative technique that enabled them to reinvent the genre from the inside out. "When I performed Aida," Leontyne Price has reflected, "the color of my skin became my costume, and that gave me an incredible freedom no other role could provide."[10] To Price, Aida was a role brimming with possibility, rooted in the shared identity of performer and character and culminating in nothing less than the attainment of freedom. "This very minute," Price elaborated, "Aida says things about where I am as a woman and as a human being, about my life and the progress, or lack of, of millions of people at home in the States—things I could not have said as eloquently in other ways."[11] Her layered claims about race, gender, and citizenship insist on *Aida*'s interpretive richness and political salience, wresting the opera into the urgency of "this very minute." Naomi André affirms this sensibility in a meditation on Price's performance of the aria "O patria mia," in which Aida yearns for her Ethiopian homeland: "I feel how real these words are: 'Oh my country, how much you have cost me.' It feels like a moment when the drama onstage and the reality offstage crash together . . . Revealed in this voice is the childhood in Mississippi during the 1930s and 1940s; the proud and puzzled receptions of her operatic singing by her family, community, and audiences around the world; the comments she must have endured."[12] As opportunities for the co-constitutive production of affective and social meaning, Black women's performances of Aida were part of a genre-spanning phenomenon in which, as Farah Jasmine Griffin writes, the Black woman's voice "is like a hinge, a place where things can both come together and break apart."[13] Both the role and the celebrity status that it afforded to its performers promised to engender new ways of understanding the relationship between the European operatic past and the African American present.

The optimistic sense of possibility generated by early performances of *Aida* was never fully realized, and racialized roles remained limited in their ability to unsettle opera's color line. To paraphrase Audre Lorde, the masterwork did not dismantle the opera house. But even under such ambivalent circumstances, Black women artists of this era would succeed in infusing Aida with a countercultural sensibility, generating critical depth from *within* the character and the resolutely canonical opera in which she appears.

Operatic Casting and the Racial Imagination

The expectation that Black singers will assume the roles of Black characters in opera is less straightforward than it may appear. Scholars including Nina Sun Eidsheim have detailed how, as opera houses became nominally desegregated in the second half of the twentieth century, Black singers were "plugged into the standard repertoire's liminal roles," normalizing the practice of racial typecasting.[14] Aida, in particular, came to be considered an expectation, even a requirement, for Black sopranos. By the mid-1950s, Wallace Cheatham writes, it was "an unspoken fact" that "if a black soprano came along she had to do *Aida*."[15] The issue persisted: Jessye Norman observed in 1973 that "it's typecasting. People look at me and say 'Aida,'" while Shirley Verrett recalled that "they looked at black sopranos in that day and said, 'You're a soprano—Aida!'"[16] If this practice subjects performers to what Rosalyn Story calls the "maid / slave-girl / gypsy syndrome," it also shows how Blackness is not just ancillary to, but also constitutive of, the operatic canon.[17] As one critic observed in 1918, "Otello—taken from Shakespeare's Othello—is a black moor of Northern Africa. Aida is a black princess from Ethiopia. The La Traviata is Colored Dumas' Camille, set to music; Meyerbeer's L'Africaine is another, in which the heroine is a black person, 'Selika.' The Negro should know what a swath he cuts, as a subject, in the operatic world."[18] But in the early twentieth century, even those roles were off-limits. In other words, the connection between character and performer was not preordained: Black performers first had to secure a place for themselves within operatic institutions that had long excluded them.

African American critics employed an array of rhetorical and tactical strategies in support of this goal, focusing especially on opera's narrative and visual components. They argued that racial representations in opera were not timeless or ahistorical, but rather intimately entangled with contemporary social and political concerns. Early critics coupled praise of African American singers' unassailable skill with acknowledgment of the barriers they faced. An American theater manager who traveled to Europe in the summer of 1911 reported that "the colored men are given leading parts in grand opera," a "freak development" that would be impossible at home given the racist proclivities of "the American public."[19] When Anita Patti Brown and Roland Hayes performed duets from *Aida* in recital in Chicago, a critic noted that "to say that these two artists are unequalled in the firmament of grand opera stars would be but putting it mildly and were it not for the color of their skin they would hold a place in the musical world second to none."[20] After Brown sang arias from the opera in a solo recital,

the *Defender* noted that "[Rosa] Raisa, who is known as the greatest Aida, does not sing it better, and it would be a pleasure to hear her sing the entire score, for the dramatic quality of the libretto and music is a fitting medium for her resonant voice."[21]

A parallel discursive thread critiqued white sopranos' use of blackface in *Aida.* (The practice was so common that its absence evinced shock among white reviewers—as when one Aida at the Met "surprised the sold-out house by bursting into view with as lily-like a complexion as a Marguerite."[22]) In 1917, Lester Walton reported that the Italian soprano Claudia Muzio was "darkening her skin to accomplish the complete impersonation of the Ethiopian princess slave."[23] What incensed Walton was not Muzio's use of blackface per se, but that the *New York Sun,* which had a policy of refusing to publish images of Black performers, printed a photograph of Muzio in full makeup. The photograph, Walton argued, "brings to one's attention the superficiality of color prejudice," because "when the opera singer darkens up to resemble a Negro she is as much of a colored person as a peroxide blond is a member of the light-haired type or a drug-store beauty is of the red-lipped, rosy-cheeked class."[24] Walton expanded his argument beyond Muzio's appearance and the *Sun's* policy, using the opportunity to point out the fundamental illogic of racism.

Critics also noted how Black men were particularly unwelcome on American operatic stages. When the white, Chicago-based tenor Charles Marshall performed the title role of Verdi's *Otello* to great acclaim in 1921, the *Defender's* critic suggested that the opera, despite its "superb" music, had previously been unpopular in the United States due to the "impossible" status of its title character vis-à-vis American racial politics: "This marrying of white women, even in history and fiction—well. It just isn't done. It is not southern and therefore not American." It was not until Marshall sang the part that "worshipers at the shrine of music" "subdued their prejudices . . . They are forgetting that [Othello] was black and have forgiven Shakespeare and Verdi for immortalizing him."[25] Directly implicating white listeners who chose to "subdue" white supremacy for their own aesthetic benefit, the critic also emphasized the inextricability of artistic works from the sociopolitical context in which they appeared. Tellingly, however, the notion of a Black singer taking on the role of Otello is virtually absent from this era's discourse on race and representation.[26] The prospect of an onstage romance between a white soprano and a Black tenor was incendiary in a context where *The Birth of a Nation* (1915) had surged to nationwide popularity for its grotesque story of terroristic violence; where the KKK had re-emerged as a national force with millions of members; and where Black men

were vilified as sexual threats to white women and remained vulnerable to extrajudicial murder.[27]

Black critics also located African American singers' struggles within a multiracial context, scrutinizing occasions on which other performers of color assumed operatic roles. When the Japanese soprano Tamaki Miura made her US debut, in 1915, as Cio-Cio-San in Puccini's *Madama Butterfly*, a laudatory editorial in the *New York Age* entertained "the possibility that some day colored singers will portray, even on the stage of the Metropolitan Opera House, the roles of the colored characters in such operas as Aida, Otello and Salambo." Acknowledging that the "first impulse will be to say that such a hope is absurd," the writer expressed defiant optimism: "we believe that the time will come when singers of our race will sing grand opera in this country, especially those roles to which they are especially adapted by race and temperament."[28] This was a risky strategy. As Mari Yoshihara has argued, the identification of performer with character on the basis of race and gender risks devaluing that singer's individual artistry. Miura was a case in point: while white women who sang the role were exalted for their "performative mastery," her suitability was presupposed—even though, as an older, divorced woman, she had little in common with the naïve teenager she portrayed.[29]

Complicating matters further, critics who praised Miura also recognized that the Japan portrayed in the opera was unrealistic and fantastical, a product of Puccini's imagination. In this sense, Miura's presence took on a compensatory function, *adding* a realistic element to the opera ex post facto rather than fulfilling a preexisting need. Moreover, one writer posited that Miura's ability to imbue the role with a feeling "true to life" reflected her training as well as her identity, arguing paradoxically that "the reason that she is so able to impress her audience in the role is that her stage training has been along occidental lines." In contrast with the "aloofness" characteristic of Eastern actors, Miura possessed "that magnetic quality called personality, which is regarded in the western world as the chief asset of an actor."[30] To establish a "natural fit" between performer and character, then, was a convoluted process that required the audience to disregard Miura's biographical details and *Madama Butterfly*'s intrinsic inaccuracies; it also required Miura to study in the Western tradition to make her performance of an imagined Japanese woman more convincing. Rather than questioning the terms on which European composers depicted non-Western characters of color, this flavor of inclusion framed gender, race, and other identity markers as realist enhancements to existing works—an essentially anti transformational practice in which performers were tasked with providing

visual specificity without challenging the aesthetic or dramatic parameters of the work as a whole.

More broadly speaking, attention to the perceived "fit" between performer and character reflected changing attitudes toward the visual politics of operatic realism. Singers were increasingly evaluated for their adherence to the "physique du rôle," or ability to "look the part."[31] Women faced particularly intense scrutiny. In 1916, one commentator postulated that whereas female opera singers of the past had been "matronly," even "fat and ugly," modern productions required "not only beautiful voices" but also "beautifully formed bodies such as the heroine of an opera should have." "The modern audience is not so inclined to accept these incongruities," the writer noted, because "the eye and the mental sense of fitness should be satisfied as well as the musical ear."[32] This development was linked to the rising popularity of film: as critic Howard Taubman observed, "Singers today . . . must look reasonably like the figures they are portraying. The cinema has set up new standards of personal appearance, and younger audiences will not compromise the eye for the benefit of the ear."[33] Modern media thus reshaped standards for live operatic performance, encouraging a slippage of aesthetic conventions between the two in which visual suitability became an ever more important consideration.

For Black performers, these attitudinal shifts coexisted and, ultimately, converged with the emergence of what Karl Hagstrom Miller calls the "authenticity paradigm," an idea that originated in the Jim Crow South and strengthened a previously weak link between "racialized music and racialized bodies" in popular music, effectively shoring up the musical color line by yoking a performer's race to their repertoire.[34] The idea had massive material ramifications in an era when, as Langston Hughes famously put it, "the Negro was in vogue": white publishers courted Black authors, record executives saw the economic potential in the work of African American blues and jazz singers, and immensely successful Broadway shows like *Shuffle Along* (1921) took the theater world by storm. But the authenticity paradigm also intensified a long-held perception that genres like opera and concert music were outside the parameters of "Black music," and thus beyond what African Americans should sing. Earlier norms regarding race and genre had accommodated a measure of performative fluidity, enabling an event like the Drury Company's performance of *Carmen,* for instance, to be perceived by white audiences as a novelty rather than a transgression. But now-fashionable versions of racial authenticity were difficult to square with Western art music's Eurocentric origins. Only concert spirituals, with their

DREAMING IN ENSEMBLE

antebellum origins and close ties to the Black musical past, might be acceptable.[35]

Black critics questioned this idea. Lester Walton argued that African American classical artists had the right to perform not only that which was "characteristically Negro," but also any other music, because "to show appreciation for your own music does not preclude a race from studying and admiring the music of the masters of other races."[36] Walton explained that if "the Negro should solely confine himself to the rendition of spirituals made famous by his race, then by the same process of reasoning it must follow that Italian opera is to be exclusively sung by the Italian, German opera by the German and French opera exclusively by the French." But this was a faulty premise: "After all, music requiring, among other things, intelligent interpretation, skill and facility of expression, is written for artists—'irrespective of color,' and I might add—irrespective of race."[37]

The implications of the "authenticity paradigm" with respect to operatic casting were ambivalent. While the genre of opera's associations with whiteness became ever stronger, there was also a new rationale for performers of color to heighten the ostensible realism of a given production by appearing in racially marked roles. The resulting paradox echoed that which had undergirded the Ferrari Fontana Vocal Trials: race both authenticated these artists' performance and rendered it transgressive. A powerful example dates from 1918, when the Metropolitan Opera presented a triple bill of Charles Wakefield Cadman's *Shanewis,* about a Native American woman; Franco Leoni's *L'Oracolo,* set in a San Francisco Chinatown; and Henry Gilbert's *The Dance in Place Congo,* a tale of enslaved people in antebellum New Orleans. All three works document how opera actively shaped what Josh Kun calls the "American audio-racial imagination": white American composers, responding to and building on European opera's longstanding fascination with depictions of "the Other" as a means of defining both self and nation, used opera as a vehicle for exoticizing explorations of nonwhite cultures.[38]

Shanewis was an exemplar of the so-called Indianist movement, which attempted to transport Native American myths and characters to the operatic stage via the interpretive lens of white composers. It was based on the life of Creek soprano Tsianina Redfeather, who attended the Met premiere in traditional dress as an audience member—a performance in its own right that, Philip Deloria suggests, was a way of "blurring the relation between frontstage performance and backstage authenticity."[39] *L'Oracolo,* an exoticist, *verismo*-inspired piece set in an opium den, appeared at a historical

juncture when the effects of the Chinese Exclusion Act had decimated a once-vibrant Chinese American opera scene. Part of a tradition of enormously popular Orientalist stage productions, it featured an all-white cast—suggesting that even if performers of color were now possible participants in opera, their presence was by no means considered imperative.[40] *The Dance in Place Congo* rounded out the program. Presented as a ballet-pantomime (a dramatic genre with ties to grand opera), its troupe of silent artists included a small group of African American dancers portraying enslaved men, alongside an all-white cast of principal dancers and a ballet corps of white dancers in blackface. This arrangement, Carolyn Guzski argues, "served to signal—rather than conceal—white male identities among the *corps,* differentiating them from actual performers of color in order to ostensibly quell audience anxieties surrounding the possibility of unsanctioned interracial intimacy."[41]

In 1926, the Met presented John Alden Carpenter's *Skyscrapers,* a ballet that celebrated the invigorating nature of modern urban life. It featured a small troupe of Black performers who both sang and danced onstage. Although the program mentioned the group's organizer, Frank Wilson, by name, it failed to acknowledge the additional individuals who comprised the troupe. Described by the *New York Times* reductively as "real Negroes from Harlem," they were established performers with a wealth of artistic experience.[42] (For example, Leviticus Lyon was a tenor and conductor who graduated from Juilliard in 1925 and helped to organize a variety of musical and theatrical groups in New York.) By contrast, the *Amsterdam News* named the performers—in addition to Lyon, they included Amos Guerrant, Annyce Francis, Electra Jackson, Eva Muse, Ralph and Joseph Northern, Mrs. O. Baker, Marle Hill, Flora Sutton, and Lloyd Grey—and wished them well. Yet this praise was accompanied by a reminder that previous efforts to desegregate American stages had yielded "nothing lasting."[43] Like *The Dance in Place Congo, Skyscrapers* offered evidence of the centrality of Blackness to the racial definition of American opera, as well as the perilously narrow paths by which African American artists reached US opera stages.[44]

Narrow, but not impenetrable. By the early 1930s, the emerging expectation that Black performers might sing the roles of Black characters catalyzed a strategic shift among artists and intellectuals who recognized the tactical importance of such roles as an important step along the journey toward full participation in the operatic mainstream. Critics began to reframe the absence of Black singers as a deliberate choice rather than an inherent property of opera. "While many of the celebrated operas by the old

composers, who knew not racial prejudice, call for colored characters, American custom has prevented Negroes from appearing in these roles," one wrote; yet it would be "common sense" to feature Black artists "instead of using only whites with their faces corked in conformity with American racial prejudice."[45] By 1933, another critic had predicted that "some day in the not too distant future, Negroes will be called upon to take leading roles with the Metropolitan and with other grand opera companies. Color lines will be erased and Negroes will sing not only in operas depicting darker peoples, but also in Wagner's 'Tristan und Isolde,' Alfano's 'Resurrection,' and many others."[46] The language almost perfectly echoed that claim printed in the *New York Age* eighteen years prior regarding "the possibility that some day colored singers will portray, even on the stage of the Metropolitan Opera House, the roles of the colored characters in such operas as Aida, Otello and Salambo." But there were two key distinctions. Whereas in 1915 such a vision seemed far-fetched, now it appeared "not too distant."[47] And while the earlier writer focused exclusively on "the roles of the colored characters," the later one called for African Americans to appear in *all* operas, from Wagner's reinvention of a medieval European legend to Alfano's adaptation of a Tolstoy novel.

That demand, in turn, evolved into a call for new forms of operatic world-making. Even as participation in opera's mainstream began to seem within reach, a commitment to Black operatic self-determination—inaugurated years prior by Freeman's dream of a Black-authored operatic canon, and Drury's of Black-led operatic institutions—endured. In a 1937 opinion piece for the *Pittsburgh Courier,* the musician Penman Lovingood praised the few African American singers who had appeared with white opera companies before offering an admonishment: "Those persons who expect such appearances by Negro artists to solve the problem of the Negro's development in the field of operatic art are headed for a disappointment." The appearance of individual stars in canonical roles was insufficient: "Alien Operas are all right as accomplishments for Negro singers, but a native Negro school of opera must eventually come, or Negroes will remain just outcasts in the truer sense . . . We dream of, we hope for the establishment of organizations that will produce the best that the Negro has to offer in the theatre and in that most sacred of artistic confines, the opera house. When we come to be producers and not just camp-followers, we will properly be regarded by those people, who have an appreciation for originality."[48] Lovingood's comments underscore that racialized roles were never the only means by which African Americans sought to enter the opera house, nor were they considered an uncontested good. Their limitations were profound, yet their

strategic and material utility was indisputable. For select singers, they represented the chance to engage in a new type of self-making, enter into interracial public spheres, and pursue artistic stardom. At various moments, they could be both chokeholds and thresholds, trap doors and entryways. The combination of reward and restriction that they offered would shape Black operatic counterculture in fundamental ways.

"Our Own Aida"

As early as the 1890s, Sissieretta Jones was praised as "like a veritable Aida"; one critic wrote that "the thought was irresistible that she would make a superb Aida, whom her appearance, as well as her voice, suggested."[49] These speculative comments illuminate the depth of the relationship between Black women's vocality and this operatic character. *Aida* originated when the Egyptian khedive, Isma'il Pasha, commissioned Giuseppe Verdi and librettist Antonio Ghislanzoni to write an opera on an Egyptian subject; having never visited Egypt, they drew heavily on the work of French Egyptologist Auguste Mariette. (Or, as Naomi André pointedly describes it, "*Aida* is a made-up story by Italians and Frenchmen set in the time of the Pharaohs with little knowledge of the historical Egyptians and Ethiopians and makes no reference to living Egyptians or Ethiopians during the late nineteenth century."[50]) The opera premiered in Cairo on Christmas Eve, 1871, and was performed for the first time in the United States at the New York Academy of Music in 1873. Like much nineteenth-century grand opera, it is at once intimate and grandiose, staging interpersonal drama within an expansive historical and political context.[51] The title character is an enslaved Ethiopian princess who falls in love with the Egyptian general Radames while their nations are at war, prompting a crisis of love, loyalty, and betrayal. When Radames is declared a traitor and sentenced to death, Aida chooses to die with him. Verdi's music combines a conservative formal structure with exoticist sonic tropes. In performance, the opera features a large chorus and orchestra, extended ballet sequences, elaborate sets, and sometimes even live animals, making it an ideal vehicle for spectacle and extravagance.

Aida is often recognized for its imperial entanglements. Edward Said famously characterized the opera as "not so much *about* but *of* imperial domination," an exemplar of the impulse to invent a static Oriental other in order to reiterate and justify European colonial power.[52] Other scholars, including Ralph Locke and Katherine Bergeron, have offered alternative analyses that account for the role of performers and others who co-create

the opera's significance onstage.[53] Most productions portray its Egyptian characters as white (or racially unmarked) and Ethiopians as Black, a convention that dates to an early production book indicating that the Ethiopian characters have "olive, dark reddish skin."[54] As a result, white singers often have performed the role of Aida (as well as that of her father, the Ethiopian king Amonasro) using skin-darkening makeup. This practice persisted throughout the twentieth century and continues to this day.[55]

If *Aida* looked backward to both the imperialist and exoticist tendencies of nineteenth-century European grand opera and the American tradition of blackface performance, participants in early twentieth-century Black operatic counterculture looked forward, identifying the opera as a touchstone for creative engagement with the European canon. The Drury Company offered the first fully staged productions of *Aida* by African American singers in 1903 and 1906; both featured soprano Estelle Pinckney Clough in the title role.[56] The vaudevillian Aida Overton Walker was likely inspired by the opera when she changed her first name from Ada to Aida around 1905.[57] Black concert singers frequently included arias from *Aida* on recital programs—including Roland Hayes, who often began his recitals with "Celeste Aida." Across the country, African American musical clubs were named in the opera's honor: the Aida Club of Musical Art, the Aida Choral Society, the Aida Choral Club.[58] The opera was also evoked by composers and writers. Thomas Riis has noted that the popular song "My Castle on the Nile," by Bob Cole, James Weldon Johnson, and J. Rosamond Johnson, quotes the chord progression from "Su! del Nilo al sacro lido," a chorus from *Aida,* while Nicole Aljoe has identified thematic and aesthetic parallels between the opera and Pauline Hopkins's 1903 novel *Of One Blood.*[59] Around 1920, W. E. B. Du Bois penned notes for a short story titled "The Secret Singer," about a "black girl . . . with a phenomenal voice" who "succeeds as Aida."[60]

Within major opera houses, *Aida*'s title role remained the purview of white singers. When Black sopranos at long last began to perform it, they faced an interpretive, even ethical, challenge. Fred Moten, in a consideration of Shakespeare's *Othello,* observes that when Black performers take on a role crafted in the white racial imaginary, both those who embrace it and those who refuse to engage with it are "enjoined to take responsibility for white fantasy and solve a problem not of their own making." "What does it mean to portray Othello," Moten asks, "when the beauty of the language of that role, or the depth of human feeling it bears, is still filtered through the protocols of blackface no matter who plays it? . . . Is it right to marshal the forces of composition, improvisation, and interpretation to

get at the soul of Othello?"[61] Aida prompts similar questions, and in the context of Verdi's opera, they refer to a figure who is both curiously generalized and intriguingly complex. Jacek Blaszkiewicz has argued that the character exemplifies the interchangeable nature of various racial and gendered stereotypes in the nineteenth-century imagination; she is a figure of "generic alterity" rather than an evocation of a specific time or place.[62] But she is also deeply multifaceted—a princess and a slave, a heroine and a tragic victim, an object and a subject, a woman plagued by divided loyalties—and thus invites a range of interpretive possibilities.[63] As feminist opera scholars since Carolyn Abbate have argued, female performers have the capacity to displace male composers to wield authorial power, or otherwise exercise interpretive agency within the genre.[64] It is in such artistic acts that what Price called the role's "incredible freedom" inheres, enabling Verdi's image of Black female subjection to become a vehicle for Black female stardom.

Black sopranos who assumed the role chose to locate Aida within their specific historical moment, in a manner that facilitated social critique and allowed for the preservation of Black operatic counterculture within mainstream institutional contexts. Both opera and US popular entertainment had long displayed an appropriative fascination with representing Blackness on the stage, but these artists insisted on the value of their own embodied artistry. Moreover, whereas educators like Azalia Hackley had focused primarily on the self-making potential of operatic vocality, these performers intervened in opera's dramatic and visual meanings as well. In turn, their achievements in opera heightened their profile within the Black public sphere, enabling them to take on the status of celebrities—figures whose stature, as Sharon Marcus argues, is co-created by media narratives, public reception, and the stars themselves.[65] Their newfound public visibility converged with their reconceptualization of Aida as a heroic and racially representative character, cementing their status as artists whose work had the potential to comment on, and even transform, the social conditions under which they performed. Tasked with spectacle, they insisted on specificity.

In 1927, in the southern Italian city of Cosenza, Florence Cole-Talbert became the first Black woman to sing *Aida* with a European company. Born in Detroit in 1890, Cole-Talbert came from a line of musical women: her grandmother, Sarah Hatfield Chandler, played the guitar and sang in a choir in nineteenth-century Cincinnati, and her mother, Sadie Chandler Cole, had been a Fisk Jubilee Singer.[66] Cole-Talbert studied music at the University of Southern California and the Chicago Musical College, where she received the prestigious Diamond Medal in 1916. She toured the Midwest

with Hann's Jubilee Singers, a group that specialized in programs of "Plantation Melodies and Opera."[67] Like many singers of her generation, Cole-Talbert was mentored by Azalia Hackley. As a teenager, she and Hackley attended together a performance of *Aida* that featured a white woman in blackface makeup as Aida. A profile of Cole-Talbert in the *Defender* recounted that

> Florence noticed the star and asked: "Why is she all blacked up."
>
> "She's supposed to be an Ethiopian," the curious teenager was informed.
>
> "But why don't they let a Negro sing the part," she pressed.
>
> "There are no Negroes who can," Florence was told.
>
> These words were a challenge and the pig-tailed teenager vowed she would someday sing the lead in "Aida."[68]

Cole-Talbert repeated this story in interviews throughout her career. "I was impressed by the opera as nothing had ever moved me before," she recalled. "I sat breathlessly watching the artists, and as the opera progressed, a desire (an impossible desire, so it seemed at the time) took possession of me. I wanted to sing the title role in Aida."[69] While this narrative highlighted the young singer's ambition, it also reiterated the naturalizing rhetoric of the Ferrari Fontana contest, implying that Aida represented both the origin and the logical culmination of her aspirations. In the summer of 1925, Cole-Talbert made her way to New York Harbor and boarded the *Conte Rosso,* an ocean liner bound for Naples, Italy. She first studied at a music school for Americans at the Villa d'Este in Tivoli, near Rome, then pursued further training in Paris and Milan before giving recitals in several Italian cities. Nearly two years later, in March 1927, she made her long-awaited debut as Aida.

What men like Ferrari Fontana assumed to be a natural fit between performer and character, Cole-Talbert denaturalized and reimagined as an opportunity for creative opposition to musical and social hierarchies. Because US-based audiences could not hear her sing Aida, the Black press was the primary means by which African Americans accessed her voice. Her creative ambitions, like those of other Black women performers, became the stuff of political critique—a process by which, as Jayna Brown writes, "disenfranchised citizens came to represent that nation's most prized claims to freedom, equality, and opportunity."[70] Before and on the occasion of her debut, she was the subject of journalistic reports, letters to the editor, and autobiographical dispatches in prominent US Black newspapers.[71] Within

Florence Cole-Talbert, ca. 1921.

these texts, Cole-Talbert emphasized the sense of duty she felt as a public figure and Talented Tenth exemplar: "I hope to be a success," she wrote. "THIS IS NOT FOR ME BUT FOR MY RACE."[72] One reporter praised her by declaring: "It is harder to become a successful opera singer than it is to become a United States Senator, and when a colored woman reaches the operatic goal one cannot speak too highly of her talent and force of will," a surprising comparison that legitimized opera as an important site of cultural politics.[73]

Cole-Talbert skillfully drew attention to the social climate in Europe that made her achievements feasible. One missive detailed how her "hateful" white American classmates in Tivoli attempted to reproduce the conditions of Jim Crow segregation when they tried to prevent her from performing with them and objected to her staying in the same hotel. Italians actively countered their racist behaviors, and Cole-Talbert's voice teacher was, she wrote, resolute in "standing by me."[74] Black journalists also exalted her ability to impress finicky Italians, "the most critical operatic audience in the world."[75] They painted an idyllic scene: "It was remarkable how she attracted attention wherever she went. The children followed her about the streets and cried, 'There is Aida, there is the new Aida.'"[76] As Kira Thurman notes, such praise should be read skeptically; it reflects the privilege that Black Americans held over other Black people in Europe, as well as the longing for acceptance that they felt.[77] Yet even if these reports represented a selective oversimplification of Italian racial politics, they conveyed the magnitude of Cole-Talbert's achievement and gave US-based readers access to a cultural scene beyond the United States, where white supremacy did not quash her operatic aspirations.

Both white and Black critics foregrounded the visual politics of Cole-Talbert's performance. The Italian press noted that she was able to sing the role "excellently without darkening her skin," while the *Amsterdam News* rejoiced, "The critics need no longer complain that Verdi made his greatest heroine black, forcing white singers to make themselves up for the role . . . we have our own Aida."[78] These characterizations essentialized Cole-Talbert's body as ideally suited to play Aida, with the implied corollary that white artists lacked a similarly legitimate claim to the role. An evocative account in the *Amsterdam News* offered additional insight into Cole-Talbert's interpretive approach: "Upon the stage Radames, the young Egyptian captain, was going off to join the army in its campaign against the Ethiopians. Aida, the Ethiopian captive in love with Radames, was bidding him Godspeed. Radames disappeared and Aida turned to the audience, and from her lips burst that most tremendous of Verdi's arias, 'Ritorna Vincitor!' Her voice soared and sank and soared again, till all the pent-up suffering of a race throbbed forth in the words 'Sempre Soffrir,' ending with a long sob."[79] This is an iconic moment in the opera: Aida stands alone, tormented by the prospect of choosing between her love for Radames and her loyalty to her Ethiopian homeland. First echoing the martial confidence of the chorus's call for victory, she slips back into the soft, longing melody with which the opera began. She loves Radames, even though in Egypt she is "oppressa e schiava" (oppressed and enslaved). The aria concludes with a pleading

prayer for peace, Aida's voice gliding over the glistening strings of the orchestra as she begs the gods for mercy.

The characterization of Cole-Talbert's voice here—bursting, soaring, throbbing, even sobbing—implies an extroverted, vigorous approach to this psychologically complex moment, a refusal of Aida's fate. As a conduit for the "pent-up suffering of a race," Cole-Talbert transformed an introspective aria into communal, quasi-cathartic expression. But curiously, the phrase "sempre soffrir" (always suffering) is not actually part of the aria; rather, the phrase is "Numi, pietà del mio soffrir!" (Gods, have pity on my suffering). The mistranslation productively transforms the aria from a resigned, individual plea to a generalized recognition of the "always suffering" status of "a race" under global white supremacy. Cole-Talbert's Aida, these critical details suggest, recognized the injustice not only of her own plight, but also of that faced by Ethiopian characters under Egyptian rule in the opera, and by African American readers in the United States.

Cole-Talbert was not the only African American woman to sing opera in Europe during these years. Lillian Evanti was a counterpart of Cole-Talbert's whose career took a divergent path. She was born Annie Lillian Evans in Washington, DC in 1890 to an elite family (Hiram Revels, the first Black US senator, was a relative). Evans studied voice at Howard University, changed her name to the Italian-sounding portmanteau "Evanti" following her marriage to Roy Tibbs, and moved to Europe.[80] She sang the title role of Léo Delibes's *Lakmé* at the Casino Theater in Nice, France in 1925 and reprised the part at the Trianon-Lyrique in Paris two years later. *Lakmé* takes up themes of "generic alterity" and tragic interracial romance similar to those of *Aida,* though it does not feature Black characters: it is set in nineteenth-century India, and the title character is a Hindu princess who commits suicide at the opera's end after her British lover abandons her. Photographed in costume for the role, Evanti cuts a glamorous figure. With her lips slightly parted and eyes cast demurely downward, she wraps her hands around an ornate vase. Her long hair flows out from behind a tightly wrapped headscarf. The flapper-esque look lends a modern sheen to her evocation of this exotic figure, linking her visually with other modern Black women performers on the popular stage.

Comparing Cole-Talbert and Evanti's trajectories elucidates that although race was central to Black women's pursuit of operatic roles, their careers were also shaped by factors including social class, education, and physical appearance, particularly in a context where both "looking the part" and extensive vocal training were of paramount significance. Even as some observers glibly connected Evanti's racial identity to the "eminently befitting"

Lillian Evanti in costume as Lakmé on the occasion of her 1925 debut.

role of an "unsophisticated Hindu maid," Evanti was soon offered other non-racially marked roles, including Violetta in *La Traviata* and Rosina in *The Barber of Seville*.[81] Her light complexion, glamorous appearance, and elite family background may have liberated her from the constraints that hindered most African American women seeking operatic careers. Her recital repertoire was also more varied than that of other African American concert singers, perhaps reflecting the diversity of training that she was able to access. A 1926 recital in Detroit, for instance, included arias from *La*

Traviata and Handel's *Rodelinda* alongside spirituals and art songs, and a 1927 concert in Washington, DC included music of Ravel and Stravinsky.[82] Her concert programs boasted of European engagements and featured the untranslated praise of French critics.[83] She tangibly embodied the possibility of a world beyond Jim Crow, and she connected her artistic success to her sense of personal and political freedom. "Thank you la belle France for my debut in Grand Opera," she reminisced. "France offered Liberte, Egalite, Fraternite [*sic*] . . . I was free!"[84]

Even as Evanti and Cole-Talbert's professional paths diverged, they were linked musically and in the public imagination by a mutual engagement with *Lakmé*. In 1923, Cole-Talbert recorded the opera's best-known aria, known as the "Bell Song," for Black Swan Records. Known as a "rite of passage, or a gauntlet" for sopranos due to its outsize technical demands, the aria begins with non-lexical, improvisatory vocalizing in which, as Ginger Dellenbaugh writes, the title character's "exotic femininity is extracted from the body and melts into air."[85] Cole-Talbert's rendition, however, prompts a different interpretation. As a recording made by an African American woman for a company dedicated to the promotion of African American artists, it does not separate the artist's voice from her (racialized) body. The aesthetic details of Cole-Talbert's singing depart from the sensuousness and pure vocality with which the aria is often associated. Her vocal timbre, precise as a fine-tip pen, is narrow but deep.[86] Her scrupulous technique evokes the training she received from Hackley and other mentors, prior to her intensive study in Europe. Just as Evanti, photographed in costume as Lakmé, visually intersperses the modern with the exotic, Cole-Talbert interrupts the presumed generic temporality and placelessness of the character by rooting the performance in a particular body, time, and place.[87] The meticulousness of her singing offers a sonic parallel to the specificity that she, Evanti, and other Black women brought to canonical operatic roles, transforming objects of the white racial imaginary into concrete opportunities for musical and social self-creation.

Race and History at the Hippodrome

On July 22, 1933, thousands of people streamed into Manhattan's Hippodrome Theater, undaunted by sweltering temperatures and teeming crowds, eager to witness a performance of *Aida* unlike anything they had seen before. The 5,300-seat theater, the largest in New York, had sold out days in advance, and patrons clambered for standing-room-only spots; still more were turned away at the door. Many in the audience were Italian

American, and about one-third were African American.[88] The evening's star, soprano Caterina Jarboro, entered to prolonged applause. Fanning their programs in the heat, the audience greeted her with a "tremendous ovation" as "Italians sat in admiration. White America gasped in amazement. And Harlem applauded its heroine in magnificent and splendorous debut."[89] By evening's end, Jarboro had become the first African American woman to appear in *Aida* with a previously all-white opera company in the United States. This was a momentous occasion. By 1933, the idea of a Black Aida was no longer new: writers had imagined that this day would come; young women in Harlem had flocked to the basement of the 135th Street branch library in pursuit of this very goal; and readers had read about Cole-Talbert's European performances in the Black press. Jarboro built on those precedents, but she further complicated what was increasingly seen as a natural relationship between Black women and Aida by crafting a glamorous, authoritative persona defined by not only her race, but also her aesthetic expertise and transhistorical social import. It seemed that she might redefine the terms of the racial logic that initially enabled her to perform the role.

The woman who would become Caterina Jarboro was born Katherine Yarborough in Wilmington, North Carolina in July 1898. Her father, John Wesley Yarborough, was a barber, an occupation that afforded the family a comfortable position in Wilmington's Black middle class. He and his wife, Elizabeth, lived in a picturesque Queen Anne cottage east of the Cape Fear River, where Katherine and her five siblings were born. But the relative stability of their life was shattered just months after Katherine's birth. In November 1898, a white supremacist mob staged a political coup and murdered dozens of African Americans in the now-infamous Wilmington Massacre, marking the beginning of a tyrannical period in which terroristic violence and economic and civic disenfranchisement threatened local Black citizens' lives.[90] This fundamental social reordering may well have shaped Jarboro's decision to leave the city at an early age, moving to New York as a teenager to live with an aunt. By 1921 she had joined the cast of the wildly successful Broadway show *Shuffle Along,* and in 1926 she moved to Europe to study opera. She followed the example of Cole-Talbert, making her debut as Aida at Milan's Puccini Theater in 1931.

As her career progressed, Jarboro engaged in acts of inventive self-making that repudiated the gendered and racialized scripts available to Black women in the Jim Crow United States. In addition to changing her name from Katherine Yarborough to the more glamorous Caterina Jarboro, she had a penchant for embellishing autobiographical details. Her great-nephew, the literary scholar Richard Yarborough, notes that her desire to "create a

mystique about her background" spoke to her "intuitive restlessness and ambition," which propelled her far from her origins and into the realm of grand opera.[91] She often downplayed her relationship to her family, even going so far as to claim that she had been an orphan and "couldn't remember" her siblings.[92] She maintained that she had never married.[93] Although she never denied her connection to Wilmington, she mentioned the city primarily in relation to well-received performances she gave there later in life—when her celebrity status allowed her to return home, in Yarborough's words, "as a sort of royalty, in a way the conquering queen."[94] The most straightforward way to contextualize Jarboro's regal persona might be to identify her as a diva, that quintessential figure of operatic grandeur and excess.[95] But as Yarborough notes, her emphasis on self-making also evoked the narrative conventions of both the celebrity memoir and the nineteenth-century slave narrative, in particular those genres' shared emphasis on the distance traveled from one's origins to one's current stature.[96] Distancing herself from (local and national) homes, family, and marriage, as well as from the popular stage, Jarboro created and claimed a persona rooted in cosmopolitan mobility and personal and artistic independence.

Upon returning to New York in 1932, Jarboro met the impresario Alfredo Salmaggi, who engaged her to sing *Aida*. An immigrant from central Italy, Salmaggi was a larger-than-life figure whose Chicago Grand Opera Company produced "popular price opera," massive and extravagant productions for which tickets cost less than a dollar.[97] Known by sobriquets like "the P. T. Barnum of bargain opera" and "the greatest producer of second-rate opera in the US," he favored spectacle and excess: parades of animals, enormous choruses, and a generally circus-like atmosphere.[98] For him, hiring a Black singer to perform the role of Aida may have been a way to heighten the production's spectacular nature and appeal to his audience's taste for novelty—an extension of the longstanding practice of hiring Black supernumeraries—rather than an entirely new or antiracist endeavor. (Indeed, in 1936, Salmaggi engaged the boxer Jack Johnson to play a [silent] Ethiopian general in *Aida,* clad in an outrageously primitivist leopard- and zebra-print costume.[99]) Despite these limitations, though, Jarboro embraced the opportunity. The circumstances of her debut suggest that her glamorous self-construction had a transgressive edge: her insistence on personal independence enabled her to push back against the spectacularizing constraints of the stages on which she appeared.

Photographed in costume, Jarboro radiates glamour. Adorned in necklaces and bracelets, a jeweled ankle-length dress, and a headband dripping with beads, she gazes into the distance with determination and confidence.

Richard Yarborough recalls that his great-aunt had a commanding presence, and that "how she carried herself physically was not stereotypically feminine." Instead, her affect was "regal, with her taking for granted that she was the center of attention. She could be raucously funny, but she didn't joke about her celebrity, which she saw as fully deserved."[100] That same self-possession emanates from this photograph, marking another way Jarboro might have used her embodied presence to contest the histrionic aesthetics of the Salmaggi production. Her Aida was not solely the feminized object

Caterina Jarboro in costume, ca. 1933.

of Radames's romantic love and Amonasro's paternal love, but also a character confident in her own dignity.

Headlines splashed across the front pages of major Black newspapers on the occasion of Jarboro's debut: "Miss Jarboro Scores in 'Aida'"; "Harlem Goes to Opera and Acclaims Its Own"; "Rises to Fame as Singer."[101] The editor of the *Amsterdam News* reported that scores of young women wrote him letters regarding Jarboro's performance, and he deemed public interest significant enough to publish a seven-hundred-word synopsis of *Aida* in the paper.[102] White critics focused primarily on the novelty of Jarboro's appearance and, to a lesser extent, her vocal technique, but they rarely contextualized the performance further or related it to broader cultural phenomena.[103] A richer and more heterogenous response emerged in the Black press, where critics marveled at Jarboro's visual and sonic suitability for the role, located her performance within a deep historical trajectory, and declared that her crossing of the color line heralded an interracially utopic musical future.

Both Black and white critics described Jarboro's body primarily in terms of the color of her skin, much as they had described Cole-Talbert's performance six years earlier. A headline in *Time* declared Jarboro an "Aida without Makeup," and many Black critics emphasized the intrinsic artificiality of white singers' appearances in the role. "Ever since the days when Verdi's great opera was produced in 1871 for the first time," one noted, "the stars who have sung the role of Aida have had to revert to the use of powder, Vaseline, and the spreading of pomade of some sort."[104] Yet "Miss Jarboro, unlike all other singers of 'Aida,' needed no grease paint to make her face brown. She did not have to use brown colored gloves to effect brown-skin arms."[105] To return to Leontyne Price's resonant phrase, Jarboro's skin was her costume.[106] In one respect, the cosmetic language of powder, grease paint, and makeup highlighted her distance from the context of blackface minstrelsy. In another, persistent attention to her visual and racial legibility as Aida assuaged deeper anxieties about Black operatic performance by suggesting that the natural relationship between performer and character was a requirement for her success. It undermined the possibility that Black singers might perform a fuller range of roles from across the operatic canon, including those for which they *did* need to apply makeup or dress in costumes.

Critical descriptions of Jarboro's voice had a different focus. Nina Sun Eidsheim has noted that Black opera singers are often evaluated in terms of the essentialist concept of "sonic blackness," but the reception of Jarboro's performance suggests a less straightforward relationship between the sonic

and visual facets of her work.[107] A few reviewers did evaluate Jarboro's voice in racialized terms; the *New York Times,* for instance, praised her "characteristically racial timbre, husky and darkly rich."[108] But most, white or Black, described her voice not as Black but as Italian. Critics highlighted her studies with Italian teachers and praised her "real understanding of the true Italian spirit," "Italian diction," and "typically Italian quality of voice."[109] When she returned from Europe, one reporter remarked that she "hasn't spoken English in years. When excited flies off into French or Italian. Is wild about Italy."[110] Another noted her taste for Italian cuisine, and one revealed that Jarboro even spoke Italian to her dog, with whom she often strolled through Harlem.[111] Her Italian voice facilitated professional success as well: when she introduced herself in fluent Italian to Salmaggi, he was reportedly so impressed by her command of the language (and her singing) that he offered her the role of Aida on the spot.[112] It also proved useful when, upon being denied entry to a segregated New York restaurant, Jarboro responded in Italian and convinced a waiter that she and her companion were actually non-Black Europeans, circumventing the restaurant's policy.[113] The minor incident suggests that Jarboro could mobilize her Italian voice strategically: whereas Blackness and Italianness together qualified her to sing Aida, she also used Italian to destabilize her racial identity and evade Jim Crow.

Jarboro's singing was never recorded, but contemporaneous and retrospective accounts give some indication of its character. At her New York debut, one critic wrote that her voice had "the range of a mountain and the clearness of a bell," a poetic description suggesting both technical excellence and authoritative presence.[114] Both qualities would have been exceptionally impressive in the cavernous Hippodrome Theater, where Jarboro had to make herself heard above the many choristers and animals crowding the stage. That same charisma and authority can be heard in an interview Jarboro gave in 1972.[115] She rarely answers the interviewer's questions directly, instead telling whatever stories she prefers to tell. Although past her vocal prime, she evokes her operatic abilities, tapping her microphone and telling the interviewer that at the Hippodrome she "didn't have one of these, because opera singers didn't need the microphone. You sang."[116] Richard Yarborough recalls that although he never heard his great-aunt sing in a formal setting, around the house she would regularly burst into operatic song: "It was almost a non sequitur. For whatever reason, she would do a snatch of a song, and of course it was always an opera." Her voice, he remembered, was "booming" and powerful. It was also deep: "If I had to identify the register it wouldn't have been soprano. It wasn't very

high. It struck me as a much deeper voice. Alto or something like that."[117] While Jarboro's lower vocal register might be attributed partially to her age and the spontaneity of these performances, this description also coheres with earlier critics' characterization of her voice as commanding and able to dominate the room she was in, be it the public space of a massive auditorium or the private space of a family member's living room.

Jarboro's performance was also situated within the long scope of post-Emancipation African American history. There was some precedent for linking Verdi and *Aida* to Black historical narratives. A review of the Drury Company's 1903 production of *Aida* suggested an affinity between Frederick Douglass and Verdi, both of whom rose from modest origins to heroic stature.[118] In 1913, W. E. B. Du Bois included two arias from *Aida* in *The Star of Ethiopia,* his diasporic pageant commemorating the Emancipation Proclamation's fiftieth anniversary.[119] Jarboro herself asserted a race-based birthright to the role, telling a reporter, "I felt very natural in the part. You see, my role was written for me sixty-two years ago by Verdi."[120] The African American critic T. R. Poston generalized this claim by describing the Harlem crowds at the theater as "descendants of Verdi's Ethiopian princess."[121] Noting that *Aida*'s 1871 premiere coincided with a post–Civil War vogue for the spirituals, Poston wrote: "Verdi and the freedmen have traveled parallel paths to immortality . . . And now, after sixty-two years, the parallel is destined to end. For, on Saturday night at the Hippodrome Theatre, the mythical Ethiopian princess will come to life through the voice and personality of a freedman's descendant."[122]

Contextualizing Jarboro's performance as part of a progressive narrative of modern Black history elided the paradox at the heart of *Aida:* namely, that Jarboro attained stardom by portraying an enslaved woman who dies at the opera's end. Poston accentuated Jarboro's status as a historical actor and aligned her with a lineage of African American achievement. This critical revision is especially notable given that *Aida*'s themes of morbidity, antiquity, and death are typically understood to be inextricable from its Orientalist origins. As Lydia Goehr explains, Said's influential critique of the opera argued that it "displac[ed] a living people into a dead civilization . . . thus denying them a living voice" in order to exert European authorial control and, by extension, imperialist power.[123] But to connect the opera to the recent African American past via Jarboro's presence was to reimagine its relationship to history writ large, refuting the idea of *Aida* as inexorably past, and instead refiguring it as historically specific and distinctly modern. Moreover, locating Jarboro within a national, African *American* history undermined the essentialist notion that race alone sufficed to connect

Jarboro, a modern Black opera singer, to Aida, a fictional character from ancient Ethiopia.

A robust debate about how to evaluate Jarboro's performance against the legacy of slavery emerged in the Black press. Arturo Alfonso Schomburg, the archivist and collector, insisted that her debut be analyzed in light of historical injustice: "In the language of Frederick Douglass," Schomburg proclaimed, "let us judge her from the depths she came, and let us bow in gratitude."[124] In a dissenting reply, the Brooklyn minister Reverend George Frazier Miller wrote: "If Miss Jarboro has attained the heights accredited to her by the musical critics of recognized competence, why 'judge her from the depths she came'? Might she not be measured by normal standards?" Miller preferred to judge Jarboro "on the intrinsic merits of her excellence and brilliancy . . . her comparison should be with those who are holding forth in a similar field of celebrated artists."[125] The exchange raised metacritical questions as to what constituted Miller's "normal standards," and whether the portrayal of Jarboro as having risen "from the depths" to overcome historical burdens enhanced or diminished her achievement. Like Schomburg and Miller, Fred Moten has characterized the Black operatic voice in terms of depth, joining together its physical and epistemological meanings in order to theorize its "disruptive" potential: "The black voice is . . . figured as 'deep,' an adjective that is both spatialised through metaphors of meaning, truth and history (as opposed to surface, as opposed to any absolute newness) and anatomized (wherein the sound is tied to a kind of deep-throatedness that is sometimes seen as a function of training but has often been linked to supposed anatomical features specific to black bodies)."[126] In contrast to the literally surface-level focus on Jarboro's skin, a focus on the deep historical resonances of her performance challenged the notion that her achievement was notable mainly because it was unprecedented. By instead showing how Jarboro evoked and contributed to a longer narrative, critics gave the performance a history of its own, recasting it as a culmination of longstanding struggle rather than merely the breaking of new ground.

Inspired by the magnitude of Jarboro's achievement, African American critics imagined the performance in what Josh Kun might call "audiotopian" terms, which cast Jarboro as concomitantly a singer, a celebrity, and a symbol.[127] In a particularly poignant framing, Salem Tutt Whitney recounted that as he read the program for Jarboro's performance, "The wonder of it all filled my eyes with tears and blinded my sight so that I could not see the names of those wonderful white artists, whose love for their art and devotion to their art ideals, completely erased all thought of racial

prejudice, and in so doing proved that art is universal and international."[128] Whitney's overwhelming emotion literally blinded him to the existence of the color line, presaging a future in which race was not authenticating but irrelevant. Importantly, this was a mode of universalism that did not require the erasure or transcendence of race, but rather insisted that racial difference could not justify inequality of musical opportunity.

Caterina Jarboro's debut as Aida was so acclaimed that it prompted an additional performance two nights later, in which she was joined by the African American baritone Jules Bledsoe in the role of Amonasro. Bledsoe was a genre-transcending artist from Waco, Texas whose career had taken off in the mid-1920s: he appeared as soloist with the Boston Symphony Chamber Players in 1926, then rose to fame as the original Joe in *Show Boat* in 1927. His extensive operatic repertoire included nearly thirty arias by composers from Scarlatti to Rimsky-Korsakov, as well as six full roles.[129] When he sang scenes from *Aida* in New York in 1929, the *Amsterdam News* deemed it "an opportunity to hear him in a greater role than that which he gives nightly [in *Show Boat*]," lamenting that in "'Aida,' 'Othello,' and other famous operas in which Negro characters are created Negro, such eligible artists are never given a chance to star in these parts."[130] His debut alongside Jarboro disrupted this trend; "the presence of dark-skinned artists," one critic rejoiced, augured a "wholly new step for America."[131]

Then, in 1935, Bledsoe made a debut—of sorts—at the Metropolitan Opera House. On the evening of May 2, he appeared in an Old South–themed "opera ball," an extravagant benefit for the Metropolitan Opera Association. The venue was transformed into the Louisiana mansion Belle Rive, circa 1855, on the occasion of an aristocratic wedding. Two thousand members of the white New York elite (tellingly described in the *Times* as the "cast" of the "pageant," their "stage names" listed in the newspaper) filed into a "luxurious setting reflecting the benign atmosphere of plantation days." They dressed in "hoop skirts," "bonnets," and "pantalettes"; some reportedly donned outfits once owned by their southern ancestors.[132] As they assumed their antebellum alter egos, attendees were greeted by the sounds of the Hall Johnson Choir, whose members took on the part of "plantation slaves [who] chant the sonorous melody of 'Deep River.'" Bledsoe "was cast as Jules, butler of the La Grange family, and he sang the famous old Foster song 'Massa's in the Cold, Cold Ground.'" The African American singer Bertha Powell also appeared, playing the role of "Mammy Liddy, the bride's personal maid."[133]

The scene provides a disquieting counterweight to the various ways in which African American singers had entered the mainstream opera house since the Ferrari Fontana Vocal Trials, ten years prior. At the Met, Bledsoe became not Amonasro but "Jules," the perceived "natural fit" between performer and character reinforced by the assignation of his given name to the butler he portrayed. He, Powell, and the Hall Johnson Choir appeared in the guise of enslaved laborers, recalling both the social order of the Old South and the supernumeraries who had worked on that same stage in productions of *Aida*. Much as the event collapsed past into present, it collapsed Black subjection into Black performance—a stark contrast to the interpretive creativity of artists like Cole-Talbert and Jarboro, who carefully rooted their performances of Aida in the specificities of their historical moment. Perhaps most significantly, Bledsoe's near-parallel appearances as Amonasro and "Jules" suggest the inadequacy of desegregation as a framework through which to assess Black participation in mainstream US opera during the 1920s and 1930s, and to assess the relationship between Black operatic counterculture and the dominant opera culture with which it became increasingly enmeshed. As Kira Thurman writes, "*how* opera houses presented Black singers on the opera stage in front of thousands of listeners often demonstrated that one step forward could mean two steps back."[134] The mere fact of inclusion did not guarantee antiracist change, much less structural transformation; Black performers could just as easily be pressed into roles that reified extant racial hierarchies.

Yet a new generation of critics and singers nonetheless found ways to critique and remake the very systems that threatened to squelch their creative work. In the pages of Black newspapers, and on stages from France to Italy to New York, they reframed the relationship between racialized roles in canonical operas and the artists who assumed those roles. Black women who sang *Aida*, in particular, profoundly reimagined Verdi's opera as a standpoint from which to advocate for Black freedom, transforming the figure of an enslaved Ethiopian princess into a symbol of collective racial progress. If singers like Cole-Talbert and Jarboro did not destabilize the color line as fully as their most optimistic listeners had hoped, they generated much from the role of Aida, both in terms of tangible progress toward the desegregation of operatic institutions and in terms of aesthetic possibility. Their performances did not dismantle the opera house, yet they built a different and more urgently relevant space through and for operatic performance.

❦ 5 ❦

Composing Afrodiasporic History

Wind back the clock from Jules Bledsoe's May 1935 appearance at the Metropolitan Opera House as an Old South butler, and a shapeshifting performance history emerges. In 1934, Bledsoe was an emperor: the power-hungry leader of an island in the West Indies, appearing in cities across Europe in the new opera *The Emperor Jones.* In 1933, he was a king: Verdi's Amonasro, singing alongside Caterina Jarboro's history-making Aida at the Hippodrome. In 1932, he was the Voodoo Man: a figure in the world-premiere opera *Tom-Tom,* grandly envisioned by the young Black composer Shirley Graham as an embodied conduit of the Afrodiasporic imagination. Bledsoe's appearances speak to the wide range of representations of Blackness that appeared in opera houses by the early 1930s. While the "controlling images" established by *Aida* and other canonical warhorses continued to exert a powerful influence, they now shared space with newly composed works.[1] Some, like *The Emperor Jones,* modernized and reworked longstanding primitivist conceits. Others, like *Tom-Tom,* offered a largely unprecedented conception of what Blackness could signify on the operatic stage.

Tom-Tom was the most visible and spectacular manifestation of a paradigm shift in Black operatic composition during the 1920s and 1930s, one that repurposed opera as a means of reinterpreting the Black past. Like the listeners, laborers, and sopranos who reshaped the racial politics of the opera house during this era, composers worked in a context informed by an upsurge of mainstream interest in African American culture and increased access to previously all-white cultural institutions. Crafting what Gayle

Murchison has described as "a tradition of African American opera . . . that reflected and embraced the aesthetics of the cultural movement known as the Harlem Renaissance," they created operas focused on historical narratives of Black freedom, from the Haitian Revolution to abolition in the United States, in ways that emphasized these episodes' contemporary resonances.[2] This dramatic emphasis was matched by an expansion of composers' musical repertoires, which increasingly drew on global styles of vernacular and popular Black music—not in lieu of, but alongside, an engagement with the European operatic canon. Embracing opera's characteristic formal and narrative capacities, including its visual and sonic grandeur, narrative complexity, and dramatic scope, they used the art form to envision alternative histories and futures.

The shifting contours of Harry Lawrence Freeman's operas exemplify this change. His earliest works, like *The Martyr,* were based on fictional plots set across the globe, and aesthetically proximate to the canon of nineteenth-century grand opera. Now he turned to pieces set in contemporary American contexts; once a Wagnerian acolyte, he began to embrace jazz and other sources of musical inspiration. He was joined by a generation of newcomers. Clarence Cameron White, a violinist long enmeshed in Black musical institutions, made his first foray into opera with *Ouanga,* a story of the Haitian Revolution that incorporated Haitian folk music. Graham, a polymathic artist and intellectual who was also new to the genre, created *Tom-Tom,* a diasporic narrative of African American history that compressed centuries and continents into an epic work featuring West African percussion, spirituals, and cabaret song. No longer content to invent potential narrative containers for Black history out of whole cloth, some composers turned to immersive ethnographic and historical research. White's opera was composed after he spent a summer conducting fieldwork in Haiti, while Graham drew on her background as a performer and scholar of Black music across genres.

In effect, Black operatic counterculture was being pulled in two directions. It became further entangled with the white operatic mainstream as Black performers appeared in principal roles on previously segregated stages and some white companies expressed interest in the work of Black composers. It also became increasingly aligned with other Black (counter)cultural formations, including the ethnographic literary impulses of the Harlem Renaissance and a corollary concern with popularizing Black historical knowledge. Daphne Lamothe has noted the prevalence of "ethnographic literature," or literary texts that drew on practices of fieldwork ethnography, among Harlem Renaissance intellectuals.[3] Musicians and artists engaged

in similarly "creative-academic" work, to borrow a term Katherine Dunham used to characterize her research-based dance practice.[4] Even as they participated in these broader trends, however, Black operatic composers maintained a productively marginal stance, predicated on opera's peripheral cultural status and its aesthetic particularities. Whereas celebrity singers like Florence Cole-Talbert and Caterina Jarboro extracted new interpretive meaning from within the art form's classic texts, composers like Shirley Graham made a more decisive break from tradition, embracing opera's potential as a site of Black world-making. They collectively embraced its capacity to articulate specific claims about the vastness of Black historical experience: its expansive narrative scope invited consideration of the complex relationship between the Black past and present, while its correspondingly broad musical scale facilitated the incorporation of musical and historical research into newly composed works.

During the 1920s and 1930s, a coterie of Black composers revitalized opera as a locus of sociopolitical worldbuilding and creative ambition. Composers negotiated a place for opera within the Black public sphere amid circumstances of increasing marginalization as other musical genres rose to prominence within Black creative life, and as new white-authored operas used Blackness as a reductive signifier of modernity that reproduced entrenched racial hierarchies rather than unsettling them. African American composers spoke back to these conditions by creating operatic worlds of their own, worlds that were both engaged with the contemporary moment *and* resonant with Black operatic counterculture's longstanding commitment to demonstrating a fundamental compatibility between opera and Black expressive culture. Consider the radically ambitious Shirley Graham and her opera *Tom-Tom*. Hurtling audiences through time and space from a premodern West African village to a plantation in the US South on the eve of Emancipation to a 1920s Harlem cabaret, *Tom-Tom* was a fundamentally hybrid work that held a tripartite status as a historical narrative, a musical work, and a music-historical archive. While most operas written by Black composers continued to go unperformed—a reminder of a persistent gap between these figures' aspirations and the material conditions under which they worked—*Tom-Tom* became the first opera by a Black woman produced by a major opera company. In practice, it also became a countercultural meeting ground, gathering myriad participants under the auspices of a single, vast production.

Tom-Tom and other operas of this era did much more than just broaden the scope of representations of Blackness available within the art form; they ultimately advanced a new conception of opera's role within African Amer-

ican life. If earlier theorists and practitioners had understood opera as a singular zenith of the Black cultural sphere, this generation—which included many composers who came to opera after developing expertise in other creative and intellectual pursuits—reframed the art form as one among many arenas through which their aesthetic and political commitments might be expressed. Relatively uninterested in opera's symbolic prestige or cultural cachet, they were less concerned with securing a place within an extant operatic tradition than they were in marshaling opera's aesthetic resources in service of ambitious creative expression.

By showing how opera might not only reflect, but also shape, public knowledge about Black diasporic history, composers also claimed a capacious political relevance for the art form. Within their compositions, opera exceeded both its established associations with uplift and respectability and its contemporary relationship to US-based struggles for desegregation, becoming imbricated with Black diasporic cultural and political life more broadly. *Tom-Tom* is a case in point. Written by a woman who would later become recognized as one of the leading Black intellectuals and activists of the twentieth century (and, in 1951, the wife of W. E. B. Du Bois), the opera anticipated and aligned with what would become Graham's lifelong commitments to diasporic racial solidarity and innovative forms of cultural production.[5] Not only did Black composers employ new methods of creating opera, but they also essentially came to understand opera itself as a creative and political method: a means of critical engagement with Black history; a medium that could foreground the vitality of Black music across genres; and an opportunity to showcase art's enduring role in a struggle not just for inclusion, but for freedom.

Being "Opera-Conscious" in a "Jazz-Crazy Age"

"Has the Negro a future in concert and grand opera?" asked a 1931 forum in the *Amsterdam News*. Why did African American singers "spend years in classic preparation," only to "end up in night clubs or theatrical productions where their training counts for little"? One respondent lamented that vocal students were "put in a limited class": "The student is told that he is too 'this' or 'that' for the concert stage. If his voice is refined and bears none of the expected traces of race, he is looked upon as a hybrid animal by both white and black."[6] Professionals were also thwarted. While white institutions tolerated the performance of spirituals, they had "no faith in their ability to 'sell' concerts of classical music where the singers are colored . . . The Metropolitan stage is therefore, 'out of the picture.'"[7] Accordingly,

classically trained singers pursued other genres, attracted to the financial rewards and "emotional tonic" of appearing on, say, the Broadway stage.[8] Another forum participant noted that the present state of Black musical organizations was equally disheartening, characterized by "a complete absence of organization" and "a discouraging lack of appreciation for good music on the part of the public."[9]

Discussions within the Black public sphere increasingly emphasized opera's residual status in relation to newly dominant genres, deeming it unprofitable and unpopular. "Jazz v. the Classics," blared one headline, bemoaning the fact that opera "earned no dough."[10] In 1932, decades after establishing his eponymous opera company, Theodore Drury lamented that African Americans were no longer "opera-conscious," having disregarded the art form's "great beauty, inspiration, and delightful pleasure."[11] The art form also risked alienating Black audiences: none other than Ethel Waters professed that she saw "no hope for a real negro drama nor negro grand opera . . . The negroes would not patronize a negro opera, as the very word 'opera' would keep them away."[12] Black opera's most visible proponents were thought to be out of step with contemporary culture. A 1930 discussion of Harry Lawrence Freeman's work observed that "Mr. Freeman . . . possesses all the qualities of genius—high ability, tenacity of purpose and unfaltering courage. In a jazz-crazy age he has remained loyal to the classical ideal . . . Steadfast in his belief, he has worked through jazz, blues and spirituals to a new form equally fine and original. He refused to follow the crowd, but with the arrogance that is the prerogative of genius demanded that the crowd follow him. When the crowd refused, he went on alone."[13] Revising a label that had accompanied the composer throughout his career, the article redefined genius not as intrinsic excellence but as chosen marginality, the decision to refuse convention and "[go] on alone." Importantly, that commitment did not require an *aesthetic* rejection of jazz, blues, or the spirituals. Rather, it stemmed from opera's *cultural* marginalization, which located it outside the logics of commodification that defined the US culture industries, and particularly Black cultural production. To be an operatic genius was to remain resolutely committed to one's art—to become a sort of martyr for the sake of opera, to borrow a theme from Freeman's own work.

Other musical and theatrical fields were flourishing. On Broadway, the breakout success of *Shuffle Along* (1921) sparked a panoply of imitators. In legitimate drama, the formation of groups like Harlem's Krigwa Players ensured that there would be theater "by us, for us, about us, and near us," as Du Bois wrote in his 1926 definition of the Black theater movement.[14] In

the concert hall, there was a flurry of symphonic premieres, including William Grant Still's Symphony no. 1, "Afro-American" (Rochester, 1931); Florence Price's Symphony in E Minor (Chicago, 1933); and William Levi Dawson's Negro Folk Symphony (Philadelphia, 1934). Such works, which drew deeply on Black folk music, fulfilled Dvořák's turn-of-the-century imperative that "Negro melodies" should be the "true basis for a distinctively American school of music," as well as a Harlem Renaissance worldview that celebrated Black vernacular traditions' potential to inspire future classical compositions.[15] But opera came to be seen as uniquely inaccessible, perhaps irrelevant. "This is not the Golden Age of the Negro in Opera," observed the singer Caska Bonds. But he maintained hope that once more singers attained excellent training, "the barriers will fall as they have always fallen, and admit us."[16]

For the time being, those barriers remained firmly in place on mainstream operatic stages. A bevy of newly composed works updated but ultimately reiterated extant operatic (mis)representations of Blackness, often invoking the legacy of blackface minstrelsy to do so. Incredibly popular among global audiences, they also prompted incisive responses from Black critics who, building on an existing tradition of opera criticism in the Black press, situated these works in relation to current debates over racial representation, cultural politics, and social critique. White composers on and off the operatic stage, Nora Holt observed, had a propensity to resort to stereotypical "caricatures" rather than multidimensional "portraits." Sardonically, she wrote, "The procedure is patented now—a quick downward intonation on a minor third, jiggling figures and syncopated rhythms in various choirs, one good spirited tune that everyone has heard . . . the shuffling of a sand bar, clap-clap of a paddle, a boom and a crash and there you are, a correct caricature of the Negro."[17]

In line with the genre-blurring norms of the era, some new productions existed in the nebulous space between opera, operetta, and musical theater. George Gershwin's one-act *Blue Monday* (1922) was a melodramatic tale of the doomed relationship between two Harlem residents. Set at the corner of 135th Street and Lenox Avenue (steps from where the actual Ferrari Fontana Vocal Trials took place), it was originally performed by white performers in blackface as part of a revue. It invoked a mélange of musical styles—*verismo* opera, jazz, ragtime—and was given the subtitle "Opera Ala Afro American" by its arranger, Will Vodery.[18] Critical reception was positive, with the exception of Charles Darnton, who disparaged the piece as "the most dismal, stupid and incredible blackface sketch that has probably ever been perpetrated."[19] *Lulu Belle* (1926) reimagined *Carmen's* plot among

African Americans in New York City (though it excised most of Bizet's music). A Broadway success featuring white actors in leading roles and a supporting cast of more than one hundred African Americans, *Lulu Belle* attracted some praise from Black critics for the material opportunities it offered to actors. Unsurprisingly, it also drew the ire of such stalwarts as Sylvester Russell, who deemed it a "white playwright's version of free common racial slander to be depicted in stage usage to blaspheme, slander, and lower rate a weaker minority race of people to the glory of an ignorant prejudiced white majority."[20] W. Franke Harling's *Deep River* (1926), another quasi-operatic Broadway show with a multiracial cast and a hybrid musical style, evinced similar critical ambivalence.[21]

In both Europe and the United States, white opera composers made forceful associations between Blackness and modernity. Austrian composer Ernst Krenek's *Jonny spielt auf* told the story of Jonny, an African American violinist and bandleader who vies for control over the musical future with a white modernist composer. An exemplar of *Zeitoper* (which made use of topical subjects, from trains to radios to flappers), *Jonny spielt auf* premiered in Germany in 1927 and become explosively popular, the most-performed opera in the country that year. Its titular character, as Jonathan Wipplinger has argued, amalgamated contradictory ideas about Blackness, from minstrel stereotype to primitivist caricature to modern cosmopolitan subject.[22] The Metropolitan Opera set out to present the opera's US premiere in 1929, but was stymied by its depiction of interracial relationships between Jonny and a series of white women.[23] (A journalist for *Musical America* reported that a white American to whom he described the opera's plot became "wrathful" at the possibility.[24]) Accordingly, the company commissioned what Paul Edwards has called a "Jim Crow translation" of the opera, which reinvented Jonny as a white vaudevillian in blackface.[25] Revealing what Edwards calls "an impulse to return Blackness to nineteenth-century minstrelsy," this revision emphasized the synergy—long normalized by supernumeraries and singers alike—between blackface and opera.[26]

It was difficult, *New York Age* writer Lucien White noted, to maintain a posture of critical "detachment" in response.[27] White distanced himself from the "amused wonder" of white reviewers, such as the *Variety* critic who cheekily described Michael Bohnen, the white singer who played Jonny, as a minstrel-like buffoon who "hoofed," "swayed to jazz," and "did the strut."[28] By contrast, an editorial in the Black periodical *Opportunity* skewered the Met's obsequious attitude toward the "delicate racial sensibilities of the lovers of opera."[29] Harry S. Keelan, a critic who was one of the era's most trenchant writers on opera and race, opined that the "extraordinary sub-

terfuges and excuses" of the proposal amounted to a "commentary on American color prejudice," in which "white supremacy is saved once more." Keelan surmised that the company's manager "knew his people," for "the audience beamed and clapped in bovine contentment."[30] In Keelan's view, the Met's approach facilitated the same voyeuristic titillation that attracted white audiences to other types of racialized entertainment, enabling the opera house to combine the enduring popularity of blackface with the illusion of sophisticated spectatorship.

An equally politicized controversy erupted when the Met staged *The Emperor Jones,* by the Russian American composer Louis Gruenberg, in January 1933. Adapted from the 1920 play by Eugene O'Neill, the opera tells the story of Brutus Jones, an African American former Pullman porter and ex-convict who overtakes a Caribbean island and declares himself emperor. His failure propels the land into chaos—a plot that, David Metzer argues, "assert[s] through the demise of its protagonist the inability of non-whites to govern themselves."[31] O'Neill's play famously featured African American actors—both Paul Robeson and Charles Gilpin had starred in productions of it during the 1920s, and Robeson appeared in the 1933 film adaptation. But although the NAACP urged the Met to consider Black singers, Robeson and Jules Bledsoe among them, for the title role, the company refused to entertain the possibility, instead casting the white singer Lawrence Tibbett, in blackface.[32] In the pages of *Opportunity,* Keelan weighed in once more. Tibbett failed to "ring true as a Negro," thus diminishing O'Neill's drama into a "farce" that "burlesqued" Blackness.[33] To those who might protest that operatic blackface was distinct from its historical counterparts, the magazine offered the rejoinder that "'black face' itself must inevitably evoke the minstrel concept. For, 'black face' in America is inextricably bound up with those fantastic distortions of the Negro character which delighted American theatre audiences for over a half-century."[34]

Jonny spielt auf and *The Emperor Jones* tethered operatic Blackness once again to blackface minstrelsy and primitivist fantasy. To some observers, their immense popularity signaled that audiences were uninterested in more holistic, accurate portrayals of the Black past. Ethel Waters archly posited that "white people would not attend" operas by Black composers, "because if it was a true expression of negro history it would be unacceptable to their vanity."[35] Duke Ellington made similar claims in relation to his long-held but ultimately unrealized plans for *Boola,* an ambitious work which he characterized as a "Negro opera." Ellington worked on the project for more than ten years, but after its completion he struggled to imagine a way out of dominant narrative and practical constraints. "It would have been easy

Jules Bledsoe in costume as Brutus Jones. This photograph was likely taken in relation to Bledsoe's brief appearance in a 1927 production of Eugene O'Neill's play. He would go on to perform the operatic role in Europe in 1934.

to have written an opera dealing with the trials, tribulations and tragedies of the group," he told a reporter. "But we've heard too much of this side of the Negro already. The things I have tried to depict in the opera are the things which should make the Negro proud of his heritage." He was also skeptical of white producers who, overly attached to the "money-making angle," might obfuscate "the correct interpretation of what I've tried to make music convey." Explaining his decision not to "peddle" the opera, Ellington insisted that "this idea must be done right or it won't be done at all."[36]

In the *Amsterdam News*, composer Edward Margetson proposed that "The Negro's day in Grand Opera is to come, but it awaits the opera made especially to accommodate him. 'Aida' might be pressed into service, some say; but lovely 'Aida' has grown gray and a Negro cast, however good, cannot rejuvenate her. Our literary lights must provide libretti that, depicting Negro life, steer nevertheless away from the sordid and silly. There may be humor, but let it be sanitary: religion, but not grotesque. A better-type Negro as hero would be a Godsend after so much buffoonery."[37] Like Ellington, Margetson envisioned a new compositional tradition that would transcend the representational and affective limitations of the contemporary stage. It would be historically accurate; focused on narratives of Black success rather than hackneyed tragedy or cheap humor; and oriented toward helping its listeners envision a better future—a sort of Afrofuturist reinterpretation of *Zeitoper,* deeply intertwined with other facets of African American culture and with the enduring presence of the Black diasporic past.

New World Operas

To compose an opera in the early twentieth-century United States was to enter the fray of contentious debates over music, race, and nation. African American critics had long hailed Black composers as destined for greatness. In 1907, Sylvester Russell wrote that the "new advent in classical music which is to come must come from a Negro composer . . . who will come up to give us grand opera and classics."[38] A 1912 profile of J. Rosamond Johnson predicted that he would be "the logical composer to create the really great American Opera."[39] In parallel, a racist counter-discourse dissociated Blackness from composition. Marshalling the trope of natural Black musicality, the Spanish novelist Vicente Blasco Ibáñez posited in the *New York Times* that "the African race has a great sense of cadence. The Negro *could never write an opera nor a symphony,* but he has an unquestioned superiority in musical emotion that can be expressed through the feet."[40] The question of whose (racial) property opera could be was bound up with

persistent cultural anxiety about its ability to flourish in the United States at all. American operas were dismissed as derivative of European models, and thereby a poor foundation for a national repertory. "There is as yet no definitely American operatic tradition," fretted music historian Edward Hipsher in *American Opera and Its Composers* (1927).[41] Nevertheless, Hipsher managed to produce a four-hundred-page survey on the topic that identified 118 individual composers—including Freeman, the lone Black composer included.[42]

Decades after the premiere of *The Martyr,* Freeman's compositional aspirations had only intensified. He established a music school and choral society when he moved to Harlem in 1910, but composition remained his central focus. Before moving to the city, he had completed seven operas; after 1910, he wrote at least fourteen more. "That's the work he loved, you see," his son, Valdo, recalled. "He stayed up half the night. He'd be composing, you know. As a matter of fact, when we lived over on 127th Street a woman was going to take us to court for disorderly conduct because he's up there composing music at midnight."[43] His imagination continued to run free and far. The never-produced *Athalia* (1917) was a "fantasy suggested by certain episodes of the Civil War."[44] *Vendetta,* set in Mexico and described by Valdo as "on the idea of Carmen," dramatizes a love triangle among the noblewoman Donna Carlotta, the toreador Alonzo, and the governor Don Castro.[45] Its premiere, at Harlem's Lafayette Theater on November 12, 1923, was facilitated by the Negro Grand Opera Company, which Freeman had incorporated in 1920.[46] Helmed by Valdo as business manager, the company sought to remedy a situation in which "the Negro composer has not had this same opportunity for public presentation," positing that "the successful presentation of these works by a superb organization of vocal and instrumental artists of color . . . will forthwith establish irrefutable proof of the Negro Races' artistic status."[47] Yet the company struggled to finance new productions, and few of Freeman's works reached the stage.

Even as Freeman established an autonomous company, he concomitantly sought the imprimatur of mainstream institutions. In the 1920s, he found a glimmer of hope in the Metropolitan Opera's purported search for a composer who could write a "jazz opera" that would meld the popular new sounds of jazz with the conventions of grand opera.[48] Spearheaded by the company's chairperson, Otto Kahn, the search mostly elicited suggestions of white composers—George Gershwin, Jerome Kern, Irving Berlin. But a 1924 article in *Billboard* proposed that Freeman was "perhaps the best fitted of all the American composers to fill the suggested need for the jazz

opera that Otto H. Kahn, millionaire patron of music, states will represent the spirit of America. Due to the African base of modern jazz a Negro composer of American birth and training no doubt will be better able to achieve this than will one of another race."[49] Valdo recalled that when Freeman received the prestigious Harmon Award (a prize honoring African American artists), Kahn told him, "I hope some day to see your operas at the Metropolitan." Freeman, his son recounted, "was thunderstruck . . . he was speechless."[50]

A glaring problem with this plan was that Freeman did not write "jazz opera." Most of his previous oeuvre, with its late-Romantic style and global subject matter, was patently unsuited to Kahn's goal. But the enticing prospect of a Met production prompted him to compose a new opera, *American Romance,* that engaged the era's jazz-inflected aesthetics directly. Set in the New York City of "today," *American Romance* is an allegorical tale of two white women, the old-fashioned Adele and the flapper-esque Joy, who represent a conflict between tradition and the new. Notably, Freeman's single "jazz opera" was also his "white opera" because he anticipated—correctly—that the Met was unlikely to produce a work requiring a Black cast.[51] Although *American Romance* was never performed, it registers Freeman's ongoing negotiation between his countercultural standing and mainstream aspirations, as well as how race inflected his response to these competing pressures.

Freeman's most successful opera from this period, *Voodoo,* demonstrates a similarly two-pronged commitment to maintaining an allegiance to his Wagnerian roots and broadening the aesthetic scope of his work. Composed in 1914, but not staged until 1928, at the height of the Harlem Renaissance, *Voodoo* premiered at the Palm Garden on West 52nd Street. Valdo, who considered *Voodoo* to be Freeman's best work, promoted the production by advertising it months in advance, selling tickets, and peddling a souvenir libretto.[52] Set on a Louisiana plantation during Reconstruction, the piece dramatizes a conflict between Cleota, a servant, and Lolo, a voodoo queen. Lolo uses voodoo to sabotage Cleota, but her plan goes horribly awry. The opera represents a departure from Freeman's previous work in its incorporation of spirituals, which a small chorus sings throughout. Rather than offering a hybridized fusion of Black and European music, though, Freeman keeps them distinct: the music of the principal characters could have been written in nineteenth-century Italy, while the spirituals evoke the "local color" of southern Black culture. Moreover, as David Gutkin notes, while Freeman referred to the work as a "Negro Grand Opera" at the time of its composition, in 1928 he rebranded it as a "Negro Jazz Grand Opera,"

despite the fact that jazz is not stylistically prominent in the piece—perhaps another attempt to catch the attention of the Met, or to invoke the "jazz vogue" of the era.[53]

Among white critics, the opera elicited a critical conundrum. At *The Martyr*'s 1893 premiere, Freeman had been hailed as "the first colored man to ever compose and produce an opera."[54] Now it was as if time had stopped: "Negro operas are a novelty," one reviewer wrote, even "complete strangers."[55] *Voodoo* was the "very first Negro grand opera the world has ever seen or heard."[56] Another critic proclaimed that "Negro opera was born into the world last evening and it proved indeed a lusty infant," reverting to the trope of characterizing Black musicality as childlike and undeveloped.[57] Other responses questioned *Voodoo*'s racial bona fides, dismissing it as "not significant": "the opera as a whole is not melodious, nor is it even faithfully Negro."[58] It was a "conglomerate rather than a homogenous, fused score. Arias harked back to an Italo-French operatic atmosphere of last century, while the composer often waxed modernistic."[59] The *New York Sun* could not decide what to think: "At the first crash of cymbals and brass, shrilling of reeds and scraping of strings that opened the piece, it was apparent that here was either almost unbelievable discord—a mad mélange that would kill a master musician—or a thing in new forms and new rhythms, a thing so hideously bizarre that it was beautiful."[60] Was this praise or fear? Was *Voodoo* too old or too new, too Black or not Black enough? Like *The Martyr* before it, *Voodoo* teetered on this dissonant edge, refusing categorical and chronological distinctions.

Black critics focused primarily on the structural challenges that *Voodoo*'s premiere elucidated. The *Amsterdam News* proclaimed it a "milestone in the history of higher Negro music," but also decried the "terrific secondary labor" Freeman was compelled to undertake, the "back-breaking task of putting it before the public unaided" without economic or infrastructural support. "The white composer does not have to face such difficulties," the writer noted. "He can give his whole energy to creation, knowing that . . . stage managers, impresarios, press agents, financing committees, wealthy music-lovers—all are ready to put the opera before the public under the best possible conditions.[61] Despite its promising start, *Voodoo* closed before the end of its scheduled run due to insufficient ticket sales, again cutting short Freeman's ambitions.

If *Voodoo* was thought to occupy a strange space between the modern and the antiquated, so was its composer. In a 1934 profile, theater critic Obie McCollum described Freeman's music studio as "the workshop of an old school music teacher who lives in the past," replete with "Elizabethan

period paintings," an "alabaster bust of Shakespeare," and "panelled walls and ceiling in ebony, red, gold, and pale green." One willing to "tarry and observe" in this anachronistic environment, however, would learn that Freeman "lives and works in an atmosphere suggesting yesterday, but his mind is on tomorrow." For example, McCollum cited Freeman's praise of Jarboro and Bledsoe's appearances in *Aida* as an indicator that white America was "becoming more willing to assign Negroes roles in the beggarly few famous operas with African environment or suggestion"—a tempered acknowledgment that celebrated these artists' success while maintaining that there was an urgent need for new operas focused on African and African diasporic life.[62] Freeman's own unfaltering commitment to opera had evolved with the times: he adapted readily to its changing aesthetic parameters in the 1910s and 1920s, maintaining a commitment to Wagner and the nineteenth-century canon while also turning newly to spirituals and jazz. Yet McCollum's evocative description of the composer in his "workshop," writing alone while surrounded by artifacts of the European past, suggests that Freeman's underlying conception of opera's cultural import remained the same. The sonic profile of his operas had changed, but his fundamental goal—to craft maximalist works that depicted and celebrated the expansive grandeur of Black diasporic life—had not.

A striking alternative to Freeman's resolute traditionalism emerged in Clarence Cameron White's *Ouanga,* an epic work about the Haitian Revolution informed by extensive ethnographic research. Born in 1880 in Clarksville, Tennessee, White was immersed in early twentieth-century Black musical networks. Educated at Howard and Oberlin, he first rose to fame as a violinist, winning the praise of Nora Holt for his impeccable technique, meticulous phrasing ("at the end of a phrase his bow leaves the strings so delicately and surely that the auditor can almost grasp the syntax of the music with his eye"), and "honesty of purpose."[63] He became acquainted with Freeman while still a teenager, and the two attended a Cleveland performance of *La bohème* while White was studying at Oberlin.[64] In 1908 (on a trip to London facilitated by funding from Azalia Hackley), he heard the overture to Afro-British composer Samuel Coleridge-Taylor's opera *Thelma.* "I did not know that the idea of some day writing an Opera was deeply buried in my subconsciousness, but it must have happened then," White later reflected. "The idea laid dormant for exactly twenty years before things began to take definite shape."[65] In the mid-1920s, while teaching at West Virginia Collegiate Institute, he and a colleague, the writer John Frederick Matheus, identified the "ideal subject": the "marvelous history" of Haiti, namely the story of Jean-Jacques Dessalines and the Haitian

Revolution. Such a work would offer an alternative to the "single characters" presented in operas like *Aida,* allowing for a multiplicity of representations of Black life on the operatic stage; just as importantly, it would foreground "Negro achievement" rather than reiterating narratives of tragedy and trauma.[66]

Unassailable in principle, these aspirations were complicated in practice. Intrigued by Haiti's privileged site in the African American imaginary, White and Matheus set out to visit the country and familiarize themselves with its folk songs and cultural traditions.[67] In the summer of 1928, they embarked on what White termed a "musical pilgrimage," a six-week trip to conduct preparatory research.[68] Their visit was entangled with the politics of the ongoing US occupation: it was facilitated by White's friends Harriet Gibbs Marshall, the founder of the Washington Conservatory of Music, and her husband, Napoleon Marshall, a member of an American committee investigating US military abuses.[69] Michael Largey contends that White and Matheus's approach to their subject matter can be understood as "'musical ethnography,' that is, first-hand observational research in a field site intended to provide fodder for an entertaining musical work."[70] This outlook risked reproducing power imbalances along the lines of class and nationality: Largey argues that while the duo's choice of subject "could be viewed as an anti-colonialist critique that holds up Haiti as an example of African liberation from European domination," it is important to consider positionality as well: as middle-class African Americans, they "maintained many of the commonly held Haitian misconceptions about lower-class Haitian culture."[71] They obtained little direct exposure to rural Haitian musical life, instead visiting tourist attractions and attending staged performances of vodou rituals. They had more contact with Haitian elites—White gave a violin recital in Port-au-Prince during the trip—than with rural populations.

The opera's creators made few claims to observational precision, preferring to frame their work more capaciously. White described Haiti as a place that defied the logics of modern time and space, a place where, immersed in "primitive African surroundings," one "gets back to the very beginning of things"—only to discover "melodies and rhythms quite akin to modern music."[72] In the rhythmic heterogeneity of drums at Haitian festivals, he heard both the nation's African history and an anticipation of "the birth of 'jazz' as we first knew it here in America."[73] Matheus made similarly atmospheric pronouncements, noting that in Haiti he aimed to "hear the songs, see the dances, catch the spirit of the African mood."[74] They seemed to be

less interested in reproducing Haitian music exactly than in repositioning it as ambient inspiration. Matheus completed the opera's libretto shortly after their return, and White composed the music while in Paris on a Rosenwald Fellowship between 1930 and 1932.

Ouanga marked a meaningful shift within the Black operatic tradition in terms of both its engagement with Black history and its compositional method. Freeman, the instigator of that tradition, had based his works on fictional narratives with general relevance to the Black past (from religious conflict in ancient Egypt to life on a Louisiana plantation), with the intention of establishing opera's formal ability to convey the grandeur of this past. *Ouanga,* by contrast, repurposed opera as a site of popular knowledge about specific historical events. Even more radically, it was publicized as a work that, due to its ethnographic orientation, could make a historiographical intervention in contemporary thinking about the Haitian Revolution. The *Pittsburgh Courier* framed it as a corrective to the fact that "most if not practically all, of the information about the lands populated by Negroes has been gathered by white men and women," and suggested that White and Matheus would produce "an unbiased study."[75] If *Ouanga* did not fully reach this standard, it nonetheless offered a significant reinterpretation. It refuted the racist primitivism of extant works like *The Emperor Jones,* giving operatic voice to what Michel-Rolph Trouillot characterizes as the "unthinkable" quality of the Haitian Revolution within Western white ideological frameworks.[76] *Ouanga* offered new ideas about where and how composers should find operatic material; the need to center stories of Black achievement; and opera's narrative and formal capacity to tell these vital stories.

Although *Ouanga* attracted attention in musical circles, earning White the American Opera Society's David Bispham Medal in 1932, audiences had minimal opportunities to engage directly with the work at the time of its composition. Its sole performance that year was an event in Chicago at which White and Matheus explained the rationale for their work and a few singers, accompanied by a pianist, performed excerpts from the score. By contrast, *Jonny spielt auf* was performed more than four hundred times during its first season onstage in Germany, in 1927; *Aida* was presented an average of ten times per year at the Metropolitan Opera between 1925 and 1935; and *The Emperor Jones* was staged fifteen times in 1933 and 1934 alone.[77] Even as composers like Freeman and White imagined expansive operatic worlds, they continued to wrestle with broader institutional constraints that hindered their work.

Tom-Tom's Historical Counterknowledge

Spectators came in droves: ten thousand on the first night, fifteen thousand more on the second. They filled the lakefront stadium, marveling at the multi-tiered stage, the elephant that lumbered across it, and the thirty-foot waterfall towering above. As the sun set, a light rain began to fall. Its rhythmic patter merged imperceptibly with the sounds emanating from a battalion of percussion instruments. Soon a quartet of soloists and a chorus of hundreds appeared. Their voices guided the audience out of the drizzly present—Cleveland, summer, 1932—and into the sweeping historical epic onstage. Those critics scattered among the crowd declared the evening a resounding success. One called *Tom-Tom* a "revolutionary project." Another deemed it an "opera which marks an epoch in the history of creative music in this country." A third proclaimed that it was "new opera. Something different from what has preceded it in history."[78]

A first-time composer of opera, Graham lacked Freeman's deep affiliation with the canon. She had not sought out operatic success as did Cole-Talbert, Jarboro, and other would-be Aidas. But her opera was realized on an exceptionally grand scale, the sort of performance opportunity that Freeman or White could only dream of.[79] Graham shared her counterparts' commitment to working in epic, historical, and diasporic narrative registers, but she created her opera under advantageous structural conditions that included a prestigious venue, excellent cast, sizeable budget, ample press coverage, and immense audience. Yet despite the brilliance of *Tom-Tom*'s premiere, her work ultimately met the fate of obscurity and nonperformance.

Over three acts and sixteen scenes, *Tom-Tom* told a historical tale of race, migration, and social transformation, fully exploiting what Colleen Renihan calls opera's "historiographical potential."[80] In contrast to Freeman's use of jazz and spirituals to evoke the respective local color of *American Romance* and *Voodoo,* or White's use of Haitian folk music to convey the atmosphere of revolutionary Haiti, Graham took a more holistic and conceptually complex approach. The opera's multifaceted musical language, which ranged from Liberian folk song to African American spirituals to Harlem jazz, amplified and extended its historical argument, calling attention to the inherent instabilities of a putatively teleological narrative arc. *Tom-Tom* became an opera that functioned as a work of critical archival practice, collecting and curating various facets of Black music history into an intricate sonic whole. Rejecting the boundaries that typically divide historical texts and musical scores; composition and arrangement; and artistic and

scholarly forms of intellectual production, Graham created what Shane Vogel calls a "repository of historical counterknowledge," or a text that functions as an alternative to normative ideologies and narrative conventions.[81] Further, she used opera's fundamentally collaborative aesthetics to diffuse authorial power among various participants, making the Black sonic archive audible on the operatic stage.

Shirley Graham's biographer, Gerald Horne, characterizes her as living multiple "lives," grounding her fluid identity in what Black feminist scholars have theorized as standpoint epistemology.[82] She was born in Indianapolis, in 1896, to Etta Bell Graham and David Graham.[83] Her father, a minister, worked itinerantly, and during Graham's childhood she and her four younger brothers moved to New Orleans, Nashville, Colorado Springs, and the Pacific Northwest. The family's mobility meant that Graham was exposed to many manifestations of racial violence and Jim Crow. When she was seven, her father organized a mass meeting at a New Orleans church to protest a lynching, and only narrowly escaped attack from a mob. At thirteen, she published her first piece of writing, an editorial, after being denied access to a segregated swimming pool.[84] Her formal education was a "pretty mixed up thing" due to the family's moves, she recalled, but her father, who "never missed an opportunity to improve the minds of his children," read them an eclectic mix of literature—the Bible, *Les Misérables,* Dickens, travelogues, *Uncle Tom's Cabin.*[85] She studied Western classical music, became a skilled pianist, and developed an interest in religious music, especially spirituals.[86] As an adult, Graham resisted the circumscribed confines of middle-class domesticity.[87] In 1921, while living in Seattle, she married Shadrach T. McCanns, a tailor. They had two sons, Robert and David, before divorcing on contentious terms in 1927.[88] Later, Graham would claim that she was a widow—perhaps a way of adhering to a certain standard of propriety, or of erasing McCanns from her life. Robert and David spent much of their childhood in the care of their maternal grandparents, including the period during which Graham wrote *Tom-Tom.* Relentlessly adventurous, she had an ambivalent relationship to her gendered roles as wife and mother, and more broadly to the patriarchal ideologies inherent in the politics of respectability and racial uplift.

Although not wealthy, Graham found sufficient funding to embark on transatlantic travel.[89] In December 1926, she sailed to Paris, where she would return multiple times over the next five years. She was accompanied by her father, uncle, and brother, who were en route to Liberia to become teachers and missionaries at the AME-affiliated Monrovia College. Residing in the Latin Quarter, she enrolled in music courses at the Sorbonne and studied

French. She soaked up Parisian cultural life, following her brother's jocular advice to "keep away from les Americaines" and attending performances of opera, jazz, and everything in between.[90] "Everyone came to Paris that summer," Graham recalled of a 1930 visit, and she luxuriated in the rich sociality that the city offered.[91] Enmeshed in a diasporic network of Black artists and intellectuals, she became particularly close with the Guyanese intellectual Eric Walrond, a prominent anticolonial thinker. Walrond introduced Graham to Paul Robeson, and she sojourned to London to see Robeson in *Othello* in 1930.[92] She became enamored with African music, which she heard from "African and Egyptian students" at the Sorbonne.[93] In short, she witnessed and engaged in what Brent Hayes Edwards calls "the practice of diaspora": the circulation of ideas, sounds, and texts across national borders, which articulated difference even as it attempted to forge transnational solidarities.[94] (Edwards also notes that many African Americans in Paris appreciated the city's welcoming atmosphere while ignoring its status as a colonial metropole, and Graham falls in this category: her writings from these years did not contend with the politics of French colonialism in Africa, even as she celebrated the presence of African students and music.) Her experiences offered ample inspiration for *Tom-Tom*: innumerable examples of Black artistry, a notion of the heterogeneity—yet connectedness—of Black identity across cultures, and a sense of how diasporic identity worked artistically and intellectually.

Between trips to Paris, Graham continued to pursue a musical career in the United States. She studied at Howard University and the Institute of Musical Arts, worked as a music librarian, taught music and drama at Morgan College in Baltimore, sang spirituals with jubilee quartets, and directed choruses. She also traveled around the country giving lectures on "the origin, history, appreciation, and spiritual message of Negro Music."[95] Earning little from these short-term positions—her monthly salary at Morgan College was a paltry one hundred dollars—Graham cobbled together a living.[96] She remained financially insecure, especially given her obligation to provide for her children as a divorced mother. The onset of the Depression only exacerbated these conditions, spurring her to take on more and more work.

In 1929, Graham wrote the first version of *Tom-Tom*: a one-act play, subtitled the "Spirit of Negro Music" and described in a program as "a drama of the development of Negro music from the first faint beatings of the African tom tom to the most finished products of our trained musicians today."[97] Intended for student performers at Morgan College, it featured compositions by Will Marion Cook, J. Rosamond Johnson, and

Samuel Coleridge-Taylor, as well as spirituals and other Black vernacular music. While the piece bore little connection to Black opera, it contributed to a contemporaneous trend of dramatizing African American history to instill racial pride.[98] One critic called it "one of the most tuneful as well as educational dramas of the current season" that "made one feel glad that he was of African descent."[99] The piece also positioned Graham within a lineage of Harlem Renaissance–era artists and authors who educated audiences about Black music history. Although such projects differed in form and scope, they typically offered a chronological, evolutionary story of Black musical progress from past to present: they would describe the distant past of African folk music or the less-distant past of spirituals; show how these evolved into popular genres like ragtime and jazz; and, finally, explain how these vernacular traditions held additional promise as the foundation of classical compositions to come.[100] At its origins, then, *Tom-Tom* was shaped by diverse pedagogical and historical imperatives rather than by an individualized desire on Graham's part to compose opera—circumstances that presaged the work's eventual formal breadth and sociopolitical significance.

In 1931, Graham moved to Ohio to attend Oberlin Conservatory. Oberlin had a long history of educating Black musicians: Clarence Cameron White had studied there, as had Harriet Gibbs Marshall and the composer Nathaniel Dett.[101] Unable to afford a dormitory room, Graham lived off campus and worked at a laundry to support herself.[102] She enrolled in six courses in a single semester, ranging from piano to essay-writing to "Opera Excluding Wagner."[103] She also became acquainted with Russell and Rowena Jelliffe, white progressive reformers and Oberlin alumni who had founded Cleveland's Playhouse Settlement, later known as Karamu House. In addition to providing social services, Karamu House was known for its robust music and theater program, and Graham hoped that the Jelliffes might produce her play, *Tom-Tom*.[104] While nothing came of this plan immediately, they remembered the work when they were approached by Laurence Higgins, a producer for the Cleveland Stadium Opera Company who was seeking a "Negro opera" for the company's 1932 summer season, to be featured as part of a "Theater of Nations" including *Carmen, Aida,* and *Die Walküre.* The Jelliffes arranged for Graham to share the play with Higgins's collaborator, the Austrian opera director Ernst Lert. Convinced of its merits, Higgins and Lert commissioned Graham to turn *Tom-Tom* into an opera. During an era when white musical institutions virtually always ignored the work of Black composers, and especially Black female composers, this was an extraordinary turn of events.

It was also a wildly difficult task. Graham took a semester's leave from her studies and rented a room equipped with an upright piano at the Phillis Wheatley House in Cleveland. Her long-held commitment to dramatizing Black history, coupled with the hypervisibility of being the first Black woman to write an opera on a grand scale, operated as both motivation and burden. In a letter inviting NAACP director Walter White to attend the production, Graham wrote breezily of how "happy and excited" she was for an opportunity that represented "the realization of many, many hopes."[105] She revealed a different perspective to her young son Robert, then in her parents' care: "My work here is getting so hard that sometimes I feel as though I just can't get it. But then, I have to just get real still and <u>think</u> harder. Even if a thing doesn't come out right away, <u>thinking</u> is the <u>only</u> thing that will ever bring it out."[106] Declining to draw a boundary between intellectual and creative work, she underscored *Tom-Tom*'s hybrid foundations. Serving as both librettist and composer, she worked ceaselessly for three months. By the end of a whirlwind spring, *Tom-Tom* was ready for the stage.

Graham gave *Tom-Tom* the subtitle "The Epic of Music and the Negro," and it is indeed epic in temporal, geographic, dramatic, and musical scope.[107] Each act depicts a moment of social transformation, articulated via interpersonal drama that stems variously from generational conflict, romantic entanglements, and religious and political difference. The principal characters are the Girl, the Boy, the Mother, and the Voodoo Man, plus a fifth figure who assumes a different identity (the Leader, the Preacher, and the Captain, respectively) in each act. Act 1 is set in an unspecified time and place in premodern West Africa. The Leader admonishes the villagers to watch out for Bantu slave traders who prowl the jungle. Following a ritual dance, Voodoo Man announces that the Girl must be sacrificed to the gods. Although the Mother accepts this fate, the Boy declares his love for the Girl and attempts to rescue her. Slave traders burst onto the scene. Act 2 takes place in 1865, on a plantation in the US South. While most of the enslaved, including the Boy, have converted to Christianity, Voodoo Man declares that he "[wants] no new gods," then murders an overseer.[108] The crisis intensifies when the Mother, evoking the notorious case of Margaret Garner, decides to kill the Girl in order to save her.[109] Only the opportune entrance of Union soldiers saves them; yet Voodoo Man mourns, reflecting rhapsodically about his African homeland. In act 3, set in the "Harlem of today," Voodoo Man reappears as the Garvey-like agent of an "Afro-Pan-American" shipping line, promising to transport the gathered crowd back

to Africa. The Mother and the Girl fight about the prospect, and the Mother disparages the Girl's less-than-respectable job as a cabaret singer. Catastrophe strikes: the ship explodes into flames, killing most on board. An enraged dancer stabs Voodoo Man. Yet as he dies, his beliefs prevail. The Boy has an ideological change of heart, eschewing his commitment to modern American Christianity, then pledges to continue Voodoo Man's mission and retain a connection to Africa. The Girl and Mother join the Boy as the opera comes to a close.

Tom-Tom offers an intricately conceived representation of the relationship between the African past and African American present. Its titular drum, the tom-tom, was a pervasive sign of African cultural retentions during the Harlem Renaissance, famously evoked in Langston Hughes's essay "The Negro Artist and the Racial Mountain," with its allusions to "the eternal tom-tom beating in the Negro soul."[110] To Graham, it was "the voice of Africa."[111] In promotional press for the opera, she elaborated: "To me African life and music always has been symbolized by the tom-tom . . . when I started out to compose an opera about Negroes, it was natural that I should choose to write music about this symbolic instrument."[112] If this was a natural choice, it was not a straightforward one. Graham placed a heavy representational burden on the instrument, which served as a recurring sonic motive, a trope in the libretto, and a sign of transhistorical connection. Its multidimensional significance rendered it a source of what Tsitsi Jaji calls "stereomodernism," a musical means of shaping transnational Black solidarity in which the "stereo effect" of slight difference within a larger collectivity creates a form of solidarity that leaves room for inherent complexity.[113]

From its opening moments, *Tom-Tom* represents Africa as an idealized Black "homeland" temporally and spatially distant from the modern United States. Some scholars have interpreted this depiction as a reductionist concession to white audiences' expectations, aligned with a transatlantic vogue for primitivist fantasy.[114] The first act begins with the stage directions "Africa. Darkness" and involves ritual sacrifice, jungles, and wild animals— hardly a challenge to stereotypes—yet its musical evocation of the continent is more ambiguous.[115] The overture conjures danger. From silence, a sound emerges: a lone tom-tom struck four times. A fermata, and the pattern repeats. Another fermata, and five more tom-toms enter at two-measure intervals. Each plays a different rhythmic figure before falling silent. The instrumentation gradually expands to include xylophone, bass drum, snare, timpani, cymbals, and a West African elephant trumpet.[116] The first vocal music is heard in scene 2. Against an ostinato played by *col legno* cellos and

basses, bass drum, and xylophone, the Leader tells the Boy to "Listen to the distant Tom Toms / And answer quickly when they call you." Diminished triads in the ostinato underlie the Leader's stentorian vocal line, and the dissonances underscore his admonitory rhetoric. Succinctly conflating instrumentation with primitivism, one white critic wrote of this act that "as existence remains at a savage level, percussion suffices."[117]

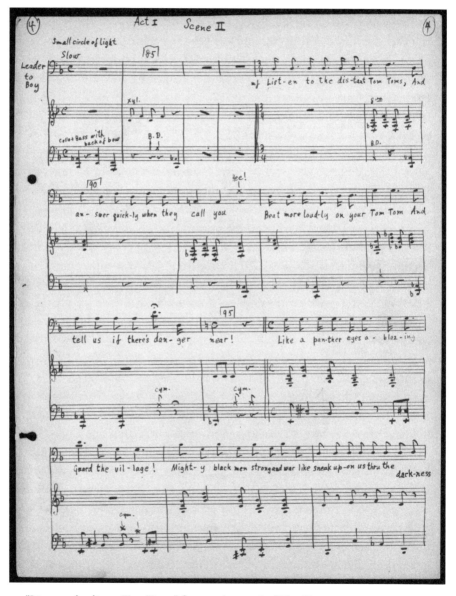

"Listen to the distant Tom Toms," from act 1, scene 2 of *Tom-Tom*.

DREAMING IN ENSEMBLE

A key intervention among Harlem Renaissance intellectuals was to re-ject racist notions of African backwardness and reclaim the continent as a source of racial pride, but the implications of this project could be ambiva-lent.[118] David Garcia argues that those who embraced the idea of Black music's African origins often reinforced binary ways of classifying Africa versus the West, or Black versus white music.[119] Graham's use of putatively African music in *Tom-Tom* risked precisely these representational hazards. Act 1, for instance, included several melodies identified as African folk songs. In program notes, the composer explained that she learned this music from her brother, who spent four years in Liberia as a missionary, and that she had also listened to the "primitive music of the French Negroes, many of them but shortly come from Algeria," while in Paris.[120] Graham's facile con-flation of Liberian and Algerian music, transcribed via second- and third-hand listening as simply the music of "Africa," risks falling into precisely the sort of binary that Garcia identifies. Yet it might be understood more generously as an expression of diasporic solidarity, an assertion in sound that the racialized connections among these musical traditions outweighed their differences.

Graham's engagement with African music can also be situated within her broader creative and intellectual worldview. In line with the literary-ethnographic approach of Zora Neale Hurston and the "creative-academic" practice of Katherine Dunham, she conceived of her work in broad terms that encompassed the varied methods of historical research, fieldwork, and composition. In 1931, prior to her arrival at Oberlin, she applied for a Guggenheim Fellowship to study "Africa's Influence on Western Music," a project she called "the dream and ambition of my life." It would involve research trips to Ethiopia, French Guinea, Liberia, Spain, and France. Writing about her plans in West Africa, where she sought "knowledge con-cerning music of American Negroes," Graham disparaged Liberia as a land of "uncivilized stupor which is far worse than a primitive state of barba-rism."[121] Such statements reiterate the imbalance of power that necessarily underscored her representation of Africa (and may also reflect a strategic appeal to the application committee amid a widespread fascination with African primitivism). But Graham also expressed interest in revising those views. Previewing the collaborative approach that would shape her oper-atic composition, she styled herself a participant-observer, noting that her "attitude of friendliness would be one of the great essentials in my work," and she reiterated her need to learn directly from Liberians.[122] Although Graham did not receive the fellowship, she pursued an analogous project in *Tom-Tom*—a convergence that emphasizes the opera's status as a work

of intellectual inquiry shaped by a scholarly method, and suggests that *Tom-Tom* can be analyzed on terms that rely less on representational accuracy and more on what Graham's interest in African music signified within the context of her intellectual development.

If *Tom-Tom* was emblematic of broader trends in Black operatic world-making in that it made a historical argument about African music and diasporic solidarity, it also made an exceptional epistemological claim about the relationship between lived experience and historical narrative.[123] Characters express vastly divergent responses to the social transformations that the opera depicts, enabling Graham to reinterpret major historical developments—the advent of transatlantic slavery, the moment of emancipation—as heterogeneously subjective experiences with different effects on different individuals. As a result, the opera offered an anti-essentialist conception of Black subjectivity and highlighted the potential of ordinary people to serve as historical actors (a conceit heightened by the generic names of the Girl, Mother, and Boy).[124] The climactic scene of act 2 exemplifies this approach. As Union soldiers announce Emancipation and the Girl is saved from imminent death, hundreds of enslaved people sing with collective joy: "Free at last! Free at last!" The Boy celebrates, but Voodoo Man mourns. His shouts of "No! No!" trouble the notion of emancipation as an uncomplicated good. After bitterly detailing the freedom that others will enjoy, he rhapsodizes about his African homeland. His melody begins with extended whole notes, creating a sense of unhurried dreaminess. The meter switches abruptly from 4/4 to 6/8 to 3/4, highlighting his musical and social difference from the chorus, whose collectively voiced spirituals proceed steadily in common time. Virtuosic and rhythmically complex, Voodoo Man's aria traverses nearly two octaves and ends on a heroic high E-flat, held for three measures and sustained through a final fermata. This is no outright celebration of freedom. Rather, the expansive emotional and musical scope of the aria acts as an ideological and aesthetic counterweight to the hundreds of voices singing spirituals together. Celebration is undercut by doubt and memory, showcasing Graham's compositional sophistication and notion of what historical progress entails.

The opera's expressive complexities converge with striking poignancy in the opera's third act, especially its final scene. The act offers a musical geography of Renaissance-era Harlem, moving from the spirituals of the church to the popular song of the cabaret to the preacher's call of the street corner. Texturally complex, with multiple simultaneous vocal lines that convey the din and clamor of a dense urban environment, it was described by one reviewer as near cacophonous: "Tonalities mix in ex-

citing confusion. The orchestra goes its way in one key, the jazz-band in another, spirituals rise from other tonal centers. And always the tom-tom beats its insidious rhythm."[125] When the ship burns at the end of the act, music gives way to sheer noise: a chorus of "Screams. Screams. Screams," as Graham scrawled in the score, accompanied by an "entire chord, chrom[atic] up and down, contrary motion."[126] As Voodoo Man takes his dying breaths, the orchestra repeats a rolled E-major chord, and he can only marvel in disbelief: "I've failed. I've failed." A portentous exchange follows:

> VOODOO MAN: Now, even my tom-tom will be silent.
> (*The stick falls from his hand. The BOY catches it*)
> BOY: No! Black Man, No! Your tom-tom shall be heard. (*He
> strikes a mighty blow upon the tom-tom.*)
> Who will go with me,
> Not to distant lands,
> But here, beating the tom-tom
> We'll find kingdoms unknown.[127]

The gathered crowd, led by the Boy, begins to sing spirituals, culminating in a rapturous rendition of "My Lord, What a Morning." Underneath the song's final two measures, the rhythmic beat of the tom-tom resounds once again. Through its combined visual, sonic, and dramatic presence, the drum endures as a stereomodern symbol of cross-generational and diasporic solidarity linking "distant lands" to "here" in the opera's closing moments. African American operagoers may well have heard themselves implicated in the Boy's "here," a final public-facing gesture in an opera concerned with the social impact of historical knowledge.

The fact that, in sonic terms, the opera ends up exactly where it began suggests that despite its chronological plot and forward-marching narrative, *Tom-Tom* requires a different theory of historical change. The reappearance of archetypal characters in each act gives *Tom-Tom* what Sarah Schmalenberger describes as "a sense of timelessness to the conflicts portrayed," but given the disparate settings of the three acts, one narrative action does not necessarily lead to the next.[128] Such dramatic and aesthetic details generate "historical counterknowledge," to return to Vogel's term. At odds with the opera's basic teleology, they suggest that Graham's commitment to celebrating Black diasporic solidarity across eras and geographies precluded a conception of historical change as inevitable or even wholly desirable. Decades earlier, works like *The Martyr* had endeavored to

claim space for African American composers, performers, and stories within the operatic canon, implying that through the involvement of Black composers and their operas, a tarnished past would give way to a more hopeful future. *Tom-Tom*'s counterhistorical approach unsettled such developmental models, using opera's formal complexity to argue against inexorable change. History and the present intermingled; modern Black life was distinct from, yet productively entangled with, its past.

Tom-Tom's cast included Augustus Grist (Leader / Preacher / Captain), Luther King (Boy), Lillian Cowan (Girl), Charlotte Murray (Mother), and Jules Bledsoe (Voodoo Man). Their diverse musical backgrounds reflected the heterogeneity of Graham's score. Grist, known as "Cleveland's favorite baritone," appeared frequently on local radio.[129] King, a tenor, was a former Fisk Jubilee Singer praised for his "beautiful timbre" and "wonderful artistry."[130] Cowan worked on the popular stage, appearing in musical theater productions including *Runnin' Wild* and *Change Your Luck*. Murray, the elder figure of the group, was from Washington, DC. In 1919, she sang Handel's *Messiah* alongside Roland Hayes and Florence Cole-Talbert, accompanied by Estelle Pinckney Clough (who had starred in Drury's productions). Bledsoe brought a wealth of experience to the production, as well as a perspective on history and culture that aligned conceptually with Graham's.[131] In a 1928 piece for *Opportunity*, he had written that the "Negro's every move is filled with drama," yoking lived experience to performance. Describing Black artistry as haunted by the trauma of slavery—one "tries to outrun his shadow by breaking into frenzied laughter, by wild and tempestuous dancing"—he recognized Black artists' ability to confront and contend with history through spectacular performance.[132] Alongside these principal performers, *Tom-Tom* featured a chorus of over two hundred—a number often exaggerated in the press to five hundred or even one thousand. All fit comfortably on the enormous stage, a multilevel behemoth with an area of fifty thousand square feet.

Locally and nationally, both the Black and white presses covered the premiere extensively, deeming *Tom-Tom* "colossal in scope and marvelous in pageantry," an "exciting spectacle," and a "racial epic."[133] Some celebrated Graham as a "distinguished composer," while others betrayed racialized and gendered suspicion. One white writer asked: "Who is the slender, twenty-eight-year-old negress, who has wended her way between Bizet and Wagner with an opera?"[134] Yet this turn of phrase was at odds with Graham's own self-presentation. In program notes, she wrote: "I cannot think of 'Tom-Tom'

as either a score of music or as a piece of literature. I cannot think in terms of having written it . . . I have been told that the polyphonic effects of 'Tom-Tom' are of unusual worth. I believe they would have been easy for any Negro who determined to write down exactly what he 'heard.'"[135] While this framing might suggest gendered modesty or ambivalence about her newfound role as an object of fascination, it also generatively reframed *Tom-Tom* as fundamentally collective. Graham's role was almost akin to that of the tom-tom itself, she implied—a vessel through which to express music history and diasporic solidarity.

Tom-Tom offered multiple opportunities for what might now be called "community engagement." These modes of participation facilitated shared affective and musical experience, fostering a collective sociality that re-called that of the Drury Company, Mundy's Opera School, and Azalia Hackley's choral festivals. The chorus comprised amateur singers from local church choirs and community groups, whose rehearsals Graham conducted in advance of the production. The Cleveland Museum of Art mounted an exhibition of Black literature and art, including the artwork of local children, to coincide with the premiere. A contest organized by the Playhouse Settlement offered cash prizes for "the best full set design submitted by a Negro for use in the opera," including "masks, costumes, tattoo designs, spear heads, shields and such."[136] Like other elements of the opera that purported to represent Africa, these efforts trod a fine line between enacting diasporic solidarity and rehashing stereotypical ideas about African primitivism. But they also served an anti-exceptionalist function, ensuring that the task of creating a "Negro opera"—the phrasing of Graham's assignment from the Cleveland Stadium Opera Company—would not express her ideas alone.

An intriguing counterpart to Graham's collectivist approach emerged in reviews. While the opera's reception was overwhelmingly positive, a recur-ring critique among white reviewers was that there was simply too much of it: that it was sprawling, unstructured, or in need of editing. The "whole thing gropes toward something extremely vital," wrote one critic, but "on the whole, there was more atmosphere than musical substance in the score."[137] *Tom-Tom* lacked a "clear cut plot, as for instance that of 'Carmen,'" and it needed "pruning and blue-penciling," especially in the overlong third act.[138] Still another noted the opera's "intentional formlessness" and wrote that Graham's "touch upon the score was not sufficiently sustained and firm, and her shaping of the entire three acts was a little too lacking in the em-phasis of a central conviction."[139] The cumulative message was ambiguous,

An artist's rendition of Graham rehearsing the chorus for *Tom-Tom*, published June 14, 1932.

recalling earlier critiques of Freeman's *Voodoo*: *Tom-Tom* was either too much or too little; it was either not operatic enough (that is, too unlike *Carmen*) or not epic enough; it either fell short or went too far.

Yet these comments do more than demonstrate how white operagoers (mis)heard *Tom-Tom*; they illuminate its status as a work of critical archival practice. The formlessness *was* intentional: as Graham stated, she did not think of the opera as a traditional score or literary work. Rather, if *Tom-Tom* was created by and about collectivities, it was also created by and about collecting: a descriptive assemblage of Black musical history that constituted an archive in the form of an opera. *Tom-Tom* is perhaps best understood as an *arrangement*, a term that links its musical and archival meanings. Rather than strategically interpolating examples of Black popular and vernacular music at opportune moments, as other composers had done, Graham arranged a musical archive comprised of the Black diasporic musical history she had learned throughout her life: music she heard from African students in Paris, Liberian folk songs transmitted through her brother, spirituals learned in childhood, operas from her Oberlin courses, cabaret songs heard

DREAMING IN ENSEMBLE

in Harlem. She aimed to organize this music in a logical fashion rather than select only its most dramatically significant elements, hence some critics' perception that the opera lacked a "clear cut plot" or "central conviction." *Tom-Tom*'s putatively unstructured nature invited the listener to engage with this music in open-ended, exploratory ways, rather than putting forth a singular narrative.

Tom-Tom's archival sensibility is inextricable from traditional archives' historical reinforcement of racist structures of knowledge production and access to information.[140] Having worked as a librarian and pursued scholarly research, Graham was well aware of the racial politics of the archive, namely the scarcity of resources related to Black life and the way those resources were hidden from Black researchers. In a 1971 interview, she recalled being turned away from an archive that claimed not to have any material about Black historical subjects, only to find out later that those materials were indeed present.[141] Under Jim Crow, she reflected, it was inconceivable for a Black researcher "to go into the archives, and the libraries in the deep south, and go get behind and go into their papers . . . it just would have been an impossibility."[142] With *Tom-Tom,* Graham refused that impossibility. Bringing the Black sonic archive into an intensely public space, immediately accessible to the listeners who filled the lakefront stadium, she created an opera whose "formlessness" belied its transformational arrangement of historical and musical knowledge.

Attending to the historical and archival politics of *Tom-Tom* helps locate the opera within Graham's intellectual life writ large. In the same interview, she noted: "My music training has influenced me a great deal in writing, I'll say that I am conscious of that fact. Before I learned to write, I learned what a symphony was. And I learned how to write, to project the music, the movement, the first movement, the theme, to go into the andante and to come down and probably to introduce another theme and kind of underneath theme and then how to weave all the themes together into the allegro and then how to pull them all together in the finale."[143] If somewhat unconventional as a description of symphonic form, this is an excellent description of the architecture of *Tom-Tom,* which does indeed culminate by "pull[ing] them all together in the finale" as spirituals, Graham's original orchestral writing, and the tom-tom sound simultaneously in the opera's final moments. This cumulative approach also marked Graham's radicalism in relation to standard narratives of Black classical composition. Departing from a model of "cultivation" or "development," which cast Black musical idioms as material to be refined before becoming

incorporated into Western art music, Graham understood those same forms—operas and symphonies—as sites for the arrangement of Black music *as it already existed.* Opera's capaciousness and extravagance allowed it to communicate the full scope of Black sonic life.

Shortly after *Tom-Tom*'s premiere, Graham reflected on the experience in a letter to Walter White. "It was for me an exquisite torture," she wrote. "Every mistake sunk like burning irons into my very flesh, yet there were a few moments of complete and utter satisfaction." She was eager to revise the piece, to make it "as near the perfect thing as is possible."[144] Reporters announced plans for future performances within the United States and internationally. Graham corroborated this plan, even giving a date—October 2, 1932—for a scheduled performance of *Tom-Tom* at Madison Square Garden in New York City.[145] She discussed potential revisions with Ernst Lert, who, upon returning to his native Vienna, requested a revised copy of the libretto and offered advice regarding orchestration. Lert also suggested that Graham's next work be a "chamber opera of the American Negro," one compact enough to travel around Europe, where, he promised, he could easily organize performances.[146]

But trouble was brewing. Following the production, Graham returned to Indiana to spend time with her parents and two sons. At the end of July, her brother Lorenz wrote her a sympathetic note: "Dear Little Sister," it read, "I am sorry to learn that you are suffering a breakdown."[147] If part of Graham's stress derived from the sheer intensity of work that *Tom-Tom* had necessitated, it also had to do with deception on the part of the opera's producers. In the devastating economic context of the Depression, the Cleveland Stadium Opera Company struggled despite the massive audiences it attracted, and its extravagant summer season ended in the red. Perhaps due to these mounting financial problems, producer Laurence Higgins misled Graham regarding the opera's copyright and the royalties that she would receive. Higgins also failed to pay some performers, including Luther King, as well as community members who sang in the chorus.[148] Jules Bledsoe expressed outrage on behalf of the "poor colored people" whom Higgins had deceived: "How my heart does burn when I think of this terrible injustice. I am able to fight my own battle; but these people. I don't know what they can do to protect themselves."[149] Lorenz urged Graham not to be too hard on herself: "We know it wasn't Tom Tom's fault nor that of Tom Tom's author . . . don't wear yourself to a frazzle."[150] But Graham was also financially vulnerable; in August, a letter from Oberlin College reminded her of an overdue balance of $77.15 that

needed to be paid as soon as possible.[151] These post-production travails demonstrate how the structural advantages that the Cleveland Stadium Opera Company offered also carried with them the risk of exploitation. The company's celebration and spectacularization of Black music and history via Graham's "Negro Opera" did not translate into treating with basic fairness and justice those people whose labor made that spectacle possible.

Graham was also frustrated that the suddenness of the commission had prevented her from completing substantive on-the-ground research. "I should have much preferred writing Tom-Tom after I had done my research work in Africa," she mused. "I want to go to Africa while I am young and strong. The work ought to be done now."[152] She remained at Oberlin for three more years, earning bachelor's and master's degrees in 1934 and 1935, respectively. Her master's thesis, "The Survivals of Africanism in Modern Music," traced Black music's development from Abyssinia to Europe and the United States. It concluded—or, more precisely, declined to conclude—with a reference to *Tom-Tom:* "Two years ago I attempted to put something of this music with its never ending beat, its striving and aspirations, upon the stage." She admitted that she could "write no conclusion for this thesis. It remains unfinished even as so much of the material which we are discussing remains undiscovered and undeveloped."[153] In addition to conveying the self-consciously provisional nature of Graham's ideas about African music, the thesis shows how access to resources, or lack thereof, shaped *Tom-Tom*'s historical and musical worldbuilding. Graham was unable to attain the well-researched, experientially grounded knowledge of African music to which she aspired, but she remained confident that opera's grand aesthetic resources could communicate the fundamental significance of African music to Black diasporic history.

The opera itself remained deeply important to Graham, and she made repeated attempts to secure the time and funding necessary to revise her work. In 1934, she drafted another Guggenheim application, seeking funding to revise *Tom-Tom.*[154] She did the calculations, estimating that it would take at least three months and $2,400.[155] In 1935, she took a job at Tennessee Agricultural and Industrial State College in Nashville. It was a demanding and underpaid position, requiring her to complete endless administrative tasks; teach Fine Arts, French, Orchestration, Piano, Music History, and Music Theory to more than five hundred students; and conduct the orchestra.[156] The school was so poorly funded that students and teachers pushed each other aside at mealtimes in a cafeteria that rarely had enough food to serve all who needed it.[157]

Under such crushing circumstances, opera became a refuge. Graham wrote to her then-mentor, Du Bois:

> This morning I am happy. For the past week I have been preparing my music classes to listen in on the Metropolitan Opera broadcast of Wagner's "Gotterdammerung." There was some amusement when it was learned I was doing this. I borrowed a Victrola from the city and with records and piano I took my one hundred and fifty young folks into Wagner's land of the gods. I told them the stories and revealed to them the glories of his music. They not only listened attentively, but their eyes shone with real excitement. They are anxiously waiting for the afternoon. Now, that is something—to have the opportunity to lead hungry, young Negroes to Wagner! What if I must spend to-morrow straightening out registration records of these hundred and fifty students—work neglected for this <u>teaching</u>? Insignificant detail! Today, for a little while, they shall glimpse Beauty.[158]

With abundant detail, Graham sketched a scene in which *Götterdämmerung* linked the Metropolitan Opera to the southern college classroom to the mythological "land of the gods." An ephemeral reprieve from the drudgery of record-keeping, Wagner's opera also became a site of shared affective experience for Graham's students, much as *Tom-Tom* had been for its community participants. Unlike Freeman, who envisioned himself as the "colored Wagner," Graham was concerned primarily with what Wagner could offer students "hungry" for both food and Beauty. She wished for her students to "listen in on" Wagner—a project that exceeded the college's vocational mandate and took them seriously as participants in an operatic culture.

By the 1940s, Graham's priorities had moved away from *Tom-Tom* in particular and the arts in general. Following her son Robert's tragic death at a military hospital in 1944, which she believed to have been the result of racist treatment he received, she became involved in organized leftist politics. Her marriage to Du Bois in 1951 dramatically altered the course of her life, catapulting her into elite political and intellectual circles across the African diaspora. She became affiliated with the Communist Party and spent decades advising political leaders and working in support of anti-imperialist and anticolonial movements. In 1961, she and Du Bois moved to Ghana, where they became Ghanaian citizens and Graham became an influential adviser to Kwame Nkrumah, a role she continued after Du Bois's death in 1963. If her time in Africa was not the research trip that she had planned

thirty years prior, it finally offered her the opportunity to travel similar routes. Having once portrayed vast historical change on the operatic stage, she now worked at the center of it.

As an early, pivotal event in Graham's long and varied life, *Tom-Tom* illuminates Black operatic counterculture's imbrications with Black diasporic cultural and political life more broadly. And as an opera of astonishing breadth and ambition, it offered performers and audiences a compelling alternative to the canonical stasis of *Aida,* the stale racism of modern white-authored compositions, or the offensive plantation nostalgia of the Met's Old South opera ball. Yet its absence from the stage made it impossible for the opera to fulfill the potential ascribed to it in 1932: that it would be not just "new opera," but "revolutionary," "epoch"-making opera. Those laudatory predictions took as a given its continued presence in the repertory and the public imagination; after all, for an opera to shape history, it must become part of the historical record. *Tom-Tom* was exceptionally dependent on performance for its full realization, due to its diffusion of creative responsibility among participants and pedagogical ambition to educate audiences about Black diasporic history. Instead, non-performance and absence became central to its history, creating a sort of ripple effect: other operas not written, other sounds not heard, other ideas not considered. These circumstances bring a more colloquial meaning of the term arrangement into play—that of "making arrangements," as for a funeral or other memorial. The archive, not the stage or canon, became *Tom-Tom*'s resting place.

This may sound like a familiar refrain. To some extent, *Tom-Tom*'s trajectory echoes the experiences of many participants in Black operatic counterculture during these years. From the entrants in the Ferrari Fontana Vocal Trials, to Florence Cole-Talbert and Caterina Jarboro, to Freeman and White and their largely unperformed operas, a pattern recurs: fleeting possibilities, aspirations thwarted by erasure, dreams deferred. The pattern raises the question of whether, despite moments of ephemeral recognition, these artists' many-sided marginalization—within opera, within African American musical life, within the US cultural mainstream—would prove to be an insurmountable obstacle, or whether it was a necessary, generative condition for the creation of their work.

Yet that same absence invites a different relationship between these works, performers, events, and their potential future audiences. Their enduring unfamiliarity facilitates another sort of historical counterknowledge, distinct from but related to that which Graham initially crafted through *Tom-Tom*. In drawing attention to the constructed limitations of opera's master

narrative and all that it does not include, they become a record of speculative possibility—of how opera could be a method of engaging with the Black past and present in creative, liberatory ways. If the structural conditions under which these artists worked were ultimately not conducive to the large-scale worldbuilding to which they aspired, their work nonetheless preserved and expanded opera's countercultural possibilities, ensuring that the art form would continue to foster transformational creativity and collective imagination.

6

The Countercultural Roots of Desegregation

On July 19, 1935, singers from the original cast of *Porgy and Bess* joined George Gershwin and a few dozen orchestral musicians in a recording studio to rehearse excerpts from the composer's new work, which was scheduled to premiere on Broadway that fall. Excerpts from the session offer the first recorded documentation of music that has become central to the American songbook; they also attest to the collaborative labor that informed its creation. In one remarkable selection, Gershwin announces that they will begin at "five bars before [rehearsal number] 9, Scene 1"; he plays the piano and sings a scratchy approximation of the choral part above. The orchestra joins in. Then Abbie Mitchell, in the role of Clara, begins to sing "Summertime." Her voice, delicate in size but deepened by a sumptuous vibrato, curves sinuously around the orchestra's accompaniment. The musicians match her phrasing as she pauses before the third syllable of "summer*time*" in her first entrance. They recede in volume as she luxuriates in the portamento between "rise" and "up," an interpretive choice that emphasizes the melancholy disjunction between the downward fall of the melody and the semantic content of the lyrics.[1]

Mitchell's performance testifies to the enduring power of Black operatic counterculture. Since beginning her career in the 1890s as a teenage star of Black musical theater, she had accumulated decades of vocal training, including an early 1900s stint to study lieder in Germany, where she gained praise for her "velvety" timbre and "splendid diction and legato."[2] In the 1920s, she sang operatic arias in recital, prompting the normally cantankerous Sylvester Russell to deem her "not only the greatest lyric soprano of

her race but the greatest figure and most talented woman of her race now before the public."[3] Her longevity and influence were such that she was thought to represent a conduit between past and present. One critic observed in 1929 that Mitchell had risen to prominence within an "earlier period in the development of the Negro in the theatre" and was "still going—indeed, lives yet for her greatest glory and hopes to be one of the pioneers in a new advancement of her race." Yet as illustrious as Mitchell's career was, she had been precluded from attaining her "major objective": "a role in grand opera." Her "long-cherished ambition" to sing a role such as Aida remained unrealized, but she was "confident that a way will be opened and that when the opportunity comes she will be ready."[4]

Porgy and Bess signified both a partial realization of these ambitions and yet another departure from them. Gershwin's composition—a "folk opera" of contested generic status, which showcased the talents of experienced African American singers even as it epitomized the representational constraints relentlessly imposed on Black artists in the white-authored American imaginary—was lauded as a cultural milestone. But its paradoxes were not new. They echoed the conundrum faced by entrants in the Ferrari Fontana Vocal Trials, by Caterina Jarboro when she made her debut as Aida, by the artists who appeared in Shirley Graham's *Tom-Tom*. Predicated on a potentially generative, yet hierarchically imbalanced relationship among a multiracial group of participants, it compelled Black artists to navigate the racial politics of white-led institutions and carve out opportunities for individualized self-making therein.

At the outset of Mitchell's career, the white US opera scene was closed entirely to Black singers, who instead engaged with opera via the ambitious countercultural performances led by Harry Lawrence Freeman and Theodore Drury, or the educational endeavors of such figures as James Mundy and Azalia Hackley. Incremental change throughout the Harlem Renaissance era had generated new possibilities for Black listeners, singers, and composers, who disrupted the Jim Crow logics of the opera house and claimed space within it. These artists argued for African Americans' centrality to the operatic canon as it stood, while seeking to remake that canon to encompass Black diasporic history and culture. Concomitantly, Black singers, intellectuals, and educators maintained a productively marginal relationship to the art form's mainstream by persisting in the creation and preservation of their own institutions, from autonomous companies to critical conversations in the Black press. But by 1935, when Mitchell sang *Porgy and Bess,* change was in the air. Increasingly, Black cultural workers found it strategically useful to link opera directly to contemporary political concerns,

from global debates over American democracy's racial hypocrisy in an era of war and fascism to the burgeoning strength of the domestic civil rights movement. In doing so, they reoriented Black operatic counterculture toward the more precise goal of desegregating operatic institutions within the United States. Opera was reconfigured as a bellwether of racial progress, a proxy for the nation's ability to live up to its democratic ideals and guarantee African Americans their civil rights.

This shift in focus galvanized immediate, tangible change in that more opportunities arose for Black artists to participate in mainstream operatic life. Yet in the longer term it risked deradicalizing effects. Whereas the political implications of previous iterations of Black operatic counterculture had been diffuse and wide-ranging—from Freeman's radical insistence that opera's grandeur was ideally suited to the expression of global Black solidarity, to Hackley's conservative suggestion that the operatic voice could facilitate the performance of respectable Black womanhood—the art form was now yoked to the attainment of the politically possible. This new understanding of opera as an indicator of "progress" required obscuring its historical roots within Black communities, its cultural marginality, and the specific aesthetic qualities that made it appealing to Black artists. Perhaps counterintuitively, advocating for Black opera's future risked the erasure of its past.

In the 1930s and 1940s, efforts to desegregate opera played out across the realms of composition, institution-building, and performance. Yet this development was not an unambiguous indicator of progress, and should not be taken as evidence that the arc of the Black operatic universe bends toward justice. While major white-authored operas, including *Four Saints in Three Acts* (1934) and *Porgy and Bess* (1935), appeared to dismantle racial barriers by virtue of their all-Black casts, they simultaneously advanced a regressive message that implied further artistic or political change was unnecessary. Black opera companies, including the newly formed National Negro Opera Company (NNOC), took on multifaceted roles as pedagogical training grounds, advocates for interracial cooperation, and sites of model Black citizenship. In the mainstream opera house, longstanding efforts to cast Black singers were reworked in relation to contemporary global politics—a process that culminated in Camilla Williams's celebrated debut in *Madama Butterfly* at New York City Opera (NYCO) in 1946.

Both scholarly and popular narratives of Black opera tend to frame this period as one of "firsts": the premiere of *Porgy and Bess* as the first time that Black singers appeared en masse in an operatic work; Williams's debut as the first time a Black woman was offered a contract by a major company.

My panoramic approach instead situates these high-profile, seemingly disparate events in relation to Black operatic counterculture writ large. I argue that instances of desegregation are best understood not as isolated, inaugural events, but rather as moments in which the longstanding tradition of Black participation in opera became more visible to mainstream onlookers—the "*most widely witnessed* transition . . . to grand opera," in the astute words of Rosalyn Story.[5] The political project of desegregation invited and required widespread recognition, and it was tactically important for these to be framed as unprecedented activities. Yet deep roots on the cultural margins made this set of events possible.

Nor was desegregation solely a story of institutional change. Black artists worked both within and beyond desegregationist frameworks, embracing opera's capacity for affective self-making—as when Anne Wiggins Brown, the first soprano to sing Bess, wrote poignantly about the deep affinities she came to feel with the character. Like Tammy Kernodle, whose work on jazz and gender eschews the trope of the "exceptional black woman" in favor of an emphasis on collaboration and offstage labor, I show how Black operatic artists took care to recognize their forebears, acknowledging that their efforts represented the culmination of decades of artistry and activism.[6] Williams, for instance, insisted that her NYCO debut was made possible by Cleota Collins, the Black soprano with whom she studied at Virginia State College. Such acts of recognition established a lineage in which performers like Williams could situate themselves. At a moment when Black operatic counterculture risked mainstream cooptation, they also served as a reminder of the tradition's deep roots and continued radical potential.

Spectacle and Authenticity in *Four Saints in Three Acts* and *Porgy and Bess*

Two new works appeared on the American cultural scene in quick succession in the mid-1930s, offering putatively novel reframings of the relationship between Blackness and opera. In 1934, *Four Saints in Three Acts*, an avant-garde collaboration by Gertrude Stein and Virgil Thomson in which Black performers played medieval Spanish saints, became a critical and popular sensation. In 1935, George and Ira Gershwin's *Porgy and Bess* enjoyed immediate recognition as a cultural landmark, acclaimed as the "first true American opera."[7] Adapted from DuBose Heyward's novel *Porgy*, it too featured a cast of Black singers, who played South Carolinians in the quasi-realistic community of Catfish Row.

These works were more ideologically similar than their divergent aesthetics might suggest. Like *Jonny spielt auf* and *The Emperor Jones*, both proved that Blackness was central to the transatlantic mainstream of early twentieth-century operatic composition. By some measures, they seemed to be harbingers of change: while those earlier works had featured white singers in blackface, *Four Saints* and *Porgy and Bess* insisted that Black artists were crucial to their success. But they simultaneously entrapped those performers within static narratives that spectacularized their appearance in opera, reiterated the notion that they were outsiders to the art form, and consigned them to ahistorical scenarios in which change was neither needed nor desirable. Both also premiered on Broadway rather than in opera houses, propagating the racially exclusionary fiction that Black performers belonged only on the popular stage—even when they sang operatic music. At a moment when Black operatic counterculture was increasingly invested in linking opera to the exigencies of contemporary politics, these works assumed a reactionary function, epitomizing the double bind that Black performers continued to face within white cultural institutions. For individual participants, however, they ultimately generated very different interpretive possibilities. Whereas *Four Saints* offered limited opportunities for its performers to revise or contest its constrictive narrative, *Porgy and Bess* became an immensely rich resource for Black interlocutors, who mined the opera's ostensibly "authentic" engagement with Black life to countercultural effect.

Four Saints was defined by its aesthetic eclecticism. Steven Watson argues that the opera, which evokes the pastoral, the new, and the absurd in equal measure, "mainstreamed" modernism in the United States, becoming the first massively popular iteration of a movement that had previously attracted niche audiences.[8] First conceptualized while Stein and Thomson were both expatriates in Paris in the mid-1920s, it premiered in Hartford, Connecticut before moving to Broadway, where it became the longest-running opera to date. The piece paired Stein's characteristically obscure poetry with arrestingly simple music by Thomson, redolent of the church hymns of his Missouri childhood. There was little plot per se. An array of medieval Spanish saints paraded amid brightly colored cellophane sets, singing lines like "Pigeons on the grass alas." Unlike other operas in which issues of plot, setting, or characterization linked Black performers to the work in which they appeared, *Four Saints* contained "no suggestion of race, color or anything along that line."[9] *Aida* or *The Emperor Jones* this was not.

The inclusion of Black performers within this heterogeneous work was not motivated by an ethical or political desire to desegregate opera; rather,

it was predicated on essentialist beliefs about musical-racial difference and natural Black musicality. Thomson initially envisioned a white cast, but after attending a performance of Hall Johnson's 1933 Broadway musical *Run, Little Chillun,* he concluded that "[Black singers] alone possess the dignity and the poise, the lack of self-consciousness that proper interpretation of the opera demands."[10] His perspective echoed that of other white commentators, such as the *New York Times*'s Olin Downes, who thought the musical offered a prototype for "real American opera," given its "genuinely racial" conflation of "speech and song, action and dance." "Quite without pretension or consciousness of the fact," Downes ruminated, "this exhibition comes nearer the practice of the dramatic principles that the old Florentine pioneers of opera entertained than might be realized. Nor is this inconsistent with Richard Wagner's conception of the union of the arts and the expressive resources of the theatre."[11] By acknowledging these parallels but concomitantly insisting that Johnson must be unaware of them, Downes paradoxically reinscribed the idea of a fundamental difference between Black music and Wagnerian opera. (This sleight of hand was also factually inaccurate, eliding Johnson's extensive classical training: he studied theory and composition at the University of Pennsylvania and Juilliard, and had accompanied Marian Anderson and Roland Hayes as the violist of the illustrious Negro String Quartet.[12]) *Four Saints* echoed Downes's characterization of Black performers as unself-consciously Wagnerian by identifying a resonance between the operatic avant-garde and Black expressivity—a superficially transgressive but ultimately essentialist move that inverted the self-making claims that Black performers themselves often made in relation to the art form.

Although *Four Saints* departed from the narrative models typical of white-authored operatic Blackness, it retained similar spectacularizing effects. As one critic succinctly put it, "The audience was white, the players were colored."[13] Many critics focused on the work's narrative nonsensicality, but their responses also contained a note of surprise at the implicitly ideologically nonsensical spectacle of Black performers taking part in a modernist opera. Lisa Barg has argued that the opera's stylistic eclecticism was "racially mediated" by way of its Black cast, a "collapsing of black difference as modernist aesthetic difference."[14] Some commentators interpreted the opera's two "narrator" figures, the Commère and Compère, as reformulations of blackface minstrelsy's "end men," and visual representations of the opera emphasized its overlap with minstrelsy.[15] Paige McGinley argues that the Spanish setting invoked the US South, linking the opera to the familiar genre of the southern pastoral and its attendant representations of

African Americans.[16] Even as the piece appeared to disrupt dominant logics of race and casting by superimposing Black performers onto a tale of medieval Spain, its reception emphasized its similarities to other racialized cultural productions.

Although *Four Saints* located Black performers within a modern aesthetic context, it also relegated them to a disturbingly static past. Stein had previously expressed the belief that "negroes were not suffering from persecution, they were suffering from nothingness . . . the african is not primitive, he has a very ancient but a very narrow culture and there it remains. Consequently nothing does or can happen," and in this light, the opera's playful nonsensicality might be understood to imply that Black performers were "blank slates" not simply because avant-garde aesthetics demanded it, but also because they inherently lacked history and culture.[17] This sense of stasis appeared not only within Stein's circuitous libretto, but also in the opera's choreography. One of the most celebrated elements of *Four Saints* was its climactic "procession scene": choreographer Frederick Ashton directed cast members to sway back and forth for four full minutes, creating an illusion of movement without actually going anywhere. The "procession" echoed a similar scene in *The Green Pastures,* but it also evoked broader notions of timelessness, even "nothingness," in its combination of putative mobility with a lack of actual change in position—an image that all but demands to be read as metaphor, particularly during an era in which Black artists demanded changes to their cultural and political status.[18] This ahistorical framework diverged sharply from contemporaneous works by Black composers: compare this scene to the urgent momentum of Graham's *Tom-Tom,* whose Black subjects embark on a quest for freedom that spans continents and centuries. Whereas *Tom-Tom* insisted on the possibility of an alternative future even as it questioned teleological conceptions of progress, *Four Saints* merged the modern and the Baroque into an out-of-time tableau in which change was effectively impossible.

Despite its conceptual limitations, *Four Saints* retained some material appeal for Black performers. In an era when the opportunity to appear in operatic productions was still exceedingly rare, it was a chance to gain further professional experience. For artists struggling to make ends meet during the Depression, it was also comparatively lucrative, offering substantial pay for both rehearsals and performances. Yet the opera's reception in the Black press suggests that few embraced its aesthetic possibilities. Although one critic praised the performers as "capable of executing the lyrics of this opera with an appreciation for the pure beauty of the sound of the words and music, unhampered by their apparent meaninglessness," another

wondered if "all of this seemed a waste of beautiful voices capable of higher attainments on a nonsensical extravaganza." The cultural critic Floyd Calvin summed it up: "That eccentric piece gave employment to colored artists, but little else."[19]

While *Four Saints* made a critical and popular splash at its premiere, it has faded from public memory in the years since. In contrast, its near-contemporary *Porgy and Bess* remains profoundly influential. The contours of the work's genesis are well known. The South Carolinian author DuBose Heyward, born to an elite white family in 1885, wrote a novel, *Porgy*, in 1925, about a disabled beggar living in Charleston's poor waterfront neighborhood of Catfish Row, and his love for the young, drug-addicted, vulnerable Bess. In 1926, George Gershwin—having completed his opera-esque *Blue Monday* a few years prior—wrote to Heyward about the possibility of adapting the novel, but when he learned that Heyward's wife, Dorothy, was already working on a stage adaptation, the plan was put on hold. The Theatre Guild's production of the Heywards' play opened in 1927, running for 217 performances in New York before touring the United States. After a 1932 proposal by Al Jolson to make a blackface adaptation of the play was, thankfully, rejected, Gershwin signed a contract in 1933 with the Theatre Guild. His opera opened in previews in Boston in September 1935 and premiered on Broadway on October 10, 1935.

At each step of this process, white authors and audiences obsessed over the work's putative authenticity.[20] In advance of the 1927 Theatre Guild production, which was advertised as "an authentic picture of Southern life," director Rouben Mamoulian and set designer Cleon Throckmorton visited Charleston to observe the city in visual and sonic detail. The resulting set contained a replica of an actual building in Charleston, and the production made use of dozens of "street sounds" from the city, even featuring a brief onstage appearance by a band of young jazz musicians from Charleston's Jenkins Orphanage.[21] White critical responses similarly focused on the issue of authenticity, creating a sort of feedback loop in which creators and audiences collectively affirmed the "truth" of the work. The *New York Times* had praised Heyward's novel for the empathetic realism conveyed by its "sympathetic and convincing interpretation of negro life by a member of an 'outside' race."[22] Two years later, the same outlet characterized the 1927 play as "always true," a "bit of folk-life [which] catches the loyalties and superstitions of the negro in what their true value must be" and "never sacrificed truth for showmanship."[23]

Gershwin, the New York–born son of Russian Jewish immigrants, undertook extensive research in an attempt to guarantee that his adaptation

of *Porgy* would plausibly evoke the sounds of Black life in Charleston. In 1934, in an excursion that recalls White and Matheus's visit to Haiti to collect material for *Ouanga,* he spent five weeks at Heyward's summer home on Folly Island, off the South Carolina coast. Motivated in part by a pragmatic need to collaborate with Heyward in person, the trip also allowed Gershwin to visit local communities and experience the musical culture of the Gullah Geechee people who Heyward's novel purported to represent. Heyward later reflected that the experience was "satisfying as well as exciting": "James Island with its large population of primitive Gullah Negroes . . . furnished us with a laboratory in which to test our theories, as well as an inexhaustible source of folk material."[24] Heyward characterized his "primitive" subjects as wholly divorced from modern life, their home as a sterile "laboratory" rather than a site of active cultural engagement.

This conceptual and critical focus on *Porgy and Bess*'s authenticity not only mistook experiential proximity for cultural knowledge and veracity, but also foreclosed the work's potential as an agent of social change. Ellen Noonan has argued that Heyward's "fundamentally conservative" novel and subsequent play, which "defined authentic blackness as southern yet apolitical," established a model in which the opera could sidestep contemporary racial politics, namely efforts to dismantle the white supremacist systems that maintained Jim Crow segregation and prohibited Black political participation.[25] Authenticity begat deradicalization: to claim that the work offered as a truthful picture of Black life in Charleston was to avoid interrogating how it should change, or how audiences should contend with their complicity in the tragedies portrayed onstage. Some white audiences applauded this romanticized portrayal, interpreting the piece as an escapist refuge. As James Baldwin famously observed, "It assuages [white Americans'] guilt about Negroes and it attacks none of their fantasies."[26]

Debates about the racial authenticity of *Porgy and Bess* were entangled with debates about its genre. The piece resurrected longstanding questions about the convergence between Black narratives and operatic form—in short, about the very definition of a "Black opera." Gershwin, famous for his aesthetic versatility and hybridized style, deemed the piece a "folk opera." Unlike Shirley Graham, who had collected and presented an intentionally "formless" array of Black sonic archival material in *Tom-Tom,* he prioritized compositional cohesion, explaining that he had opted not to use "original folk material because I wanted the music to be all of one piece."[27] Among Black commentators, there was little consensus on the work's genre, or, for that matter, its overall merits: critics both praised the beauty of its music and critiqued its stultifying images.[28] But even those who appreciated the

work often declined to recognize it as opera per se. Hall Johnson found that it displayed "faulty operatic technique" due to its lack of "consistent thematic development." Distinguishing between a "good Negro opera" and a "good opera *about* Negroes," Johnson concluded that Gershwin's "much-publicized visits to Charleston for local color do not amount even to a matriculation in the preparatory-school that he needed for his work." This was "not a Negro opera by Gershwin, but Gershwin's idea of what a Negro opera should be."[29] Others were similarly skeptical. Harry Lawrence Freeman wrote that "at no time does the work attain the calibre or scope of grand opera," while Graham wrote to W. E. B. Du Bois, "No doubt you have heard 'Porgy and Bess' . . . I left 'Porgy' more than ever firm in the conviction that there is work for me to do."[30] How dispiriting it must have been for Graham to see her epic pushed aside as *Porgy and Bess* was hailed as the exemplary opera about African American life, the diasporic and historical scale of *Tom-Tom* replaced by the stagnant time and constricted space of Gershwin's work.

Among other Black interlocutors, the same factors that catalyzed the opera's entry into the cultural mainstream—its emphasis on racial authenticity, basis in a well-known novel and play, and stylistic hybridity—also enhanced its countercultural expressive potential. An array of writers and musicians took up the question of how the Heywards' play and Gershwin's opera might become a creative wellspring, a jumping-off point for thinking about opera's relationship to self-making and formal appeal to Black artists. Take, for example, a remarkable June 1928 *Opportunity* essay by the African American writer Harry S. Keelan, which imagines an opera based on Heyward's play.[31] Published several years before Gershwin's plans to compose an opera were made public, Keelan's speculative piece suggests that opera is an ideal medium through which to narrate epic stories of Black life. Keelan professed himself an admirer of Heyward's "beautiful" work. But rather than proposing that a Black composer adapt it into a newly composed opera, he took a collage-like approach that repurposed the Western classical canon to illustrate the milieu of Catfish Row. For the prelude, he imagined that the Andante from Beethoven's Symphony no. 7, whose "beauty and majesty" "fade into . . . utter hopelessness," could presage the tragedies to come. The bustle of the neighborhood would be best expressed by way of "Stravinsky at his most fortzando [*sic*] moments—with every instrument in the orchestra at full blast." Conveying the "unconventionality" of the love between Porgy and Bess would require a "Wagnerian cello" overlaid with "Debussy." There would be three instances of a "Wagnerian climax": the death of Serena's husband, Robbins; the emotional

DREAMING IN ENSEMBLE

release that follows the exit of the undertaker; and Crown's boastful challenge to God to kill him before he goes out into the storm. The final scene would compel "one of the grandest arias of all opera," music so spectacular as to have no analog.[32]

Keelan's musical references remade Porgy, Bess, and their compatriots as modern, cosmopolitan subjects. By way of Stravinsky, he connected the ostensibly "timeless" Catfish Row to contemporary European modernity; by way of Wagner, he reframed its inhabitants as majestic, even godlike. He supplemented these allusions with loving attention to the spirituals, through which he sought to illustrate the characters' moral excellence. The opera, Keelan explained, would also feature "Lord, I want to be like Jesus in my heart," a message that conveys Porgy's "radiant idealism," and "Who'll be a witness for my Lord," which ennobles Bess by showing how her love for Porgy "was more faithful than Isolde's or Elsa's or Sieglinde's."[33] If Heyward and Gershwin tethered Porgy and Bess to a particular time, place, and attendant set of challenges in a manner that forestalled the possibility of change, Keelan stripped away those elements, wresting the characters out of Catfish Row and into an expansive musical world. Where Gershwin's work assumed a fundamental incommensurability between Black "original folk material" and the genre of opera—one that could be reconciled only through his compositional prowess—Keelan comingled spirituals, symphonies, and operas, reframing Heyward's play in maximally capacious terms.

The artists who ultimately brought *Porgy and Bess* to life followed in Keelan's creative footsteps, contending actively with its combination of opportunity and constraint. The premiere cast featured approximately seventy singers. Several were already luminaries within Black classical circles, even if they appeared as newcomers to white audiences: Abbie Mitchell, Howard University voice professor Todd Duncan, soprano Anne Wiggins Brown. Fresh off their work in *Four Saints in Three Acts* came choral director Eva Jessye and baritone Edward Matthews (as well as white musical director Alexander Smallens). Others brought varied stage experience to their roles, from Juilliard-trained soprano Ruby Elzy to vaudeville star John W. Bubbles. Some white critics framed these performers' diverse training as evidence of their outsider status in relation to opera: they "knew no stuffy traditions" and were not "handicapped at the start by having real grand opera ways."[34] In contrast, African American critics hoped that *Porgy and Bess* might augur an era in which Black artists could succeed professionally in serious roles. To the *New York Age*'s Lucien White, it offered incontrovertible proof of "Negroes' ability in interpreting and portraying the operatic forms."[35] The *Baltimore Afro-American*'s Ralph Matthews noted that the love duets between

Porgy and Bess "call upon all the technical training of both artists to get the best out of the intricate score of Gershwin."[36] This focus on technical excellence was sometimes coupled with an uplift-oriented emphasis on performers' social class or educational attainments. One critic, for instance, clarified that Brown, in the role of Bess, played "a hussy on stage but she's really serious in life," linking operatic training to elite status.[37]

Indeed, Bess was the work's most controversial figure: hypersexualized, and unflatteringly construed as an addict and victim, she offended those who interpreted her as a generalized symbol of Black womanhood, and she especially raised the hackles of critics invested in the notion of opera as a proxy for respectability. The Baltimore-based educator (and erstwhile supernumerary) W. Llewelyn Wilson made sense of this conundrum by situating Bess within the broader operatic canon. Wilson denied that "there has been any attempt on the part of the writers and producers of 'Porgy and Bess' to establish the character of Bess as typical of American Negro womanhood." Even if Bess was a "strumpet," opera was rife with less-than-perfect women, from Faust's "bad heroine" Marguerite to Bizet's "fickle flirt" Carmen. Further, if Black sopranos were "sullied by essaying such parts as Bess of 'Porgy and Bess,' they would assume just as great a risk portraying Aida, the Ethiopian captive slave girl who dies buried in a sealed vault."[38] If this perspective failed to critically interrogate the prevalence of misogynistic representation within the genre, it nonetheless redirected the critical conversation by suggesting that Bess was exemplary not of African American women, but of operatic women.

For Brown, the soprano who created the part, the negative connotations of Bess's character were subsumed by the role's capacity for self-making. Growing up in a middle-class family in Baltimore, Brown adored listening to opera but was discouraged by the racism she anticipated she would face. As she recalled in a memoir, "It was opera of which I dreamed when I thought about the future. Not a chance! The opera scene . . . was closed to me." Undaunted, she pursued her love for the art form from the security of her own home: "Before I ever sang an operatic aria, I 'played' opera. At the age of 11 or 12, I would dress myself in some kind of costume—perhaps a gay bedspread draped around my body, or a dress belonging to Mama and with invented words and melody I could sing and act for perhaps an hour." She deepened her knowledge as a student at Douglass High School, where Black operatic counterculture operated in full force. Often taking on a "leading part" in the school's productions, which were "rehearsed and rehearsed for months," she gained an intimate knowledge of the art form. "In retrospect, I realize how good and how vital these performances were,"

she recalled. "Ambition was great in us, we young people, who had so little chance to show what we could do."[39]

Brown enrolled at Juilliard, where she learned of Gershwin's plans to write the opera from her classmate (and future co-castmate) Ruby Elzy. Initially concerned that her skin was too light for her to convincingly play Bess, Brown nonetheless requested an audition. She won the part and began to practice in secret, using a score that Gershwin insisted she show to no one; as a result, her first encounter with the character occurred on an atypically intimate basis. Her perspective on Bess reflects that closeness. Like Keelan in his *Opportunity* essay, she strategically elided the details of Bess's struggles, musing that Bess was "weak—but not in all ways," and that her love for Porgy helped her become "part of the little community" of Catfish Row.[40] Her musical expertise also became fundamental to the production's development. As Gwynne Kuhner Brown has shown, interracial collaboration was central to the rehearsal process for *Porgy and Bess,* and Gershwin relied on Brown's deep knowledge of opera, consulting with her on questions of vocal range and other technical matters.[41]

Brown was not overly quixotic. After the premiere, her father, though "excited by [her] success," was "a little sad, he told us, to see Negroes revealed in such violence, such 'lack of decorum,' such superstition and primitiveness . . . It furthers the myth that all black people are like that." But she ultimately redeemed Bess as a site of affective identification. After countless hours of study and rehearsal, Brown finally found "a space inside me—a space which could take in the whole world. *I knew what to do,* and I knew it was right. I no longer had any fear, it was simply to listen to the instructions, and with complete attention 'live out' the situation. I <u>was</u> that person—the one I was playing."[42] In creating Bess, she also recreated herself.

Many years after Brown first appeared in *Porgy and Bess,* the opera continued to shape her identity. During a tumultuous period late in her life, she developed an imaginary companion named Johan, a "clairvoyant" confidante who used a wheelchair or cane and offered unconditional "comfort and support." Brown even bought him an actual cane, which she kept in her home. When she confided in a friend about Johan, he

> Laughed and laughed.
> "Porgy!" he said.
> "What?"
> "Yes, Porgy! You've let crippled Porgy save Bess again. Don't you see?
> "Yes, of course, now that you say it, but it was not conscious."[43]

The opera had become personally significant to Brown in a way that far exceeded the limitations of its authors' imaginations. Moving beyond the preoccupation with authenticity that pervaded *Porgy and Bess*'s origins, and the static image of Black life it presented, she emphasized its power to assuage her struggles and contribute to her evolving sense of self.

The Black Opera Company in an Age of Integration

As African Americans entered onto modern, mainstream stages, they also continued to perform within institutions explicitly dedicated to the advancement of Black opera. Earlier Black opera companies, including those led by Theodore Drury and James Mundy, had worked within Jim Crow–era high culture, an environment defined by both the growing sacralization of opera and Black cultural workers' investment in collective artistic self-determination. But as those catalyzing conditions changed, so did companies' institutional aspirations. Newer efforts were often framed as self-consciously historical attempts to fulfill the dreams of past impresarios, but they also embraced the possibility of interracial collaboration—a tactic that dovetailed with other integrationist projects in which Black-led institutions pursued the politicized goal of formal equality. These organizations crafted a new rationale for their existence: the Black opera company could be an agent of democratic social change, providing a literal and figurative stage on which the drama of national racial progress could play out.

The self-determinist model inaugurated by Freeman, Drury, Mundy, and others persisted, but it proved difficult to implement on a consistent basis. The Federal Music Project sponsored a Black-cast production of *Il trovatore* in Harlem in 1936, led by the versatile singer Minto Cato. Like her predecessors, Cato merged pedagogy with performance, instructing a group of "eager amateurs" so expertly that "would-be singers who hadn't known *fa* from *do* were trying their voices on arias and choruses." In the *Crisis,* a reviewer marveled at "the amateur cast of 55, by day houseworkers, porters, seamstresses and laborers," whose "sincere and sympathetic interpretation of the opera [left] no doubt in the minds of the audience of the artistry of the performers."[44] In 1938, a Detroit group (known alternately as the Detroit Negro Opera and Detroit Civic Opera) presented a Black-cast *Aida;* they followed up with *Carmen* the next year.[45] The Chicago Negro Opera Guild also staged *Aida* in 1943, promising audiences a "history-making, extraordinary musical event."[46] Although they received effusive critical praise, these efforts, too, were short-lived.

Drury's own company reappeared in the 1930s after a long hiatus. Having ceased yearly productions in 1906 and suffered a calamitous train crash during a tour later that year, Drury moved from New York to Boston, where his productions became smaller and more sporadic. By 1919, he was in taxing circumstances. He moved to Kansas City, where he placed an advertisement in a local paper: "Let me help you raise money for your church. Who wants me? Theodore Drury, Tenor Singer."[47] Upon resurrecting his company in Philadelphia, in 1930, Drury staged familiar repertoire, presented in humble venues with minimal staging: *Aida* (1930), *Carmen* (1931), *Cavalleria Rusticana* (1932), *Carmen* (1933 and 1936), *Aida* (1937), and *Carmen* yet again (1938). The company struggled artistically and financially. "How the mighty have fallen," remarked Harry Lawrence Freeman.[48] "We have all the essentials necessary for opera, such as voice, the gift of acting, etc.," Drury mused. But "the greatest drawback, is, of course, the finance . . . Personally, I have never been able to solve it."[49] Despite these challenges, the company remained an important training ground for aspiring artists. Its members were now increasingly—if still infrequently—likely to be engaged by the white opera establishment: for instance, tenor Embry Bonner sang Radames (1930) and Don José (1931) with the Drury Company, then joined the cast of *Four Saints in Three Acts* in 1934.

A few predominantly white companies hired Black singers. In 1934, the Italian American musician Peter Creatore established an interracial venture, the Aeolian Opera Association, in New York. The company held only one performance, an intriguing double bill of *Cavalleria Rusticana* and *The Emperor Jones* that featured Abbie Mitchell alongside two stars of *Tom-Tom*, Charlotte Murray and Jules Bledsoe. The *Defender* raved about Bledsoe's performance as Brutus Jones, a vast improvement over Tibbett's "somewhat minstrel showish" rendition at the opera's Met premiere one year prior.[50] Bledsoe also appeared in both *Aida* and *The Emperor Jones* with the New York–based Cosmopolitan Opera Association in November 1934; Ernst Lert, who had directed *Tom-Tom*, led both productions. In 1937, two African American singers, La Julia Rhea and William Franklin, sang Aida and Amonasro, respectively, with the Chicago Civic Opera Company. Building on the triumph of Caterina Jarboro, impresario Alfredo Salmaggi cast other Black singers in the role of Aida, including Minto Cato in 1937 and Edith Dixon Sewell in 1943. These events largely followed an established model in which Black singers appeared in white-authored racialized roles. Works by Black composers seemed to generate little interest: for example, when Freeman requested that the Cosmopolitan

Opera Association consider producing *Voodoo,* he received a politely non-committal response.[51]

Some interracial efforts retained an unequal power dynamic that disadvantaged Black participants. In 1941, the Black musician Edward Boatner offered a scathing critique of the Cooperative Opera Club, organized by a white woman named Elizabeth Wachtel. In a review of a recital by the club's members, Boatner wrote that Wachtel assumed that her African American students were "very ignorant and need a white light to guide and rescue them." Rather than assessing the quality of the singing, Boatner focused on systemic issues: Wachtel's selection of "moth-eaten" repertoire, printed program full of "mistakes," and "ignorance really remarkable." Given that opera companies still shut out Black singers, "anyone who encourages Negroes to study for opera is taking advantage of them," he concluded; it was imperative to "discourage any kind of organization that misrepresents the possibilities of the Negro in opera."[52] The transgressive potential of Black operatic singing could easily be coopted within institutional structures that remained racially discriminatory.

The era's most ambitious, enduring, and visible attempt at Black operatic institution-building was the National Negro Opera Company (NNOC), established in 1941.[53] Premised on a faith in opera's ability to advance racial progress, the company fostered a multi-pronged public image that celebrated Black artistry, embraced interracial cooperation, and emphasized the art form's democratic bona fides. Its founder, Mary Cardwell Dawson, was born in 1894 in rural North Carolina and moved with her family during the Great Migration to the outskirts of Pittsburgh, where her male family members worked at a brickyard. Around 1920, she moved to Boston to study piano, conducting, and stage production at the New England Conservatory. She found the culture of classical music in the urban North oppressive, later recalling that the "complete discrimination or exclusion" she experienced when seeking to attend opera and symphony performances in Boston "weighed heavily upon" her, making her "wonder why even she had chosen this field for her life's work."[54] Upon returning to Pittsburgh in the mid-1920s, she established the eponymous Cardwell School of Music and founded the Cardwell Dawson Choir. Beginning in 1931, Dawson served as president of a local chapter of the National Association of Negro Musicians (NANM). She was elected national president of NANM in 1938, and in 1941 she mounted a staging of *Aida* in connection with the annual NANM convention, held in Pittsburgh. The production served as the impetus for the NNOC's official establishment later that year.

The company's first production illustrated both its deep roots within Black operatic counterculture and its orientation toward contemporary political concerns. In the role of Amneris was Nellie Dobson Plante, who, twenty years prior, had sung a principal role with Mundy's South Side School of Grand Opera in Chicago. In the audience was the critic Carl Diton, whose review recalled "the age-old dream of Theodore Drury, the pioneer opera producer of a genuine grand opera with an all-colored cast" (Drury himself attended at least one early production).[55] Yet whereas Drury's company had downplayed the occasional involvement of non-Black artists, the NNOC celebrated its links to the white operatic mainstream. Promotional materials proudly noted that its inaugural production was directed by Frederick Vajda, an assistant conductor at the Met. Press coverage walked a fine line between foregrounding the contributions of its Black artists and impresario, on the one hand, and emphasizing its potential to exemplify interracial cooperation, on the other. In 1944, the Pittsburgh arts critic P. L. Prattis mused that the company, "through its excellence, becomes a medium of social significance." He elaborated: "Mrs. Dawson's undertakings may be measured in terms of art or in terms of their social significance . . . what are these grand operas by Negro casts to mean in increasing appreciation for the Negro in this country and in making friends for him? Will they have any effect in dispelling the false beliefs about Negro inferiority and will they come to be recognized as a distinguished contribution which the Negro is making to the world of music? I think the answers to both questions must be affirmative if the promoters strive for artistic success in every way."[56] Earlier companies had certainly situated their work in relation to racial uplift, but Prattis's rhetoric intensified and foregrounded that priority, insisting that opera could be a vehicle of, or even proxy for, the advancement of civil rights.

The NNOC's rise in the early 1940s coincided with both World War II and signal early events of the civil rights movement, including A. Philip Randolph's 1941 March on Washington Movement, the establishment of the Fair Employment Practices Commission, and the Double V campaign. To emphasize its resonance with these urgent political struggles, the company made rhetorical connections between its endeavors and the success of American democracy—starting with its name, which yoked race to nation.[57] "Opera is now a national distinction," boasted one fundraising circular.[58] Soprano Lillian Evanti (who, years after her European debut, become one of the NNOC's stars) avowed that the company was "best proof of democratic processes," evidence that the United States was moving

toward racial equality.[59] In this context, Black opera singers could become model citizens: if they were to succeed in opera, they "would be the first Americans to perform the feat. Thus they would have made a distinct contribution to America which could not be taken from them."[60]

The company's programmatic focus on canonical European operas performed in English translation—in addition to *Aida,* they performed *Carmen, La Traviata, Il trovatore,* and *Faust*—might seem at odds with this Americanizing effort.[61] Annegret Fauser suggests that this repertory afforded the company "symbolic capital," which secured it a place within the operatic mainstream, but it also located the company within a specifically Black genealogy of operatic performance reaching back to the Drury Company.[62] More pointedly, it was a rebuttal to the modernist primitive works that had dominated recent operatic portrayals of Blackness. By performing Verdi, Gounod, and Bizet, the NNOC claimed space not just within opera's present, but also in its past—a seemingly traditionalist move that, somewhat like Keelan's imagined *Porgy,* actually departed from contemporary aesthetic imperatives.

Although the NNOC enjoyed atypical longevity, producing opera for nearly two decades, it contended with serious obstacles. The company faced financial challenges from its inception. With little cash on hand, but high costs related to space rentals and travel, unlucky occurrences (such as weather-related cancellations of outdoor performances) could spell disaster. In 1944, the company was sanctioned by the American Guild of Musical Artists, the musicians' union, for failing to pay singers. So severe were its trials that they prompted Nora Holt to ask, in a 1945 article: "Are Negro Artists Ready For Opera? Will Public Back Them?" After recounting previous companies' efforts, Holt despaired at the NNOC's instability and lack of support. She ended pessimistically: "Yes, there is a need for a Negro opera company, but until it is founded on the principles of culture, with a Guild of supporters, clean, sincere business dealings, and an aim to actually benefit the people, the artist and the community for interracial good, it will go—except in a few isolated cases—into another 70 years of mediocrity, empty and unworthy of documentation."[63] Holt cast doubt on the very notion of a Black opera company, suggesting that under present conditions such institutions were bound to fail.

If the company's promotional materials and press coverage elucidate its progressive aspirations, and the fact of its financial struggles directs attention to its eventual institutional failure, the question of what the NNOC meant to its participants remains more difficult to answer. Because it offered its ensemble a site of collective sociality, and its audiences an extravagant

Charles "Teenie" Harris. American, 1908–1998. Portrait of William Franklin wearing Egyptian costume, standing against painted stonework backdrop in Syria Mosque for National Negro Opera Company performance of *Aida,* October 30, 1941. Black and white: Agfa safety film. H: 3in.×W: 4 in. (7.60×10.20 cm).

Charles "Teenie" Harris. American, 1908–1998. Informal group portrait of men and women wearing Egyptian costumes, seated in stairwell in Syria Mosque for National Negro Opera Company performance of *Aida,* October 30, 1941. Black and white: Agfa safety film. H: 3 in.×W: 4 in. (7.60×10.20 cm).

entertainment, the NNOC's experiential significance exceeded both its stated ideological parameters and its material constraints. The esteemed Black press photographer Charles "Teenie" Harris documented several of the company's Pittsburgh performances, photographing its artists on and off the stage. In one image from the company's inaugural production, William Franklin poses in costume as Amonasro. Photographed against a painted stone wall that formed part of the set, Franklin offers a dramatic self-presentation, his hands-on-hips pose suggesting the depth of his commitment.

Another image, of cast members clustered on a set of stairs backstage, beautifully captures the group's closeness, epitomizing the intensive collaboration that opera entails. The singers are in full costume, and their expressions range from regal distance to mild amusement to full-fledged smiles. At left, two singers tilt their heads and bodies together, sharing a comfortably intimate moment. Surrounding the performers are quotidian reminders

Charles "Teenie" Harris. American, 1908–1998. La Julia Rhea wearing costume for National Negro Opera Company production of *Aida,* October 30, 1941. Black and white: Agfa Superpan Press safety film. H: 3 in.×W: 4 in. (7.60×10.20 cm).

of the backstage setting: a row of doors, signage with messages of "no smoking please" and "handle with care." The image locates these performers simultaneously within the extravagance of the production and the rhythms of daily life. A similarly multilayered effect emerges in a backstage portrait of the company's first Aida, La Julia Rhea. In contrast to previous Aidas like Caterina Jarboro, who sat for elaborately posed studio portraits in costume, Rhea appears in a humanized, even vulnerable light. Adorned with ornate jewelry, she echoes the glamour of her predecessors. But her arms are slightly askew, and she glances upward rather than outward. The image captures her in a moment of introspection, even uncertainty. Collectively, the portraits suggest the experiential possibilities that Black opera companies, and Black operatic counterculture in general, afforded within and beyond public performance. Rather than conveying opera's status as a catalyst for political progress, they foreground the individuals whose labor and artistry enabled

that status. In a moment when opera was increasingly abstracted as a bell-wether of change, it remained an intensely personal, affective endeavor for those who chose to take part in it.

Race, War, and Politics in the Opera House

As African American performers triumphed on Broadway in *Four Saints* and *Porgy and Bess,* and performed canonical works with the NNOC, the longstanding struggle to desegregate opera's most visible stages continued apace. The earliest efforts in this vein had relied on narrow discourses of realism and representation: put simply, that Black performers were best suited to play Black characters. During the Harlem Renaissance, this premise was reformulated as a strategic step on the path toward fuller integration, with critics and intellectuals arguing that Black performers' artistic talent qualified them to sing *all* operatic roles. In the 1930s and 1940s, a more audacious and more politicized rationale took hold: desegregating the opera house was a democratic imperative in an age of war, fascism, and global geopolitical strife.

The Black theater critic Edgar Rouzeau set his sights on the Met. The economic crisis of the Depression had prompted major changes at the company. Rather than continuing to rely financially on a small group of stockholders, it cultivated a broader donor base, inaugurating a "Save the Met" campaign in 1932 and transferring ownership of the building to the newly formed Metropolitan Opera Association in 1940. Edward Johnson, appointed as the new general manager, adopted a vision for the house that entailed adding American singers to its roster, lowering ticket prices, and democratizing its image. To Rouzeau, this endeavor necessitated the inclusion of Black singers. Noting that President Roosevelt had praised the reorganized Met as the "people's opera," he argued that only "when the fact is once established that race and creed are no longer barriers on the stage of the Metropolitan, then, in truth, will grand opera become the 'people's opera' rather than the possession of only a privileged few."[64] In an age of war and fascism, this was an urgent matter. Observing in 1939 that "the singers with the greatest box office appeal today" were Kirsten Flagstad, widely rumored to be a Nazi supporter, and the celebrated contralto Marian Anderson, Rouzeau asked the hypothetical "white stockholder" to decide: "how would you vote?"[65]

In an article titled "'Met' Turns Down Negro Stars," Rouzeau relayed that he had corresponded directly with Johnson on the topic, only to have his entreaties summarily dismissed. "You have probably heard of a hot po-

tato being picked up and hurled back in the direction from whence it came," he harrumphed. "When the Big Day arrives and Negro singers are admitted to the Met, I am going to remind Mr. Johnson about his letter and have my laugh."[66] He urged readers to produce "a thousand pieces of mail" demanding the hiring of Black singers.[67] Nora Holt joined Rouzeau in calling for the Met to live up to its stated democratic ethos. In March 1945, she reported on an interracial group of forty-four "Germans, Poles, English, Bohemians, Negroes and many others" employed at a wartime manufacturing plant who attended an opera at the Met together, "working and playing together under the common banner of Democracy."[68] Holt insisted that "the day of opera as a luxurious institution designed for the social few who can afford it, and ruled high and mightily by a clique of 'stars,' is fast fading from the musical scene." African American singers must be added to the Met's "cosmopolitan" roster, cementing its ability to "[strike] a sonorous tone in democratic principles."[69]

If Rouzeau and Holt characterized the opera house as a desegregationist battleground, other intellectuals made a humanistic call for egalitarian access to the art form. In October 1936, W. E. B. Du Bois published two columns on German opera in the *Pittsburgh Courier*. Du Bois had first visited Germany in the 1890s, where he developed an intimate attachment to Western art music and realized, as Kira Thurman writes, that "he could love and lay claim to the same cultural works as white Americans but on different grounds."[70] In 1936, he traveled to Bayreuth, the German town with a theater fully devoted to Wagnerian opera. Du Bois described it as a "shrine" where one could pursue "an interest in the development of the human soul and for the spirit of Beauty," a paradise where those "who know little of music" found themselves "glimpsing the unknown world."[71] It is startling that he failed to mention the Nazis' appropriation of Wagner, even while writing from Germany in 1936.[72] In a second column, "Opera and the Negro Problem," Du Bois mused: "I can see a certain type of not unthoughtful American Negro saying to himself: Now just what has Bayreuth and opera got to do with starving Negro farm tenants in Arkansas or black college graduates searching New York for a job? It may be all right for the fortunate to rest and play, but is it necessary to pretend that this has any real vital connection with our pressing social problems?"[73] Like Shirley Graham, who had joyfully introduced her Tennessee students to Wagner, Du Bois exalted Wagner's capacity to "tell of human life as he lived it": "No human being, white or black, can afford not to know [his operas], if he would know life."[74] There was a quixotic cast to this statement, which clung faithfully to the idea of artistic transcendence even as it acknowledged that,

in the face of modern economic and social crises, others might regard such faith as untenable.

Other critical voices emphasized the continued need for Black-authored operas. After the premiere of *Porgy and Bess,* the *Amsterdam News* issued a strategically timed call to "revive *Abyssinia,*" the hugely successful Williams and Walker musical of 1906. Recalling that white critics had dismissed *Abyssinia* as overly operatic ("Their very slurs were compliments: they said that Negroes were impudently aspiring to produce grand opera"), the article suggested that a revival could function as "a clever piece of propaganda for Ethiopia" in the context of the 1935 Italian invasion of that nation.[75] This multilayered claim triangulated a dissatisfaction with *Porgy and Bess,* an acknowledgment of the long history of Black operatic composition that preceded it, and a conviction that Black opera could speak to immediate political concerns. Nora Holt enjoyed *Porgy and Bess*—she saw it four times—and rebuffed those who were "reading into it the stigma of ridicule," but she acknowledged a need for "other plays and operas . . . depicting the finer side of the Negro which would in turn balance the influence of these risibilities."[76] "Where, if any, are our younger composers?," she wondered. Even as she celebrated Black performers, Holt maintained that new compositional voices would "live long after those purveyors of song have passed, signally giving to the world the soul thoughts of a race."[77] The politicization of opera as a vehicle for desegregation was never disentangled from long-standing struggles for Black musical and social self-determination.

Although much ink was spilled about desegregation at the Met, many years would pass before that company revised its exclusionary policies. Change came sooner at New York City Opera (NYCO), founded in 1943 as a more populist alternative to the Met with lower ticket prices, a commitment to producing opera in English, and a willingness to cast lesser-known singers in major roles.[78] In October 1945, the company engaged baritone Todd Duncan in two productions: first Tonio in *Pagliacci,* then Escamillo in *Carmen.* In 1946, it hired soprano Camilla Williams to sing Cio-Cio-San in *Madama Butterfly.* Widely celebrated in the Black and white presses, these occasions epitomized how the opera house was increasingly understood as a symbol for democratic social organization and racial progress. For Duncan and Williams, they also prompted a more complex reckoning with the politics of inclusion and the public impulse to exceptionalize, and thus decontextualize, their work. Both singers strove to balance a rhetorical focus on their work's democratic social import with recognition of the countercultural forces that were fundamental to their success.

Duncan, an acclaimed educator and musician, came to NYCO with a wealth of experience. A decade earlier, he had starred as Porgy in the first production of *Porgy and Bess*. (Anne Brown characterized him as "the one person in the cast who <u>never</u> made a musical mistake").[79] He sang in *Cavalleria Rusticana* opposite Abbie Mitchell with the short-lived Aeolian Opera Company in 1934, then appeared on Broadway and in film during the early 1940s, all while continuing to teach voice at Howard University. His debut with NYCO was celebrated in the Black press as both the realization of a long-held dream and an unprecedented breakthrough, the result not of white companies' belated beneficence but of Duncan's "many years of hard study, grim experiences and disappointments he has weathered to secure the coveted role of a top-flight singer."[80]

As the *Afro-American* noted, Duncan's debut as Tonio was also "the first example of such casting in opera, that is, in which a colored person appears in a role not specifically designated as calling for a colored performer."[81] The singer had long sought to evade the parameters of what Nina Sun Eidsheim calls "sonic blackness": when he auditioned for the part of Porgy, he recounted, Gershwin was flummoxed by the "paradox" of a "a Negro singing for a Jew and singing an old Italian aria of the eighteenth century, auditioning for an opera whose site was to be in South Carolina."[82] By 1945, Duncan proudly reflected that while he "used to study the 'dark-skinned' roles—'Aida,' 'L'Africaine,' 'Lakme,'" he subsequently "forgot all about [them] and began to work on any that I liked," as "an artist sings roles best suited to his voice regardless of nationality or colour."[83] His NYCO debut suggested that the rationale of a "natural fit" between performer and character could at long last be replaced by a putatively raceless focus on vocal type and quality.

This ostensibly universalist approach to casting may have aligned with Duncan's own ambitions, but it was also fueled by historical circumstances that repositioned the Black opera singer as a symbol of American democracy. Limiting Black singers to racialized roles—effectively, reproducing the logic of segregation onstage—would no longer suffice. The Hungarian-born director of NYCO, Laszlo Halasz, lauded Duncan as "the best of American talent," eliding race to showcase national unity.[84] Critic E. B. Rea cited a recent occasion in Germany when Afro-Caribbean conductor Rudolph Dunbar led the Berlin Philharmonic in a program of "The Star-Spangled Banner," Tchaikovsky, and William Grant Still's Symphony no. 1, "Afro-American." "Dunbar already has struck a blow for democracy and tolerance with his performance," Rea proclaimed, and "Mr. Duncan's performance will be equally as significant" in proving that "music can destroy racial

bigotry."[85] Kira Thurman has argued that Dunbar's appearance served to idealize the United States amid German denazification efforts, with his presence harnessed to mask the persistence of US racism.[86] Duncan's operatic performance raised similar issues in a domestic context, by denoting the possibility of a racially inclusive democracy during a time of antifascist politics and postwar patriotism.

Camilla Williams's 1946 debut in *Madama Butterfly* marked the first time that a Black woman obtained a contract with a major opera company. The occasion prompted celebratory rhetoric around civil rights ("Many ways are open to Negroes to crack the color line. Voting is one; excellence in music is another"), but it also compelled consideration of how operatic casting engaged with race beyond a Black-white binary.[87] Appearing at NYCO alongside an "array of racial adjuncts" including Greek and Italian performers, Williams comprised part of a "cultural and interracial experiment" to democratize opera.[88] While critics predicted that her debut, like Duncan's, could indicate "the beginning of a new trend in grand opera casting," they also suggested—oddly—that "her presence in the title role of 'Madame Butterfly' gave it an authenticity that it has previously lacked."[89] Conflating Williams, a twenty-six-year-old African American soprano, with Cio-Cio-San, a fictional, tragically fated Japanese teenager, this claim showed how Black singers continued to be perceived through racializing lenses even when they appeared in non-Black roles. Williams was not the first African American singer to assume an Orientalist role in opera, as Josephine Lee has shown: *L'Africaine,* a longstanding favorite of African American concert singers, and *Lakmé,* in which Lillian Evanti made her European debut in 1925, similarly carried "a degree of racial ambiguity" and conveyed the "sexual allure and high passion . . . associated with oriental and African heroines."[90] Rosalyn Story has argued that "the idea of a black Butterfly onstage was revolutionary," but more recently scholars have suggested that casting Williams as Butterfly relegated her to the "safe" space of an exotic, sexually desirable woman—a variation on racial typecasting rather than a subversion of it.[91]

In 1915, the Japanese soprano Tamaki Miura's US debut as Butterfly had prompted Black critics to make a case for the appearance of Black performers in racialized roles.[92] Now, it was suggested that Williams was an "authentic" Butterfly, a "real find" who could "portray Puccini's heroine with a vividness and subtlety unmatched by any other artist who has essayed the part here in recent years."[93] Williams herself reinforced this perspective, suggesting that she "became Butterfly" and that "the Japanese in the audience thought I was actually Japanese!"[94] Revising the rhetoric of self-making that

had long accompanied Black women's operatic vocality, Williams implied that her identification with Cio-Cio-San was such that it enabled her to essentially change her race, to "become" onstage "actually" Japanese. This was an especially audacious claim given the postwar context, and the fact that the opera had been banned from major US houses during World War II. Williams's appearance in *Madama Butterfly*'s return to the stage thus embodied a democratic victory in multiple senses, deploying a Black performer in an Asian role as a symbol of American triumph.

Williams's debut also offers a prime example of how Black artists continued to honor and recognize the marginalized roots of their work. Born and raised in Danville, Virginia, Camilla Williams began singing as a child. Black social and musical networks were fundamental to her training, identity, and career. At Virginia State College, her teacher was Cleota Collins—a soprano who worked with Nora Holt at *Music and Poetry*, helped found NANM in 1919, and became a protégé of Azalia Hackley. Williams later recalled that after she lost a singing contest as a student, Collins assuaged her disappointment by taking her to visit her "close friend" Camille Nickerson, another esteemed vocal teacher who "supported young black performers at Howard University and beyond."[95] Williams also enjoyed the support of Beatrice Godfrey, a fellow Virginian who starred as Saint Teresa in *Four Saints in Three Acts*. Indeed, Williams first studied the score of *Madama Butterfly* while sitting on Godfrey's front porch in Virginia.[96] The scene offers a striking contrast to the notion of Williams being thrust into the position of triumphant democratic symbol, instead suggesting how Puccini's opera could foster intergenerational countercultural connection within and beyond the mainstream opera house.

An especially influential figure in Williams's life was none other than Nora Holt. Holt attended both Williams's NYCO debut and the rehearsals that preceded it, an experience Williams recalled as "quite special for me."[97] In an interview on the eve of the performance, Williams implored Holt, "Whatever you do, don't forget to mention Miss Collins in the story about me, as the teacher at Virginia State College who gave me invaluable instruction in voice production and interpretation. She was wonderful and I can never forget her."[98] The repeated invocation of "forgetting" cautioned against the erasure of Black women's musical networks, and it shows how carefully Williams located herself within this lineage. It made an impression on Holt, who, years later, recalled that "before [Williams] made her debut on that memorable night, this writer interviewed her during one of the rehearsals, and with great loyalty she expressed a wish that credit be given the teachers and college where she received her early training."[99]

A photograph of Williams in *Madame Butterfly,* autographed "To the Hackley Memorial Collection. Sincerely, Camilla Williams '51." Williams's words, overlaid on the image, suggest her multifaceted efforts to locate her performance within Black musical genealogies.

The multiple narratives that emerge around Williams's debut as But-terfly—her symbolic role as a figure of postwar desegregation, appearance in a non-Black racialized role, and enduring relationship to Black operatic counterculture—are inextricably linked. Collectively, they demonstrate how framing Black singers' performances as proxies for racial progress can have an obfuscating effect. Considering Williams exclusively as a notable "first" or harbinger of change minimizes not only her own past experiences, but also those of the figures who mattered most to her. The resulting erasure exceptionalizes Williams, portraying her as a singular star rather than a member of a musical and cultural community. In this light, we might read Williams's insistence that we "don't forget" her past as not just a gesture of intergenerational respect, but also as a political claim that pushed back against the incoming tide of erasure that accompanied the mainstream rec-ognition of Black operatic singing.

In 1951, sixteen years after Abbie Mitchell first sang "Summertime," Camilla Williams made a recording of the same song. The circumstances were very different. "Summertime" had become iconic, the subject of covers by singers and instrumentalists from Billie Holiday (1936) to Sidney Bechet (1939) to Helen Dowdy (1942). Williams sang it in the context of the first full recording of *Porgy and Bess*.[100] Wary of associating herself with the stereotype-laden Bess, she had never sung the part onstage.[101] As she later explained, "I loved the music in *Porgy and Bess* but I thought then, and still think, it should be restaged. If works by Wagner and Mozart can be restaged, why can't they restage *Porgy and Bess*? Black folks don't live like that anymore, playing craps and living the low life. We've moved on from that. African Americans have made great steps from that sort of existence. Why should we allow ourselves to be portrayed like that? *Porgy and Bess* is so popular and every time it is performed, it perpetuates the stereotypes."[102] Williams's comments, notwithstanding their elitist tone, emphasize the opera's static plot, inability to be reimagined in the manner of other canonical operas, and reproduction of racist images. Her dissatisfaction—"why should we allow ourselves to be portrayed like that?"—highlights the limitations of Gershwin's vision and positions her voice as racially representative.

Williams's comments suggest that in the age of desegregation, to be a "first" was to walk down a precarious path. If disparate events of this era, from the premiere of Gershwin's opera to Williams's NYCO debut, were framed as unambiguous symbols of democratic political change, they actually revealed how tenuous the connection between art and politics could be. Aesthetic novelty could accompany political revanchism, as when the ensembles who assembled on Broadway for *Four Saints* and *Porgy and Bess* were tasked with reproducing stale tropes about Black life. Paradoxically, the canon seemed to offer more promise as an agent of social change. The NNOC's productions of Verdi creatively repositioned the Black opera singer as a model citizen, while the NYCO's postwar soloists used Puccini, Leoncavallo, and Bizet to dismiss the racialized role as a relic of Jim Crow. To make sense of these apparent contradictions requires turning to these events' shared countercultural roots. Decades of activity among Black operatic artists created the conditions under which they could enter onto mainstream stages, establish new autonomous institutions, and maintain a nuanced perspective on the relationship between these two goals. Across institutional contexts, artists remained aware of their indebtedness to extant Black musical networks, as well as their ability to wrest affective and social meaning from their work.

Williams's interpretation of "Summertime" offers a powerful illustration of this commitment. Like the many Black women artists past and present who have, as Daphne Brooks argues, "navigated, complicated, and transformed the charged aesthetics of *Porgy and Bess*," Williams makes Bess her own.[103] She imbues the character with authority. Freed from the imperative to embody the character onstage, Williams sings with a lyrical, light sound that befits the work's ambiguous status between opera and musical theater. Whereas she had attempted to "become" Butterfly on the NYCO's stage, her rendition of "Summertime" uses timbral precision to maintain a critical distance from Bess.[104] Eschewing any hint of improvisatory freedom in her phrasing, Williams elects to sing the aria in an almost stern, aloof style, one in which both performer and character appear entirely in control.[105] Her steady pacing, impeccably placed high notes, and evenly paced diminuendo at the end of the aria create a sound that might be described as authoritative, even authorial: a style that maintains fidelity to Gershwin's music but "restages" his ideas. In Williams's voice, "Summertime" makes audible the promise of its lyrics: she refuses the harm of stereotype, making it possible to "rise up singing" to a place of self-possession.

❧ 7 ☙

Open Doors and Shadow Archives

The day was near, and the anticipation was high. "Never before had so many librettos been seen lying around Harlem homes," observed a local columnist, as residents "boned up on their Verdi" in preparation for the occasion to come.[1] At dawn on January 7, 1955, those who had not yet secured tickets to the sold-out performance began lining up outside the Metropolitan Opera House as early as 5:30 A.M., hoping to secure a standing-room-only spot. Undeterred by bitterly cold temperatures, they were determined to see Marian Anderson make her long-awaited Met debut as Ulrica in Verdi's *Un ballo in maschera*—the first time the company would engage a Black singer in a leading role. The *New York Times* circulated the news of Anderson's engagement under the triumphalist headline "A Door Opens," using a spatial metaphor frequently invoked in relation to operatic desegregation. It had been predicted that the Ferrari Fontana Vocal Trials, in 1925, would "open [the] door of fame to colored girl[s] in opera"; that Caterina Jarboro's debut as Aida, in 1933, would engender an "open door of opportunity"; that the Aeolian Opera Company, in 1934, would unlock "the Open Door, for Negroes to walk into the field of Opera." Nora Holt rightfully noted, in 1950, that although "Negro artists have been knocking at the door of grand opera since the turn of the century," they still had not reached its most prestigious stages.[2] The Vocal Trials' winners never sang at the Met; Jarboro appeared with no other American companies; and the Aeolian disbanded after just one performance. Had the moment of more lasting change finally arrived?

Yes and no. For a small coterie of African American artists—exceptionally talented singers, mostly women—the 1950s did inaugurate what one observer called a "deluge" of opportunities, including engagements to sing full roles at elite opera houses.[3] But little changed for those who already maintained a lower-frequency presence in the opera house: the countless supernumeraries who appeared at the Met in hundreds of productions of *Aida,* or people like Edward "Black Carl" Johnson (whose job, beginning fifty-one years prior to Anderson's debut, was quite literally to stand at the threshold of the opera house and open its doors). For Black composers, the mainstream opera house remained generally out of reach, as companies continued to produce almost exclusively white-authored, canonical operas. Even as the achievements of figures like Anderson were deservedly celebrated, progress and stasis intermingled: moments of meaningful change were set against a backdrop of an enduring reliance on white-authored representations of Blackness onstage and the continued exclusion of Black listeners and composers from the art form's mainstream.

The rhetorical figure of the "open door" had additional limits. It had served a crucial purpose during the early twentieth century, foregrounding the injustice of a Jim Crow regime that excluded African Americans from critical facets of public life, but it took on a different valence as the long civil rights movement gathered speed. While it demanded inclusion in existing institutional spaces, it did not necessarily demand more than that. It elided questions of representation: whether, once inside the opera house, Black singers would be compelled to sing the same limited roles over and over, or be subject to what Nina Sun Eidsheim calls "phantom genealogies" that primed audiences to hear their voices as interchangeable and inherently racialized.[4] By privileging entrance into historically white spaces as the primary or most significant form of Black artists' engagement with opera, it effaced the art form's capacious history within the Black public sphere, as well as the Black musical networks whose collective labor and advocacy made a moment like Anderson's debut possible. Further, in equating the desegregation of the opera house with the appearance of a single Black singer therein, the "open door" elevated the star over the collective. Inclusion and exceptionalism became conceptually linked, as the figure of the individual Black opera singer came to stand in for the entire past and present of Black operatic artistry.

The years that passed between Camilla Williams's NYCO debut in 1946 and Marian Anderson's appearance at the Met in 1955 were a period of celebration, ambivalence, and reinvention. Efforts to gain entrance into the mainstream opera scene, premised on a fundamental demand

DREAMING IN ENSEMBLE

for racial justice, proved successful: Jim Crow segregation in the opera house was being dismantled, piece by piece. But at the same time, increased participation in previously segregated endeavors prompted the decline of Black operatic counterculture as a distinct cultural phenomenon—a manifestation of what Gerald Horne calls the "Jim Crow paradox," in which the success of Black institutions in a segregated society ultimately created the conditions for their own irrelevance.[5] Having long staked out a marginal position in relation to opera's mainstream, African Americans were now compelled to renegotiate that relationship as they considered how they might continue to reinvent opera from within its central institutions. In parallel, those who remained outside the opera house's doors—composers, singers, and impresarios who were unwilling or unable to join the mainstream—strove to preserve a place for Black artistic self-determination.

The story of Black opera during the 1940s and 1950s is one in which success and frustration coincide, inclusion and confinement are linked, and the relationship between the margins and the mainstream is perpetually in flux. Black artists and activists led the charge for major companies to add African American singers to their rosters. Yet white institutions remained far less likely to produce an opera by a Black composer than to engage an individual singer, and those productions that did occur could represent a sort of pyrrhic victory, as composers with long-held commitments to the art form, including Harry Lawrence Freeman and William Grant Still, met with unsatisfactory performance conditions and critical responses. Beyond the stage, many artists, especially those nearing the end of their careers, began to think in self-consciously archival terms about their individual and collective legacies, aiming to secure a place in the historical record via memoirs, collages, scrapbooks, and scores.

But even though midcentury desegregation was uneven and piecemeal, Black operatic artistry continued to coalesce around a shared set of aesthetic and social priorities. The desegregation of major institutions became especially visible during these years, yet it never became the singular or ultimate focus of Black artists' engagement with the art form. They remained invested in thinking about opera in capacious ways; the projects of transforming existing operatic institutions, creating new ones, *and* remaking the art form in the process were not incompatible, but intertwined. If conditions of exclusion had long informed the relationship between Blackness and opera, they had never dictated the contours of that relationship. Rather than understanding the open door as an endpoint in and of itself, Black artists continued to embrace opera's speculative and fantastical aesthetics,

imagining operatic worlds in excess of those that then existed. Rather than settling comfortably into the opera house, they continued to work collaboratively, both within and beyond mainstream institutions, to find opportunities for meaningful sociality within the art form. Most fundamentally, they retained a vital focus on what opera meant to the people who took part in it—from Anderson herself, at long last appearing on the Met stage, to the hundreds of listeners who lined up to hear her sing.

Activism, Performance, and the "Aida Pattern"

In 1949, the concert manager Dick Campbell observed that the "top rung of the ladder that leads to glory and success for the Negro in America is crowded to the point of congestion these days . . . Sports, music, art, theatre, movies, radio, sculpture, politics, diplomacy, medicine, science, chemistry, military, law, and education are goals where the score has been made, the touchdown accomplished, the victory won. But look closely and you'll find one category missing—opera. True, Negroes have achieved a modicum of success in this greatest of all forms of musical art, but they have yet to crash the majors, 'the Met.'"[6] As African American "firsts" snowballed across the US cultural scene, opera was gaining a reputation as a "last bastion" of racial exclusion, an elite exception to the rule of societal transformation.[7] Seeking to remedy this situation, operatic artists and activists aligned their work with the rhetoric and tactics of other struggles for civil rights. During World War II, Black critics and singers had framed the desegregation of US stages as a democratic imperative. In the immediate postwar era, they both furthered this line of thinking *and* resurrected an earlier emphasis on the racialized role—a strategically useful but ultimately more conciliatory approach that offered activist campaigns a cohesive focus while implicitly proposing a pathway toward desegregation that did not upend opera's extant racial hierarchies.

There was no shortage of excellent singers. A group of extraordinarily talented, classically trained young artists—Dorothy Maynor, Carol Brice, Inez Matthews, and others, collectively characterized by Rosalyn Story as the "mid-century divas"—gained a foothold as recitalists.[8] Established figures like Caterina Jarboro continued to attract critical praise. When Jarboro gave a recital in New York in 1942, Virgil Thomson provocatively deemed her "the Last of the Divas," whose vocal prowess was matched by "a truly great dramatic temperament." Her rendition of arias from *Aida* and *Die Walküre* prompted effusive admiration: "No soprano at the Metropolitan Opera House is doing that kind of dramatic singing today," Thomson

raved. "I had thought the species was extinct; but there she is, a diva, no less, grand and glamorous and beautiful and a thoroughgoing professional."[9] But Jarboro was a diva without an opera house, because opportunities for Black singers remained scarce.

Efforts to desegregate opera once again coalesced around the racialized role. By 1951, one critic identified an "Aida pattern" in operatic casting, in which Verdi's opera remained "the only operatic vehicle in which most Negro singers were featured."[10] Although Camilla Williams's 1946 NYCO debut (and subsequent appearances in two other non-Black parts, Nedda in *Pagliacci* and Mimì in *La bohème*) had seemed to presage an expansion of possibilities, Williams was engaged to sing Aida with the company in 1948, alongside bass-baritone Lawrence Winters. The *Amsterdam News* observed: "The opera of 'Aida' is a natural for singers of African blood to portray Amonasro, the captured king of Ethiopia and his princess daughter Aida, held as a slave by Egyptians. It has taken seventy-seven years for an opera company to bridge the gap between precedent and comparable artistry to highlight Verdi's magnificent work with a touch of realism which gives the opera an authentic impact never before achieved . . . The appearance of Camilla Williams as Aida and Lawrence Winters as Amonasro gave credence to the production and made it a living epic of social significance which must have crossed the minds of those who saw the stirring performance."[11] The review relied on the familiar trope that Black performers would lend a "natural," "authentic" "realism" to Verdi's opera. But it updated that idea by suggesting that their appearance also served a politically salient purpose. Transforming Verdi's opera into a "living epic of social significance," these artists could illustrate its relevance to the contemporary struggle for Black freedom.

When soprano Ellabelle Davis made her debut as Aida in 1946, she employed a similar strategy. Born in 1907 in New Rochelle, New York, Davis began her singing career by performing duets with her sister, Marie. While working as a seamstress to support herself, she earned a role in a 1941 production of an eighteenth-century operetta, *The Chaplet*, at the Museum of Modern Art.[12] She sought opportunities beyond the United States, touring Latin America in the mid-1940s.[13] In 1946, Davis sang *Aida* with the Opera Nacional in Mexico City, attracting an audience that included such political heavyweights as the US ambassador and the president of Venezuela.[14] In a *Time* profile, she explicitly characterized her performance as an activist effort aligned with the civil rights movement: "I want to prove that a Negro singer doesn't have to stay in his own backyard. In a singer, it is the color of the voice and not of the face which matters. If I'm a success in Aida I will

carry the fight to the doors of the Met."[15] Eleanor Roosevelt dedicated her syndicated "My Day" column to Davis's performance, amplifying this message. Appealing to national and cultural pride, Roosevelt argued that the failure to desegregate opera houses was a national embarrassment. "We in the United States," she admonished, "let our prejudices spoil our enjoyment of talent."[16] Reprinted in leading Black newspapers, Roosevelt's column cast Davis's debut as a galvanizing call for change.

In support of her barrier-breaking ambitions, Davis meticulously crafted a public persona that emphasized her exceptional talent, respectable background, and history-making potential. One promotional booklet foregrounded the incomparable nature of her voice, which was of a caliber heard "once in a century," "never before," "rarely in a lifetime," "seldom within memory," and "only a few times in history."[17] She was situated within a "long and illustrious tradition" of Black singers, encompassing nineteenth-century divas like Sissieretta Jones, who had been excluded from operatic stages—and whose dreams she was thus well-positioned to fulfill.[18] Rejecting the presumption that her race would dictate her repertoire, Davis explained that she did not sing spirituals on recital programs because while "a Negro who grew up in a rural Southern community, with spirituals as an integral part of his religious life, would sing those songs spontaneously and with genuine feeling," she, as a "professional musician," "would have to be taught." Davis elaborated, "I grew up and was educated in New Rochelle, on the commuter's line from New York City . . . all I know about spirituals I learned from the same white teacher who coaches me for concert and operatic work."[19] If these remarks pushed back against racialized generic norms, they also implied that as a professional trained by white experts, and as a respectable Black singer distinct from her rural, vernacular counterparts, Davis would not disrupt the aesthetic norms of the opera house. This notion was echoed in press coverage of her Mexico City debut. Whereas reviews of previous Aidas, including Cole-Talbert and Jarboro, had engaged deeply with matters of interpretation—how these artists chose to portray an enslaved princess, caught between love and country—critical accounts of Davis's performance contained curiously few details regarding vocality or characterization. Its functional utility to the civil rights movement superseded its creative dimensions.

When disentangled from the project of US desegregation, though, *Aida* remained a generatively open text. In 1948, the soprano Mayme Richardson traveled to Addis Ababa, where she performed scenes from the opera in recital and found herself "completely overcome by the spirit of freedom."[20] A reporter recounted that "her rendition of the aria from the opera, 'Aida,'

dressed in native Ethiopian costume, captivated her audience as she poured out Aida's sorrow song over being a captive far from her blue skies of Ethiopia. This may in part be attributed to the fact that an announcer gave a brief historical sketch of Aida as having been an Abyssinian princess in the national Amharic language . . . the audience got the point and responded accordingly."[21] Remade as a Du Boisian "sorrow song," the aria sidestepped the opera's colonialist origins, instead emphasizing its potential to articulate African diasporic solidarity.[22]

In the United States, Aida was at the center of a sustained campaign for desegregation helmed by the soprano and activist Muriel Rahn. Born in Boston in 1911, Rahn began acting and singing as a teenager, and she reached the finals of the Ferrari Fontana Vocal Trials in 1925. Her breakthrough role was Carmen in the 1943 Broadway production of *Carmen Jones,* the Americanized version of Bizet's opera. An outspoken advocate for racial justice who also worked as an educator, theater director, and union organizer, Rahn articulated her artistic and political ethos with forceful clarity: "Negro artists who 'retreat' into a rarified musical atmosphere and cover up their feelings with 'art' had better come down out of their ivory towers and face the bitter truth . . . Well, I am a Negro first and an artist second . . . Any Negro artist who fails to throw her moral, physical, financial and militant support to every fight that deserves it, is losing a great opportunity to contribute to racial progress."[23]

When, in August 1948, Rahn became the fourth Black singer to appear as Aida with Salmaggi's Chicago Grand Opera Company, she seized the opportunity to advocate for the desegregation of opera's biggest stage: the Met. In a letter addressed to the company's general manager, Edward Johnson, and reprinted widely in the Black press, she invited Johnson to hear her sing and asserted she would make a "pretty good Aida for the Met." She was "confident, willing, qualified, and able. All I want is a chance."[24] The press bolstered her efforts with headlines that critiqued the company by name: "The Met Bows Out as Salmaggi Soars"; "Singer Challenges Metropolitan Opera"; "Singer Seeks to Crash Metropolitan Opera Bias."[25] These efforts came to partial fruition in December 1948, when Rahn sang the second act of *Aida* on the Met stage at a benefit for the American Guild of Musical Artists (AGMA), the influential musicians' union on whose board she served.[26] The performance was lauded as an artistic triumph and strategic turning point. One critic wrote that Rahn had "wormed her way" into the Met, advancing her "'campaign' to open up operatic fields to colored artists."[27] In the *Courier,* Billy Rowe lauded Rahn's "precedent-establishing performance" as "the culmination of a long and untiring fight

to break the lily-white bonds which kept democracy out of the historic old house." In pointedly militaristic language that linked Rahn's work to the larger Black freedom struggle, he termed the event part of a "battle" "inspired . . . by the press"; Rahn had taken "individual shots at the Metropolitan and its governors," and the "result of that counter attack . . . shattered the barrier."[28]

Between 1949 and 1954, Rahn was engaged to sing Aida nearly a dozen times, including return appearances with Salmaggi's company and new engagements with the San Carlo Opera Company, New York Opera Society, and NNOC. She became a well-respected public figure, taking first place in a poll of who had "done the most for Harlem" ahead of Lena Horne, Marian Anderson, and Jackie Robinson.[29] Although she never appeared in a full role at the Met, she did audition privately for the company four times; her audition record shows, with dismaying concision, that she was judged "pleasant" and "artistic," "but not good enough for us."[30] (A similar response befell Caterina Jarboro, who, upon auditioning in 1951, was evaluated as an "intelligent artist with experience" who had a "rather shaky middle range and no *piano*. Not for us except possibly chorus."[31]) But Rahn understood that even if her effort to sing with the company was not wholly successful, her 1948 appearance at the house retained great symbolic significance: as she later reflected, it "conditioned Met audiences they would soon be seeing Negroes singing there."[32]

Beyond the stage, Rahn was at the forefront of an organized effort to desegregate the Met, conducted primarily through direct correspondence with administrators. She was "quietly and without fanfare waging a powerful 'behind the scenes' fight," intimated one reporter.[33] In a 1952 letter to company administrator Max Rudolf, for example, she praised the company for hiring soprano Tomiko Kanazawa to sing Cio-Cio-San during a tour of Minnesota. "Such a fine demonstration of democratic principles toward an American-Japanese vocalist," Rahn wrote, "makes me feel that the time is not too far distant when an American-Negro soloist will be found who meets the high artistic demands of the world's most celebrated Opera Company."[34] Rahn was not alone in her efforts. In the *Courier*, George F. Brown castigated the Met's "ironclad policy of excluding Negro singers" and called for "sustained criticism." Given the institution's conservatism, he advised, "Picketing, mass meetings, lobbies, cajoling and the other devices of pressure groups would not be the proper strategy." Instead, he recommended a "long, intelligent, not-too-vociferous campaign" of boycotts, "conferences with the officials," and gaining donors' support.[35] In another article, "Public Opinion Could Change Metropolitan Policy," Brown wrote: "Wires and

Muriel Rahn in costume as Aida for her 1949 performance of the role with the San Carlo Opera Company in Boston.

letters to the Metropolitan Opera Company in New York will get results . . . The people throughout the United States can break their silence and bring this taboo subject into the open. There must be a constant hammering at the sensibilities of the officials of the Metropolitan. Another blow for democracy will be struck when the Metropolitan lets down its bars. It's your fight!"[36]

Answering this call, dozens of ordinary citizens wrote to the company. Rachel Leib, Iowa City, 1943: "Surely it could not be that their voices are

unsuited to opera?" Dean Murem, Long Island, 1944: "I'm sure that they would fit into opera perfectly if given a chance. I think that it's time society loosened up—don't you honestly think so too?" Morris Carrell, from a Navy ship in Nova Scotia, 1944: "Why is a negro or negress never permitted to sing at the Metropolitan Opera? . . . If steps such as this are not taken soon then I must feel that I am fighting for the wrong cause." Ernest Phillips, Harlem, 1946: "Dear Mr. Johnson . . . Marian Anderson cannot become a singer at the Met because she is a different color than you are. This is racial discrimination." A 1949 letter from Reginald Farrow of Philadelphia stands out for its angry conviction: the Met was "the most Nazi-like, Fascist-like organization on earth!" "The whole world knows," he wrote, "that while you profess 'opportunity' on one hand, you deny it on the other. They know that the American white man knows nothing about democracy." A company staffer annotated the letter: "This delicate—want Rudolf to handle?" The general manager, Edward Johnson, responded: "<u>Don't answer!</u>"[37]

The company maintained a posture of innocence. A reply to Rachel Leib insisted, "We here at the Metropolitan . . . have not shown the slightest prejudice." When Sylvia Golden, of the Committee for the Negro in the Arts, appealed directly to Johnson—"Mr. Johnson, it is people of your power who can help to break down discrimination against minorities"—his secretary replied stonily that "there is no discrimination shown." Administrators went so far as to craft a form letter to respond to expressions of support for Black singers. "While I have the greatest admiration for [their] voices," it read, "I have never heard, or learned, that they are qualified to fill important operatic roles . . . Our doors are thrown open wide to all who show promise of operatic possibilities, regardless of race, color or creed."[38] This blanket declaration disproved the very claim it made, effectively revealing that racial discrimination *was* a matter of policy. Black singers' agents received similar responses. When a representative for Caterina Jarboro suggested several singers whom the Met might engage, he was told: "Of the artists you mention, both Miss Anderson and Miss Brice have appeared in the Opera House during the last year, although not in opera, which, to our knowledge, neither has ever been interested in singing . . . There is no 'tradition' that Negroes are not 'permitted' on the Metropolitan stage—very few have studied for opera, and those who have must expect to be judged on the competitive basis which governs the engagement of any other singer."[39] Another letter claimed that "only comparatively recently have negro artists evinced interest in operatic careers, and it is probable that, with experience, in the future, they will achieve increasing prominence in the field."[40] Confronted with the undeniable prominence of Black artists on concert stages (and in countless

other fields), the company flatly rejected the notion that it had a social obligation to desegregate, turning instead to the rhetoric of colorblind meritocracy and the disingenuous suggestion that the absence of Black singers from its stage reflected a lack of interest and experience.

For evidence of the falsity of this claim, the Met did not need to look further than its own ranks. In 1954, the company hired pianist and vocal coach Sylvia Olden Lee, the first African American member of the organization's artistic staff. Lee's family history exemplified the depth and longevity of Black musicians' operatic aspirations. Her father had been a member of Fisk University's Jubilee Quartet who, she recalled in memoirs, spent "every day of his life for five years" with Roland Hayes as they toured with the group.[41] Her mother, Sylvia Olden, adored opera; as a teenager in New Orleans, she took a job cleaning at the city's French Opera House so that she could afford tickets to hear Enrico Caruso. She cherished a copy of *Madama Butterfly* that her brother had given her with the inscription, "To Sylvia, hoping someday."[42] When she joined the Fisk Jubilee Singers as a college student, Olden attracted the admiration of Paul Cravath, a lawyer whose father had been the president of Fisk University, and who became board chairman of the Metropolitan Opera in 1931. In 1912, Cravath proposed that she could sing at the Met if she were willing to pass as white; she refused the offer because it would mean abandoning her family and community.[43] Her daughter, Sylvia Olden Lee, grew up in Washington, DC, where she attended recitals by Abbie Mitchell and accompanied Todd Duncan's vocal students at Howard. In 1943, she served as pianist for the NNOC's production of *La Traviata*. When she first moved to New York with her husband, the violinist and conductor Everett Lee, she practiced the piano on an instrument that had belonged to Scott Joplin.[44]

Olden Lee became a vociferous advocate for institutional desegregation. When her husband began to study conducting with Max Rudolf, the couple was invited to dinner at Rudolf's home. She recounted: "The first thing I did when I met this man, came to his house informally, I said: 'I want to know, when is a Negro . . . going to get a chance to sing at the Metropolitan?' And I told him about my mother." Olden Lee suggested that desegregation was both a matter of present-day equity and a reparative measure, given the Met's historical treatment of Black singers. Rudolf assured her, "It'll happen, Sylvia, but you know, the first singer, at the Met, of color, has got to have the greatest voice, the finest talent, training, and be an absolutely incontestible, excellent musician, and the first part that he or she sings, must be visually believable."[45] In response, Olden Lee, who had recently listened to *Un ballo in maschera* on the radio, suggested

that the company cast a Black singer as Ulrica—the precise role in which Marian Anderson would soon appear. "Since it was my idea to cast the role of Ulrica with a Negro contralto," she later avowed, "Maestro Rudolf presented me with box one for Miss Anderson's debut on January 7, 1955."[46] Olden Lee's ability to advocate directly to Rudolf on Anderson's behalf stemmed from her insider status at the Met, but her impulse to do so emerged from her roots in Black musical circles.

When Anderson's debut at long last arrived, it represented the culmination of decades of activist efforts forged by Davis, Rahn, Olden Lee, and countless others, named and unnamed. The occasion is typically regarded as the result of overdue, but admirable, choices on the part of Met administrators. More recently, scholars have emphasized the incremental nature of this shift (showing, for instance, how Anderson's debut followed on the heels of African American dancer Janet Collins's 1951 appearance in *Aida* and subsequent engagement as prima ballerina with the company), as well as the role of Black political organizations like the NAACP in putting pressure on the Met to act.[47] But such accounts nonetheless privilege institutional actors in the political and cultural spheres as agents of change. A shift in focus to the less visible efforts of Black women artists elucidates that those individuals who gained a foothold within mainstream institutions—Rahn through her work with AGMA, Olden Lee through her position at the Met—worked proactively to desegregate these institutions from within, a process crucial to the eventual incorporation of Black singers in leading roles.

In many ways, the selection of Anderson to sing at the Met made both political and musical sense. A celebrity of international renown with impeccable artistic credentials, she had previously established a connection in the national consciousness between desegregation and the Black classical voice.[48] Her 1939 performance at the Lincoln Memorial, arranged after the Daughters of the American Revolution's notorious refusal to allow her to sing at Constitution Hall, served as what Gayle Wald calls a moment of "political theater of the highest order," in which musical performance functioned "as an instrument of oppositional consciousness."[49] Howard Taubman called it "no longer a concert but a democratic manifestation."[50] In the years that followed, she became involved in various desegregationist campaigns. The NAACP had arranged for Anderson to perform recitals on the Met stage multiple times, literally and figuratively setting the stage for her role debut.[51] Although she performed for segregated audiences during much of her career, she sometimes engaged in quiet gestures of resistance: for instance, at a segregated hall in Houston, Texas, she "bowed perfunctorily straight in front of her, then turned deliberately toward those of her own

race and bowed very low and long." Critic Harry Keelan, who was in the audience, called it "the most beautiful and queenly gesture I have ever seen."[52] When her debut was announced, the *Amsterdam News* observed that for decades, "the voice of Jim Crow was far more influential than the most admirable baritone or coloratura soprano in America's most distinguished hall of music."[53] Now that injustice would be remedied.

But in other ways, Anderson was a less obvious fit. Less overtly invested in political change than Muriel Rahn or Ellabelle Davis, she was tightlipped about her extramusical opinions. She had expressed ambivalence about the Lincoln Memorial event, reflecting, "I could see that my significance as an individual was small in this affair. I had become, whether I liked it or not, a symbol, representing my people."[54] Anderson had also never expressed a desire to sing at the Met, nor had she ever performed a full operatic role. Decades earlier, her performance at NANM's first convention, in 1919, prompted Nora Holt to compare her voice to "that of Rosa Raisa, the wonderful contralto of the Chicago Grand Opera Company."[55] But while she occasionally sang operatic arias, she was more drawn to lieder and spirituals, and although she received a handful of tentative offers to sing roles such as Carmen and Amneris in Europe, these never materialized. Her voice was not suited for racially marked soprano roles like Aida or Bess; moreover, she may not have wanted to risk undermining her ultrarespectable persona by portraying operatic characters that linked Black women to scandal, abjection, and disrepute.

At the Met, the central paradox of entrance into opera via racialized roles remained. As Nina Sun Eidsheim has noted, Ulrica was a character marked as nonwhite and exotic, described in the libretto as a mysterious sorceress with "negro blood."[56] In an article published in the *Times* just days before Anderson's debut, the company's newly appointed general manager, Rudolf Bing, suggested that racialized casting remained a precondition for Black singers. In one paragraph, he proudly touted Anderson's upcoming appearance; in the next, he scaled back, writing, "Eva in 'Die Meistersinger' might be difficult with a Negro singer; nor could I easily envisage a Negro Elsa in 'Lohengrin.'"[57] This was a precarious basis for further change. Bing's approach, which was predicated on the putatively "colorblind" recognition of artistic aptitude yet was still indebted to the logic of the racialized role, created unprecedented opportunities for an exceptional few, but it concomitantly diminished the commitment to collective engagement and systemic transformation that had long animated Black operatic counterculture.

Observers within Black musical circles situated Anderson's debut within a more expansive history. The NNOC's Mary Cardwell Dawson commented

Marian Anderson in her role of Ulrica at the Metropolitan Opera, 1955.

that although the Met had "belatedly opened its doors to the internationally famous contralto Marian Anderson," this was insufficient, as "within
our race thousands of singers and musicians with rare operatic gifts seek
to be heard." Her aim, in contrast, was to "open *wide* the door," ensuring
that opera remained a collective endeavor.[58] The critic Carl Diton reminded readers that Anderson's achievement—while momentous—was "no
sudden thing," given that "around 1900, it was Theodore Drury, himself
an ambitious Negro singer, who made pioneer promotion experiments
with such operas as Carmen."[59] Diton's comments articulated how Anderson's exceptional, ostensibly groundbreaking performance relied on decades
of collective learning and labor. Another commentator deemed Drury the

"father of Negroes in opera," a turn of phrase that, paradoxically, performed its own sort of erasure, by obscuring the ensembles that had participated in his productions in relative anonymity.[60]

A rejoinder to that erasure might be heard in the sound of Anderson's voice. She studied the role extensively, and the performance was rapturously received, with the audience applauding for nearly five minutes as soon as she appeared onstage.[61] But she was in her mid-fifties by 1955, and widely perceived to be past her vocal prime. Although her acting was exactingly intense ("there was no moment in which Miss Anderson's interpretation was commonplace or repetitive in effect," one critic wrote), there was an "unexpected tremulousness in her voice."[62] Typically construed as a symptom of nervousness or technical decline, this vocal quality also offered sonic evidence of how Anderson singularly embodied the longevity of Black operatic counterculture and the belated date of her own arrival on this stage. Sounding out decades of thwarted aspirations, it relayed what Daphne Brooks calls the "revolutionary potential" of the "Black feminist curatorial performer," who "boldly alters our relationship to the sonic past, ferociously jolts dominant perceptions of history, and consistently awakens listeners to the meaning and value of Black women's lives and livelihood that undergirds that history."[63] The grain of her voice conveyed a half-century of efforts to reach the Met, an aural reminder that she was roughly the same age as Jessie Zackery and Marguerite Avery, the women who had won the Ferrari Fontana Vocal Trials thirty years prior. Anderson became not only a barrier-breaking performer, but also an embodiment of the dreams and aspirations of those artists whose collective efforts led to this moment.

Margins and Martyrs

As major opera companies began to engage Black performers, the work of Black composers stayed largely outside their purview. The Harlem Renaissance–era surge of interest in operas by Black composers and white-authored works about Black lives, from *Tom-Tom* to *Porgy and Bess,* diminished in the postwar era. Canonical repertory remained dominant: the Met season during which Anderson made her debut, for instance, featured eight performances of *Aida,* ten of *La bohème,* and twelve of *Carmen.*[64] The sharply differentiated trajectories of performance and composition reflected the racial politics of mainstream desegregation. Economic support for Black opera companies remained scarce, and for white institutions, producing an opera by a Black composer was a far more involved project, one requiring a greater

financial and artistic commitment than engaging an individual singer for a handful of performances. Moreover, operas by Black composers, which were likely to require multiple African American artists and possibly no white ones, failed to offer the portrait of harmonious interracial music-making that liberal integrationist logics demanded. When works by Black composers were staged, the process could be rife with difficulties, from material constraints to critical skepticism to interpretive disagreements. Under such circumstances, it became increasingly difficult for Black operatic composition to serve as a site of political critique or creative worldbuilding.

A 1947 production of Harry Lawrence Freeman's *The Martyr* epitomized the conditions under which Black composers now worked. Fifty-four years had passed since the opera's Denver premiere, and the composer, now in his late seventies, had composed nearly two dozen more operas. His son, Valdo, arranged for the rental of Carnegie Hall on a Sunday afternoon in late September. Promotional materials emphasized the enduring presence of Freeman's grand operatic vision by featuring the same image of a scene from *The Martyr* that had accompanied decades' worth of materials for his Negro Grand Opera Company. But much had changed since the opera's initial production. Whereas in 1893 Freeman had directed a cast of African American amateurs with no operatic experience—singers who also worked as cooks, schoolteachers, waiters, and clerks—he now engaged an interracial cast of professional singers. Muriel Rahn (billed as the "former 'Carmen Jones' star") starred in the role of Shirah, alongside Betty Voorhees as Meriamum, Italian American tenor Louis Rocca as Pharaoh, Loys Price as Platonus, and Paul Robinson as the high priest Rei.[65]

The performance was, Valdo recalled, "the last opera we did," and it was marked by the financial challenges that had dogged Freeman's career. Although a promotional poster advertised "Elaborate Scenery!" it was still unclear, just days before, whether the group would be able to afford sets evoking the ancient Egyptian setting.[66] The advertised "symphony orchestra" (supervised by Sylvia Olden Lee's husband, Everett Lee) was not to be found, so some scenes were accompanied by a small group of instrumentalists, and others by piano alone. One reviewer noted that Shirah's virtuosic "farewell aria" "would have been infinitely more effective if accompanied by full orchestra rather than by piano," implying that the production's constraints hindered the realization of the composer's artistic vision. The reviewer also felt it necessary to clarify that though *The Martyr* was not a new opera, Black operatic composition as a whole "still remains in the experimental stage," associating Freeman's music with unmet potential rather than lifelong accomplishment.[67]

THE MARTYR
An Original Grand Opera
By H. LAWRENCE FREEMAN
DEAN OF AMERICAN GRAND OPERA COMPOSERS

Featuring

Muriel Rahn

Former
"Carmen Jones" Star
as Prima Donna
Soprano

Will be Produced at

Carnegie Hall

SUNDAY
AFTERNOON

SEPT. 21st
At 2:00 O'clock

Elaborate Scenery!

Georgeous Costumes!

BETTYE VOORHEES, Noted Canadian Contralto.

LOUIS ROCCA, Celebrated Italian Tenor.

LOYS PRICE, Famous American Baritone.

PAUL ROBINSON, Sterling Young Negro Basso.

WAILERS: Emma Francis, Thelma Andrews, Johnie Parker and Violet Barker.

GRAND CHORAL ENSEMBLE under the Direction of Van Sylvester Whitted and Wesley Henderson.

MAGNIFICENT BALLETS by the Katherine Dunham Experimental Group.

A SYMPHONY ORCHESTRA of renowned personnel supervised by Everett Lee, Brilliant Violinist.

✒ **The Composer will Conduct** ✒

Scale of Prices : Orchestra $3.60 1st Tier Boxes $3.60. 2nd Tier Boxes $3.00
Dress Circle $2.40   Balcony A to H $1.80, J to N $1.20

Tickets on Sale at Carnegie Hall Box Office, 7th Avenue and 57th Street.
Also at the Opera Studio, 214 West 127th Street.

VALDO FREEMAN, Manager   Phone MOnument 2--8432

A poster for the 1947 Carnegie Hall performance of *The Martyr*, featuring the image of the opera that had accompanied Freeman's work throughout his career.

In the press, the opera was refigured less as an exemplar of Freeman's wide-ranging theoretical vision for Black opera or considerable achievements as a composer, and more as evidence of contemporary performers' worthiness to desegregate mainstream stages. Critics seized on the thematic parallels between *The Martyr* and *Aida,* both set in ancient Egypt. "'Martyr' Uncovers Star for Role in Met's 'Aida,'" one wrote, in an article that described Rahn as the "logical candidate for the Metropolitan's next production."[68] Performers—including Rahn herself—advocated more proactively for Freeman's compositions, albeit with limited success. Rahn included arias from *The Martyr* and *Vendetta* on national concert tours, and she became a personal friend to Freeman as well, sending him cheerful postcards from the road.[69] Another cast member, Paul Robinson, encouraged the Met to produce Freeman's work, even inviting Edward Johnson to come hear him sing excerpts from the operas in Freeman's studio.[70] There is no record of Johnson's response.

In 1949, two years after *The Martyr*'s showing at Carnegie Hall, New York City Opera presented William Grant Still's opera *Troubled Island.* Born in Mississippi in 1895, raised in Little Rock, and educated at Wilberforce and Oberlin, Still was among the most prominent Black composers in the United States by the 1940s. His early musical career had been stylistically heterogenous: he studied with the French modernist composer Edgard Varèse; played clarinet in the pit orchestra for *Shuffle Along;* arranged songs for Jewish vaudevillian Sophie Tucker and blues pioneer W. C. Handy; and composed pop songs under the pen name Willy M. Grant. In 1931, his well-received Symphony no. 1, "Afro-American," prompted a bevy of performances and additional orchestral commissions.[71] Yet he longed for greater attention to his operas, which he considered core to his compositional identity. "My love has always been opera," he wrote. "This love of operatic music, stimulated in my early youth by listening to operatic records, was the thing that first aroused the desire to compose. All my other work has been a means to this end."[72] Opera was "the dream of my life," he confided in a letter to fellow composer Clarence Cameron White: "I have tried every possible way to get a production—through musical people and through socially influential people. But I am convinced that the Metropolitan firmly intends to keep all of us out, and now I am sure that they are deeply prejudiced against Negroes . . . It may be that someday I'll see one of my operas performed. If so, I've told my wife that I won't believe it until I see the curtain go down on the last act."[73]

This pessimism proved prescient. Unlike Freeman, who spent much of his career at a real distance from the operatic mainstream, Still was beset

by a tantalizing closeness: productions of his work remained just out of reach. Fleeting expressions of interest often failed to materialize into real opportunities. When conductor Leopold Stokowski publicly affirmed his intention to produce one of Still's operas in 1944, for example, Still was "electrified," anticipating that it "ought to prove to someone that we can do things—that we don't have to have as vehicles some of the things other people 'cook up' for us all the time—as, for instance, 'Porgy and Bess,' 'Green Pastures,' and so on."[74] The performance never occurred. His frustrations mounted: in 1946, he wrote to White that with respect to opera, "as yet I have no news, and have despaired of ever getting any . . . I have waited over thirty years for this, and it always eludes me."[75]

But if the 1949 premiere of *Troubled Island* signaled the attainment of a long-sought goal for Still, it also represented both the possibilities and the perils that Black composers might encounter when they stepped through the opera house's open door. The opera, which tells the story of Jean-Jacques Dessalines's role in the Haitian Revolution, had a thorny origin story. Its libretto was by Langston Hughes, who adapted it from a play, *Emperor of Haiti,* which premiered in 1936 at the Playhouse Settlement in Cleveland (the same venue that helped facilitate Shirley Graham's commission for *Tom-Tom*). As Hughes worked to adapt the play into a libretto, he met occasionally with Still, but the collaboration was challenging; at one point, Hughes wrote to Still, "I am beginning to wish we were one person, like Wagner, so that our creativeness would be a single powerful force, indissoluble in its beauty and strength."[76] After Hughes left the United States to cover the Spanish Civil War as a correspondent for the Black press in 1937, the project fell by the wayside, and Still's wife, Verna Arvey, completed additional revisions to the libretto in Hughes's absence. Still dreamed of having the work staged, even constructing miniature sets while he orchestrated the piece so that he could visualize it fully. But when he submitted the score to the Met for consideration in 1939, it was rejected. Attempts to interest other companies throughout the 1940s failed, and Still and Hughes tussled over how to divide potential earnings. Music from the opera was heard only on scattered occasions: Ellabelle Davis and Muriel Rahn sang excerpts on recital programs, and a group of high-school students in Port-au-Prince performed arias.[77] By the time it arrived at NYCO, its reputation preceded it: Nora Holt, announcing the planned performances, noted the "siege" of "production troubles" that had plagued the work for years.[78]

Still's esteemed status as a composer of orchestral music no doubt shaped NYCO's eventual interest in his work, but so, perhaps, did his professed

apolitical stance. Although *Troubled Island* aligns with *Ouanga* in its focus on Dessalines's heroic role in Haitian history, and echoes *Tom-Tom* in its depiction of Africa as a utopian homeland, Still distanced himself from the world-making ambitions of earlier Black composers. He claimed no ideological investment in Black revolutionary history, insisting that the piece was best understood as an apolitical tale of love and patriotism.[79] He made the startling assertion that in *Troubled Island,* "there weren't great political implications. The rebellion is used merely as exposition. In substance, it's a love story."[80] He also avowed that the work was "American rather than Negroid," a surprising claim about an opera focused on Haitian history. This perspective suggests how an abiding concern with mainstream recognition might defang Black operatic counterculture's political edge, even with respect to an opera that dramatized the Black radical past. It also put Still at odds with Hughes. Philip Kaisary has argued that Hughes's play and libretto represent the "radical political path" that the author came to pursue in the 1930s, and that the subject matter offered a "heroic counternarrative of black freedom" in line with Hughes's increasingly outspoken anticapitalist and anticolonial politics.[81] By contrast, Still was an ardent anticommunist, and he and Hughes had what one scholar has called "genuine and unconcealed philosophical differences," particularly with respect to race.[82] While this ideological distance between librettist and composer was not intrinsically unworkable, it became a point of contention in a context where Black-authored operas were expected to serve as indicators of progress on civil rights, and thereby to advance legible political messages.

For Still, the premiere proved an exercise in frustration and disappointment. Its critical reception was famously mixed: while Nora Holt generously praised its "stirring drama, gripping music and moving text," other reviewers, including those writing for the Black press, bemoaned its unmemorable music, derivative qualities, and reliance on "old operatic patterns."[83] Responses to its political implications were similarly muddied. The *Amsterdam News* noted that the story of the Haitian Revolution had "overtones . . . significant of today," and it characterized *Troubled Island* in generalizing terms as about "man's search for freedom"—a phrase that might be read as Cold War–era praise of American democracy or, more subversively, as an endorsement of the struggle for Black freedom.[84] To Still, these critiques were evidence of racist misreading. He wrote to the conductor, Laszlo Halasz, that critics "failed to comprehend the opera—possibly because they expected the work to follow the lines of the stereotype which I abhor because of its falseness."[85] Eventually, Still came to believe that there

had been a critical conspiracy to denigrate the opera, claiming he had been told that "the critics have had a meeting to decide what to do about your opera. They think that the colored boy has gone far enough, and they voted to pan *Troubled Island*."[86] In the immediate aftermath of the premiere, he came to see Hughes's involvement as an additional liability, due to Hughes's outspoken leftist views and the friction they might prompt with presenting institutions. In effect, Still's commitment to opera, political conservatism, and disappointment with the reception of his work collided, culminating in an event that he understood as a profound failure.

The opera itself remains a more ambiguous document. Its best-known aria, "I Dream a World," appears in act 2, when the African elder Martel sings to Dessalines of his vision for a better future for Haiti. It is set to Hughes's utopian words:

> I dream a world where man
> No other man will scorn,
> Where love will bless the earth
> And peace its paths adorn.
> I dream a world where all
> Will know sweet freedom's way,
> Where greed no longer saps the soul
> Nor avarice blights our day.
> A world I dream where black and white,
> Whatever race you be,
> Will share the bounties of the earth,
> And ev'ry man is free,
> Where wretchedness will hang its head
> And joy, like a pearl,
> Attends the needs of all mankind—
> Of such I dream, my world![87]

Still's music is gently authoritative. The aria toggles between declarative phrases that return repeatedly to the tonic ("I dream a world where man no other man will scorn"), and more fanciful figures that rise higher into the singer's range ("where love will bless the earth and peace its paths adorn"). Mirroring the text's progression from a straightforward call for the absence of "scorn" to a more idealized vision of peace, love, and blessings—yet ultimately returning, melodically and conceptually, to the "world" where it began—the music never quite breaks into the free reverie that its text implies.

As Tammy Kernodle has observed, its "lush sonorities . . . convey little of the emotion and tension these words project."[88] Its earthbound affect suggests that there is minimal distance between the dreamed-of world and the actual one; that a world of racial harmony is firmly within reach.

Hughes's text, by contrast, is brilliantly double-voiced. While in the context of the opera it seems to call explicitly for Black liberation, it might also be understood as a plea for racial integration within a liberal democracy, allowing it to retain multi-signifying potential for a variety of audiences. Hughes had completed the poem prior to its incorporation into *Troubled Island,* and after the opera's fraught premiere, he repurposed the text in situations more aligned with his radical politics. It became his "signature poem": he would often end public readings by declaiming it, and he included it in a written statement to the House Un-American Activities Committee when he was called to testify in 1953.[89] His continued engagement with the text suggests that beyond the challenging circumstances of its premiere, and beyond the doors of the opera house, *Troubled Island* remained a rich aesthetic resource for Hughes. Separated from the institutional context in which it had first appeared, the aria gained additional significance and made meaning out of opera beyond the opera house—a gesture deeply resonant with Black operatic counterculture's past.

Commemoration as Counterculture

In the era of the open door, performers like Marian Anderson were celebrated as "firsts," exceptional cases whose extraordinary talent catalyzed their success. While such successes made clear the patent indefensibility of Jim Crow, these artists' ascendance also led to a pernicious new way of answering the question of who deserved a place on the operatic stage. The rationale of basic racial justice was superseded by a focus on conceptually slippery and fundamentally inegalitarian notions of merit and talent. Black artists took care to ensure that inclusion was not predicated on erasure, as when Camilla Williams honored her roots within Black musical networks upon her NYCO debut, or when critics showed how Anderson's Met appearance was indebted to Theodore Drury's pioneering efforts. Collectors and archivists maintained a creative, generatively marginal relationship to these developments. In personal and institutional archives, they cataloged the difficulties that aspiring operatic artists encountered, the experiential meanings they derived from the art form, and their hopes for its future. While some community-driven archival endeavors were openly invested in dismantling singular narratives of Black operatic achievement, others did their own

exceptionalizing work, commemorating not only the breadth of Black operatic history writ large, but also the role of particularly influential figures within that history.

Archives had been fundamental to Black operatic counterculture since its inception, from Freeman's creation of grandiose visual accompaniments to *The Martyr* to Shirley Graham's dramatization of Afrodiasporic sonic history in *Tom-Tom*. But in an era of putatively greater inclusion, commemorative and archival projects related to opera increased in both scope and significance. In his study of the Black "musician-writer," Brent Hayes Edwards redefines "jazz literature" to encompass writing influenced by jazz music as well as "writing *by* musicians . . . an enormous range of work, including not only autobiography but also music criticism, history, interviews, philosophy, fiction, poetry, drama, technical and instruction manuals, liner notes, and magazine and newspaper articles," which collectively exemplify a "persistent impulse" to refuse a neat divide between music and writing.[90] Black operatic artists' heterogenous print-cultural work at midcentury might be understood in analogous terms as "opera literature." Signaling a persistent connection between opera and the project of history-making, they evoked what Jean-Christophe Cloutier calls the "shadow archives" of twentieth-century African American literature—a conceit that builds on Kevin Young's notion of African American "shadow books," comprising texts that "fail to be written," those that have been "removed" from public view, and those that are lost: "written and now gone."[91] Memoirs, biographies, collages, scrapbooks, histories, libraries, and special collections conveyed the extent of Black artists' operatic ambitions and their commitment to documenting those ambitions for future generations.

A series of texts published in the late 1940s and early 1950s offered a counternarrative to the perception that Black participation in opera was new, unprecedented, or previously undesired. J. Rosamond Johnson, who completed an unpublished memoir in 1947, characterized opera as an unattainable dream: "I had dreams of composing Grand Opera and Symphonies, based on the native elements and themes from the songs of my people," he reflected, "but the necessity of raising monies to carry on the maintenance of the school, and the many hours devoted to teaching, my duties as organist at Salem Church, I was unable to carry out all of my dreams, in all of the things I dreamed of."[92] Nora Holt observed in 1950 that "the current opera craze is not new among Negro musicians," citing Drury and Freeman's endeavors as precedent.[93] Marguerite Davenport's 1947 biography of Azalia Hackley described her as "one of America's outstanding pioneers

in the field of serious music, who reached her apogee in the early twentieth century."[94] In testifying to generations of operatic artistry, these texts unsettled the fiction that segregation had been equivalent to absence.

Artists also documented the place of opera in their broader creative lives. In two remarkable and eclectic collages, the soprano Minto Cato commemorated her wide-ranging career. Cato's popular reputation rested largely on her work in musical theater, but her collages gave opera pride of place, emphasizing its centrality to her artistic sense of self. The first, if read left to right, suggests a chronological and generic progression from Cato's work in *Show Boat,* at the Cotton Club, and on television to her NNOC engagements. Conveying the scope of Cato's career as an "international musician" through its mention of various locales in which she appeared—New York, Paris, Israel, Hawaii, Egypt—it devotes nearly half the page to her work in opera. The second collage highlights major productions in which Cato performed: Lew Leslie's *Blackbirds of 1930,* in which she debuted the song "Memories of You"; *Aida,* which she performed with Salmaggi's company in 1937 and with the NNOC in Chicago in 1944; and *La Traviata,* which she sang with the NNOC in 1944. Glamorous images of Cato in costume are overlaid with a clipping from a review that praises her as a "dramatic soprano" who "compares to Rosa Ponselle of the Metropolitan

Two collages by Minto Cato documenting her career.

DREAMING IN ENSEMBLE

Opera Company" as well as "the world's greatest Negro singer, Mme. Sissieretta Jones."[95] A curatorial performance in their own right, the collages celebrated Cato's versatility while also locating opera at the forefront of her work.

Other, community-driven efforts honored the collective work of Black operatic counterculture, reflecting what Cloutier describes as the dual motivation of "private self-construction and public-minded group unity" characteristic of Black archival practice at midcentury.[96] In 1942, two prominent members of Detroit's Black classical community—Jerene Macklin, a founder of the Detroit Civic Opera, and Fred Hart Williams, president of the NANM-affiliated Detroit Musical Association—began a fundraising drive to create a collection honoring Azalia Hackley. Holding benefit concerts to support their efforts, they donated a collection of scores, manuscripts, and books to the Detroit Public Library in 1943. This repository, intended to offer "adequate evidence of the musical talent and potentialities

of colored American composers and musicians," became the first special collection dedicated to Black music in the United States.[97] Initially comprised of just a few dozen items, it grew to encompass more than one thousand by 1951.[98] Various local musicians joined in the collecting effort, and their personal investment in the preservation of Black musical history informed their work. One collector, Carlotta Franzell, was a coloratura soprano who, in 1938, appeared in the role of the High Priestess in the Detroit Civic Opera's production of *Aida;* in the early 1940s, she moved to New York City, joining the cast of *Carmen Jones* on Broadway. In an image that shows her gathering materials for the collection in a New York record store, she peruses the shelves with a record of *Porgy and Bess* tucked under her arm. Likely captured during the period when Franzell was appearing in *Carmen Jones,* the image powerfully conveys the offstage labor that Black operatic artists undertook to preserve their past.

Collective preservation and operatic sound also converged at the James Weldon Johnson Collection at Yale, founded by Carl Van Vechten in 1941. In 1959, Nora Holt hosted a "party for singers" at the collection, wherein "the guests were amazed and delighted to see that Mr. Van Vechten had been sending historical material on their achievements to the collection for the past decade or more." The guest list included Camilla Williams, Betty Allen, Carol Brice, Lawrence Winters, William Warfield, Charlotte Holloman, Margaret Tynes, and Margaret Bonds. After viewing the collection, the group traveled to the Milford, Connecticut home of Godfrey Nurse, an Afro-Caribbean doctor, for a meal and performance: "The grand surprise was the inspiring idea to have each artist sing the operatic aria which had brought him fame. With Margaret Bonds at the piano, opera star Camilla Williams began with 'Un bel di' from 'Madame Butterfly,' and soon there followed 'Opera on the Sound' and a rapport between the artists which happens once in a lifetime."[99] In contradistinction to mainstream opera's exceptionalizing impulse, Holt built on the collective ethos that had guided her work for decades, refiguring opera as a means of access to the archive and to a broader community of Black musicianship.

The most sustained attention to commemorating and archiving Black opera came from Harry Lawrence Freeman. Events like the 1947 production of *The Martyr* offered only a partial realization of his operatic vision, and it was clear that performance would not be a cornerstone of his legacy. Valdo, when asked if Freeman felt "unhappy or bitter or anything that he didn't get the kind of recognition [he desired]," responded, "Well, he eventually got to the place where he said he'd compose his operas for the generation that was coming after him."[100] While print had always been

Carlotta Franzell purchases records for the E. Azalia Hackley Memorial Collection, 1945. A clipping appended to the photograph notes that her visit also yielded recordings by Marian Anderson, Roland Hayes, Paul Robeson, and Dorothy Maynor.

meaningful to Freeman, from the extravagant calligraphy of his score for *The Martyr* to his commissioning of brilliant costume designs, it eventually became his primary creative medium. Nonperformance became a crucial factor in shaping his operatic imagination—but not necessarily a limiting one. Perhaps counterintuitively, the marginalization of his work and ensuing unlikeliness of performance enabled a different relationship to opera's

characteristic qualities of grandeur, extravagance, and fantasy. Exempt from the various conceptual and practical limitations imposed by the material realities of operatic production, he imagined operatic worlds of ever-expanding scope. By the twilight of his career, he had accumulated an archive of thousands of pages, composing his own archival legacy. As Brent Hayes Edwards has argued, for many Black musicians the material archive "itself is equally an arena of practice, a medium immanent with 'its own story,' parallel to or interwoven with music as well as literature."[101] Freeman's archive became an arena of grand aesthetic practice, an expressive vehicle more readily available than the operatic stage and, ultimately, a means of self-creation through which the composer could insist on his own historical significance.

A 1944 profile of Freeman by Nora Holt conveyed the "stupendous, and almost unbelievable" scale of his work:

> An estimate of the singing time and number of pages of scores present staggering figures. Eight operas running two or three hours represent an average of over thirty hours, nearly a day. This does not include six unfinished operas (not orchestrated). The tetralogy is arranged to run for four hours each. All of Mr. Freeman's compositions are orchestrated and notated by him. The tetralogy contains 2150 pages; Leah Kleschna, adapted from the Smith play made famous by George Arliss and Katherine Fisk, some 800 pages and an average of 200 to 300 pages to the other works, finished and unfinished, brings the total to about 6,000 pages of manuscript, not including symphonies and smaller works. All of these he has written in his own hand, done with meticulous detail and painstaking care.[102]

Holt's statistics conveyed the sheer space the operas took up, in performance and in print. She paid particular attention to Freeman's massive *Zululand* tetralogy, a Ring-like set of four operas (*Chaka*, *The Ghost-Wolves*, *The Stone Witch*, and *Umslopogaas and Nada*) based on the fantastical novels of H. Rider Haggard. The manuscript, which Freeman worked on over the course of multiple decades, was conscientiously marked with the dates on which he completed various parts. These markings, David Gutkin argues, betrayed "a keen time-consciousness bound up with Freeman's self-conception as a pathbreaking figure"; they also conveyed an awareness that prospective audiences were more likely to see Freeman's scores than to hear them.[103] To Valdo, they were evidence that "he's writing this for those who follow him. And I knew he must have gone through his scores and he put down certain

dates he finished this section and that section, which showed he knew some day someone would look at those things and they'd know when he did these things."[104] As Holt concluded, Freeman remained confident in his work's legacy despite the scarcity of performances, maintaining "faith that his works will be heard and recognized not only by his race, but by the world."[105]

Freeman's scrapbooks provide additional evidence of his dedication to archival self-making. Ellen Garvey has shown how scrapbooking was a way of "performing archivalness" in the early twentieth-century United States, with particular relevance for African Americans whose scrapbooks served as alternative historical records.[106] Freeman's scrapbooks (six are extant in his papers) contain items created over a period of more than sixty years. Overflowing with material, and profusely annotated in his own hand, they create meaning through accumulation and abundance.[107] A document misleadingly titled a "brief" resume stretches on for far more than the length of a standard piece of paper. There are so many press clippings that there is no room to paste them all into the book, and some lie wedged between the pages instead. The scrapbooks offer useful information about Freeman's career, but they are also material objects that convey his sense of his own historical standing and intention to convey that standing to future students of his work. As Valdo advised when he handed one of the scrapbooks to an oral-history interviewer: "Take good care of this as a valuable American historical document."[108]

While Freeman was undoubtedly concerned with his individual legacy, he also embraced the anti-exceptionalist potential of archival work. He wrote a number of articles in the Black press about African American musical history, including a 1936 series titled "Down Memory Lane." Even more monumental was, of course, *The Negro in Music and Drama,* the unpublished book manuscript of four hundred pages that he completed around 1940. Tellingly, the manuscript concludes with praise for the recently opened Schomburg Collection at the New York Public Library and its "marvelous idea of garnering every scrap of documentary data extant for future compilation."[109] Optimistically noting the collection's plans to expand—"The budget has been increased, the organization departmentalized, a phonograph record collection documenting the history of the Negro in music has been begun"—Freeman conveyed an investment in the broader project of archival institution-building, suggesting a commitment to establishing not only his own historical significance, but also that of Black musicians more generally.[110]

As he worked assiduously to craft a material archive, Freeman also continued to speculate about the possibilities of performance. Around 1953,

he wrote a long letter to Eleanor Roosevelt, inviting her to join the board of his latest venture, called the Aframerican Opera Foundation. Confidently insisting that his own works were "of the dimensions and calibre of those of the great European masters," Freeman drew attention to the institutional constraints that continued to hinder his success. Poignantly, he observed that although he had lived for forty-five years "within 20 minutes of the Metropolitan Opera House," his operas were never heard in that symbolic center of American opera.[111] The five-page letter also contains a richly imagined description of performances-to-be of *The Martyr,* complete with a proposed program:

THE AFRAMERICAN OPERA FOUNDATION
Presents
"THE MARTYR," an original GRAND OPERA
by
H. Lawrence Freeman, Distinguished Negro Composer
at the Cleveland Auditorium, Sunday Evening, May 4,
1954, with the Cleveland Symphony Orchestra
George Szell, conductor
Hazel Scott, piano virtuoso
Staging by Margaret Webster

· · · · · · · · · · ·

THE CAST

Platonus	{Lawrence Tibbett, Todd Duncan, Lawrence Winters}
Shirah	{Muriel Rahn, Camilla Williams, Charlotte Wesley}
Meriamum	{Marian Anderson, Zelma George, Carol Brice}
Pharaoh	{Lorenz Melchoir, Louis Rocca, Andrew Watson}
Rei	Kenneth Spencer
Priestess	{Katherine Dunham, Jeanette Collins}

Wailers and chorus ensembles from the Carimu
Theatre, the Katherine Dunham Ballet Dancers

Reproduced in full, this speculative program conveys the detail and precision of Freeman's imagined operatic universe, the granularity of what Kira Thurman calls his "grandiose visions."[112] He proposed that following the opening performance in Cleveland, the tour would continue for two more months, with additional performances in Chicago on May 11, Pittsburgh on May 18, Washington, DC on May 24, Philadelphia on June 2, Boston

on June 9, Westchester on June 23, and Brooklyn on June 30.[113] Revenue from the tour would fund his "ultimate plans": the creation of his own opera house on the outskirts of New York City. The space would have a scale befitting the operas to be performed within its doors: seats for seven thousand operagoers, parking for two thousand cars, and, most importantly, a long-term home for the realization of his work.[114] As he had throughout his life, Freeman created on paper the world he wished to see built around him, his aspirations remaining far ahead of reality.

Freeman died at his home in Harlem on March 24, 1954. He did not live to see Marian Anderson perform at the Met, and as he had predicted, his own compositions remained unheard within that opera house and others. The abundance of his archive is starkly at odds with the fact that his operas are so little-known today. With one notable exception, a 2015 production of *Voodoo* at Columbia University's Miller Theatre, his music has not been heard since his death in 1954.[115] As Kira Thurman writes, these operas constitute "an entire world of music that had been sealed off to succeeding generations."[116] They offer a powerful reminder of how Black operatic counterculture endured in settings beyond the open doors of the mainstream opera house, even—perhaps especially—in an age of institutional desegregation.

Typically, the silence imposed on Freeman's work might be considered a hindrance or stumbling block: it forecloses knowledge of how his music sounds, and makes it impossible to know how his operas might have impacted other composers and audiences, had they been performed. Yet paradoxically, perhaps the partiality of contemporary listeners' knowledge of Freeman's work actually brings us closer to the lived experience of listeners in his own time. They, too, hardly would have heard his music. Freeman himself, even, did not hear much of this music beyond what he could play on the piano. In accessing his work via methods that relied on the print archive and acts of partial performance, as I did in the course of my research—by paging through scores, playing through passages on the piano, singing along tentatively, using that experience to assess his work, and leaving the rest to my imagination—I experienced these operas in a way that is appropriate to their history. Listening is, of course, historically contingent, and my experience cannot fully approximate that of early twentieth-century listeners; nevertheless, this partial means of engagement was strangely illuminating.[117] If the archive is always a site of partial access to the past, here that partiality becomes its own sort of closeness, a way of foregrounding the persistently unrealized nature of Freeman's—and so many others'—grand operatic universe.

Conclusion

Ralph Ellison's virtuosic essay "The Little Man at Chehaw Station" concludes with a surprising argument over opera. Written in 1975, the essay recounts Ellison's time working for the Federal Writers' Project in New York City during the late 1930s. While circulating a petition among Black residents of a tenement building in San Juan Hill, Ellison was waiting outside a door on the "basement level" when he heard four "foulmouthed black workingmen . . . locked in verbal combat over which of two celebrated Metropolitan Opera divas was the superior soprano!"[1] Yet what first seemed to be a "mystery," "incongruous, outrageous, and surreal," was soon explained. "Where on earth," Ellison asked, "did you gentlemen learn so much about grand opera?":

> "Hell, son," he laughed, "we learned it down at the Met, that's where . . ."
>
> "You learned it *where*?"
>
> "At the Metropolitan Opera, just like I told you. Strip us fellows down and give us some costumes and we make about the finest damn bunch of Egyptians you ever seen. Hell, we been down there wearing leopard skins and carrying spears or waving things like palm leafs and ostrich-tail fans for *years!*"

His "sense of order restored," Ellison now understood that "the men were products of both past *and* present; were both coal heavers *and* Met extras; were both workingmen *and* opera buffs . . . there was no contradiction."[2]

They exemplified the pluralistic heterogeneity that Ellison understood to be a hallmark of US democratic culture, one that persisted despite the hierarchies of race and genre that attempted to stifle it.

Like the 1925 Ferrari Fontana Vocal Trials, with which this book opened, this subterranean scene invokes Black artists' relationship to the institutional space of the Metropolitan Opera House and the canonical *Aida*. Rather than spotlighting young women who aspired toward stardom, though, it asks us to listen to the anonymous supernumeraries who—outfitted in primitivist "leopard skins," and wielding markers of exoticism like "spears" and "palm leafs"—nevertheless responded to the opera on their own terms, their vigorous "verbal combat" a sharp contrast to their silent, spectacularized labor onstage. Both examples illuminate the breadth of African Americans' early twentieth-century engagements with opera, which flourished on the underground lower frequencies. But when Ellison recalled this encounter decades after its occurrence, the dominant affective note of his narrative was surprise, even shock, regarding these men's familiarity with and enthusiasm for the art form.

Who did these men name as they quarreled over the identity of the "superior soprano"? Perhaps the contenders included Dusolina Giannini, Elisabeth Rethberg, or Maria Caniglia—to name just a few of the white European and American sopranos who sang Aida at the Met during the 1930s. But by 1975, the ranks of "celebrated Metropolitan Opera divas" included Gloria Davy, who became the first Black woman to sing Aida with the company in 1958; Martina Arroyo, who sang the part beginning in 1965; and Leontyne Price, who first sang Aida at the Met in 1961 and became the role's most storied interpreter, reveling in what she called its "incredible freedom."[3] They also included Grace Bumbry, who first sang Amneris in the same opera in 1967; and Shirley Verrett, who made her debut in 1970. As this litany of celebrities suggests, exceptional Black singers were firmly established on opera house stages by the time of Ellison's writing. Marian Anderson's 1955 debut had been a "catalyst," the *New York Times* avowed, on the occasion of a 1982 Carnegie Hall recital honoring her legacy. It had compelled opera houses around the world to desegregate their rosters, and although "utopia has not yet arrived," it was undeniable that "today, black singers of both sexes are taken for granted in every opera house and on every concert stage of the world."[4]

Yet while the rise of a generation of elite singers marked a hard-won victory, deep inequities endured, as did opera's pervasive cultural associations with whiteness and elitism. Successful Black singers continued to face overt and subtle forms of racial discrimination; Black men remained unlikely to

be cast alongside white women, and Black women were often consigned to racially marked roles. Mainstream institutions engaged vanishingly few African Americans to compose, conduct, or direct opera, or to serve as administrators. An observer in the *Crisis* lamented that for the "thousands of young black students in music schools and conservatories of the nation [who] are busy studying to become serious musicians," the future looked bleak. "The supertalented black youth may eventually be singled out for 'token' success," the writer observed, "but thousands of others whose talent may be equal to that of young whites will fail to get the nod from the music establishment and never make it in the area of his choice, unless there is change."[5]

Black operatic counterculture had flourished within a particular moment in US cultural and social history: one marked by the paradox of extreme repression under Jim Crow and extreme African American cultural creativity during and beyond the Harlem Renaissance; by opera's visibility within US culture more broadly; and by a cultural landscape in which Black formalism thrived, enabling opera to become interwoven with a variety of other aesthetic and political projects. Working under such conditions, diverse ensembles of Black artists theorized and enacted opera across a dazzlingly broad array of contexts, from Sylvester Russell's grandiose vision that the art form would become a zenith of Black culture to Shirley Graham's crafting of an Afrodiasporic historical epic in *Tom-Tom*. Embracing opera's grand aesthetics and ability to foster new social arrangements, African Americans conceptualized and experienced the art form as a rich creative, intellectual, and political resource: a locus of the Black public sphere, a place for collective sociality and individual self-making, and a formal vehicle for ambitious worldbuilding. These efforts vitally reshaped opera's relationship to Blackness as artists transformed existing operatic institutions, created new ones, and reimagined the art form's aesthetic and social possibilities.

But as the bemused tone of Ellison's account implies, the conditions that had both constrained Black opera and facilitated its growth throughout the first half of the twentieth century changed in the decades that followed. The long-sought "open door" admitted just a few, leaving the fundamental racial politics of the mainstream opera house largely unaltered. At the same time, the "Jim Crow paradox" resulted in the dissipation of many institutions in which more autonomous facets of Black operatic activity had thrived: the newspapers in which critics had maintained a vibrant discourse about opera, for example, began to decline in circulation and significance.[6] In a creative landscape marked by the ascent of new popular music genres and the rise of the Black Arts Movement, many artists found themselves

drawn to other expressive practices. Growing up in Los Angeles in the 1940s and 1950s, Odetta Holmes trained for a career in opera as a teenager, "being groomed as the next Marian Anderson."[7] But she then turned to folk music, reinventing herself as Odetta, the outspoken, politically progressive "voice of the civil rights movement."[8]

To be sure, Black operatic counterculture did not simply disappear. In spaces both apart from and intertwined with the operatic mainstream, Black artists continued to generate new meaning from the art form's aesthetic capaciousness and collaborative ethos. Nora Holt adapted her criticism to new technologies, moving from newspaper to radio. Beginning in 1945, she curated and hosted an American Negro Artist Program as part of WNYC's annual American Music Festival. The program celebrated the longevity and vitality of the Black classical tradition, as music that Holt had showcased in her *Defender* column, such as the compositions of Nathaniel Dett, now shared space with works by young composers like Julia Perry.[9] After the NNOC disbanded in 1962, following the untimely passing of its founder, Mary Cardwell Dawson, a number of new Black opera companies emerged, including Opera / South (established in 1971) and Opera Ebony (established in 1973). Devoted to fostering the collective work of not only African American singers, but also directors, impresarios, and audiences, they preserved a space for opera within the Black public sphere.

These companies also provided vital support to Black composers, who continued to create new, aesthetically innovative works that repurposed opera's maximalist aesthetics to narrate key episodes of African American history. In 1976, Opera / South commissioned Ulysses Kay's *Jubilee,* based on a historical novel by Margaret Walker that recounts her great-grandmother's experiences during slavery and Reconstruction; in 1985, Opera Ebony presented Dorothy Rudd Moore's *Frederick Douglass,* a monumentally ambitious work that took its composer more than ten years to write. More recent histories of Black radicalism reached the stage as well. NYCO, which remained the rare mainstream company attentive to Black composers, premiered Anthony Davis's *X: The Life and Times of Malcolm X* in 1986. In an interview, Davis observed how some press coverage not only misunderstood the opera as "just a polemic," but also neglected to mention how its mostly African American audience reshaped the social arrangements of the opera house beyond the stage. "Think how strange it must have been to *be* a white critic in that audience," he meditated. "They were in another world—a world they'd never been in before. *We* were in another world—let's face it—that most of us certainly haven't been in very often. But it was ours."[10]

Since its inception, Black operatic counterculture had prioritized the (counter)historical preservation of its own significance, and this work persisted as well. Like Harry Lawrence Freeman, who proactively created print archives to ensure his own legacy, Black operatic artists resisted the conditions of their own erasure. In one poignant example, soprano La Julia Rhea wrote a letter published in the *Chicago Tribune* in 1980. "In December, 1937, I became the first black major opera star in the United States by singing the lead in 'Aida' with the Chicago City Opera Company," Rhea wrote. "I would like for future musical history to record my name and valid achievements. Any information you can give me to make this dream a reality would be greatly appreciated."[11] The Black press, once a vibrant record of operatic goings-on, maintained a commitment to documenting Black operatic history, even as it was ignored or minimized in other venues. Music critics, including Earl Calloway at the *Defender* and Raoul Abdul at the *Amsterdam News,* reminded their readers of this legacy in columns about the achievements of early Black operatic artists.[12] Yet they also remained aware that opera's profound experiential meanings sometimes exceeded the scope of textual preservation, even—perhaps especially—for those who had borne witness to Black artists' decades-long quests for recognition. Two decades after Anderson's 1955 appearance at the Met, Abdul reflected, "I was a witness to Miss Anderson's debut that night, and I am grateful that I did not have to review the performance. It was a shattering emotional experience that made me want both to shout with joy and cry at the same time. It was a great moment in operatic history."[13]

If the trajectory of Black opera since the mid-twentieth century has been shaped by the mainstream ascent of renowned singers and the enduring presence of a countercultural operatic scene, it has also entailed a complex historical reckoning. The deferred dreams of an earlier generation of African American artists have garnered renewed attention, and long-unheard operas by Black composers have returned to the stage—or, in some cases, been heard for the first time. Such revival efforts are rich with creative potential, but they also bear a considerable burden. Not only must they present aesthetically compelling productions of operas that are unfamiliar to both performers and audiences, but they are also tasked with a variety of extramusical imperatives. To counteract a history of nonperformance, new productions must educate operagoers about the conditions that governed these works' initial genesis, as well as the reasons for their subsequent absence from the stage. To move long-unheard works from the margins to the mainstream, they must advocate for inclusion within the contemporary

opera scene without losing sight of the experimental aesthetic and social qualities that marginalization initially engendered. The recuperation of these works, in other words, is inextricable from their past.

The first opera to undergo this process of revival was Scott Joplin's *Treemonisha,* which, in the 1970s, became a focal point of inquiries into Black opera's history. Composed in 1911, and set in Reconstruction-era Arkansas, the opera tells the uplifting story of a young woman, Treemonisha, who guides her rural community toward enlightenment, rejecting the superstitious chicanery of local "conjurers" to promote the value of education. Modeled structurally after nineteenth-century European grand opera, the piece teems with attractive melodies and syncopated rhythms, reflecting Joplin's immersion in Black popular musical cultures. Although the opera was the subject of much excitement during Joplin's lifetime, it was sidelined after planned productions fell through. Joplin self-published the score, and its only performance was a read-through with piano accompaniment in a rented hall in Harlem, for an audience of scarcely more than a dozen people.[14] *Treemonisha* then, in the words of one scholar, "slumbered in oblivion for more than half a century" before being performed in full for the first time.[15] Its January 1972 premiere, in Atlanta, was led by the African American composer T. J. Anderson, who arranged Joplin's music for a fifteen-piece ensemble, featuring the Afro-American Music Workshop of Morehouse College and the Atlanta Symphony. Later that year, a version for a larger ensemble, orchestrated by William Bolcom, premiered in northern Virginia. A still more elaborate version, arranged by Gunther Schuller, was presented by the Houston Grand Opera in May 1975 before reaching Broadway that fall.

This flurry of performances raised questions regarding race, genre, and reception that echoed fundamental debates within Black operatic counterculture. Its premiere was facilitated primarily by Joplin's centrality within the "ragtime revival" of the era: recordings of his piano rags became a surprise hit, and the appearance of "The Entertainer" in the 1973 movie *The Sting* further popularized his work, generating what one critic called a "ragtime tidal wave currently deluging America."[16] As a result, some listeners heard *Treemonisha* as a songwriter's excursion into another genre rather than evidence of Joplin's specific aesthetic investment in grand opera. It is no surprise that, within this context, one critic termed the piece "little more than beguiling entertainment."[17] But another perceptively observed that when an audience is entirely unfamiliar with a work and the (counter)cultural context of Black operatic composition from which it emerged, "even a masterpiece might seem just a curiosity."[18] A history of nonperformance was not

necessarily an impediment: if some heard *Treemonisha* as a mere curiosity, for others, it may have enabled a productive consideration of how the opera unsettled entrenched cultural norms of race and genre. Yet the fact remained that *Treemonisha* could not simply make a delayed entry into the repertoire, unencumbered by the conditions that had first prevented it from being heard.

The varying institutional contexts in which *Treemonisha* was performed also raised familiar questions about the possibilities and limits of mainstream inclusion. Raoul Abdul observed that following the immense critical success of the Atlanta production, which was led by a Black composer and creative team, the newly celebrated *Treemonisha* risked becoming yet another spectacle, beholden to opera's existing representational norms and racialized power dynamics rather than challenging them from the margins. In the subsequent Virginia production, he observed, "some rich white folks" adorned its title character in "a brand new gown," "much to the surprise of her Black friends." The Texas production, by "white orchestrator Gunther Schuller and white director Frank Corsaro, with Black choreographer Louis Johnson tagging along," prompted the question of whether "Treemonisha was the victim of the classic ripoff."[19] From Abdul's perspective, the revival of Joplin's work was not an uncontested good; misrepresentation and cooptation remained urgent concerns as a work long relegated to the archive was now ushered through the opera house's belatedly open door.

In the twenty-first century, interest in the Black operatic past has intensified. Although the broader programmatic landscape is still dominated almost entirely by white composers—the Met did not stage its first opera by a Black composer, Terence Blanchard's *Fire Shut Up in My Bones,* until 2021—a number of companies on the institutional margins have mounted ambitious revivals. In 2012, the UK company Surrey Opera presented the posthumous premiere of Samuel Coleridge-Taylor's *Thelma* (1909) after it was excavated from the British Library's archives. In 2015, New York City's now-defunct Morningside Opera produced Freeman's *Voodoo*—the opera's first performance since 1928. The year 2017, the centennial of Joplin's death, brought several additional performances of *Treemonisha,* in locales from Virginia to Louisiana to Mississippi.[20] The most tenacious attention to this history comes from the New Orleans company OperaCréole. Founded in New Orleans in 2011 by Givonna Joseph and Aria Mason, the company notes on its website that "opera and classical music in New Orleans and around the world have always included the contributions of persons of color," a statement whose axiomatic tone belies its subversive implications.[21] OperaCréole has presented Edmond Dédé's *Françoise et tortillard* (1866),

Lucien-Léon Guillaume Lambert's *La flamenca* (1903), and William Grant Still's *Minette Fontaine* (1958), among others. Such a sustained focus on the work of composers of color does much more than return individual operas to the repertoire; it disproves the enduring perception that opera is an art form from which Blackness has historically been absent.

In a commemorative landscape focused largely on male composers, Mary Cardwell Dawson has become the rare African American woman to receive renewed attention. A speculative "play with music" titled *The Passion of Mary Cardwell Dawson,* created by playwright Sandra Seaton and composer Carlos Simon, premiered in 2021. Starring the mezzo-soprano Denyce Graves, it narrates Dawson's work with the NNOC: her meticulous guidance of the singers under her tutelage, her struggles to secure performance venues for the company.[22] A conceptually related project seeks to restore the Pittsburgh home that was the company's headquarters. I visited the site, a majestic Queen Anne house perched high on a hill, in the summer of 2023. It was a quiet, sunny morning, and from the third floor I could glimpse a striking view of the city. At present, only a small historic marker outside the building notes the site's significance. Jonnet Solomon, who purchased the home in 2000 with the late Miriam White and is leading the effort to restore it, envisions that it will one day become a vibrant gathering place that extends Dawson's work, "doing exactly as she did" by hosting performances, providing space for music lessons, and offering a "space where artists can explore and create freely."[23] Years in the making, Solomon's endeavor has gained the support of major institutional donors, and a ground-breaking took place in 2022.

Treemonisha remains a touchstone among these efforts. But aesthetic engagements with Joplin's work have changed significantly since its re-introduction into the repertoire in the 1970s, as have the broader educational and cultural imperatives that accompany its revival. Some recent productions, less interested in the notion of historical fidelity than their 1970s predecessors, have reinterpreted *Treemonisha* as an opportunity to showcase the global scope and diasporic aesthetics of contemporary Black operatic production.[24] In 2022, South Africa's Isango Ensemble presented a "reminiscence" of the piece during a tour of France and Luxembourg. The company, which specializes in what it terms "reimaginations" of classic works of Western theater and has previously presented adaptations of *Carmen* and *The Magic Flute,* arranged Joplin's music for an orchestra of marimbas and other South African instruments, and made use of South African dance styles.[25] A 2023 *Treemonisha* by the Volcano Ensemble, in Toronto, offered a "musical reimagining" of the work. Adapted by a creative

team including the librettists Leah-Simone Bowen and Cheryl L. Davis, and the composers and arrangers Jessie Montgomery and Jannina Norpoth, the production is framed by the history of slavery: an opening "flashback" shows a young fugitive who leaves her newborn child under a tree to save her from enslavement. Its musical language is pointedly heterogenous, incorporating Afrodiasporic instruments and singers trained in traditions other than opera.[26] Rather than attempting to evoke the opera as it might have sounded in its own time, or as Joplin might have imagined it, they take the piece as a foundation on which to make a claim—musical and political—about what Black opera can sound like today.

In the United States, *Treemonisha* has become a means of reckoning with the politics of the contemporary moment. As social movements like Black Lives Matter have demanded an end to systemic racism, and particularly in the aftermath of George Floyd's murder in May 2020, some opera companies have begun reckoning publicly with their histories of racist exclusion. There have been halting steps toward change as companies have hired new artists and staff; introduced myriad diversity, equity, and inclusion initiatives; and commissioned and performed new works by composers of color. Within this context, the revival of Joplin's early twentieth-century opera offers an opportunity to reshape the art form's dominant cultural connotations, and to catalyze creative inquiry into the relationship between the Black operatic past and the art form's present. (*Treemonisha*'s enduring appeal also exemplifies a trend in which opera companies continue to favor works by Black composers who have already attained recognition in another genre: consider Terence Blanchard's acclaimed career in jazz and film music, or the folk-inflected, genre-crossing expertise of Rhiannon Giddens, whose opera *Omar*, co-commissioned by some of the country's most prominent companies, was awarded the Pulitzer Prize in 2023.[27]) Yet new productions also introduce tensions between the project of institutional legitimization and the experimental ethos that guided *Treemonisha*'s creation.

In June 2023, I attended Opera Theatre of Saint Louis's production of *Treemonisha*, which approaches these questions with immense creativity and candor. Rather than reimagining Joplin's score outright, the production resituates his music within a newly created frame. A prologue and epilogue, by librettist Karen Chilton and composer Damien Sneed, bring biography to the fore by focusing on Joplin's relationship with his wife, Freddie Alexander, whose tragic death, just ten weeks after they married, weighed on Joplin as he worked on *Treemonisha*.[28] This biographical framing is both emotionally compelling and pedagogically useful. Twenty-first-century operagoers might recognize Joplin's name, but they are unlikely to know

much about the details of his life. "Even some opera singer friends of mine who had done this production at other places," Chilton divulged to me, "told me they never knew anything about him, which really helped confirm for me why it was important" to flesh out the emotional texture of Joplin's life.[29] The prologue begins with their wedding celebration, then shows Joplin hard at work at the piano, completing his opera, while Freddie grows frail from illness. He credits her with inspiring the work's thematic focus on education and enlightenment: "Freddie! You were my Treemonisha," he cries upon her death.[30] The singers playing Freddie and Joplin then assume the roles of Treemonisha and her love interest Remus, respectively, and *Treemonisha* itself is presented as an "opera within an opera." The epilogue has a tragic mood. Joplin struggles, "distraught and discontent" that his contemporaries have not recognized his opera's greatness. Freddie reappears as an apparition, reassuring Joplin of the beauty and worth of his "wondrous creation." "My dear, Maestro / You must know / You are ahead of your time," she sings.[31]

The inclusion of this frame narrative is a bold interpretive move, disrupting art-for-art's-sake conventions in its insistence on situating *Treemonisha* within a particular historical and biographical context. It serves an essential educational purpose: audiences are asked to consider Joplin not simply as a forgotten historical figure, but as someone who, even as his creative aspirations were thwarted, maintained a deep commitment to opera, faith in education, and conviction in his own artistic excellence. But the narrative also made me curious about the potential challenges of revival as a way of introducing contemporary audiences to the Black operatic past—about whether, in seeking to add someone like Joplin to the pantheon of operatic composers, it is possible to simultaneously contest the terms on which that list is constructed. Joplin and Freddie fell rather neatly into the gendered dichotomy of great male artist and supportive female muse, reproducing a familiar trope. Although Joplin acknowledges Freddie's influence on his thinking, his obsession with his art is coupled with seeming obliviousness to her failing health. "I've borne witness / To greatness / In you," Freddie assures her husband, even as she struggles to breathe. Her words reflect an overarching emphasis, prevalent throughout the narrative, on *Treemonisha*'s "masterwork" status. "This work will stand tall among the masters!" Joplin avers, in a restless passage situated low in the singer's range.[32] While this framing might be an especially legible way to persuade an audience of the opera's worth, it does not necessarily convey the versatility and scope of Joplin's expertise. Like so many operas by early twentieth century Black composers, from Freeman's *Voodoo* to Graham's *Tom-Tom,*

Treemonisha reimagines the very notion of a "masterwork": it remixes Joplin's songwriting talents with opera's maximalist aesthetics to transformative effect, creating a piece that is alternately serious and giddy, righteous and charming. If Joplin aspired not only to contribute to the operatic canon, but also to remake it, then a preoccupation with legitimizing the opera for a contemporary audience may elide that transformative impulse.

Freddie assures Joplin in the opera's epilogue that he is "ahead of [his] time," and that he will one day attain the recognition that he deserves.[33] But as I watched the production, I became curious about how a revival might not only generate belated appreciation of a single figure, but also prompt new ways of thinking about the historical scene from which that figure emerged. I found myself wondering anew about the creative environment that had shaped *Treemonisha* in the time of its creation, and the careful attention paid to Joplin by the communities in which he worked. I wondered about the singers who took the time to sing through the piece with the composer at the piano even after his plans to stage the work failed, and about the Black critics who praised the overture as being "great as anything ever written by Mr. Wagner"—even before it was complete.[34] A story that Harry Lawrence Freeman's son, Valdo, shared in an oral history interview also came to mind. His father knew Joplin "very well," Valdo recounted, and they crossed paths occasionally when Joplin was living in New York toward the end of his life. On a cold winter day, they came across Joplin huddled on the street in distress: he had been "knocked on the head and robbed." "My father took his coat off and put it around him," Valdo said, "and we took him home."[35] I read Valdo's story long before attending the production, and it had initially struck me as disheartening, a sad commentary on the difficult circumstances of Joplin's later life. But the experience of seeing that life dramatized onstage shifted my thinking, prompting me to reconsider the story as a testament to how Joplin benefited from the support of a broader musical and social community. It would be fascinating, I thought, to see how a future revival of *Treemonisha* could accommodate such stories of intracommunal care, situating Joplin's aspirations (or, for that matter, Freeman's) within the countercultural sphere in which they both worked.

Given his longstanding dream of seeing the opera staged, Joplin would no doubt have been delighted by the scene in St. Louis. Before the performance, operagoers gathered outside to eat at picnic tables scattered within a lush garden, or to sip champagne at the outdoor bar. Indoors, the hall was packed, and the excitement was palpable. At the opera's end, the

audience rose for a hearty standing ovation, and a voice over the speaker system invited us to move outdoors for dessert and discussion. I recalled Nora Holt's warm invitation to readers of her *Defender* column to join her in the lobby after symphony performances, disrupting the institutional space of the Chicago Symphony to create their own community of listeners.

For the artists involved in its creation, *Treemonisha* continues to offer powerful opportunities for individual and collective self-making. The afternoon following the performance, I spoke with three members of the opera's cast and creative team—baritone Justin Austin (who appeared in the dual role of Scott Joplin / Remus), composer Damien Sneed, and soprano Brandie Inez Sutton (Freddie / Treemonisha)—about their relationship to Joplin's work. For Austin and Sneed, the connections run deep. Sneed is the godson of the late Jessye Norman, who vociferously encouraged him to honor and recognize Joplin's work. As an undergraduate at Howard University, he accompanied vocal lessons for Carmen Balthrop, the soprano who sang the role of Treemonisha in Houston Grand Opera's 1975 production. Austin is the son of two opera singers; his mother, Alteouise DeVaughn, appeared as Monisha in an early production. If presumed unfamiliar to most audiences, the opera was rooted in their own familial and educational histories—a striking reminder of where and how Black operatic counterculture has been preserved, even as it has been made absent from most narratives of US opera history.

Sutton's introduction to Joplin came later, and it was not until she began rehearsing the opera in community with other singers that its full creative scope became clear to her. "To me, it reminds me of Black culture," she explained. Her relationship to the piece stemmed from a realization that Joplin's devotion to *Treemonisha* in particular, and opera in general, was premised less on an investment in external recognition, and more on its ability to "bring our culture to the world."[36] Sutton shared the story of an audience member who, after the previous night's performance, told her that the opera's penultimate scene, "We will trust you as our leader," brought to mind examples of contemporary Black leadership, such as the presidency of Barack Obama. This observation prompted me to reevaluate an element of the opera that has often been criticized as a weakness: its simply phrased libretto and uncomplicated plot. A far cry from the elaborate vocabulary of Harry Lawrence Freeman's works, Joplin's language is strikingly direct. "We will trust you as our leader," the community assures Treemonisha, in words set to a melody of radiant, Schubertian simplicity. "We want you to lead. / You should lead us." Such language is often taken as a sign of Joplin's

inexperience as a librettist, but it could also be read as generative of social meaning. By declining to conform to conventional expectations of what "operatic" language sounds like, Joplin imbues the piece with a radical generalizability that, as Sutton's experience suggests, ultimately lends the opera its allegorical and social power.[37]

As valuable and generative as revivals can be, the past is well-charted territory in opera, and new productions of works composed more than a century ago are unlikely to serve, in the long term, as primary avenues of new aesthetic experimentation and political expression. When Sylvester Russell averred, in 1907, that the "futurity of American music" would flow from the pen of a Black composer, he looked not to the past, but to the present, in search of the horizon on which "some spark of hidden genius suddenly alarms the universe."[38] The optimistic tone of Russell's prediction merits further consideration. "How does it feel to be a problem?," W. E. B. Du Bois asked in *The Souls of Black Folk* (1903), an acerbic retort to white interlocutors unable to see him as anything but. Mainstream operatic institutions' reckonings with the art form's history have tended toward the contrite, describing race as a "problem" that needs to be overcome. It is crucial to acknowledge the harmful ways that anti-Black racism has structured opera's past. But it is equally important to attend to how African American artists have long transformed the art form into a source of profound aesthetic creativity. Even more fundamentally, it is imperative to invest in new artists—composers, critics, performers, teachers, listeners—who are working to create a future in opera, both within and beyond its mainstream iterations, that is equitable, joyful, and abundant.[39]

To engage with the Black operatic past, whether as a musician, a listener, or a critic, is to contend with a legacy of absence. If there is something inspirational to be found in the image of a composer's dreams at long last fulfilled, or of the contemporary operagoer hearing their own experiences reflected in his work, such examples also necessarily evoke the many instances in which opportunities to write, sing, and hear opera were denied to those who ardently desired them. But it is also a history of enduring presence: of the individuals who made meaning out of opera across the first half of the twentieth century, and of the communities that have celebrated, protected, and preserved their artistry in the years since. To Chilton, the librettist, one of the most remarkable features of *Treemonisha* is Joplin's choice to set the opera in 1884: a hopeful moment before the confines of Jim Crow had fully set in, when the emancipatory promise of Reconstruction still held sway. In rehearsals, she encouraged the cast to think "sociopolitically" about "where these people are, how they were living, what their

desires were, what their aspirations were . . . now that we have freedom, what do we do with it?" The opera's fundamental question, she believes, is a profound one: "How do we become ourselves?"[40]

This question was at the heart of Black operatic counterculture, for Joplin and for the countless others who found in opera an opportunity to remake their artistic and political lives. If no single act of historical recuperation can fully convey the entirety of this cultural phenomenon, each has the potential to gesture toward its sheer breadth and expanse: the generative possibilities of operatic aesthetics, the productive potential of marginalization, and the significance of the ensemble. As they engaged with opera in basements and on stages, in print and in performance, participants in this collective endeavor found opera meaningful not only because of what it might offer in some speculative, future world unlike their own, but also because of what it offered to them in the concrete reality of the present. Experimenting with the art form's near-infinite possibilities, Black operatic artists mapped out new ways of singing, hearing, writing, dreaming, thinking, and living.

Notes

Introduction

1. "Greatest Musical Offer Ever: Ferrari-Fontana Seeks Negro Voice for Grand Opera," *New York Amsterdam News,* July 1, 1925.

2. "Greatest Musical Offer Ever." I am grateful to Eric K. Washington, a Harlem community historian who first made me aware of the Ferrari Fontana Vocal Trials in a talk delivered at "Restaging the Harlem Renaissance: New Views on the Performing Arts in Black Manhattan," Columbia University, June 2015.

3. "Preliminary Tryout of Soprano Voices Well Under Way," *New York Amsterdam News,* July 15, 1925.

4. "Fontana Selects Two Voices Instead of One," *New York Amsterdam News,* August 12, 1925.

5. Although neither Avery nor Zackery had a career in opera, both pursued music professionally. Avery was a founding member of the Hall Johnson Choir who toured nationally as a chorus member for *The Green Pastures* in 1930. Zackery worked as a teacher and concert artist in New York.

6. There is no record of Fontana fulfilling his promise. He moved to Toronto shortly after the contest. Laura Macy, ed., *The Grove Book of Opera Singers* (New York: Oxford University Press, 2008), 158.

7. "Fontana Selects Two Voices."

8. In the years following the Vocal Trials, the basement lecture hall became a space for theatrical performance, often used by groups associated with the Little Theater Movement. On the 135th Street branch library, see Sarah A. Anderson, "'The Place to Go': The 135th Street Branch Library and the Harlem Renaissance," *Library Quarterly* 73, no. 4 (2003). 383–421.

9. On Black women performers during the late nineteenth and early twentieth centuries, see Daphne A. Brooks, *Bodies in Dissent: Spectacular Performances of Race and Freedom, 1850–1910* (Durham, NC: Duke University Press, 2006); and Jayna Brown, *Babylon Girls: Black Women Performers and the Shaping of the Modern* (Durham, NC: Duke University Press, 2008).

10. "Profoundly absent" is from Tammy Kernodle, review of *Blackness in Opera*, ed. Naomi André, Karen M. Bryan, and Eric Saylor, *Women and Music: A Journal of Gender and Culture* 17 (2013): 78–81, 78. Samuel Floyd described classical music and opera as the "last frontier of black music research," a situation resulting in "gaping holes in music historiography." Samuel Floyd with Melanie Zeck and Guthrie P. Ramsey, Jr., *The Transformation of Black Music: The Rhythms, the Songs, and the Ships of the African Diaspora* (New York: Oxford University Press, 2017), xxviii. In a different but rhetorically related context, Alex Ross characterizes early twentieth-century Black composers as the "absent center" of American classical composition. Alex Ross, *The Rest Is Noise: Listening to the Twentieth Century* (New York: Farrar, Straus and Giroux, 2007), 123.

11. Toni Morrison, "Unspeakable Things Unspoken: The Afro-American Presence in Americanist Literature," *Michigan Quarterly Review* 28, no. 1 (1989): 1–34, 11. See also Toni Morrison, *Playing in the Dark: Whiteness and the Literary Imagination* (Cambridge, MA: Harvard University Press, 1992).

12. Samuel R. Delany, *Silent Interviews: On Language, Race, Sex, Science Fiction, and Some Comics* (Middletown, CT: Wesleyan University Press, 1994), 289. This quotation comes from an interview that Delany conducted with the composer Anthony Davis in 1986, following the premiere of Davis's *X: The Life and Times of Malcolm X*. Davis responded to Delany's query about how he and his collaborators felt working in "a field in which blacks have traditionally been the *objects* of white operas" as follows: "Well, we felt very good about it. We said: This is an opportunity to have our own voice—to deal with our own history, our own characters, and with our own people, in our own voice." Delany, *Silent Interviews,* 290.

13. Samuel Dwinell, "Blackness in British Opera" (PhD diss., Cornell University, 2017), 24–27.

14. On the use of these concepts within opera studies, see W. Anthony Sheppard, "Exoticism," in *The Oxford Handbook of Opera,* ed. Helen Greenwald (New York: Oxford University Press, 2014), 795–816. See also Timothy Taylor, *Beyond Exoticism: Western Music and the World* (Durham, NC: Duke University Press, 2007); Susan McClary, *Georges Bizet: 'Carmen,'* Cambridge Opera Handbooks (Cambridge: Cambridge University Press, 1992); and Mari Yoshihara, "The Flight of the Japanese Butterfly: Orientalism, Nationalism, and Performances of Japanese Womanhood," *American Quarterly* 56, no. 4 (2004): 975–1001.

15. Quoted in Wallace Cheatham, "Racism and Sexism: Melodies That Continue to Soar on the Operatic Landscape," in *Opera in a Multicultural World: Coloniality, Culture, Performance,* ed. Mary Ingraham, Joseph So, and Roy Moodley (New York: Routledge, 2015), 178.

16. Ingraham et al., "Introduction," in *Opera in a Multicultural World,* 7.

17. As Karl Hagstrom Miller observes, "The study of black music has tended to produce stories of racial difference because of the high political stakes involved in writing African American cultural history." Karl Hagstrom Miller, *Segregating Sound: Inventing Folk and Pop Music in the Age of Jim Crow* (Durham, NC: Duke University Press, 2010), 12. Similarly, Emily Lordi argues that scholars often follow in the tradition of *Blues People* (1963), by Amiri Baraka (aka Leroi Jones), which "treats black music as a metaphor for black life." *Black Resonance: Iconic Women Singers and African American Literature* (New Brunswick, NJ: Rutgers University Press, 2013), 12.

18. Kira Thurman, "Singing against the Grain: Playing Beethoven in the #BlackLivesMatter Era," *The Point,* Fall 2018, https://thepointmag.com/2018/examined-life/singing-against-grain-playing-beethoven-blacklivesmatter-era.

19. Lawrence Schenbeck, *Racial Uplift and American Music, 1878–1943* (Jackson: University Press of Mississippi, 2012), 6, 8.

20. See Evelyn Brooks Higginbotham, *Righteous Discontent: The Women's Movement in the Black Baptist Church, 1880–1920* (Cambridge, MA: Harvard University Press, 1993). Kevin Gaines offers a sustained critique of uplift ideology in *Uplifting the Race: Black Leadership, Politics, and Culture in the Twentieth Century* (Chapel Hill: University of North Carolina Press, 1996).

21. James Monroe Trotter, *Music and Some Highly Musical People* (Boston: Lee and Shepard, 1878). On Trotter's significance within Black music scholarship, see Guthrie P. Ramsey Jr., "Cosmopolitan or Provincial? Ideology in Early Black Music Historiography," *Black Music Research Journal* 16, no. 1 (1996): 11–42, 16–18.

22. Eileen Southern, *The Music of Black Americans: A History* (New York: W.W. Norton, 1971).

23. Willia Daughtry, "Sissieretta Jones: A Study of the Negro's Contribution to Nineteenth Century American Concert and Theatrical Life" (PhD diss., Syracuse University, 1968); Hansonia Caldwell, "Black Idioms in Opera as Reflected in the Works of Six Afro-American Composers" (PhD diss., University of Southern California, 1974); Celia Davidson, "Opera by Afro-American Composers: A Critical Survey and Analysis of Selected Works" (PhD diss., Catholic University of America, 1980); Mildred Denby Green, *Black Women Composers: A Genesis* (Boston: Twayne, 1983); Antoinette Handy, *Black Women in American Bands and Orchestras* (Lanham, MD: Scarecrow Press, 1981); Doris Evans McGinty, "'As Large as She Can Make It': The Role of Black Women Activists in Music, 1880–1945," in *Cultivating Music in America: Women Patrons and Activists since 1860,* ed. Ralph P. Locke and Cyrilla Barr (Berkeley: University of California Press, 1997); and Josephine Wright, "Black Women and Classical Music," *Women's Studies Quarterly* 12, no. 3 (1984): 18–21.

24. On questions of absence, presence, and the limits of archival "recovery," see Laura Helton, Justin Leroy, Max Mishler, Samantha Seeley, and Shauna Sweeney, eds., *Social Text* 33, no. 4 (special issue on "The Question of Recovery:

Slavery, Freedom, and the Archive," 2015). For a perspective specific to Black classical musicians, see A. Kori Hill, "To Be Rediscovered When You Were Never Forgotten: Florence Price & the 'Rediscovered' Composer," *Harry T. Burleigh Society Blog,* 2018, https://burleighsociety.com/blog/2018-11-29/florence-price-part-one.

25. Naomi André, Karen M. Bryan, and Eric Saylor, eds., *Blackness in Opera* (Urbana: University of Illinois Press, 2012). The collection joins an array of recent work in opera studies investigating the art form's entanglements with questions of race, gender, and imperialism. Other significant collections include Pamela Karantonis and Dylan Robinson, eds., *Opera Indigene: Re/presenting First Nations and Indigenous Cultures* (Farnham, UK: Ashgate, 2011); Philip Purvis, ed., *Masculinity in Opera: Gender, History, and New Musicology* (New York: Routledge, 2013); and Ingraham et al., *Opera in a Multicultural World.*

26. Kira Thurman, *Singing Like Germans* (Ithaca, NY: Cornell University Press, 2021); Nina Sun Eidsheim, *The Race of Sound: Listening, Timbre, and Vocality in African American Music* (Durham, NC: Duke University Press, 2019), 61–90; Naomi André, *Black Opera: History, Power, Engagement* (Urbana: University of Illinois Press, 2018).

27. Christopher Brooks and Robert Sims, *Roland Hayes: The Legacy of an American Tenor* (Bloomington: University of Indiana Press, 2014); see also, for example, Maureen Lee, *Sissieretta Jones: "The Greatest Singer of Her Race," 1868–1933* (Columbia: University of South Carolina Press, 2012). This work is grounded in an important biographical tradition; see Rosalyn Story, *And So I Sing: African-American Divas of Opera and Concert* (New York: Warner Books, 1990); Wallace Cheatham, ed., *Dialogues on Opera and the African-American Experience* (Lanham, MD: Scarecrow Press, 1997); and Darryl Glenn Nettles, *African American Concert Singers before 1950* (Jefferson, NC: McFarland, 2003).

28. See Kristen M. Turner and Gina Bombola, "Respectability, Prestige, and the Whiteness of Opera in American Popular Entertainment from 1890 to 1937," *Musical Quarterly* 105, nos. 3–4 (2022): 274–319; Siel Agugliaro, "Imagining Italy, Surviving America: Opera, Italian Immigrants, and Identity in Philadelphia, 1870–1924" (PhD diss., University of Pennsylvania, 2021); Samantha M. Cooper, "Emma Goldman, An Anarchist at the Opera," *American Jewish History* 106, no. 2 (2022): 113–142; and Nancy Yunhwa Rao, *Chinatown Opera Theater in North America* (Urbana: University of Illinois Press, 2017).

29. See Daphne A. Brooks, *Liner Notes for the Revolution: The Intellectual Life of Black Feminist Sound* (Cambridge, MA: Harvard University Press, 2021); Brent Hayes Edwards, *Epistrophies: Jazz and the Literary Imagination* (Cambridge, MA: Harvard University Press, 2017); Farah Jasmine Griffin, *Harlem Nocturne: Women Artists and Progressive Politics during World War II* (New York: Basic Books, 2013); and Gayle Wald, *Shout, Sister, Shout! The Untold Story of Rock-and-Roll Trailblazer Sister Rosetta Tharpe* (Boston: Beacon Press, 2007).

30. Imani Perry, *May We Forever Stand: A History of the Black National Anthem* (Chapel Hill: University of North Carolina Press, 2018), 7–13. See also

Brittney Cooper, *Beyond Respectability: The Intellectual Thought of Race Women* (Urbana: University of Illinois Press, 2017).

31. "Patti's Home Town Recalls Her as Cousin, Sis, Choir Singer's Daughter," *Baltimore Afro-American,* July 22, 1933.

32. Daughtry, "Sissieretta Jones," 133.

33. This perception is exemplified by Eileen Southern's contention that by "the mid-1890s the black prima donna had almost disappeared from the nation's concert halls because of lack of public interest." Southern, *Music of Black Americans,* 302.

34. Ronald Radano, *Lying Up a Nation: Race and Black Music* (Chicago: University of Chicago Press, 2003); Jon Cruz, *Culture on the Margins: The Black Spiritual and the Rise of American Cultural Interpretation* (Princeton, NJ: Princeton University Press, 1999); David Gilbert, *The Product of Our Souls: Ragtime, Race, and the Birth of the Manhattan Musical Marketplace* (Chapel Hill: University of North Carolina Press, 2015). See also Hagstrom Miller, *Segregating Sound.*

35. Lawrence Levine charted the trajectory of what he called opera's "sacralization" in *Highbrow/Lowbrow: The Emergence of Cultural Hierarchy in America* (Cambridge, MA: Harvard University Press, 1988). Many scholars argue convincingly that Levine failed to account for myriad forms of operatic music-making outside the opera house. Yet sacralization remains a useful, if incomplete, paradigm for understanding the general arc of opera's shifting cultural status. For an example of scholarship that augments Levine's conclusions, see Larry Hamberlin, *Tin Pan Opera: Operatic Novelty Songs in the Ragtime Era* (New York: Oxford University Press, 2011).

36. See Taylor, *Beyond Exoticism,* 15–72. See also Jonathan Glixon and Beth Glixon, *Inventing the Business of Opera: The Impresario and His World in Seventeenth-Century Venice* (New York: Oxford University Press, 2006). Joseph Roach hinted at this notion in *Cities of the Dead,* noting how Purcell's *Dido and Aeneas* was first produced in Chelsea in 1689 by "expensive young women" within "an economy of slave-produced abundance." Pointedly describing Dido as an "Afro-Phoenician queen," Roach notes that the chaconne on which Dido's famous lament is based derives has Caribbean origins; a musical product of diaspora underlies a work central to European opera. Joseph Roach, *Cities of the Dead: Circum-Atlantic Performance* (New York: Columbia University Press, 1996), 42–47.

37. See Renee Lapp Norris, "Opera and the Mainstreaming of Blackface Minstrelsy," *Journal of the Society for American Music* 1, no. 3 (2007): 341–365.

38. Marvin McAllister, *White People Do Not Know How to Behave at Entertainments Designed for Ladies & Gentlemen of Colour: William Brown's African and American Theater* (Chapel Hill: University of North Carolina Press, 2003), 161.

39. Jennifer Lynn Stoever, *The Sonic Color Line: Race and the Cultural Politics of Listening* (New York: New York University Press, 2016), 98. Italics in original.

40. Quoted in Schenbeck, *Racial Uplift and American Music,* 31.

41. Quoted in Ivy Wilson, ed., *Whitman Noir: Black America and the Good Gray Poet* (Iowa City: University of Iowa Press, 2014), viii.

42. Brooks, *Bodies in Dissent,* 313.

43. On bel canto and racialized vocality, see Marti Newland, "Sounding 'Black': An Ethnography of Racialized Vocality at Fisk University" (PhD diss., Columbia University, 2014), 47.

44. See Ann Satterthwaite, *Local Glories: Opera Houses on Main Street, Where Art and Community Meet* (New York: Oxford University Press, 2016).

45. For example, the Boston Symphony Orchestra was established in 1881, the Metropolitan Opera in 1883, the Chicago Symphony Orchestra in 1891, and the Philadelphia Orchestra in 1900. Benefactors wielded both artistic and economic influence: at the Met, for instance, boxholders made decisions about programming, ticket prices, and the house's design. See Paul DiMaggio, "Cultural Entrepreneurship in Nineteenth-Century Boston," in *Rethinking Popular Culture: Contemporary Perspectives in Cultural Studies,* ed. Chandra Mukerji and Michael Schudson (Berkeley: University of California Press, 1991).

46. Katherine Preston, *Opera for the People: English-Language Opera and Women Managers in Late 19th-Century America* (New York: Oxford University Press, 2017), 498–499.

47. Stuart Hall, "What Is This 'Black' in Black Popular Culture?" *Social Justice* 20, no. 1 / 2 (1993): 103–114, 106.

48. Gayle Wald, "Soul Vibrations: Black Music and Black Freedom in Sound and Space," *American Quarterly* 63, no. 3 (2011): 673–696, 690. On the "lower frequencies" as theoretical lens, see also Tina Campt, *Listening to Images* (Durham, NC: Duke University Press, 2017); and Tavia Nyong'o, "Afro-philo-sonic Fictions: Black Sound Studies after the Millennium," *Small Axe* 18, no. 2 (2014): 173–179.

49. William Grant Still to Clarence Cameron White, August 9, 1944, box 2, Clarence Cameron White Papers (Additions), 1906–1972, Sc MG 492, Schomburg Center for Research in Black Culture, Manuscripts Archives and Rare Books Division, New York Public Library; souvenir program for *Aida,* National Negro Opera Company Programs and Promotional Materials, Henry P. Whitehead Collection, Anacostia Community Museum Archives, Smithsonian Institution; Anne Wiggins Brown, *Sang fra frossen gren* (Song from a frozen hilltop), 30–31, typescript, box 1, Peabody Institute Anne Brown Collection, Arthur Friedheim Library Special Collections, Peabody Institute, The Johns Hopkins University.

50. Nathaniel Mackey, "Other: From Noun to Verb," *Representations* 39 (1992): 51–70.

51. This term evokes Paul Gilroy's paradigm-shifting theorization of the Black Atlantic as a "counterculture of modernity." Given Gilroy's critique of Eurocentrism and prioritization of vernacular musical forms, my application of this term to opera might seem surprising. That is deliberate. I mean to call attention to how Black operatic musicians, like vernacular artists, were shaped by the condition of marginalization and by a fraught relationship to Western modernity. In addition, I take inspiration from Gilroy's assertion that the "power of music in developing black struggles by communicating information, organising consciousness, and testing out

or deploying the forms of subjectivity which are required by political agency, whether individual or collective, defensive or transformational, demands attention to both the formal attributes of this expressive culture and its distinctive *moral basis.*" Paul Gilroy, *The Black Atlantic: Modernity and Double-Consciousness* (Cambridge, MA: Harvard University Press, 1993), 36. For an analysis of how Black classical and operatic musicians participated in a "counterculture of modernity," see Katherine Zien, *Sovereign Acts: Performing Race, Space, and Belonging in Panama and the Canal Zone* (New Brunswick, NJ: Rutgers University Press, 2017), 99–118.

52. Anthony Reed cautions against interpreting all Black art through the "romance of resistance," particularly when formal innovations are central to its oppositional potential. Anthony Reed, *Freedom Time: The Poetics and Politics of Black Experimental Writing* (Baltimore: Johns Hopkins University Press, 2014).

53. Matthew Aucoin, *The Impossible Art: Adventures in Opera* (New York: Farrar, Straus and Giroux, 2021); Alison Kinney, *Avidly Reads Opera* (New York: New York University Press, 2021), 10.

54. Robin D. G. Kelley, *Freedom Dreams: The Black Radical Imagination* (Boston: Beacon Press, 2002).

55. Farah Jasmine Griffin, "When Malindy Sings: A Meditation on Black Women's Vocality," in *Uptown Conversation: The New Jazz Studies,* ed. Robert O'Meally, Brent Hayes Edwards, and Farah Jasmine Griffin (New York: Columbia University Press, 2004), 119.

56. See Linda Hutcheon, "Interdisciplinary Opera Studies," *PMLA: Publications of the Modern Language Association of America* 121, no. 3 (2006): 802–810.

57. Samantha Ege, "Composing a Symphonist: Florence Price and the Hand of Black Women's Fellowship," *Women and Music: A Journal of Gender and Culture* 24 (2020): 7–27, 23.

58. Marvin McAllister, in his work on "whiting up," observes that "one could potentially read whiting up as black theatrical and extra-theatrical artists strategically investing in whiteness and attempting to progress up the racial ladder toward opportunity, wealth, and prestige," but he takes a more nuanced approach in his theorization of "stage Europeans" and "whiteface minstrels." Marvin McAllister, *Whiting Up: Whiteface Minstrels and Stage Europeans in African American Performance* (Chapel Hill: University of North Carolina Press, 2011).

59. "Operas and Cabarets," *The Messenger,* February 1924, 71. On this editorial's distillation of racial uplift ideology, see Shane Vogel, *The Scene of Harlem Cabaret: Race, Sexuality, Performance* (Chicago: University of Chicago Press, 2009), 6–12.

60. Joshua Berrett, "Louis Armstrong and Opera," *Musical Quarterly* 76, no. 2 (1992): 216–241; Matthew Frye Jacobson, *Odetta's One Grain of Sand,* 33 1/3 Series (New York: Bloomsbury, 2019); Mark Burford, *Mahalia Jackson and the Black Gospel Field* (New York: Oxford University Press, 2018), 228.

61. André applies the notion of "shadow culture" to a wide range of case studies from the United States and South Africa in the twentieth and twenty-first centuries.

She cautions that the term is not meant to imply a "second-tier" status, and she is careful not to "inadvertently give an impression that the thing fully illuminated is the true art, and that which is obscured is of lesser importance." André, *Black Opera,* 9–10.

62. Raymond Williams, *Marxism and Literature* (New York: Oxford University Press, 1977).

63. See Amy Absher, *The Black Musician and the White City: Race and Music in Chicago, 1900–1967* (Ann Arbor: University of Michigan Press, 2014).

64. Gilroy, *Black Atlantic;* Brooks, *Liner Notes for the Revolution,* 27.

65. Brooks, *Liner Notes for the Revolution,* 6.

66. My thinking here is informed by Fredara Hadley's comments during the panel "Constructing the Operatic Afrodiaspora" at the International Contemporary Ensemble's Afrodiasporic Opera Forum, May 27, 2021, https://vimeo.com /563712306.

67. On these methodological approaches, see, for example, Saidiya Hartman, "Venus in Two Acts," *Small Axe* 26, no. 2 (2008): 1–14, 3; and Alexandra T. Vazquez, *Listening in Detail: Performances of Cuban Music* (Durham, NC: Duke University Press, 2013).

68. Frederick Douglass, *Narrative of the Life of Frederick Douglass, an American Slave* (Boston: Anti-Slavery Office, 1845), 14.

1. The Dawning of Black Operatic Counterculture

1. Piano-vocal score, *The Martyr,* box 18, H. Lawrence Freeman Papers, Rare Book and Manuscript Library, Columbia University (hereafter Freeman Papers).

2. Piano-vocal score, *The Martyr.* For an analysis of Platonus's aria, see Austin Stewart, "'The Opera Is Booming. This Is a City': Opera in the Urban Frontier of Denver, 1864–1893" (PhD diss., University of Michigan, 2019), 262–275.

3. Piano-vocal score, *The Martyr.*

4. Untitled clipping, *Denver Rocky Mountain News,* in Scrapbook, box 59, Freeman Papers.

5. Elise Kirk, *American Opera* (Urbana: University of Illinois Press, 2001), 386, 111. On Delos Mars, see Eileen Southern, *The Music of Black Americans: A History* (New York: W. W. Norton, 1971), 193; and Helen Walker-Hill, *From Spirituals to Symphonies: African American Women Composers and Their Music* (Urbana: University of Illinois Press, 2007), 23. The scores for Delos Mars's operettas have been lost.

6. Lewis argues that "the entry into classical music, rather than being a form of bourgeois assimilationism as it is often portrayed, becomes an oppositional stance. In fact, the very existence of the black classical composer not only problematizes dominant conceptions of black music, but challenges fixed notions of high and low, black and white." George Lewis, *A Power Stronger Than Itself: The*

AACM and American Experimental Music (Chicago: University of Chicago Press, 2008), 367–368.

7. Harry L. Freeman, "African Grand Opera," *Washington Post,* May 15, 1898. Although Freeman would later describe *The Martyr* as his first opera, he also composed at least one earlier work, a "romantic work in three acts" titled *Epthelia.*

8. W. E. B. Du Bois, *The Souls of Black Folk* (Chicago: A.C. McClurg, 1903), 4.

9. James Parakilas, "The Operatic Canon," in *The Oxford Handbook of Opera,* ed. Helen M. Greenwald (New York: Oxford University Press, 2014), 873.

10. See Saidiya Hartman, *Wayward Lives, Beautiful Experiments: Intimate Histories of Social Upheaval* (New York: W. W. Norton, 2019).

11. On uplift ideology's internally contradictory logic, see Kevin Gaines, *Uplifting the Race: Black Leadership, Politics, and Culture in the Twentieth Century* (Chapel Hill: University of North Carolina Press, 1996).

12. Fred Moten, *Black and Blur* (Durham: Duke University Press, 2017), 142–143.

13. For instance, Larry Hamberlin shows how Tin Pan Alley songs featuring operatic allusions demonstrate that "the notion of opera as the exclusive property of the social and economic elites was hotly contested. Whether or not audiences were enjoined to view the opera-loving African, Irish, Italian and Jewish American protagonists of these songs as outsiders, those characters do not see themselves that way; they simply love opera." Larry Hamberlin, *Tin Pan Opera: Operatic Novelty Songs in the Ragtime Era* (New York: Oxford University Press, 2011), 7.

14. Imani Perry, *May We Forever Stand: A History of the Black National Anthem* (Chapel Hill: University of North Carolina Press, 2018), 7.

15. Perry, *May We Forever Stand,* 7–13.

16. On African American musicians at the World's Fair, see Marva Griffin Carter, *Swing Along: The Musical Life of Will Marion Cook* (New York: Oxford University Press, 2008).

17. Cook, born and raised in an elite family in Washington, DC, began his musical career as a violinist by studying at Oberlin and the Berlin Hochschule für Musik. He later turned his efforts toward ragtime, which he believed offered a more authentic pathway toward Black musical modernity. See Carter, *Swing Along.*

18. See Lynn Abbott and Doug Seroff, *Out of Sight: The Rise of African American Popular Music, 1889–1895* (Jackson: University Press of Mississippi, 2002), 279–284.

19. "Antonin Dvorak on Negro Melodies," *New York Herald,* May 28, 1893.

20. Eric Lott, *Love and Theft: Blackface Minstrelsy and the American Working Class* (New York: Oxford University Press, 1993). See also Douglas Shadle, *Antonín Dvořák's New World Symphony* (New York: Oxford University Press, 2021), 113–136. A hagiographic approach toward Dvořák's pronouncement, which centers the authority of white composers and discounts that of Black musicians, continues to

hold sway into the present day; see, for example, Joseph Horowitz, *Dvořák's Prophecy and the Vexed Fate of Black Classical Music* (New York: W.W. Norton, 2021).

21. "An African School of Music," *Baltimore Sun,* June 3, 1893.

22. See Hazel Carby, *Race Men* (Cambridge, MA: Harvard University Press, 2000).

23. Valdo Freeman, interview by Vivian Perlis, December 28, 1971, Major Figures in American Music Collection, Oral History of American Music, Music Library of Yale University. On Freeman's biography, see H. Lawrence Freeman, *The Negro in Music and Drama* typescript, box 50, Freeman Papers (hereafter Freeman, *Negro in Music and Drama*). See also David Gutkin, "The Modernities of H. Lawrence Freeman," *Journal of the American Musicological Society* 72, no. 3 (2019): 719–779.

24. Freeman, *Negro in Music and Drama,* 4.

25. Freeman, *Negro in Music and Drama,* 5.

26. Freeman, *Negro in Music and Drama,* 36–37. The prevalence of colorist terms ("sepian" or "Creole") in Freeman's account may speak to the fact that lighter-skinned Black artists, especially women, often enjoyed greater fame on the stage.

27. Freeman, *Negro in Music and Drama,* 15, 341.

28. The city's Black population more than doubled in size during the 1880s. By 1890, Denver had just over six thousand Black residents, representing 5.8 percent of the city's total population.

29. Stewart, "Opera Is Booming."

30. Stewart, "Opera Is Booming."

31. See Jocelyn Buckner, "'Spectacular Opacities': The Hyers Sisters' Performances of Respectability and Resistance," *African American Review* 45, no. 3 (2012): 309–323.

32. "Amusements," *Rocky Mountain News,* July 24, 1893.

33. Katherine Preston, *Opera for the People: English-Language Opera and Women Managers in Late 19th Century America* (New York: Oxford University Press, 2017). On the Emma Juch Grand Opera Company, see Kristen M. Turner, "'A Joyous Star-Spangled Bannerism': Emma Juch, Opera in English Translation, and the American Cultural Landscape in the Gilded Age," *Journal of the Society for American Music* 8, no. 2 (2014): 219–252. On Wagner's popularity in the United States, see Joseph Horowitz, *Wagner Nights: An American History* (Berkeley: University of California Press, 1994).

34. Freeman, "African Grand Opera."

35. Freeman recounts this tale both in the *Washington Post* article and in a letter to author Edward Hipsher, who requested information about Freeman's work in preparation for his 1927 book *American Opera and Its Composers.* The quotation is from his letter to Hipsher. H. Lawrence Freeman to Edward Hipsher, undated, box 49, Freeman Papers.

36. Gutkin, "Modernities of H. Lawrence Freeman," 726.

37. H. Lawrence Freeman, synopsis for *The Martyr,* box 50, Freeman Papers.

38. See David Charlton, "Introduction," in *The Cambridge Companion to Grand Opera*, ed. David Charlton (Cambridge: Cambridge University Press, 2003), 1–18.

39. Celia Davidson, "Opera by Afro-American Composers: A Critical Survey and Analysis of Selected Works" (PhD diss., Catholic University of America, 1980), 51.

40. Charlton, "Introduction," *Cambridge Companion to Grand Opera*, 1.

41. Scott Trafton, *Egypt Land: Race and Nineteenth-Century Egyptomania* (Durham, NC: Duke University Press, 2004). The opera's religious subject matter also linked it to the popular genre of Afro-Christian race histories. See Laurie Maffly-Kipp, *Setting Down the Sacred Past: African-American Race Histories* (Cambridge, MA: Harvard University Press, 2010).

42. Trafton, *Egypt Land*, 239.

43. Freeman, *Negro in Music and Drama*, 2–3. The book is dedicated to the historian Benjamin Brawley, a friend of Freeman's who died shortly before the completion of the manuscript.

44. See Stewart, "Opera Is Booming," 261.

45. Valdo Freeman, interview.

46. On Ernest Hogan and the *Rufus Rastus* shows, see Lynn Abbott and Doug Seroff, *Ragged but Right: Black Traveling Shows, "Coon Songs," and the Dark Pathway to Blues and Jazz* (Jackson: University Press of Mississippi, 2009), 47–53.

47. "The Martyr at the Columbus Theatre," *Broad Ax*, April 29, 1905.

48. Sylvester Russell, "The Pekin Stock Company in Captain Rufus," *Indianapolis Freeman*, September 7, 1907.

49. "Glory Hair Pomade," *Cleveland Gazette*, December 17, 1904.

50. Paul Allen Anderson, *Deep River: Music and Memory in Harlem Renaissance Thought* (Durham, NC: Duke University Press, 2001), 33–41.

51. Freeman, *Negro in Music and Drama*, 40.

52. Untitled clippings in Scrapbook, box 59, Freeman Papers.

53. Charles L. Burnham, "Here and There," *Colored American Magazine*, June 1901, 147.

54. See Stewart, "Opera Is Booming," 264.

55. Valdo Freeman, interview. One review of the premiere of Freeman's opera *Voodoo* offered an alternative perspective: "Somebody called Freeman the negro Wagner; maybe he is the negro Monteverde [*sic*]." The implication was that Freeman stood at the beginning of an inchoate tradition of Black operatic composition. "Negro Opera Makes First Appearance," *Morning Telegram*, in Scrapbook, box 59, Freeman Papers.

56. H. Lawrence Freeman to Edward Hipsher, undated, box 49, Freeman Papers.

57. "A Brief Resume of the Status of H. Lawrence Freeman, composer of eighteen original Grand Operas," box 36, Freeman Papers.

58. Kira Thurman, "Wagnerian Dreams, Grandiose Visions: Lawrence Freeman's *Voodoo* at the Miller Theater," *Opera Quarterly* 32, no. 2 / 3 (2016): 226–232, 227. Italics in original.

59. H. Lawrence Freeman, "The Musical Outlook," box 50, Freeman Papers.

60. H. Lawrence Freeman, "The Negro in Grand Opera," *Master Musician* (1920), in Scrapbook, box 55, Freeman Papers.

61. Valdo Freeman, interview.

62. Davidson, "Opera by Afro-American Composers," 128–129; Kirk, *American Opera,* 188.

63. H. Lawrence Freeman, "The Negro in Grand Opera," *Master Musician* (1920), in Scrapbook, box 55, Freeman Papers.

64. Untitled clipping, *Cleveland Press,* March 25, 1898, in Scrapbook, box 59, Freeman Papers.

65. Valdo Freeman, interview.

66. For an overview of Black musical theater portrayals of Africa, see Karen Sotiropoulos, *Staging Race: Black Performers in Turn of the Century America* (Cambridge, MA: Harvard University Press, 2009), 123–162.

67. H. Lawrence Freeman, "The Negro in the Higher Altitudes of Music in This Country and throughout the World," *A.M.E. Review* (1915), clipping in Scrapbook, box 59, Freeman Papers.

68. Tsitsi Jaji, *Africa in Stereo: Modernism, Music, and Pan-African Solidarity* (New York: Oxford University Press, 2014), 7.

69. Prospectus for the Negro Grand Opera Company, box 36; and Freeman, "The Negro in Grand Opera," *Master Musician* (1920), in Scrapbook, box 55, Freeman Papers.

70. "Racial opera" and "Negro opera": untitled clippings, 1897; "Sacred opera": Johann Beck to H. Lawrence Freeman, April 9, 1903; "Egyptian opera," caption of photograph of shoebill stork in Freeman's handwriting; "Original grand opera": advertisement for a planned 1920 production of *The Martyr* (which never occurred); "Egyptian grand opera": Freeman, "Higher Altitudes"; all in Scrapbook, box 59, Freeman Papers. The location of all these descriptors within the pages of a single scrapbook conveys just how varied the terminology surrounding *The Martyr* was, and suggests Freeman's awareness of that confusion.

71. Program, "The Story of Negro Music," May 10, 1930, in Scrapbook, box 57, Freeman Papers.

72. Freeman, *Negro in Music and Drama,* 342–343. Italics mine. As Carol Oja has written, William Grant Still faced similar racialized critiques of his early compositions. See Carol J. Oja, *Making Music Modern: New York in the 1920s* (New York: Oxford University Press), 331–336.

73. Freeman, *Negro in Music and Drama,* 346. See also Gutkin, "The Modernities of H. Lawrence Freeman," 728.

74. Piano-vocal score, *The Martyr.* Freeman's play on musical Black-and-white might be compared to that of James Weldon Johnson's *The Autobiography of*

an Ex-Colored Man, in which the narrator recalls playing the piano with his mother: "I used to stand by her side, and often interrupt and annoy her by chiming in with strange harmonies which I found either on the high keys of the treble or low keys of the bass. I remember that I had a *particular fondness for the Black keys.*" (Boston: Sherman, French, and Co., 1912), 6. Italics mine.

75. Naomi André, *Black Opera: History, Power, Engagement* (Urbana: University of Illinois Press, 2018), 7.

76. Jayna Brown, *Babylon Girls: Black Women Performers and the Shaping of the Modern* (Durham, NC: Duke University Press, 2008), 95. See also Jennifer Brody, *Impossible Purities: Blackness, Femininity, and Victorian Culture* (Durham, NC: Duke University Press, 1998); and Daphne A. Brooks, *Bodies in Dissent: Spectacular Performances of Race and Freedom, 1850–1910* (Durham, NC: Duke University Press, 2006).

77. See Stewart, "The City Is Booming," 256–258.

78. Freeman, *Negro in Music and Drama,* 40.

79. For an important analysis of the Drury Company, see Kristen M. Turner, "Class, Race, and Uplift in the Opera House: Theodore Drury and His Company Cross the Color Line," *Journal of Musicological Research* 34, no. 4 (2015): 320–351.

80. On the rarity of studies of rehearsal within musicology in general and opera studies in particular, see John Rosselli et al., "Rehearsal," in *Grove Music Online* (1992), ed. Deane Root. Scholars of theater and performance studies have explored the subdiscipline of "rehearsal studies," which often utilizes ethnographic research. See Gay McAuley, *Not Magic but Work: An Ethnographic Account of a Rehearsal Process* (Manchester, UK: Manchester University Press, 2012). See also Marti Newland's excellent account of the Fisk Jubilee Singers' rehearsal practices in "Sounding 'Black': An Ethnography of Racialized Vocality at Fisk University" (PhD diss., Columbia University, 2014), 82–118.

81. Hartman, *Wayward Lives, Beautiful Experiments,* 334–335, 302. Similarly, Nancy Yunhwa Rao argues that close engagement with archival fragments—for instance, a creased scrap of paper containing lyrics for an aria—enables her to "dream the everyday life" of opera and consider the interiority of Chinese immigrant performers who participated in the art form. Nancy Yunhwa Rao, *Chinatown Opera Theater in North America* (Urbana: University of Illinois Press, 2017), 4.

82. Thomas Riis, *Just before Jazz: Black Musical Theater in New York, 1890–1915* (Washington, DC: Smithsonian Institution Press, 1989).

83. Cole's comments stemmed from a pay dispute with the white managers of Black Patti's Troubadours, the vaudeville troupe led by Sissieretta Jones. Bob Cole, "The Colored Actors' Declaration of Independence of 1898"; and William Foster, "Pioneers of the Stage: Memoirs of William Foster," in *The Official Theatrical World of Colored Artists,* ed. Theophilus Lewis (New York: Theatrical World Publishing, 1928).

84. H. S. Fortune, "Grand Opera as We See It," *Colored American Magazine,* June 1900, 79.

85. "Men of the Hour," *Colored American* (newspaper), February 28, 1903. Drury may have studied at the National Conservatory of Music in New York during Dvořák's tenure as director, although evidence is inconclusive. See Turner, "Class, Race, and Uplift in the Opera House," 327–328.

86. James Weldon Johnson, *Black Manhattan* (New York: Viking, 1930), 118. On the Marshall Hotel, see David Gilbert, *The Product of Our Souls: Ragtime, Race, and the Birth of the Manhattan Musical Marketplace* (Chapel Hill: University of North Carolina Press, 2015), 47–73.

87. "Theodore Drury as a Dramatic Tenor," *Colored American* (newspaper), May 28, 1900.

88. "Zion Church Concert," *Yonkers Statesman,* June 17, 1887.

89. Marvin McAllister, *Whiting Up: Whiteface Minstrels and Stage Europeans in African American Performance* (Chapel Hill: University of North Carolina Press, 2011), 4. In a related context, Diana Paulin has argued that Black-cast productions featuring non-Black characters provided "an opportunity to participate in the ongoing dialogue about racial dynamics by challenging the racist belief that nonwhites should be segregated, civilized, and contained." Diana Paulin, *Imperfect Unions: Staging Miscegenation in U.S. Drama and Fiction* (Minneapolis: University of Minnesota Press, 2012), 169.

90. Daphne A. Brooks, *Liner Notes for the Revolution: The Intellectual Life of Black Feminist Sound* (Cambridge, MA: Harvard University Press, 2021), 17.

91. Hartman, *Wayward Lives, Beautiful Experiments.*

92. "Passing Events," *Irish Times,* May 19, 1900; "Musical Notes," *Washington Post,* May 13, 1900.

93. "Only Negro Opera Company in the World," *New York Sun,* May 14, 1905.

94. "Colored Singers in Opera," *Boston Globe,* May 12, 1907.

95. Turner, "Class, Race, and Uplift in the Opera House," 330. Because few conservatories admitted African Americans, these students may have recognized that joining the company represented one of the only pathways by which they might learn about opera.

96. "Only Negro Opera Company in the World."

97. "Colored Singers in Opera."

98. Robert W. Carter, "The Drury Opera Company in Verdi's 'Aida,'" *Colored American Magazine,* August 1903, 596.

99. The exact rate of pay is unknown. Drury stated in 1906 that "I cannot pay my principals extravagantly . . . You see, we give only one performance a year, and though the rehearsing may take from two to three months, I am not able to pay my company during that time." "Black Melbas and De Reszkes: Negroes in Grand Opera," *The Sketch,* January 17, 1906.

100. "Only Negro Opera Company in the World."

101. George Ruffin, son of Josephine and George Lewis Ruffin, sang principal roles in *Faust* (1902), *Aida* (1903), and *Cavalleria Rusticana/Pagliacci* (1904). Mary

Terrell, daughter of Mary Church Terrell, sang in *Carmen* and *Aida* in 1906. Turner, "Class, Race, and Uplift in the Opera House," 349–350.

102. "Only Negro Opera Company in the World." Performances featuring white singers often attracted negative coverage in the Black press, a rare exception to the company's generally glowing reception. For instance, a review of the 1903 production of *Aida* described the casting of Alfrida Wegner, a German American mezzo-soprano, as Amneris as "an impossibility owing to conditions over which Drury has no control." "The Drury Opera Co.," *Colored American* (newspaper), May 16, 1903.

103. Information about the cast is from "Negroes to Sing 'Carmen,'" *New York Sun,* May 6, 1900.

104. Preston, *Opera for the People,* 346.

105. These quotations are from, in order: *New York Evening Post,* May 5, 1900; "The Stage," *Indianapolis Freeman,* July 21, 1900; *Chicago Tribune,* May 11, 1900; "Negroes to Sing 'Carmen,'" *New York Sun,* May 6, 1900; "'Carmen' Sung by Colored Singers," *New York Herald,* May 15, 1900; "Passing Events," *Irish Times,* May 19, 1900.

106. "Here and There," *Colored American Magazine,* June 1900, 190.

107. See Susan McClary, *Georges Bizet: 'Carmen,'* Cambridge Opera Handbooks (Cambridge: Cambridge University Press, 1992). The opera has been reimagined in relation to Black life in several contexts, from the Broadway show (1943) and film *Carmen Jones* (1954), to the 2001 MTV production *Carmen: A Hip Hopera,* starring Beyoncé Knowles. In 2005, the South African film *U-Carmen eKhayelitsha* transposed the opera to Cape Town. See André, *Black Opera,* 120–166; and Susan McClary, "*Carmen* as Perennial Fusion: From Habanera to Hip Hop," in *Carmen: From Silent Film to MTV,* ed. Chris Perriam and Ann Davies (Amsterdam: Rodopi, 2005), 205–216.

108. See Paige McGinley, "'A Southern, Brown, Burnt Sensibility': *Four Saints in Three Acts,* Black Spain, and the (Global) Southern Pastoral," in *Creating and Consuming the American South: Borderlands and Transnationalism in the United States and Canada,* ed. Martyn Bone, Brian Ward, and William A. Link (Gainesville: University of Florida Press, 2015), 235–236.

109. "'Carmen' Sung by Colored Singers," *New York Herald,* May 15, 1900.

110. "Drury Company in 'Carmen,'" *American Citizen,* May 25, 1900.

111. James Parakilas, "The Chorus," in *The Cambridge Companion to Grand Opera,* ed. David Charlton (Cambridge: Cambridge University Press, 2003), 76.

112. The best-known example is the nationalist "Va pensiero," the lament of the Hebrew slaves in Verdi's *Nabucco.* Ryan Minor, "The Chorus," in *The Oxford Handbook of Opera,* ed. Helen M. Greenwald (New York: Oxford University Press, 2014), 270.

113. Fortune, "Grand Opera as We See It," 78.

114. "Carmen Sung by Negroes," *New York Dramatic Mirror,* May 26, 1900.

115. "'Carmen' Sung by Colored Singers."

116. "Music and Musicians," *San Francisco Call,* June 13, 1900.

117. "'Carmen' Sung by Colored Singers."

118. "Carmen Sung by Negroes."

119. Freeman, *Negro in Music and Drama,* 161.

120. James Weldon Johnson, *Along This Way: The Autobiography of James Weldon Johnson* (New York: Viking, 1933), 174.

121. Hartman, *Wayward Lives, Beautiful Experiments;* Minor, "The Chorus."

122. Hartman, *Wayward Lives, Beautiful Experiments,* 301.

123. Hartman, *Wayward Lives, Beautiful Experiments,* 348.

124. Patrick Washburn, *The African American Newspaper: Voice of Freedom* (Evanston, IL: Northwestern University Press, 2006), 48–49.

125. Elizabeth McHenry, *Forgotten Readers: Recovering the Lost History of African American Literary Societies* (Durham, NC: Duke University Press, 2002), 112–113.

126. Eric Gardner and Jocelyn Moody, "Introduction: Black Periodical Studies," *American Periodicals* 25, no. 2 (2015): 105–111, 107.

127. On Black music critics, see Mark Grant, *Maestros of the Pen: A History of Classical Music Criticism in America* (Boston: Northeastern University Press, 1998), 319–320.

128. Anna Everett, *Returning the Gaze: A Genealogy of Black Film Criticism, 1909–1949* (Durham, NC: Duke University Press, 2001), 35.

129. Jennifer Lynn Stoever, *The Sonic Color Line: Race and the Cultural Politics of Listening* (New York: New York University Press, 2016), 79.

130. Brooks, *Liner Notes for the Revolution,* 61.

131. Clifford E. Watkins, *Showman: The Life and Music of Perry George Lowery* (Jackson: University Press of Mississippi, 2003), 19. On Black performers and the *Freeman,* see Rachel Miller, "Capital Entertainment: Stage Work and the Origins of the U.S. Creative Economy, 1830–1920" (PhD diss., University of Michigan, 2018), 289–349.

132. William Henry Davis, "A Historic Account of Sylvester Russell," *Indianapolis Freeman,* January 1, 1910.

133. Davis, "Sylvester Russell."

134. "Russell Song Recital," *Seneca County News,* February 4, 1898; Advertisement, *Boston Globe,* March 6, 1892. Russell's stints with minstrel companies included tours with the Hicks and Sawyer Georgia Minstrels in 1891 and 1892, and with Mahara's Eastern Minstrels in 1899. Advertisement, *Boston Globe,* March 6, 1892; "The Stage," *Indianapolis Freeman,* September 23, 1899.

135. Anna Everett notes that the inclusion of this photo was unusual, because most critics were identified through bylines alone. Everett, *Returning the Gaze,* 41.

136. Sylvester Russell, "Chicago Weekly Review," *Indianapolis Freeman,* September 25, 1915.

137. See Hazel Carby, *Race Men* (Cambridge, MA: Harvard University Press, 1998); and Gaines, *Uplifting the Race.*

138. Everett, *Returning the Gaze,* 41; Paige McGinley, *Staging the Blues: From Tent Shows to Tourism* (Durham, NC: Duke University Press, 2014), 50; and Thomas Bauman, *The Pekin: The Rise and Fall of Chicago's First Black-Owned Theater* (Urbana: University of Illinois Press, 2014), 65.

139. Du Bois, *Souls of Black Folk,* 3. This interpretation of double-consciousness is informed by Brittney Cooper, who reframes Du Bois's portrayal of the Black body as a site of internal conflict by contrasting it with Anna Julia Cooper's understanding of competing identities as a site of "generative tension." Brittney Cooper, *Beyond Respectability: The Intellectual Thought of Race Women* (Urbana: University of Illinois Press, 2017), 6.

140. See David Monod, "Double-Voiced: Music, Gender, and Nature in Performance," *Journal of the Gilded Age and Progressive Era* 14, no. 2 (2015): 173–193. Nineteenth-century Black female concert singers like Elizabeth Taylor Greenfield and Flora Batson Bergen were also described as "double-voiced." Jennifer Stoever notes the racialized implications of the term, which implies that these women were excessive or unnatural. Stoever, *Sonic Color Line,* 119.

141. McGinley, *Staging the Blues,* 49–50.

142. Sylvester Russell, "A Review of the Stage," *Indianapolis Freeman,* February 15, 1902.

143. Sylvester Russell, "Review of the Stage."

144. Sylvester Russell, "Smart Set in Hartford," *Indianapolis Freeman,* October 24, 1903.

145. Sylvester Russell, "Review," *Chicago Defender,* December 24, 1910.

146. Sylvester Russell, "Should Respectable Girls Adopt the Stage?" *Indianapolis Freeman,* April 23, 1904.

147. Sylvester Russell, "A Novel Innovation in Vocal Culture," *Indianapolis Freeman,* October 13, 1906.

148. Sylvester Russell, "Sylvester Russell's Review," *Pittsburgh Courier,* December 28, 1929.

149. Stoever, *Sonic Color Line,* 111.

150. Sylvester Russell, "The Futurity of American Music," *Indianapolis Freeman,* August 24, 1907; "Theodore Drury in Carmen," *Indianapolis Freeman,* July 7, 1906.

151. Russell, "Futurity of American Music."

152. Sylvester Russell, "Chicago Weekly Review," *Indianapolis Freeman,* May 13, 1916; "Ernest Hogan Goes West," *Indianapolis Freeman,* March 24, 1906.

153. Handwritten draft signed by Russell, in Scrapbook, box 59, Freeman Papers.

154. Sylvester Russell, "The Vocal Music of Three Great Composers," *Indianapolis Freeman,* November 10, 1906.

155. Sylvester Russell, "The Theodore Drury Opera Company in Verdi's Opera Aida," *Indianapolis Freeman,* June 23, 1906; Sylvester Russell, "Theodore Drury in Carmen," *Indianapolis Freeman,* July 7, 1906.

156. Sylvester Russell, "A Review of the Stage," *Indianapolis Freeman*, May 24, 1902.

157. Sylvester Russell, "A Review of the Stage," *Indianapolis Freeman*, February 15, 1902.

158. Russell, "The Theodore Drury Opera Company in Verdi's Opera Aida."

159. Sylvester Russell, "Special Stage Review," *Indianapolis Freeman*, August 6, 1913.

160. Sylvester Russell, "Why the Great Singers Are Declining," *Indianapolis Freeman*, June 27, 1903; "Decline of Art and Lack of Appreciation for Real Artists," *Indianapolis Freeman*, September 13, 1913; "Lack of Appreciation for the Classics," *Indianapolis Freeman*, December 25, 1915.

161. Sylvester Russell, "The Theatrical World," *Pittsburgh Courier*, December 19, 1925.

162. Evelyn Brooks Higginbotham, "African-American Women's History and the Metalanguage of Race," *Signs* 17, no. 2 (1992): 266–273.

163. Russell, "The Futurity of American Music."

164. Valdo Freeman, interview.

165. Valdo Freeman, interview.

166. "Seven Killed in Bad Wreck at Vergennes," *Barre Daily Times*, December 1, 1906.

2. New Selves, New Spheres

1. Harry Bradford, "What the Colored Vaudevillians Are Doing in New York City and the East," *Indianapolis Freeman*, November 13, 1909.

2. Many sources attribute Joplin's interest in opera to his childhood piano teacher, Julius Weiss. See Edward Berlin, *King of Ragtime: Scott Joplin and His Era*, 2nd ed. (New York: Oxford University Press, 2016).

3. The brief tour was truncated after the company's money was stolen. The score to *A Guest of Honor* is now lost.

4. Lester Walton, "Composer of Ragtime Now Writing Grand Opera," *New York Age*, March 5, 1908.

5. "New York News," *Indianapolis Freeman*, August 9, 1913.

6. Lester Walton, "Things Theatrical," *New York Age*, April 5, 1917.

7. W. Fitzhugh Brundage, "Working in the 'Kingdom of Culture': African Americans and American Popular Culture, 1890–1930," in *Beyond Blackface: African Americans and the Creation of American Popular Culture, 1890–1930*, ed. Brundage (Chapel Hill: University of North Carolina Press, 2011), 7.

8. J. Rosamond Johnson, "A Treasury of American Negro Music," typescript, 25, box 19, MSS 21, J. Rosamond Johnson Papers, Irving S. Gilmore Music Library, Yale University.

9. "Samuel Coleridge-Taylor," *Indianapolis Freeman*, September 14, 1912.

10. On Black performance cultures during this era, see David Krasner, *A Beautiful Pageant: African American Theater, Drama, and Performance in the Harlem Renaissance, 1910–1927* (New York: Palgrave Macmillan, 2002); and Karen Sotiropoulos, *Staging Race: Black Performers in Turn of the Century America* (Cambridge, MA: Harvard University Press, 2009).

11. See Ethan Michaeli, *The Defender: How the Legendary Black Newspaper Changed America* (Boston: Houghton Mifflin Harcourt, 2016).

12. See Kristen M. Turner, "'A Joyous Star-Spangled Bannerism': Emma Juch, Opera in English Translation, and the American Cultural Landscape in the Gilded Age," *Journal of the Society for American Music* 8, no. 2 (2014): 219–252; and Larry Hamberlin, *Tin Pan Opera: Operatic Novelty Songs in the Ragtime Era* (New York: Oxford University Press, 2011).

13. Scholars of African American literature have noted the ways in which "the privileging of white readership as a marker of African American literary success" has shaped what we consider to be the key features of Black literature in the pre-Harlem Renaissance era. Similar dynamics shape the reception of music and performance. See Shirley Moody-Turner, "Introduction," in *African American Literature in Transition, 1900–1910* (Cambridge: Cambridge University Press, 2021), 4.

14. Samantha Ege, *South Side Impresarios: How Race Women Transformed Chicago's Classical Music Scene* (Urbana: University of Illinois Press, 2024); A. Kori Hill, "Florence Price and the Self-Determinist Mission of the National Association of Negro Musicians," paper presented at the American Musicological Society Annual Meeting, November 2021.

15. Angela Davis, *Blues Legacies and Black Feminism: Gertrude "Ma" Rainey, Bessie Smith, and Billie Holiday* (New York: Vintage Books, 1998), 5. Davis contrasts this focus on individuality with the collective desire for freedom prioritized in the spirituals.

16. See Nina Sun Eidsheim, *The Race of Sound: Listening, Timbre, and Vocality in African American Music* (Durham, NC: Duke University Press, 2019), 39–60.

17. See, for example, Lawrence Schenbeck, *Racial Uplift and American Music, 1878–1943* (Jackson: University Press of Mississippi, 2012); Willard Gatewood, *Aristocrats of Color: The Black Elite, 1880–1920* (Fayetteville: University of Arkansas Press, 2000), 197; and Kevin Gaines, *Uplifting the Race: Black Leadership, Politics, and Culture in the Twentieth Century* (Chapel Hill: University of North Carolina Press, 1996), 76.

18. Masi Asare, "Vocal Colour in Blue: Early Twentieth-Century Black Women Singers as Broadway's Voice Teachers," *Performance Matters* 6, no. 2 (2020): 52–66.

19. Freeman also established a group called the Negro Choral Society that performed, according to one advertisement, "Anything from NEGRO FOLK SONG to GRAND OPERA." Undated clipping, Scrapbook, box 59, H. Lawrence Freeman Papers, Rare Book and Manuscript Library, Columbia University

20. "H. Lawrence Freeman, Composer of Operas, Traces Climb of Negro Musicians," *New York Amsterdam News,* November 16, 1935.

21. Darryl Glenn Nettles, *African American Concert Singers before 1950* (Jefferson, NC: McFarland, 2003), 49.

22. Sidney Woodward, *Out of Bondage to a Place of Esteem and Trust: The Story of a Career Unique in Musical History* (New York: Merchantile Press, 1918), 14–15.

23. "Madame Bertha Tyree in Recital," *Chicago Defender,* May 25, 1918; "Miss Maude J. Roberts in Recital," *Chicago Defender,* March 10, 1917.

24. Kira Thurman, *Singing Like Germans* (Ithaca, NY: Cornell University Press, 2021), 53. Thurman notes that far more instrumentalists than singers sought out training in Europe. Terrell recounted these memories in her 1940 memoir: Mary Eliza Church Terrell, *A Colored Woman in a White World* (Washington, DC: Ransdell, 1940).

25. Scott Carter, "Forging a Sound Citizenry: Voice Culture and the Embodiment of the Nation, 1880–1920," *American Music Research Center Journal* 22 (2013): 11–34.

26. Louis C. Elson, *The Realm of Music: A Series of Musical Essays, Chiefly Historical and Educational* (Boston: New England Conservatory, 1892), 275.

27. Carter, "Forging a Sound Citizenry." On the racial politics of vocal timbre and vocal pedagogy, see Grant Olwage, "The Class and Colour of Tone: An Essay on the Social History of Vocal Timbre," *Ethnomusicology Forum* 13, no. 2 (2004): 203–226; Marti Newland, "Sounding 'Black': An Ethnography of Racialized Vocality at Fisk University" (PhD diss., Columbia University, 2014); and Eidsheim, *Race of Sound.*

28. "Minutes of the Second Annual Meeting of the National Association of Negro Musicians," 1920, box 2, Collection of Materials on the National Association of Negro Musicians, Center for Black Music Research, Columbia College Chicago.

29. Advertisement, *The Crisis* 4, no. 3 (July 1912): 108.

30. J. Gray Lucas, "The Song Recital by Madam M. Calloway-Byron at Quinn Was a Very Artistic Affair," *Broad Ax,* June 29, 1918.

31. Advertisement, *The Crisis* 9, no. 6 (April 1915): 266.

32. See Stephanie Doktor, "Finding Florence Mills: The Voice of the Harlem Jazz Queen in the Compositions of William Grant Still and Edmund Thornton Jenkins," *Journal of the Society for American Music* 14, no. 4 (2020): 451–479, 457. On Black women's classical singing as "powerful," see Julia J. Chybowski, "Becoming the 'Black Swan' in Mid-Nineteenth-Century America," *Journal of the American Musicological Society* 67, no. 1 (2014): 125–165, 144–146; and Stoever, *Sonic Color Line,* 111 and 297n88.

33. "Florence Cole-Talbert Appears," *New York Times,* April 17, 1918; Eidsheim, *Race of Sound,* 61–90.

34. Nora Douglas Holt, "Music," *Chicago Defender,* February 12, 1921.

35. Lucas, "Song Recital by Madam M. Calloway-Byron."

36. Louise Henry, "A History of Negro Music and Musicians in Chicago: Anita Patti Brown," October 11, 1939, Illinois Writers Project, Chapter 5: Divas and Divans, 2, https://cdm16818.contentdm.oclc.org/digital/collection/IllWriters/id/9927/rec/1. Italics mine.

37. Jon Cruz, *Culture on the Margins: The Black Spiritual and the Rise of American Cultural Interpretation* (Princeton, NJ: Princeton University Press, 1999).

38. Henry, "History of Negro Music and Musicians," 2.

39. On racial segregation in the early recording industry, see Karl Hagstrom Miller, *Segregating Sound: Inventing Folk and Pop Music in the Age of Jim Crow* (Durham, NC: Duke University Press, 2010).

40. Quoted in David Suisman, *Selling Sounds: The Commercial Revolution in American Music* (Cambridge, MA: Harvard University Press, 2009), 218.

41. Alexandra T. Vazquez, *Listening in Detail: Performances of Cuban Music* (Durham, NC: Duke University Press, 2013).

42. "Black Swan Phonograph Company Celebrates Second Anniversary," *New York Amsterdam News,* June 6, 1923. Who was actually the first African American singer to record opera is a matter of some debate. Anita Patti Brown reportedly made a test recording of an aria from *Mignon* for Victor in 1916, and E. Azalia Hackley made a handful of recordings for an unidentified European company that same year, but those recordings are now lost. On Brown, see Tim Brooks, *Lost Sounds: Blacks and the Birth of the Recording Industry, 1890–1919* (Urbana: University of Illinois Press, 2004), 504. On Hackley, see Juanita Karpf, *Performing Racial Uplift: E. Azalia Hackley and African American Activism in the Postbellum to Pre-Harlem Era* (Jackson: University of Mississippi Press, 2022), 64.

43. "Antoinette Garnes in Concert," *Chicago Defender,* November 6, 1920. On Garnes's biography, see Emil Pinta, "Addendum," *ARSC Journal* 51, no. 2 (2020): 279–281.

44. Nora Douglas Holt, "Diamond and Gold Medal to Local Artists," *Chicago Defender,* June 28, 1919.

45. "An Opera Star," *Chicago Defender,* May 13, 1922.

46. "Mrs. Garnes to Sing," *Chicago Defender,* June 9, 1923.

47. Nora Douglas Holt, "News of the Music World," *Chicago Defender,* July 22, 1922. It also seems that Garnes may have concealed her racial identity (or been misunderstood by listeners) at certain moments during her career. In 1921, the *Music News* described her as a "charming little Spanish-American singer from Panama." Fascinatingly, this reviewer heard her voice as "of unusually pure, clear quality . . . lovely, flexible, if not extraordinarily powerful"—qualities more often attributed to white female singers. Yet her identity was certainly no secret, as periodicals like the *Crisis* and the *Defender* regularly hailed her as a "race singer" during the same years. Agnes Beldon, "Antoinette Garnes Gives Notable Vocal Recital," *Music News,* January 28, 1921.

48. John Graziano, "The Early Life and Career of the 'Black Patti': The Odyssey of an African American Singer in the Late Nineteenth Century," *Journal of the American Musicological Society* 53, no. 3 (2000): 543–596, 556.

49. Like many of her contemporaries, Garnes later transitioned from performance to teaching, including stints at Wilberforce University, Hampton Institute, and Lincoln University.

50. Lynn Abbott and Doug Seroff, *To Do This, You Must Know How: Music Pedagogy in the Black Gospel Quartet Tradition* (Jackson: University Press of Mississippi, 2013), 4.

51. On Black choral societies, see N. Lee Orr, "The United States," in *Nineteenth-Century Choral Music,* ed. Donna M. Di Grazia (New York: Routledge, 2013), 485–486; and Abbott and Seroff, *To Do This, You Must Know How,* 223–230.

52. "Mixed Audience Sees Bible Opera," *New Journal and Guide,* October 3, 1925.

53. "Douglass Amateurs Please in First Opera Offering," *Baltimore Afro-American,* June 1, 1929.

54. W. Llewelyn Wilson, "Concords and Discords," *Baltimore Afro-American,* August 9, 1930.

55. J. Logan Jenkins, "Douglass High School Opera," *Pittsburgh Courier,* June 1, 1929.

56. Jenkins, "Douglass High School Opera."

57. Brown is quoted in Sarah Thomas, "A Message of Inclusion, A History of Exclusion: Racial Injustice at the Peabody Institute," 9, essay accompanying online exhibit, Sheridan Libraries and Museums, Johns Hopkins University, September 2019, https://jscholarship.library.jhu.edu/server/api/core/bitstreams/664f1e92-60e4 -4e97-9b9b-31dab5c30b3e/content.

58. On classical music pedagogy at Black colleges, see Thurman, *Singing Like Germans,* 21–41. Thurman notes that "many institutions discouraged the study of opera, especially for Black women, on the grounds that it was not respectable enough for an aspiring student of a middle-class background" (36).

59. R. G. Doggett, "An Undeveloped Musical Genius," *Howard University Journal* 8, no. 19, February 17, 1911, Howard University Archives, https://dh.howard .edu/cgi/viewcontent.cgi?article=1018&context=huj_v8. Alexander later moved to St. Louis and became an actress.

60. Hill, "Florence Price and the Self-Determinist Mission of the National Association of Negro Musicians." On the founding of the NANM, see Willis Patterson, "A History of the National Association of Negro Musicians (NANM): The First Quarter Century, 1919–1943" (PhD diss., Wayne State University, 1993).

61. Nora Douglas Holt, "Music," *Chicago Defender,* February 21, 1920.

62. Anna Everett, *Returning the Gaze: A Genealogy of Black Film Criticism, 1909–1949* (Durham, NC: Duke University Press, 2001), 2.

63. On Black critics and the refutation of white writers' racist perspectives on Black music, see Doris Evans McGinty, "'As Large as She Can Make It': The Role of Black Women Activists in Music, 1880–1945," in *Cultivating Music in America: Women Patrons and Activists since 1860,* ed. Ralph P. Locke and Cyrilla Barr (Berkeley: University of California Press, 1997), 227–228.

64. The Black press also lacks the exceptionalizing bias of primary sources like programs and playbills, which tend to single out notable individual performers.

65. Nathan Hopkins, "Barbers Flock to Hear Opera; Elite Missing," *Chicago Defender,* December 15, 1923.

66. Nora Douglas Holt, "News of the Music World," *Chicago Defender,* January 27, 1923.

67. R. G. Doggett, "The Lady of Lyons," *New York Age,* March 6, 1913; and "The Mikado a Success," *New York Age,* March 13, 1913.

68. Lester Walton, "The Critic Criticised," *New York Age,* March 27, 1913.

69. On Walton's biography, see Everett, *Returning the Gaze;* and Susan Curtis, *Colored Memories: A Biographer's Quest for the Elusive Lester A. Walton* (Columbia: University of Missouri Press, 2008).

70. Lester Walton, "Stop German Opera; Un-American Film Allowed on Screen," *New York Age,* March 15, 1919.

71. "Lena James Holt Takes High Honors at Chicago Musical College," *Chicago Defender,* June 29, 1918. "The tragedy of my life" is from Nora Douglas Holt to Donald Gallup, July 24, 1952, box 44, Donald Clifford Gallup Papers, Yale Collection of American Literature, Beinecke Rare Book and Manuscript Library, Yale University. Holt's byline varied: at different points in her life, she went by Lena James, Lena James Douglas, Lena Douglas, Nora Holt, Nora Douglas Holt, and Nora Holt Ray.

72. In *Music and Poetry,* Holt noted that one of NANM's inaugural meetings took place at her home, and that she had encouraged Black musical leaders to come together in "musicianal unity" in the interest of collective progress. "A Chronological History of the NANM," *Music and Poetry,* July 1921, James Weldon Johnson Memorial Collection of African American Arts and Letters, Beinecke Rare Book and Manuscript Library, Yale University. On Holt's role as co-founder, see Schenbeck, *Racial Uplift and American Music,* 195–201.

73. On Holt's biography and criticism, see Lucy Caplan, "'Strange What Cosmopolites Music Makes of Us': Classical Music, the Black Press, and Nora Douglas Holt's Black Feminist Audiotopia," *Journal of the Society for American Music* 14, no. 3 (2020): 308–336.

74. W. E. B. Du Bois, *The Souls of Black Folk* (Chicago: A. C. McClurg, 1903), 4.

75. Nora Douglas Holt, "News of the Music World," *New York Age,* October 22, 1921.

76. Nora Douglas Holt, "Walters Zion Church Has Brilliant Recital," *Chicago Defender,* April 13, 1918.

77. Lena James Holt, "Chicago an Art Center," *Chicago Defender,* January 19, 1918.

78. Lena James Holt, "The Symphony Concert," *Chicago Defender,* March 9, 1918.

79. Hagstrom Miller, *Segregating Sound.*

80. "Munday [*sic*] Honored at Home and Abroad," *Chicago Defender,* July 15, 1916.

81. "Musical and Dramatic," *Chicago Defender,* May 11, 1912.

82. "The Fiftieth Anniversary Celebration of the Emancipation Proclamation of President Abraham Lincoln," *Broad Ax,* February 15, 1913. The program also featured Mundy's own composition, "Ethiopia," and spirituals.

83. "George Garner Stars in Patriotic Music Festival," *Chicago Defender,* June 22, 1918; "YWCA Recital a Success," *Chicago Defender,* May 4, 1918.

84. "In Recital at Bethel," *Chicago Defender,* April 12, 1919. For other examples of Mundy's students appearing in grand opera excerpts, see "Free Recital at 'Y' Thursday Eve., April 22," *Chicago Defender,* April 17, 1915.

85. "Mundy's Opera School," *Chicago Defender,* November 6, 1920.

86. "100 Opera Enthusiasts," *Chicago Defender,* March 5, 1921.

87. Calculated from information provided in "Opera Financially Supported," *Chicago Defender,* April 23, 1921.

88. "Samuel Insull a Box Holder for S. S. Opera," *Chicago Whip,* February 18, 1922.

89. Mildred Bryant-Jones, "Music Notes," *Chicago Whip,* February 19, 1921.

90. Nora Douglas Holt, "News of the Music World," *Chicago Defender,* December 10, 1921; Mildred Bryant-Jones, "Opera Effort Worthy of Praise," *Chicago Whip,* December 17, 1921.

91. Jarvis R. Givens, *Fugitive Pedagogy: Carter G. Woodson and the Art of Black Teaching* (Cambridge, MA: Harvard University Press, 2021), 63.

92. See, for example, "Mundy Scores Big Hit in Springfield," *Chicago Whip,* June 17, 1922. Many singers from *Martha* appeared in this production as well.

93. Mundy remained highly present in the world of Black opera in Chicago. By 1943, he had become an officer of the Chicago Negro Opera Guild, which hosted costumed "opera teas" and planned to mount full productions. At a 1944 event, singers from *Martha* appeared in his honor. "Opera Guild Costume Tea a Unique, Colorful Event," *Chicago Bee,* July 18, 1943; "Prof. Mundy to be Honored for 30 Yrs. Progress in Music," *Chicago Bee,* December 10, 1944.

94. Freeman was acquainted with Hackley's husband, Edwin, who had lived in Denver since the mid-1880s, but he left the city before Azalia arrived, and there is no evidence that they interacted there. On Hackley's biography, see Lisa Pertillar Brevard, *A Biography of E. Azalia Smith Hackley, 1867–1922, African-American Singer and Social Activist* (Lewiston, NY: Edwin Mellen Press, 2001); and Karpf, *Performing Racial Uplift.*

95. W. Lewis, "A New Star in the Musical Firmament," *Indianapolis Freeman,* March 9, 1901.

96. Azalia Hackley, "Hints to Young Colored Artists," *New York Age,* March 14, 1915.

97. Karpf, *Performing Racial Uplift,* 65.

98. Brevard, *Biography of E. Azalia Smith Hackley,* 58.

99. "A New Singer," *Indianapolis Freeman,* February 16, 1901.

100. Juanita Karpf, "The Vocal Teacher of Ten Thousand: E. Azalia Hackley as Community Music Educator, 1910–22," *Journal of Research in Music Education* 47, no. 4 (1999): 319–330.

101. Sylvester Russell, "Madam Hackley Triumphs at Orchestra Hall in a Song and Lecture Recital," *Indianapolis Freeman,* November 4, 1911.

102. Russell, "Madam Hackley Triumphs at Orchestra Hall."

103. Quoted in Karpf, *Performing Racial Uplift,* 95–96.

104. Brevard, *Biography of E. Azalia Smith Hackley,* 39.

105. Karpf, "Vocal Teacher of Ten Thousand," 322.

106. Karpf, *Performing Racial Uplift,* 166, 162.

107. Eidsheim, *Race of Sound,* 45.

108. Azalia Hackley, "Hints to Young Colored Artists: Demonstration in Voice Culture No. 1," *New York Age,* December 24, 1914.

109. Karpf posits that this change may have been due to not only Hackley's evolving pedagogical outlook, but also her increasingly poor health. Later in life, she suffered from respiratory ailments and a hearing disability that would have prevented her from singing more technically demanding repertoire. Karpf, *Performing Racial Uplift,* 158.

110. Karpf, *Performing Racial Uplift,* 102.

111. Quoted in Karpf, *Performing Racial Uplift,* 95.

112. Azalia Hackley, *The Colored Girl Beautiful* (Kansas City, MO: Burton Publishers, 1916), 11.

113. Hackley, *Colored Girl Beautiful,* 58.

114. Hackley, *Colored Girl Beautiful,* 18. On Hackley's eugenicist rhetoric, see Brevard, *Biography of E. Azalia Smith Hackley,* 225–226; and Katharine Capshaw Smith, "Childhood, the Body, and Race Performance: Early 20th-Century Etiquette Books for Black Children," *African American Review* 40, no. 4 (2006): 795–811. On eugenics and Black elite intellectuals, see Daylanne K. English, *Unnatural Selections: Eugenics in American Modernism and the Harlem Renaissance* (Chapel Hill: University of North Carolina Press, 2004).

115. Hackley, "Hints to Young Colored Artists: Demonstration in Voice Culture No. 1," *New York Age,* December 24, 1914.

116. Hackley, *Colored Girl Beautiful,* 34–36.

117. Hackley, *Colored Girl Beautiful,* 81–82.

118. Hackley, *Colored Girl Beautiful,* 66–67.

119. Lucien White, "Mme. E. Azalia Hackley Is Dead after Months of Illness," *New York Age,* December 23, 1922.

120. Nathaniel Mackey, "Other: From Noun to Verb," *Representations* 39 (1992): 51–70.

121. Samuel R. Delany, *Silent Interviews: On Language, Race, Sex, Science Fiction, and Some Comics* (Middletown, CT: Wesleyan University Press, 1994), 289.

3. "The Forgotten Man of the Opera"

1. Paul J. Banker, "Opera Season Closes with L'Africana [*sic*]," *Baltimore Sun,* April 21, 1932.

2. Quoted in Andrew Joseph Carl Fields, "William Llewellyn Wilson: A Biography" (master's thesis, Morgan State University, 1990), 49.

3. Robin Kelley, *Race Rebels: Culture, Politics, and the Black Working Class* (New York: Free Press, 1994); Saidiya Hartman, *Wayward Lives, Beautiful Experiments: Intimate Histories of Social Upheaval* (New York: W. W. Norton, 2019).

4. Henry James, *The American Scene* (London: Chapman & Hall, 1907), 164.

5. Edith Wharton, *The Age of Innocence* (New York: Windsor, 1920), 1, 5.

6. See, for example, Suzanne Aspden, ed., *Operatic Geographies: The Place of Opera and the Opera House* (Chicago: University of Chicago Press, 2018).

7. "Received Five Thousand Dollars," *Indianapolis Freeman,* April 21, 1894; "Here and There," *Colored American,* July 9, 1898.

8. Lester Walton, "Music and the Stage," *New York Age,* May 16, 1912.

9. Shannon King, "The Unmaking of the New Negro Mecca," in *African American Literature in Transition, 1920–1930,* ed. M. Thaggert and R. Farebrother (New York: Cambridge University Press, 2022), 137. See also Alyssa Lopez, "'Eternal Vigilance Is the Price of Liberty': Resistance to Segregated Seating in New York City's Theaters," *Gotham* blogpost, Gotham Center for New York History, Graduate Center, CUNY, September 24, 2020, https://www.gothamcenter.org/blog/eternal -vigilance-is-the-price-of-liberty-resistance-to-segregated-seating-in-new-york -citys-theaters.

10. Quoted in King, "The Unmaking of the New Negro Mecca," 137–138.

11. Because operas were often performed in venues other than opera houses— and because so-called opera houses featured various types of performances—it is difficult to determine whether operagoing was segregated in precisely the same way that other types of theatrical attendance were. On Black audiences' experiences under Jim Crow, see Eric Ledell Smith, *African American Theater Buildings: An Illustrated Historical Directory, 1900–1955* (Jefferson, NC: McFarland, 2003).

12. "Long Grand Opera Line Waits Night for Sale Opening," *Atlanta Constitution,* March 3, 1921.

13. "Pay Higher Price for Jim Crow Seats," *Chicago Defender,* April 19, 1930.

14. Charles Affron and Mirella Joan Affron, *Grand Opera: The Story of the Met* (Berkeley: University of California Press, 2014), 206.

15. Howard Taubman, *Music on My Beat: An Intimate Volume of Shop Talk* (New York: Simon and Schuster, 1943), 185.

16. Jacqueline Stewart, *Migrating to the Movies: Cinema and Black Urban Modernity* (Berkeley: University of California Press, 2005), 109.

17. Kristin Moriah, "Sounding: Black Print Culture at the Edges of the Black Atlantic," in *New Directions in Print Culture Studies: Archives, Materiality, and Modern American Culture,* ed. Jesse W. Schwarz and Daniel Worden (New York: Bloomsbury, 2022), 170.

18. Robert Abbott, "Refinement Sadly Lacking in Modern Youth, Says Editor," *Chicago Defender,* March 10, 1934.

19. Lena James Holt, "The Opera," *Chicago Defender,* November 17, 1917.

20. Nora Douglas Holt, "Umbrian Glee Club Presents Fine Program," *Chicago Defender,* February 3, 1923.

21. Lena James Holt, "The Symphony Concert," *Chicago Defender,* February 9, 1918.

22. Stewart, *Migrating to the Movies,* 17.

23. "Music and the Stage," *New York Age,* October 7, 1909.

24. J. A. Jackson, "Flowney [*sic*] Miller Pays Tribute to 'Black Carl,'" *New Journal and Guide,* July 12, 1924.

25. H. Lawrence Freeman, *The Negro in Music and Drama,* 285, typescript, box 50, H. Lawrence Freeman Papers, Rare Book and Manuscript Library, Columbia University.

26. Lester Walton, "Head Carriage Man Recalls Opera Glory," *Topeka Plaindealer,* November 26, 1928.

27. "Old 'Black Carl,' Twenty-Five Years Opera Doorman, Dies," *New York Herald Tribune,* January 22, 1930.

28. Jackson, "Flowney [*sic*] Miller Pays Tribute to 'Black Carl.'"

29. "Old 'Black Carl.'"

30. "'Black Carl' Dies as Opera He Loved Opens," *Chicago Defender,* November 30, 1929.

31. "*Crisis* Prizes in Literature and Art," *The Crisis* 33, no. 12 (December 1926), 70. In the 1970s, Bagley published a well-received collection of African folktales, titled *Candle-lighting Time in Bodidalee.* Julian Bagley, *Candle-Lighting Time in Bodidalee* (Rockville, MD: American Heritage Press, 1971).

32. Julian Bagley, "Welcome to the San Francisco Opera House," interviews by Suzanne Riess, July 1972–February 1973, transcript, Arts and Letters Oral Histories Individual Interviews, Bancroft Library Oral History Center, University of California, Berkeley, 13, https://digicoll.lib.berkeley.edu/record/217271?ln=en.

33. Blake Green, "The Unofficial Host of the Opera House," *San Francisco Examiner,* October 23, 1966.

34. Bagley, "Welcome to the San Francisco Opera House," 25.

35. Bagley, "Welcome to the San Francisco Opera House," 31, 76, 25, 66.

36. Bagley, "Welcome to the San Francisco Opera House," 88.

37. Bagley, "Welcome to the San Francisco Opera House," 73.

38. Bagley, "Welcome to the San Francisco Opera House," 47.

39. Bagley, "Welcome to the San Francisco Opera House," 81.

40. "Chico Woman Finds Handy Man at SF Opera House Virtuoso of Sorts Too," *Chico Enterprise-Record,* November 14, 1957.

41. Lucien H. White, "A Race Musician," *New York Age,* May 18, 1916.

42. James Weldon Johnson, *Along This Way: The Autobiography of James Weldon Johnson* (New York: Viking, 1933), 205.

43. James Weldon Johnson to E. Azalia Hackley, August 13, 1915, box 8, James Weldon Johnson and Grace Nail Johnson Papers, Yale Collection of American Literature, Beinecke Rare Book and Manuscript Library, Yale University (hereafter Johnson Papers). Johnson, *Along This Way,* 316.

44. Program for the Metropolitan Opera House, 1915–1916, box 82, Johnson Papers.

45. "'Goyescas' Brings Colored Man to Front in New Role," *Colored American Review,* March 1, 1916, box 82, Johnson Papers.

46. Hackley wrote to Johnson, "We are so proud of you, when I read about what you had done to my chorus, they cheered and were very proud." E. Azalia Hackley to James Weldon Johnson, August 17, 1915, box 8, Johnson Papers.

47. "'Goyescas,'" Johnson Papers.

48. Johnson attended performances of operas in New York, Caracas, and Paris. See Johnson, *Along This Way.*

49. Wayne Koestenbaum, *The Queen's Throat: Opera, Homosexuality, and the Mystery of Desire* (New York: Poseidon Press, 1993), 71–72.

50. Howard Taubman, *Opera Front and Back* (New York: Scribner, 1938), 196.

51. These numbers are calculated using information available in the MetOpera Database, Metropolitan Opera Archives, https://archives.metopera .org/MetOperaSearch/search.jsp?titles=Aida&&&sort=PDATE.

52. Black supernumeraries may have been part of the opera's production history from its 1873 premiere in Cairo, which featured what a reviewer called "Negroes armed with spears . . . true and superb specimens of their race." See Ralph Locke, "*Aida* and Nine Readings of Empire," *Nineteenth-Century Music Review* 3, no. 1 (2006): 45–72, 54. The 1880 Paris production seems also to have employed supers of African descent. These details cast new light on early criticism of the opera, such as a notorious early review by Viennese critic Eduard Hanslick that attributed his distaste for this "too strange" opera to its representation of Blackness: "We do not feel at ease among a lot of brown and black painted men . . . Think of nothing but dark-colored singers on the stage! Then, besides, the ugly, vaulting Negroes and the dancing women dressed and painted in the most repulsive manner!" Might Hanslick have been alluding to the presence of both white

performers in blackface and Black performers "vaulting" across the stage? (This English translation of Hanslick's 1874 review was reprinted in the Boston-based *Dwight's Journal of Music,* December 18, 1880.)

53. "Castle Square Opera Company," *Musical Courier,* October 10, 1898, 45.

54. "The Opera Season: Verdi's 'Aida,'" unsigned review in an unidentified Philadelphia newspaper, 1900, MetOpera Database, Metropolitan Opera Archives, https://archives.metopera.org/MetOperaSearch/record.jsp?dockey=0359295.

55. Charles Woodman, "Gentle Scores with Palet, Carrara in Big Roles," *San Francisco Call,* September 30, 1921. "Rosa Raisa in Aida, Egyptian Grand Opera," *Philadelphia Tribune,* November 6, 1926.

56. "Around the Clock at the Metropolitan," *Opera News* 3, no. 17 (February 27, 1939). The Met was also where the actor Earle Hyman first appeared onstage, as a super in *Aida* clad in an "abbreviated leopard skin. "'Anna Lucasta' Player Made Stage Debut as an Extra in Grand Opera," *Boston Globe,* April 6, 1947.

57. Deems Taylor, "An Impressive Home for the Metropolitan Opera Company," *Musical America,* October 8, 1927. Urban's designs were not ultimately implemented.

58. Woodman, "Gentle Scores."

59. "Golden Gate Opera Season," *Musical America,* November 25, 1935.

60. Olin Downes, "First 'Aida' Given with New Singers," *New York Times,* December 21, 1935.

61. Aime Gerber and Rose Heylbut, *Backstage at the Opera* (New York: Thomas Y. Crowell, 1937), 271–272, 111.

62. Howell Foreman, "Did You Recognize Your Son Dressed as Plumed Knight or Dusky Slave, in Operas?" *Atlanta Constitution,* April 29, 1912.

63. "Music and Musicians," *Boston Globe,* January 18, 1925.

64. Arthur Chapman, "Supers Who Welcome the Opening of the Opera Season," *New York Tribune,* November 8, 1925.

65. Taubman, *Opera Front and Back,* 196.

66. "New York's Super-Standee," *New York Times,* July 23, 1922.

67. Meyer Berger, "Aïda Through the Looking-Glass," *New Yorker,* January 1, 1938.

68. Arthur Chapman, "Supers Who Welcome the Opening of the Opera Season," *New York Tribune,* November 8, 1925.

69. "Aïda Through the Looking-Glass."

70. Lena James Holt, "The Opera," *Chicago Defender,* January 5, 1918. Holt continued to critique the use of blackface in *Aida* throughout her career. In 1952, she wrote that "most Aidas of the white race look as ludicrous as a circus clown with face blackened and white rims around the eyes." Nora Holt, "Scotching the Myth That Negro Singers Are Unqualified for Opera or Top Concerts," *New York Amsterdam News,* May 31, 1952.

71. Taubman, *Opera Front and Back,* 32.

72. Arthur Chapman, "Supers Who Welcome the Opening of the Opera Season," *New York Tribune*, November 8, 1925.

73. "'Aida' Audience Sees 'Supes' Walking across River Nile," *Chicago Daily Tribune*, November 30, 1913.

74. Chapman, "Supers Who Welcome the Opening of the Opera Season."

75. Juanita Morrow, "'Seeing Grand Opera' from the 40th Row," *Cleveland Call and Post*, August 21, 1943. The experience may have informed her consciousness of Jim Crow segregation and future activism. Just months later, Morrow participated in a sit-in as a student at Howard, and she would later become an activist for civil rights.

76. Saidiya Hartman, *Scenes of Subjection: Terror, Slavery, and Self-Making in Nineteenth-Century America* (New York: Oxford University Press, 1997), 4.

4. "My Skin Was My Costume"

1. "Greatest Musical Offer Ever: Ferrari-Fontana Seeks Negro Voice for Grand Opera," *New York Amsterdam News*, July 1, 1925.

2. "Ferrari Fontana Offers Assistance to All Contestants," *New York Amsterdam News*, August 7, 1925, clipping in scrapbook, box 59, H. Lawrence Freeman Papers, Rare Book and Manuscript Library, Columbia University.

3. "Preliminary Tryout of Soprano Voices Well Under Way," *New York Amsterdam News*, July 15, 1925.

4. "Final Audition to Be in Town Hall August," *New York Amsterdam News*, July 29, 1925.

5. "Greatest Musical Offer Ever"; "Final Audition."

6. "Town Hall Friday Evening," *New York Amsterdam News*, August 5, 1925.

7. From 1919 to 1931, between five hundred and one thousand African American musicians migrated to Europe. Rachel Gillett, "Jazz and the Evolution of Black American Cosmopolitanism in Interwar Paris," *Journal of World History* 21 no. 3 (2010): 471–495, 476. On Black artists in Europe generally, see Tyler Stovall, *Paris Noir: African Americans in the City of Light* (Boston: Houghton Mifflin, 1996); and Brent Hayes Edwards, *The Practice of Diaspora: Literature, Translation, and the Rise of Black Internationalism* (Cambridge, MA: Harvard University Press, 2003).

8. Jarvis R. Givens, *Fugitive Pedagogy: Carter G. Woodson and the Art of Black Teaching* (Cambridge, MA: Harvard University Press, 2021), 104.

9. Daphne A. Brooks, *Bodies in Dissent: Spectacular Performances of Race and Freedom, 1850–1910* (Durham, NC: Duke University Press, 2006), 3; see also Jayna Brown, *Babylon Girls: Black Women Performers and the Shaping of the Modern* (Durham, NC: Duke University Press, 2008).

10. Leontyne Price, "Aida," in *The Metropolitan Opera Encyclopedia: A Comprehensive Guide to the World of Opera*, ed. David Hamilton (New York: Simon and Schuster, 1987), 16–17. Price used the phrase "my skin was my costume" in various contexts, including a 1990 children's book about the opera and conversa-

tions with young audiences. See Leontyne Price, Leo Dillon, and Diane Dillon, *Aida* (New York: Voyager Books, 1990); and Anthony Tommasini, "Aida Takes Her Story to Harlem; Leontyne Price Reads Her Book and Sings for Schoolchildren," *New York Times,* May 30, 2000. Although Price's final appearance at the Metropolitan Opera, in 1985, was in *Aida,* she declined to make her 1961 Met debut in the role, wary of being associated only with racialized roles. Instead, her debut was in Verdi's *Il trovatore.*

11. Leontyne Price, interview by Helena Matheopoulos, in *Diva: Great Sopranos and Mezzos Discuss Their Art* (Boston: Northeastern University Press, 1991), 163.

12. Naomi André, *Black Opera: History, Power, Engagement* (Urbana: University of Illinois Press, 2018). 6, 19–20.

13. Farah Jasmine Griffin, "When Malindy Sings: A Meditation on Black Women's Vocality," in *Uptown Conversation: The New Jazz Studies,* ed. Robert O'Meally, Brent Hayes Edwards, and Farah Jasmine Griffin (New York: Columbia University Press, 2004), 104.

14. Nina Sun Eidsheim, *The Race of Sound: Listening, Timbre, and Vocality in African American Music* (Durham, NC: Duke University Press, 2019), 84. On racial typecasting in opera, see also Kira Thurman, *Singing Like Germans* (Ithaca, NY: Cornell University Press, 2021), 225–239. See also Angela Pao, *No Safe Spaces: Re-casting Race, Ethnicity, and Nationality in American Theater* (Ann Arbor: University of Michigan Press, 2011).

15. Wallace Cheatham, "African-American Women Singers at the Metropolitan Opera before Leontyne Price," *Journal of Negro History* 84, no. 2 (1999): 167–181, 176, 177.

16. Donal Henahan, "Jessye Norman—'People Look at Me and Say Aida,'" *New York Times,* January 21, 1973. Verrett is quoted in Rosalyn Story, *And So I Sing: African-American Divas of Opera and Concert* (New York: Warner Books, 1990), 167.

17. Story, *And So I Sing,* 184.

18. "Madam M. Calloway Byron at Auditorium Captivates Audience," *Broad Ax,* June 22, 1918.

19. "American and Foreign Negroes Honored in Europe," *Chicago Defender,* July 29, 1911.

20. "A Rare Musical Treat," *Chicago Defender,* October 2, 1915.

21. "Anita Patti Brown Stars in Recital at Quinn Chapel," *Chicago Defender,* October 5, 1918.

22. Noel Straus, *New York World,* February 23, 1929, in Metropolitan Opera Archives, https://archives.metopera.org/MetOperaSearch/record.jsp?dockey =0365564.

23. "Opera Singer Creates Sensation in Dark Makeup," *New York Age,* February 1, 1917.

24. Lester Walton, "The Silent Menace," *New York Age,* March 29, 1917.

25. "Music Hath Charms," *Chicago Defender,* January 8, 1921.

26. Naomi André notes that the technical difficulty of the role is also a factor. André, *Black Opera,* 13.

27. Tenor George Shirley comments on this trend ("many white people still have a problem accepting black males in romantic roles opposite white females") in Wallace Cheatham and George Shirley, "A Renowned Divo Speaks," *The Black Perspective in Music* 18, no. 1/2 (1990): 141–178, 144. On Black male singers' experiences with casting, see Jason Oby, *Equity in Operatic Casting as Perceived by African American Male Singers* (Lewiston, NY: Edwin Mellen Press, 1998). On interracial relationships on American stages, see also Diana Paulin, *Imperfect Unions: Staging Miscegenation in U.S. Drama and Fiction* (Minneapolis: University of Minnesota Press, 2012).

28. "Who Can Tell," *New York Age,* November 11, 1915.

29. Mari Yoshihara, "The Flight of the Japanese Butterfly: Orientalism, Nationalism, and Performances of Japanese Womanhood," *American Quarterly* 56, no. 4 (2004): 975–1001, 981.

30. "Grand Opera without Fat," *Washington Herald,* February 6, 1916.

31. Some scholars attribute this development to the popularity of *Salome* and its infamous Dance of the Seven Veils, which required the singer to embody a particular type of female beauty. See Linda Hutcheon and Michael Hutcheon, *Bodily Charm: Living Opera* (Lincoln: University of Nebraska Press, 2000), 117.

32. "Grand Opera without Fat."

33. Howard Taubman, *Opera Front and Back* (New York: Scribner, 1938), 129.

34. Karl Hagstrom Miller, *Segregating Sound: Inventing Folk and Pop Music in the Age of Jim Crow* (Durham, NC: Duke University Press, 2010), 4.

35. See Sandra Graham, *Spirituals and the Birth of a Black Entertainment Industry* (Urbana: University of Illinois Press, 2018).

36. Lester Walton, "Negro Music," *New York Age,* January 1, 1914.

37. Lester Walton, "Irrespective of Color," *New York Age,* October 1, 1921.

38. Josh Kun, *Audiotopia: Music, Race, and America* (Berkeley: University of California Press, 2005), 22–23.

39. Philip Deloria, *Indians in Unexpected Places* (Lawrence: University Press of Kansas, 2005), 215. Composed based in part on Cadman's interactions with Redfeather, *Shanewis* was an atypically collaborative work. On the Indianist movement, see Michael Pisani, *Imagining Native America in Music* (New Haven: Yale University Press, 2005); and John Troutman, *Indian Blues: American Indians and the Politics of Music, 1879–1934* (Norman: University of Oklahoma Press, 2012). For a transnational perspective on opera and indigeneity, see Pamela Karantonis and Dylan Robinson, eds., *Opera Indigene: Re/presenting First Nations and Indigenous Cultures* (Farnham, UK: Ashgate, 2011).

40. See David Choo, "Franco Leoni's *L'Oracolo:* A Study in Orientalism" (DMA diss., Peabody Conservatory of the Johns Hopkins University, 1998). *The Mikado,* an exemplar of this Orientalist tradition, was a popular choice among

Black opera groups and music clubs. See Josephine Lee, *The Japan of Pure Invention: Gilbert and Sullivan's "The Mikado"* (Minneapolis: University of Minnesota Press, 2010), 83–120. Lee argues that while there is a troubling dimension to Orientalist and yellowface performance by Black artists, it "does clear a space for the advancement of African American performers beyond their own racial caricatures; beyond that, the best we might hope for is that it also dislocates both racial stereotypes of 'blackness' and 'yellowness' through playing on the disjunction of the actor's body and the racial stereotype" (94).

41. Carolyn Guzski, "Harlem Renaissance Man: Frank Wilson at the Metropolitan Opera," *American Music Review* 45, no. 1 (2015): 13–17, 15.

42. H. I. Brock, "Jazz Is to Do a Turn in Grand Opera," *New York Times,* February 14, 1926.

43. "American Ballet by Negroes at Opera House," *New York Amsterdam News,* February 17, 1926.

44. Notably, neither *The Dance in Place Congo* nor *Skyscrapers* was an opera per se, even though both were productions of the Metropolitan Opera Company.

45. Ralph Matthews, "Salmaggi Kisses Caterina before 12,000 Eyes," *Baltimore Afro-American,* July 29, 1933; Ralph Matthews, "Looking at the Stars," *Baltimore Afro-American,* August 5, 1933.

46. "The Negro in Opera," *New York Amsterdam News,* July 26, 1933.

47. "Who Can Tell," *New York Age,* November 11, 1915.

48. Penman Lovingood, "Negro Opera Singers Will Win World Recognition When They Learn to Evolve, Produce Own Operas," *Pittsburgh Courier,* April 24, 1937.

49. *Chicago Inter Ocean,* undated; *Philadelphia Times,* December 3, 1892. Quoted in Willia Daughtry, "Sissieretta Jones: A Study of the Negro's Contribution to Nineteenth Century American Concert and Theatrical Life" (PhD diss., Syracuse University, 1968), 148.

50. André, *Black Opera,* 10.

51. David Charlton, "Introduction," in *The Cambridge Companion to Grand Opera,* ed. David Charlton (Cambridge: Cambridge University Press, 2003), 1–18.

52. Edward Said, "The Empire at Work: Verdi's *Aida,*" in *Culture and Imperialism* (New York: Knopf, 1993), 115.

53. Other scholars critique the totalizing nature of Said's argument and offer alternative analyses of what musicologist Gabriela Cruz calls *Aida's* "imperial genealogy." Gabriela Cruz, "*Aida's* Flutes," *Cambridge Opera Journal* 14, no. 1/2 (2002): 177–200, 177. Ralph Locke argues that Verdi critiques and even refutes the imperialist impulses Said identifies, rather than simply propagating them. Katherine Bergeron notes that Verdi should not be regarded as the sole source of the opera's meaning, given the various collaborators involved in its genesis, as well as the many participants who feature in any given production. Ralph P. Locke, "Beyond the Exotic: How 'Eastern' is *Aida?*" *Cambridge Opera Journal* 17, no. 2 (2005): 105–139; Ralph Locke, "*Aida* and Nine Readings of Empire," *Nineteenth-Century*

Music Review 3, no. 1 (2006): 45–72; Katherine Bergeron, "Verdi's Egyptian Spectacle: On the Colonial Subject of *Aida*," *Cambridge Opera Journal* 14, no. 1 / 2 (2002): 149–159. See also John Drummond, "Said and *Aida:* Culture, Imperialism, Egypt and Opera," *Critical Race and Whiteness Studies* 10, no. 1 (2014): 1–12; Paul Robinson, "Is *Aida* an Orientalist Opera?" *Cambridge Opera Journal* 5, no. 2 (1994): 133–140; and Lydia Goehr, "*Aida* and the Empire of Emotions," *Current Musicology* 87 (2009): 133–159. Scholars have also discussed how Blackness functions in the opera. Jennifer McFarlane-Harris and Christopher Gauthier, for example, assess the racial politics of its reception by Egyptian audiences. Jennifer McFarlane-Harris and Christopher Gauthier, "Nationalism, Racial Difference, and 'Egyptian' Meaning in Verdi's *Aida*," in *Blackness in Opera,* ed. Naomi André, Karen M. Bryan, and Eric Saylor (Urbana: University of Illinois Press, 2012), 55–77.

54. Hans Busch, *Verdi's* Aida*: The History of an Opera in Letters and Documents* (Minneapolis: University of Minnesota Press, 1978), 558–559.

55. In 2018, Naomi André wrote that "the opera stage is the only stage in the world today where this practice of using blackface makeup for nonblack singers to portray black roles is a regular feature that is practiced, accepted, and—until very recently—never discussed." André, *Black Opera,* 4. She refers in part to the Metropolitan Opera's 2015 decision to abandon, for the first time in its history, the use of blackface makeup in *Otello.*

56. See Darryl Glenn Nettles, *African American Concert Singers before 1950* (Jefferson, NC: McFarland, 2003), 49.

57. One white critic wondered, "Is the change from 'Ady' to 'A-e-da' meant to make a musical advance by Williams and Walker from negro melody to operatic music?" Mary Simonson, *Body Knowledge: Performance, Intermediality, and American Entertainment at the Turn of the Twentieth Century* (New York: Oxford University Press, 2013), 208n53.

58. Advertisement, *New York Amsterdam News,* February 3, 1926; "Dallas Club Sings," *Baltimore Afro-American,* January 16, 1926; "'Ruth the Gleaner' at New Star," *Chicago Defender,* May 4, 1918.

59. Thomas Riis, *Just before Jazz: Black Musical Theater in New York, 1890–1915* (Washington, DC: Smithsonian Institution Press, 1989), 88–89; Nicole Aljoe, "Aria for Ethiopia: The Operatic Aesthetic of Pauline Hopkins's *Of One Blood*," *African American Review* 45, no. 3 (2012): 277–290. In Irving Berlin's "Ragtime Opera Medley," from the musical *Watch Your Step* (1914), the ghost of Verdi mounts a futile protest as musicians "rag" music from *Aida* and *Rigoletto*. See Larry Hamberlin, *Tin Pan Opera: Operatic Novelty Songs in the Ragtime Era* (New York: Oxford University Press, 2011), 233–242.

60. The story was never completed. W. E. B. Du Bois, "The Secret Singer [notes]," W. E. B. Du Bois Papers, MS 312, Special Collections and University Archives, University of Massachusetts Amherst Libraries.

61. Fred Moten, "Letting Go of *Othello*," *Paris Review,* November 1, 2019.

62. Jacek Blaszkiewicz, "Verdi, Auber and the Aida-type," *Cambridge Opera Journal* 34, no. 2 (2022): 157–182, 164.

63. See Geoffrey Edwards and Ryan Edwards, *Verdi and Puccini Heroines: Dramatic Characterization in Great Soprano Roles* (Lanham, MD: Scarecrow Press, 2001), 40–59.

64. Carolyn Abbate, "Opera; or, the Envoicing of Women," in *Musicology and Difference: Gender and Sexuality in Music Scholarship,* ed. Ruth Solie (Berkeley: University of California Press, 1993). On women and operatic performance, see also Corinne E. Blackmer and Patricia Juliana Smith, eds., *En Travesti: Women, Gender Subversion, Opera* (New York: Columbia University Press, 1995); Mary Ann Smart, ed., *Siren Songs: Representations of Gender and Sexuality in Opera* (Princeton, NJ: Princeton University Press, 2000); Susan Rutherford, *The Prima Donna and Opera, 1815–1930* (Cambridge: Cambridge University Press, 2006); Susan Rutherford, *Verdi, Opera, Women* (Cambridge: Cambridge University Press, 2013); Rachel Cowgill and Hilary Poriss, eds., *The Arts of the Prima Donna in the Long Nineteenth Century* (New York: Oxford University Press, 2012); Karen Henson, *Opera Acts: Singers and Performance in the Late Nineteenth Century* (Cambridge: Cambridge University Press, 2013); and Simonson, *Body Knowledge.*

65. Sharon Marcus, *The Drama of Celebrity* (Princeton, NJ: Princeton University Press, 2019).

66. Sadie Chandler Cole later became a civil rights activist in Los Angeles. See Douglas Flamming, *Bound for Freedom: Black Los Angeles in Jim Crow America* (Berkeley: University of California Press, 2005), 273–274.

67. "Hann's Jubilee Singers Please Los Angeles People," *Chicago Defender,* January 2, 1915. See also Tim Brooks, *Lost Sounds: Blacks and the Birth of the Recording Industry, 1890–1919* (Urbana: University of Illinois Press, 2004), 453.

68. Lee Blackwell, "Madame Florence Cole Talbert Met Challenge and Became Opera Star," *Chicago Defender,* August 1, 1953.

69. Ruby Goodwin, "She Aimed at the Stars and Hit Her Mark," undated interview, *The Bronzeman,* quoted in Patricia Turner, "Our Divine Florence," *The Black Perspective in Music* 12, no. 1 (1984): 57–79, 59. For another telling of this story, see Daniel W. Chase, "Mme. Cole Talbert to Sing in Philly," *Baltimore Afro-American,* January 28, 1928.

70. Brown, *Babylon Girls,* 8. See also Carrie Teresa, *Looking at the Stars: Black Celebrity Journalism in Jim Crow America* (Lincoln: University of Nebraska Press, 2019).

71. Some of Cole-Talbert's supporters critiqued the Black press for its sexist tendency to valorize male singers like Roland Hayes over women like Cole-Talbert: "Every time Hayes takes a walk in the park an account of it is conspicuously featured in our newspapers," one wrote in a letter to the editor. Edna Rosalyne Heard, "Mme. Talbert in Grand Opera," *Chicago Defender,* May 21, 1927. Heard's criticism apparently was taken to heart, as an extensive report on Cole-Talbert

appeared in the *Defender* the following month. Ivan H. Browning, "Across the Pond," *Chicago Defender,* June 18, 1927.

72. "Mme. Cole-Talbert May Sing before King of Italy," *Baltimore Afro-American,* February 27, 1926.

73. "Madame Florence Cole-Talbert Returns after Three Years in Europe," *New York Amsterdam News,* October 26, 1927.

74. "Cole-Talbert Is Success in Italy," *Baltimore Afro-American,* October 31, 1925.

75. "Madame Florence Cole-Talbert Returns."

76. "Mrs. Asbury Tells of European Tour," *Pittsburgh Courier,* July 2, 1927.

77. Thurman, *Singing Like Germans.*

78. "Cole-Talbert Is Success in Italy"; "Madame Florence Cole-Talbert Returns."

79. "Madame Florence Cole-Talbert Returns."

80. On Evanti's biography, see Nettles, *African American Concert Singers,* 65–66; and T. Denean Sharpley-Whiting, *Bricktop's Paris: African American Women in Paris between the Two World Wars* (Albany: State University of New York Press, 2015), 38–39.

81. E. H. Lawson, "Lillian Evanti in Opera," *Washington Post,* March 31, 1929.

82. Promotional flyer, Lillian Evanti American Concert Tour, 1927, box 32, Evans-Tibbs Collection, Anacostia Community Museum Archives, Smithsonian Institution, gift of the Estate of Thurlow E. Tibbs Jr.

83. Promotional flyer, Lillian Evanti American Concert Tour.

84. Lillian Evanti, "Where My Caravan Has Rested," Autobiography of International Concert and Opera Soprano Lillian Evanti, typescript, 6 leaves, undated, given as a speech in 1963, Lillian Evanti Collection, Center for Black Music Research, Archives and Special Collections, Columbia College Chicago.

85. Ginger Dellenbaugh, *Maria Callas's* Lyric and Coloratura Arias (London: Bloomsbury Academic, 2021), 109, 115. Carolyn Abbate theorizes this moment of "wordless coloratura" as emblematic of the way that the character becomes "a body emanating sonority," a reminder of music's affective power in excess of characterization and narrative. Carolyn Abbate, *Unsung Voices: Opera and Musical Narrative in the Nineteenth Century* (Princeton, NJ: Princeton University Press, 1996), 4.

86. The lightness of Cole-Talbert's voice is unusual for a soprano who takes on the role. Indeed, George Shirley, upon hearing these recordings, commented that "this was not an *Aida* voice. She had high notes, but certainly not the heft that *Aida* requires. Nevertheless she was black; her debut had to be as Aida." Wallace Cheatham, ed., *Dialogues on Opera and the African-American Experience* (Lanham, MD: Scarecrow Press, 1997), 104.

87. This argument is informed by Fred Moten, "The Phonographic *Mise-en-Scéne*," *Cambridge Opera Journal* 16, no. 3 (2004): 269–281, 278–279.

88. T. R. Poston, "Harlem Goes to Opera and Acclaims Its Own," *New York Amsterdam News,* July 26, 1933. Located on 6th Avenue between 43rd and 44th

Streets, the Hippodrome opened in 1905 and had a stage twelve times larger than that of any Broadway theater. Its size ultimately made it unprofitable, and the building was razed in 1939. Rebecca Read Shanor, "Hippodrome," in *The Encyclopedia of New York City*, 2nd ed., ed. Kenneth T. Jackson, Lisa Keller, and Nancy Flood (New Haven: Yale University Press, 2010), 597–598.

89. Geraldine Thornton, "Gotham Thunders Praise of Mme. Jarboro," *Chicago Defender*, July 29, 1933.

90. On the Wilmington Massacre, see Glenda Gilmore, *Gender and Jim Crow: Women and the Politics of White Supremacy in North Carolina, 1896–1920* (Chapel Hill: University of North Carolina Press, 1996); and David Cecelski and Timothy Tyson, eds., *Democracy Betrayed: The Wilmington Race Riot of 1898 and Its Legacy* (Chapel Hill: University of North Carolina Press, 2000).

91. Richard Yarborough, telephone interview with the author, May 26, 2018. I also draw on Professor Yarborough's keynote address, "From Katherine Yarborough to Caterina Jarboro to Aunt Catherine: Memory, Legacy, and Family History," at the Celebrating Caterina Jarboro Symposium, University of North Carolina, Wilmington, February 24, 2018.

92. Caterina Jarboro, interview by James V. Hatch, February 29, 1972, Sc Audio CD-685 (2 discs), Hatch-Billops Collection, Schomburg Center for Research in Black Culture, New York Public Library.

93. Various reports disputed this contention, and it is probable that Jarboro married at least once. One article reports that she married a fellow Wilmingtonian named Elijah Mosely as a teenager, then divorced him before moving to New York. Ralph Matthews, "Forgotten Husbands," *Baltimore Afro-American*, December 22, 1934. See also Maurice Dancer, "Famous Star of 'Aida' Reveals Domestic Life," *Pittsburgh Courier*, August 12, 1933, which claims that Jarboro divorced a man named John Crawford shortly after her debut as Aida, due to her desire to pursue an international operatic career and Crawford's desire to remain in New York.

94. Richard Yarborough, interview.

95. On the diva, see Brooks, *Bodies in Dissent*, 281–342; Lauren Berlant, "The Queen of America Goes to Washington City: Notes on Diva Citizenship," in *The Queen of America Goes to Washington City: Essays on Sex and Citizenship* (Durham, NC: Duke University Press, 1997); Wayne Koestenbaum, *The Queen's Throat: Opera, Homosexuality, and the Mystery of Desire* (New York: Poseidon Press, 1993), 84–133; and Deborah Paredez, "Lena Horne and Judy Garland: Divas, Desire, and Discipline in the Civil Rights Era," *Drama Review* 58, no. 4 (2014): 105–119.

96. Richard Yarborough, interview.

97. On Salmaggi, see Edward Ansara, *The Fabulous Maestro: A Remembrance of Alfredo Salmaggi and His Legacy* (Bloomington, IN: AuthorHouse, 2001). On relationships among African American and Italian American musicians, see John Gennari, *Flavor and Soul: Italian American at Its African American Edge* (Chicago: University of Chicago Press, 2017), 25–72.

98. See Victoria Etnier Villamil, *From Johnson's Kids to Lemonade Opera: The American Classical Singer Comes of Age* (Boston: Northeastern University Press, 2004), 69, 70.

99. "Jack Goes Martial for Opera," *Baltimore Afro-American,* October 10, 1936.

100. Richard Yarborough, interview.

101. Poston, "Harlem Goes to Opera"; A. White, "Jarboro Scores in 'Aida,'" *New Journal and Guide,* July 29, 1933; "Rises to Fame as Singer," *Chicago Defender,* July 22, 1933.

102. Romeo Dougherty, "Story of 'Aida,'" *New York Amsterdam News,* August 23, 1933.

103. See, for example, "Soprano Applauded at Debut as Aida," *New York Times,* July 23, 1933.

104. "As Others See Us," *Pittsburgh Courier,* December 17, 1932. This comment refers to Jarboro's 1931 performance of the role in Italy.

105. Thornton, "Gotham Thunders Praise of Mme. Jarboro."

106. Performance studies scholars have theorized skin, and especially Black skin, as not simply a marker of racial difference, but rather a permeable boundary or a site of intersubjective encounter. See Michelle Ann Stephens, *Skin Acts: Race, Psychoanalysis, and the Black Male Performer* (Durham, NC: Duke University Press, 2014); and Anne Anlin Cheng, *Second Skin: Josephine Baker and the Modern Surface* (New York: Oxford University Press, 2011). See also Uri McMillan, "Introduction: Skin, Surface, Sensorium," *Women and Performance: A Journal of Feminist Theory* 28, no. 1 (special issue on "Surface Aesthetics: Race, Performance, Play," 2018): 1–15.

107. Eidsheim, *Race of Sound,* 75.

108. "Soprano Applauded at Debut as Aida."

109. Thornton, "Gotham Thunders Praise of Mme. Jarboro"; "Soprano Applauded at Debut as Aida"; "Critic Says Jarboro Sings Like Claudio Muzio," *San Antonio Register,* June 8, 1934.

110. "'God Sent Me Brown Song Bird,' Says Italian Maestro," *Baltimore Afro-American,* March 19, 1932.

111. Deal Moore, "Kathi Jarboro Gives Interview for the Afro," *Baltimore Afro-American,* December 2, 1933; T. R. Poston, "Caterina Jarboro to Sing 'Aida' Saturday Evening," *New York Amsterdam News,* July 19, 1933.

112. Poston, "Caterina Jarboro to Sing 'Aida.'"

113. Moore, "Kathi Jarboro Gives Interview."

114. Thornton, "Gotham Thunders Praise of Mme. Jarboro."

115. Caterina Jarboro, interview.

116. Caterina Jarboro, interview.

117. Professor Yarborough was careful to note that these recollections are retrospective and do not reflect the language he would have used as a child to describe what he heard. But I found it striking how closely they cohered with contemporaneous accounts of Jarboro's performance. Richard Yarborough, interview.

118. Robert W. Carter, "The Drury Opera Company in Verdi's 'Aida,'" *Colored American Magazine,* August 1903, 596.

119. *The Star of Ethiopia*'s 1913 premiere coincided with both the fiftieth anniversary of the Emancipation Proclamation and the centennial of Verdi's birth. In a 1974 speech given to the fourth International Verdi Congress in Chicago, theater critic Earl Calloway noted that through characters including Aida, Otello, and Ulrica, Verdi "without trying, identified with the black experience in America . . . His tremendous emotional romantic expression had a special appeal to the black singer." Calloway, "Verdi and the Black Experience," *Tri-State Defender,* September 28, 1974.

120. Edgar Rouzeau, "Jarboro Lauded by Whites in Company," *New York Amsterdam News,* July 26, 1933. She even went so far as to claim that "before singing *Aida* I went up the Nile. I had Ethiopian friends and lived alongside them, because I wanted to know how Aida would feel." Caterina Jarboro, interview. While this may be an example of Jarboro's tendency to stretch the truth, it nonetheless indicates her investment in understanding the opera from the perspective of the Ethiopian people it purports to represent, rather than that of its European creators and the Italian American director under whom she worked.

121. Poston, "Harlem Goes to Opera."

122. Poston, "Caterina Jarboro to Sing 'Aida.'"

123. Goehr, "*Aida* and the Empire of Emotions," 137. See also Cruz, "*Aida*'s Flutes."

124. Arturo Alfonso Schomburg, "Caterina Jarboro at the Hippdrome!" *Cincinnati Union,* August 24, 1933, in Arturo Alfonso Schomburg Papers, box 11 (microfilm), Schomburg Center for Research in Black Culture, New York Public Library (hereafter Schomburg Papers). Jarboro and Schomburg were personal friends, and their correspondence is located in Schomburg Papers, boxes 5 and 8 (microfilm).

125. George Frazier Miller, "Frazier Replies to Schomburg!" *Cincinnati Union,* September 8, 1933, in Schomburg Papers, box 11 (microfilm).

126. Moten, "The Phonographic *Mise-en-Scéne,*" 272, 278–279. Moten's essay analyzes Jessye Norman's performance of *Erwatung.* Norman's visual and haptic presence, Moten argues, disrupts the ideal of structural listening by introducing a plaintive, deep, Black voice and making the body from which it emanates integral.

127. Kun, *Audiotopia.*

128. Gayle Wald, "Soul Vibrations: Black Music and Black Freedom in Sound and Space," *American Quarterly* 63, no. 3 (2011): 673–696, 692; Salem Tutt Whitney, "Timely Topics: Caterina Jarboro and Jules Bledsoe," *Chicago Defender,* August 5, 1933.

129. Clifford W. MacKay, "Going Backstage with the Scribe: Bledsoe in London," *Chicago Defender,* May 30, 1931. See also "Repertoire of Jules Bledsoe," box 4, Jules Bledsoe Papers, The Texas Collection, Baylor University.

130. Frankye A. Dixon, "Bledsoe Applauded in Role from 'Aida,'" *New York Amsterdam News,* January 30, 1929.

131. Eva Jessye, "Jarboro-Bledsoe Triumph in Aida," *New York Amsterdam News,* July 26, 1933.

132. "Opera Ball Gayety Recalls Old South," *New York Times,* May 3, 1935.

133. "Opera Ball Gayety Recalls Old South."

134. Thurman, *Singing Like Germans,* 225.

5. Composing Afrodiasporic History

1. Patricia Hill Collins, *Black Feminist Thought: Knowledge, Consciousness, and the Politics of Empowerment* (New York: Hyman, 1990).

2. Subjects included African cultural retentions; the history of slavery and abolition; and religious traditions, especially voodoo. Gayle Murchison, "New Paradigms in William Grant Still's *Blue Steel,*" in *Blackness in Opera,* ed. Naomi André, Karen M. Bryan, and Eric Saylor (Urbana: University of Illinois Press, 2012), 142–143.

3. Daphne Lamothe, *Inventing the New Negro: Narrative, Culture, and Ethnography* (Philadelphia: University of Pennsylvania Press, 2005).

4. "Creative-academic" is quoted in David Garcia, *Listening for Africa: Freedom, Modernity, and the Logic of Black Music's African Origins* (Durham, NC: Duke University Press, 2017), 70.

5. On the relationship between *Tom-Tom* and Graham's politics, see Sarah Schmalenberger, "Debuting Her Political Voice: The Lost Opera of Shirley Graham," *Black Music Research Journal* 26, no. 1 (2006): 39–87.

6. Eva Jessye, "Does the Negro Singer Have a Future?" *New York Amsterdam News,* August 5, 1931. This was the first installment of a three-part forum.

7. Eva Jessye, "To Sing for Annual Baha'i Convention," *New York Amsterdam News,* August 12, 1931.

8. "Music News," *New York Amsterdam News,* August 19, 1931.

9. Jessye, "To Sing for Annual Baha'i Convention."

10. "Jazz vs. the Classics," *Baltimore Afro-American,* September 7, 1935.

11. "Race Must Be Made Opera-Conscious," *Baltimore Afro-American,* July 2, 1932.

12. "Jazz Is Race Heritage of Negro, Says Ethel Waters," *American Guardian* (Oklahoma City), June 29, 1928.

13. "And Now We Turn to Opera," *Inter-state Tattler,* June 13, 1930, in Scrapbook, box 57, H. Lawrence Freeman Papers, Rare Book and Manuscript Library, Columbia University (hereafter Freeman Papers).

14. W. E. B. Du Bois, "Krigwa Players Little Negro Theater," *Crisis,* July 1926, 134.

15. See Eileen Southern, *The Music of Black Americans: A History* (New York: W. W. Norton, 1971), 447–452; and Paul Allen Anderson, *Deep River: Music and*

Memory in Harlem Renaissance Thought (Durham, NC: Duke University Press, 2001).

16. "Music News," *New York Amsterdam News,* August 19, 1931.

17. Nora Holt, "Caricatures and Portraits," *Music and Poetry,* April 1921, 65.

18. On *Blue Monday*'s eclectic influences, see Kristen Turner, "*Blue Monday* and New York Theatrical Aesthetics," in *The Cambridge Companion to Gershwin,* ed. Anna Harwell Celenza (Cambridge: Cambridge University Press, 2019). Vodery, a successful Black composer and arranger, was a mentor of Gerhswin's. As Turner notes, Vodery's "caption is rather poignant because Vodery knew black composers, including Will Marion Cook and H. Lawrence Freeman, who had tried to get their operatic work taken seriously for years with little success." Turner, "*Blue Monday,*" 73.

19. Charles Darnton, "'George White's Scandals' Lively and Gorgeous," *New York World,* August 29, 1922.

20. Sylvester Russell, "Connotation Script Jeopardized Belasco Publicity Interests," *Pittsburgh Courier,* February 13, 1926.

21. Freeman was, perhaps predictably, skeptical of the work's operatic bona fides, deeming it "shorn of all operatic potentialities as a whole, seeing as its only consecutive musical exigencies are confined to the second act alone." H. Lawrence Freeman, *The Negro in Music and Drama,* 47, typescript, box 50, Freeman Papers (hereafter Freeman, *Negro in Music and Drama*).

22. Jonathan O. Wipplinger, "Performing Race in Ernst Krenek's *Jonny spielt auf,*" in *Blackness in Opera,* ed. Naomi André, Karen M. Bryan, and Eric Saylor (Urbana: University of Illinois Press, 2012), 236–259.

23. Kira Thurman argues that Jonny "embodies Central European anxieties about jazz, race, and sex in the interwar era." Kira Thurman, *Singing Like Germans* (Ithaca, NY: Cornell University Press, 2021), 105.

24. Henry Casson Becker, "Krenek's 'Jonny' Journeys West," *Musical America,* February 25, 1928, 5.

25. Paul J. Edwards, "The Circumstances of Colour: The Jim Crow Translation of *Jonny spielt auf,*" *Modern Drama* 64, no. 2 (2021): 151–172, 153. The Met also initially planned to remove mentions of race from the libretto, but ultimately used the original text.

26. See Edwards, "Circumstances of Colour," 167–168.

27. Lucien White, "New Opera Comes from Europe," *New York Age,* January 26, 1929. White's commentary appeared directly above an advertisement for Jules Bledsoe's forthcoming appearance in scenes from *Aida*—a tangible reminder of the Black singers excluded by the Met's continued reliance on white performers.

28. "Met's Black and Tan Opera," *Variety* (January 1929): 48.

29. "Jonny spielt auf," *Opportunity* 7, no. 2 (1929): 38.

30. Harry S. Keelan, "Jonny Tunes Up," *Crisis* 36, no. 6 (June 1929): 208.

31. David Metzer, "'A Wall of Darkness Dividing the World': Blackness and Whiteness in Louis Gruenberg's *The Emperor Jones,*" *Cambridge Opera Journal* 7, no. 1 (1995): 55–72, 58.

32. Charles Affron and Mirella Joan Affron, *Grand Opera: The Story of the Met* (Berkeley: University of California Press, 2014), 205. The Met's production featured a few other Black performers onstage: the dancer Hemsley Winfield took the non-singing role of the Congo Witch-Doctor, and a handful of additional dancers and singers also appeared. In 1934, Bledsoe performed the role in a highly successful European production, touring England and the Netherlands. On his complex relationship to the character of Brutus Jones, see Katie N. Johnson, "Brutus Jones's Remains: The Case of Jules Bledsoe," *Eugene O'Neill Review* 36, no. 1 (2015): 1–28.

33. Harry S. Keelan, "The Emperor Jones," *Opportunity* (February 1933): 45, 58.

34. "Editorials," *Opportunity* (February 1933): 40.

35. "Jazz Is Race Heritage of Negro."

36. "Ellington's Negro Opera Not Being Peddled," *Pittsburgh Courier,* December 10, 1938.

37. Jessye, "To Sing for Annual Baha'i Convention."

38. Sylvester Russell, "The Futurity of American Music," *Indianapolis Freeman,* August 24, 1907.

39. Biographical sketch, box 2, J. Rosamond Johnson Papers, MSS 21, Irving S. Gilmore Music Library, Yale University.

40. Vicente Blasco Ibáñez, "Night Life in Paris," *New York Times,* January 30, 1921. Italics mine.

41. Edward Ellsworth Hipsher, *American Opera and Its Composers* (Philadelphia: Theodore Presser, 1927), 16.

42. Hipsher also discusses Maurice Arnold Strothotte, who studied with Dvořák at the National Conservatory. Strothotte was Black but, later in his career, decided to pass for white, living in a German neighborhood in New York and teaching music. See Alex Ross, *The Rest Is Noise: Listening to the Twentieth Century* (New York: Farrar, Straus and Giroux, 2007), 134–135.

43. Valdo Freeman, interview by Vivian Perlis, December 28, 1971, Major Figures in American Music Collection, Oral History of American Music, Music Library of Yale University.

44. Freeman, *Negro in Music and Drama,* 75.

45. Valdo Freeman, interview. See Celia Davidson, "Opera by Afro-American Composers: A Critical Survey and Analysis of Selected Works" (PhD diss., Catholic University of America, 1980), 52–71.

46. While the music was praised as "attractive," critics lamented that "amateurish" acting and "poor" dancing detracted from the production's quality. "'Vendetta' Pleases at the Lafayette Theatre," *New York Age,* November 17, 1923.

47. Pamphlet on the Negro Grand Opera Company, box 49, Freeman Papers.

48. See Jennifer Fleeger, *Sounding American: Hollywood, Opera, and Jazz* (New York: Oxford University Press, 2014), 7–14.

49. "Prof. H. Lawrence Freeman, the Composer of Eight Grand Operas," *Billboard,* December 13, 1924.

50. Valdo Freeman, interview.

51. David Gutkin argues that the opera's ambiguous portrayal of jazz is simultaneously an attempt to "capitalize on the jazz vogue" and a "critique of the Jazz Age." David Gutkin, "The Modernities of H. Lawrence Freeman," *Journal of the American Musicological Society* 72, no. 3 (2019): 719–779, 756–767.

52. "Souvenir Programme," box 36, Freeman Papers.

53. Gutkin, "Modernities of H. Lawrence Freeman," 755.

54. Untitled clipping, *Denver Rocky Mountain News,* in Scrapbook, box 59, Freeman Papers.

55. Pierre Key, "Sharps and Flats," *Hartford Courant,* September 23, 1928.

56. Untitled clipping, September 10, 1928, in Scrapbook, box 59, Freeman Papers.

57. "Realm of Music," *New York Evening World,* 1928, in Scrapbook, box 57, Freeman Papers.

58. "Realm of Music."

59. "Negro Grand Opera Company Pleases in First Performance," *New York Herald Tribune,* September 11, 1928, in Scrapbook, box 57, Freeman Papers.

60. "Negro Opera," *New York Sun,* 1928, in Scrapbook, box 57, Freeman Papers.

61. "Lawrence Freeman's Opera," *New York Amsterdam News,* September 19, 1928, in Scrapbook, box 57, Freeman Papers.

62. Obie McCollum, "The Trail Blazer," *New York Amsterdam News,* October 20, 1934.

63. Lena James Holt, untitled review in scrapbook, box 5, Clarence Cameron White Papers (Additions), 1906–1972, Sc MG 492, Schomburg Center for Research in Black Culture, Manuscripts Archives and Rare Books Division, New York Public Library. Hereafter White Papers (Additions).

64. Freeman, *Negro in Music and Drama,* 57.

65. Clarence Cameron White, "'Ouanga!': Haitian Opera," 1950, box 4, White Papers (Additions).

66. White, "'Ouanga!': Haitian Opera."

67. See Brandon Byrd, *The Black Republic: African Americans and the Fate of Haiti* (Philadelphia: University of Pennsylvania Press, 2019).

68. Clarence Cameron White, "A Musical Pilgrimage to Haiti, the Island of Beauty, Mystery, and Rhythm," *The Etude* (July 1929), 505.

69. See Mary Renda, *Taking Haiti: Military Occupation and the Culture of U.S. Imperialism, 1915–1940* (Chapel Hill: University of North Carolina Press, 2001).

70. Michael Largey, "*Ouanga!*: An African-American Opera about Haiti," *Lenox Avenue: A Journal of Interarts Inquiry* 2 (1996): 35–54, 36.

71. Largey, "An African-American Opera about Haiti," 36. See also Largey, *Vodou Nation: Haitian Art Music and Cultural Nationalism* (Chicago: University of Chicago Press, 2006), 147–185.

72. White, "A Musical Pilgrimage to Haiti," 505. White's commentary aligns with a trend of identifying Black music with the African past. See Garcia, *Listening for Africa.*

73. White, "Musical Pilgrimage to Haiti," 505.

74. John Frederick Matheus, "'Ouanga': My Venture in Libretto Creation," *CLA Journal* 15, no. 4 (1972): 428–440, 433.

75. "Studying Haitian Life," *Pittsburgh Courier,* September 1, 1928.

76. Michel-Rolph Trouillot, *Silencing the Past: Power and the Production of History* (Boston: Beacon Press, 1995).

77. On the performance history of *Jonny spielt auf,* see Edwards, "Circumstances of Colour," 151. On *Aida* and *The Emperor Jones,* see MetOpera Database, Metropolitan Opera Archives, https://archives.metopera.org/MetOperaSearch/search.jsp?titles=Aida&sort=PDATE and https://archives.metopera.org/MetOperaSearch/search.jsp?titles=The%20Emperor%20Jones&sort=PDATE.

78. "World Famous Opera Stars Gather to Hear Singing of 'Tom-Tom,'" *Baltimore Afro-American,* July 2, 1932; "Former Richmond Woman Writes Opera Presented at Cleveland," *Richmond (IN) Item,* July 10, 1932; Archie Bell, "Largest Throng of Week Cheers Rebuilt Tom Tom," July 10, 1932, clippings, box 23, Shirley Graham Du Bois Papers, Schlesinger Library, Radcliffe Institute, Harvard University (hereafter SGD Papers).

79. Freeman did not attend *Tom-Tom,* but he knew of it. Shortly after the premiere, Valdo Freeman received a letter that discussed the performance and contained press clippings. Harry Ford to Valdo Freeman, July 12, 1932, box 49, Freeman Papers. While *The Negro in Music and Drama* includes a synopsis of *Tom-Tom* and information about the production, it also expresses gendered condescension, referring to Graham as "Miss Shirley," a "lady composer." Freeman, *Negro in Music and Drama,* 77–78.

80. Colleen Renihan, *The Operatic Archive: American Opera as History* (New York: Routledge, 2020). See also George Jellinek, *History through the Opera Glass: From the Rise of Caesar to the Fall of Napoleon* (White Plains, NY: Pro / Am Music Resources, 2004); Herbert Lindenberger, *Opera in History: From Monteverdi to Cage* (Palo Alto, CA: Stanford University Press, 1998); and Sarah Hibberd, *French Grand Opera and the Historical Imagination* (Cambridge: Cambridge University Press, 2009).

81. Vogel uses this term to theorize Langston Hughes's queer poetics, asking how Hughes's poetry inscribes knowledge that "is impossible to archive under the official regimes of documentation and verification." Shane Vogel, *The Scene of Harlem Cabaret: Race, Sexuality, Performance* (Chicago: University of Chicago Press, 2009), 110.

82. Gerald Horne, *Race Woman: The Lives of Shirley Graham Du Bois* (New York: New York University Press, 2000), 10. Scholars increasingly recognize Shirley Graham as one of the leading activists and intellectuals of her era. See Vaughn Rasberry, *Race and the Totalitarian Century* (Cambridge, MA: Harvard University Press, 2016); and Robeson Taj Frazier, *The East Is Black: Cold War China in the Black Radical Imagination* (Durham, NC: Duke University Press, 2014).

83. Graham gave different birthdates throughout her life, sometimes claiming to be five or ten years younger than her true age. Horne, *Race Woman,* 38.

84. Horne, *Race Woman,* 41–46. See also Robert Dee Thompson Jr., "A Socio-Biography of Shirley Graham Du Bois: A Life in the Struggle" (PhD diss., University of California, Santa Cruz, 1997), 41.

85. Shirley Graham Du Bois, interview by Ann Shockley, Fisk University, October 7, 1971, box 1, SGD Papers; Shirley Graham Du Bois, *His Day Is Marching On* (Philadelphia: Lippincott Press, 1971), 18; Horne, *Race Woman,* 41–42.

86. Horne, *Race Woman,* 46. Graham wrote in program notes for *Tom-Tom* that her "father instilled in me a deep love and reverence for the spirituals. He gave me a pride in them and a full realization of their deep meaning to those who in their sorrow fashioned the melodies." Program, *Tom-Tom,* box 23, SGD Papers.

87. Graham gravitated toward male role models and interlocutors. Her parents modeled traditional gender roles, and both her writings and those of her biographers emphasize her father's outsized role in her life. Yet even if Shirley Graham did not cite her mother as a source of political or intellectual inspiration, Etta Graham's domestic labor and care for Shirley's children effectively enabled Shirley's myriad endeavors, particularly her ability to travel widely in pursuit of her goals. On David Graham, see Horne, *Race Woman,* 42–43. See also Alesia McFadden's thoughtful consideration of Etta Bell Graham in "The Artistry and Activism of Shirley Graham Du Bois: A Twentieth Century African American Torchbearer" (PhD diss., University of Massachusetts, Amherst, 2009), 126–151.

88. McCanns had no further relationship with their children, and Graham changed her older son's first name from Shadrach Jr. to Robert following the divorce. McFadden, "The Artistry and Activism of Shirley Graham Du Bois," 102.

89. Horne, *Race Woman,* 54.

90. In a scrapbook, Graham pasted ticket stubs from events including shows at the Danton Cinema Palace and Cinéma du Pantheon, as well as an opera recital followed by dancing and jazz at Le d'Harcourt, an "American-Bar," box 1, SGD Papers. Lorenz Graham to Shirley Graham, May 31, 1930, box 11, SGD Papers.

91. Shirley Graham Du Bois, *Paul Robeson: Citizen of the World* (New York: Messner, 1946), 209.

92. James Davis, *Eric Walrond: A Life in the Harlem Renaissance and the Transatlantic Caribbean* (New York: Columbia University Press, 2016), 244–258.

93. Autobiographical sketch, *Current Biography,* 1946, box 1, SGD Papers.

94. Brent Hayes Edwards, *The Practice of Diaspora: Literature, Translation, and the Rise of Black Internationalism* (Cambridge, MA: Harvard University Press, 2003).

95. "Afro Chorus Conductor Here," *Baltimore Afro-American,* November 12, 1927.

96. Employment contract, Morgan College, box 15, SGD Papers.

97. Program, Morgan College Choral and Dramatic Club, box 23, SGD Papers.

98. African Americans embraced the tradition of community pageantry, a then-popular feature of civic life in which amateur casts reenacted past events. Often excluded from municipal pageants, African Americans reinvented the tradition to celebrate Black achievement. See David Glassberg, *American Historical Pageantry: The Uses of Tradition in the Early Twentieth Century* (Chapel Hill: University of North Carolina Press, 1990); and Errol Hill and James Hatch, *A History of African American Theatre* (New York: Cambridge University Press, 2003), 199–202.

99. J. Stanley, "Local College Talent in Music Drama," *Baltimore Afro-American,* March 2, 1929.

100. See Lucy Caplan, "'All These Songs Help Us to Trace History': Black Women and the Black Music History Narrative in the Harlem Renaissance Era," in *The Oxford Handbook of Music and the Middlebrow,* ed. Christopher Chowrimootoo and Kate Guthrie (New York: Oxford University Press, 2022).

101. See Roland M. Baumann, *Constructing Black Education at Oberlin College: A Documentary History* (Athens: Ohio University Press, 2014); and Thurman, *Singing Like Germans,* 31–32.

102. Horne, *Race Woman,* 64.

103. Oberlin Conservatory of Music Course Catalog, 1931–32, box 2, SGD Papers.

104. See Melanie N. Blood, "Theatre in Settlement Houses: Hull-House Players, Neighborhood Playhouse, and Karamu Theatre," *Theatre History Studies* 16 (1996): 45–70.

105. Shirley Graham to Walter White, May 4, 1932, Personal Correspondence of Selected NAACP Officials, 1919–1939, reel 15, part 2, NAACP Papers, Library of Congress (hereafter NAACP Papers).

106. Shirley Graham to Robert Graham McCanns, March 1, 1932, box 12, SGD Papers.

107. A piano-vocal score for *Tom-Tom* in Graham's hand includes scattered annotations regarding orchestration. Some sections are more fully orchestrated, including choral arrangements of the spirituals that appear in act 2. Nearly four hundred pages in length, the score is basically complete throughout acts 1 and 2, while only parts of act 3 are preserved. Score for *Tom-Tom,* box 23, SGD Papers.

108. Leo Hamalian and James V. Hatch, *The Roots of African American Drama: An Anthology of Early Plays, 1858–1938* (Detroit: Wayne State University Press, 1991), 249.

109. The basis of Toni Morrison's *Beloved* (1987), the case also inspired the opera *Margaret Garner* (2005), with a libretto by Morrison and score by Richard Danielpour. See La Vinia Delois Jennings, *Margaret Garner: The Premiere Performances of Toni Morrison's Libretto* (Charlottesville: University of Virginia Press, 2006).

110. Langston Hughes, "The Negro Artist and the Racial Mountain," *The Nation,* June 23, 1926, 692–694.

111. "'Tom-Tom Basis of Negro Music,' Says Author," *Baltimore Afro-American,* May 25, 1929.

112. "Girl Writer of Opera Thrilled," *Atlanta Daily World,* June 29, 1932.

113. See Tsitsi Jaji, *Africa in Stereo: Modernism, Music, and Pan-African Solidarity* (New York: Oxford University Press, 2014).

114. See, for example, Kathy A. Perkins, "The Unknown Career of Shirley Graham," *Freedomways* 25, no. 1 (1985): 6–17, 10.

115. Hamalian and Hatch, *African American Drama,* 238.

116. Following the opera's premiere, Graham composed two overtures that are more standard in form. As Sarah Schmalenberger notes, these alternative overtures were likely suggested by Mary White Ovington, a patron of Black artists who advised Graham to make the work more accessible. Their exchange suggests the extent to which some listeners heard Graham's overture as a break from convention. Schmalenberger, "Debuting Her Political Voice," 60–61.

117. Denoe Leedy, "New All-Negro Opera Framed at Stadium," *Cleveland Press,* box 23, SGD Papers.

118. See John Gruesser, *Black on Black: Twentieth-Century African American Writing about Africa* (Lexington: University Press of Kentucky, 2000), 62–67.

119. Garcia, *Listening for Africa.*

120. Program book for *Tom-Tom,* box 23, SGD Papers.

121. Shirley Graham, "Statement of Project: Africa's Influence on Western Music," application to Guggenheim Memorial Foundation, 1931, enclosed in Shirley Graham to Walter White, Personal Correspondence of Selected NAACP Officials, 1919–1939, part 2, reel 15, NAACP Papers.

122. Graham, "Statement of Project."

123. As Colleen Renihan argues, opera's "historiographical potential" derives from its endemic temporal and structural capabilities, particularly its focus on characters over events and resulting ability to draw attention to the subjective dimensions of historical narrative. See Renihan, *Operatic Archive.*

124. See Soyica Diggs Colbert's argument that, in *The Star of Ethiopia,* Du Bois "imbued the quotidian definition of actor—one who performs an action—with purpose by having ordinary citizens play the part of revolutionary historical actors." Colbert, *The African American Theatrical Body: Reception, Performance, and the Stage* (Cambridge: Cambridge University Press, 2011), 49.

125. Leedy, "New All-Negro Opera," SGD Papers.

126. Score for *Tom-Tom,* box 23, SGD Papers.

127. Hamalian and Hatch, *African American Drama,* 285.

128. Schmalenberger, "Debuting Her Political Voice," 55.

129. "Baritone Wins W. Va. Audience," *Pittsburgh Courier,* March 8, 1930.

130. Cleveland Allen, "Music," *Chicago Defender,* December 28, 1929.

131. Bledsoe was also invited to sing Amonasro in the festival's concurrent production of *Aida,* anticipating his appearance alongside Caterina Jarboro one year later.

132. Jules Bledsoe, "Has the Negro a Place in the Theatre?" *Opportunity* 6 (July 1928): 215.

133. "Opera Composer," press clipping in scrapbook, box 1, SGD Papers; Leedy, "New All-Negro Opera"; Elrick B. Davis, "'Tom-Tom' Book a Racial Epic, True, Moving," *Cleveland Plain Dealer,* June 30, 1932, box 23, SGD Papers.

134. Harriet Blackburn, "Distinguished Composer Gains New Stature," *Christian Science Monitor,* undated; Eleanor Greenwood, "An American Opera," *The Front Rank,* February 12, 1933; clippings in box 23, SGD Papers. Graham was thirty-five at the time of *Tom-Tom*'s premiere, but she often claimed to be younger.

135. Program book for *Tom-Tom,* box 23, SGD Papers.

136. "'Tom-Tom' to Be Given in Ohio Opera Season," *Baltimore Afro-American,* June 4, 1932.

137. "Our Stars in the New Opera, 'Tom-Tom,'" undated press clipping, box 23, SGD Papers.

138. Leedy, "New All-Negro Opera"; Davis, "'Tom-Tom' Book a Racial Epic"; Archie Bell, "'Tom-Tom' Scores in Premiere," *Cleveland News,* undated, clippings in box 23, SGD Papers. Reviews suggest that the third act was shortened prior to the opera's second performance.

139. Maude Roberts George, "News of the Music World," *Chicago Defender,* July 23, 1932. The cited text comes from a review by the white *Chicago Daily News* critic Eugene Stinson, which George quoted.

140. On the racial politics of archives, see Laura E. Helton, "On Decimals, Catalogs, and Racial Imaginaries of Reading," *PMLA: Publications of the Modern Language Association of America* 134, no. 1 (2019): 99–120. For a contemporary reflection, see Ashley Farmer, "Archiving while Black," *Black Perspectives* (blog), African American Intellectual History Society, June 18, 2018, https://www.aaihs.org/archiving-while-black/.

141. Shirley Graham Du Bois, interview.

142. Shirley Graham Du Bois, interview.

143. Shirley Graham Du Bois, interview.

144. Graham to White, August 4, 1932, Personal Correspondence of Selected NAACP Officials, 1919–1939, part 2, reel 15, NAACP Papers.

145. Shirley Graham to Rev. D. A. Graham and Etta Bell Graham, June 14, 1932, box 25, SGD Papers.

146. Ernst Lert to Shirley Graham, October 18, 1932, box 15, SGD Papers.

147. Lorenz Graham to Shirley Graham, July 30, 1932, box 11, SGD Papers.

148. "'Tom-Tom' Ghost Fails to Walk, Is Rumor," *Baltimore Afro-American,* July 30, 1932; Jules Bledsoe to Shirley Graham, July 20, 1932, box 11, SGD Papers.

149. Bledsoe to Graham, July 20, 1932. Bledsoe implies that he was not paid in full, either. He urged Graham to keep pressuring Higgins, and to make her concerns public if Higgins refused to pay her. There is no further evidence indicating whether Higgins ever paid the performers.

150. Lorenz Graham to Shirley Graham, July 30, 1932, box 11, SGD Papers.

151. Oberlin College Office of the Dean to Shirley Graham, August 5, 1932, box 12, SGD Papers.

152. Graham to White, August 4, 1932.

153. Shirley Graham, "The Survivals of Africanism in Modern Music" (master's thesis, Oberlin College, 1935). Graham wrote the thesis under the direction of Oberlin professor James H. Hall, and she received additional guidance from an illustrious set of interlocutors including James Weldon Johnson, W. E. B. Du Bois, William Grant Still, Florence Price, and William Levi Dawson. I am grateful to Fredara Hadley for sharing a copy of Graham's thesis with me.

154. Shirley Graham, Fellowship Application Form, Guggenheim Foundation, box 11, SGD Papers. Tellingly, Graham wrote in her application that "The project lies both in the fields of Music-History and of Music-Composition." The archive contains only the application form and not the more detailed "Plan of Study," so it does not reveal specific plans for revision. It is unclear whether Graham submitted the application.

155. Shirley Graham to W. E. B. Du Bois, October 1, 1937, W. E. B. Du Bois Papers, Special Collections and University Archives, University of Massachusetts Amherst Libraries, https://credo.library.umass.edu/view/full/mums312-b082-i221.

156. Horne, *Race Woman,* 71; Shirley Graham to W. E. B. Du Bois, October 30, 1935, W. E. B. Du Bois Papers, https://credo.library.umass.edu/view/full/mums312 -b074-i172.

157. Graham to Du Bois, October 30, 1935.

158. Shirley Graham to W. E. B. Du Bois, January 11, 1936, W. E. B. Du Bois Papers, https://credo.library.umass.edu/view/full/mums312-b078-i290.

6. The Countercultural Roots of Desegregation

1. Abbie Mitchell and George Gershwin, "Summertime," *Gershwin Performs Gershwin: Rare Recordings, 1931–1935* (Ocean, NJ: Jazz Heritage, 1991).

2. Carl Diton, "Abbie Mitchell Scores Again in N.Y. Recital," *Pittsburgh Courier,* December 5, 1931. On Mitchell, see Marva Griffin Carter, *Swing Along: The Musical Life of Will Marion Cook* (New York: Oxford University Press, 2008).

3. Sylvester Russell, "Abbie Mitchell's Recital," *Pittsburgh Courier,* February 16, 1929.

4. "Abbie Mitchell in New Role?" *New York Amsterdam News,* January 30, 1929. "Long-cherished ambition" is from "Seeks Opera Role," *Baltimore Afro-American,*

February 2, 1929. One critic, upon hearing Mitchell in recital, was so enthused by the possibility that he resorted to all capital letters: "WHAT AN 'AIDA' THIS WOMAN WOULD MAKE!" Maud Cuney Hare, *Negro Musicians and Their Music* (Washington, DC: Associated Publishers, 1936), 370.

5. Rosalyn Story, *And So I Sing: African-American Divas of Opera and Concert* (New York: Warner Books, 1990), 63. Italics mine.

6. Tammy Kernodle, "Black Women Working Together: Jazz, Gender, and the Politics of Validation," *Black Music Research Journal* 34, no. 1 (2014): 27–55.

7. Danton Walker, "'Porgy and Bess' First True American Opera," *Sunday Daily News,* October 13, 1935.

8. Steven Watson, *Prepare for Saints: Gertrude Stein, Virgil Thomson, and the Mainstreaming of American Modernism* (Berkeley: University of California Press, 2000).

9. "All-Negro Cast for New Opera Creates Stir," *Baltimore Afro-American,* January 20, 1934.

10. Thomson attended the performance with Carl Van Vechten. See Van Vechten, "Introduction," *Four Saints in Three Acts: An Opera to Be Sung* (New York: Random House, 1934), 7–8.

11. Olin Downes, "Final Scene of Hall Johnson's 'Folk-Play' Indicates One Direction for Developing Native Genre," *New York Times,* April 2, 1933. See also Judith Weisenfeld, "'The Secret at the Root': Performing African American Religious Modernity in Hall Johnson's *Run, Little Chillun,*" *Religion and American Culture* 21, no. 1 (2011): 39–79. Downes made a near-identical claim in a review of Johnson's *The Green Pastures* (1930), positing that Johnson's arrangements of spirituals operated on Wagnerian principles but insisting that the performers' "unstudied, racial musical spontaneity" made them effective. Olin Downes, "Future Opera," *New York Times,* June 29, 1930.

12. Johnson later reflected that his background in chamber music informed his approach to conducting the Hall Johnson Choir. See Marva Griffin Carter, "The New Negro Choral Legacy of Hall Johnson," in *Chorus and Community,* ed. Karen Ahlquist (Urbana: University of Illinois Press, 2006), 189.

13. "Opera Goes Hi-De-Ho," *Baltimore Afro-American,* February 17, 1934.

14. Lisa Barg, "Black Voices / White Sounds: Race and Representation in Virgil Thomson's *Four Saints in Three Acts,*" *American Music* 18, no. 2 (2000): 121–161, 123. Relatedly, Nadine Hubbs suggests that Blackness in the opera "visibly represented identity difference," and alluded to "a queer sexual freedom associated with Harlem and projected onto black bodies." Nadine Hubbs, *The Queer Composition of America's Sound: Gay Modernists, American Music, and National Identity* (Berkeley: University of California Press, 2004), 33.

15. See Barg, "Black Voices / White Sounds," 144–149.

16. See Paige McGinley, "'A Southern, Brown, Burnt Sensibility': *Four Saints in Three Acts,* Black Spain, and the (Global) Southern Pastoral," in *Creating and Consuming the American South: Borderlands and Transnationalism in the United*

States and Canada, ed. Martyn Bone, Brian Ward, and William A. Link (Gaines-ville: University of Florida Press, 2015), 235–236.

17. Gertrude Stein, *The Autobiography of Alice B. Toklas* (New York: Har-court, Brace, 1933), 292. See also Barbara Webb, "The Centrality of Race to the Modernist Aesthetics of Gertrude Stein's *Four Saints in Three Acts," Modernism / modernity* 7, no. 3 (2000): 447–469.

18. For an excellent analysis of the procession scene, see McGinley, "Southern, Brown, Burnt Sensibility," 241–243. While McGinley reads this scene as evocative of "diasporic movement," I understand it more indicative of the *limits* of move-ment within the opera.

19. "World Premiere Set for Opera, 'Four Saints,'" *Harlem Heights Daily Cit-izen,* January 9, 1934; "Reviewer Finds Gamut of Emotions in Opera," *New York Amsterdam News,* February 28, 1934; Floyd Calvin, "Broadway Now Takes Its Opera from Former Negro Spiritual Singers," *New Journal and Guide,* December 28, 1935.

20. See Ellen Noonan, *The Strange Career of* Porgy and Bess: *Race, Culture, and America's Most Famous Opera* (Chapel Hill: University of North Carolina Press, 2012).

21. Noonan, *Strange Career,* 103.

22. "A Romance of Negro Life," *New York Times,* September 27, 1925.

23. Brooks Atkinson, "Negro Lithography," *New York Times,* October 11, 1927.

24. Dubose Heyward, "Porgy and Bess Return on Wings of Song," originally published in *Stage* (October 1925), in Merle Armitage, *George Gershwin* (New York: Da Capo Press, 1995), 39.

25. Noonan, *Strange Career,* 19, 76.

26. Baldwin made this observation in relation to the 1959 film version of the opera. James Baldwin, "On Catfish Row," *Commentary* (September 1959).

27. George Gershwin, "Rhapsody in Catfish Row," *New York Times,* October 20, 1935.

28. See Ray Allen and George Cunningham, "Cultural Uplift and Double-Consciousness: African American Responses to the 1935 Opera *Porgy and Bess," Musical Quarterly* 88, no. 3 (2005): 342–369.

29. Hall Johnson, "Porgy and Bess—A Folk Opera," *Opportunity,* January 1936, 24–28.

30. H. Lawrence Freeman, "Marian, Caterina Tops among Music Celebrities during 1936," *Baltimore Afro-American,* January 9, 1937; Shirley Graham to W. E. B. Du Bois, January 11, 1936, W. E. B. Du Bois Papers, Special Collections and Uni-versity Archives, University of Massachusetts Amherst Libraries.

31. Although Gershwin had already indicated his interest to Heyward, these plans were not made public until November 1933. "To Present 'Porgy' as a Mu-sical Show," *New York Times,* November 3, 1933. As noted in Chapter 5, Keelan also wrote perceptive commentary on *Jonny spielt auf* and *The Emperor Jones.*

32. Harry S. Keelan, "Porgy: An Impression," *Opportunity,* June 1928, 180–181.

33. Keelan, "Porgy: An Impression," 181.

34. Quoted in Noonan, *Strange Career,* 153.

35. Lucien White, "Porgy and Bess," *New York Age,* October 26, 1935.

36. Ralph Matthews, "Porgy and Bess Given Ovation on Broadway," *Baltimore Afro-American,* October 19, 1935.

37. Sally MacDougall, "Porgy's Bess a Hussy on Stage but She's Really Serious in Life," *Pittsburgh Courier,* January 18, 1936.

38. W. Llewellyn Wilson, "Bess the Strumpet of Catfish Row," *Baltimore Afro-American,* November 9, 1935.

39. Brown lived in Norway beginning in 1948, and her memoir was published only in Norwegian, with the title *Sang fra frossen gren* (Song from a frozen hilltop). A typescript of an English translation is in box 1, Peabody Institute Anne Brown Collection, Arthur Friedheim Library Special Collections, Peabody Institute, Johns Hopkins University. Brown, *Hilltop,* 30–31.

40. Brown, *Hilltop,* 56.

41. Gwynne Kuhner Brown, "Performers in Catfish Row: *Porgy and Bess* as Collaboration," in *Blackness in Opera,* ed. Naomi André, Karen M. Bryan, and Eric Saylor (Urbana: University of Illinois Press, 2012), 168–170.

42. Brown, *Hilltop,* 62–63.

43. Brown, *Hilltop,* 136.

44. Levi C. Hubert, "Harlem WPA Group Sings Opera," *Crisis,* July 1936, 214.

45. Press clippings, Detroit Civic Opera Company File, E. Azalia Hackley Collection of African Americans in the Performing Arts, Detroit Public Library.

46. Press clippings, Detroit Civic Opera Company File, Hackley Collection.

47. Advertisement, *Kansas City Sun,* May 10, 1919.

48. H. Lawrence Freeman, *The Negro in Music and Drama,* 42, typescript, box 50, H. Lawrence Freeman Papers, Rare Book and Manuscript Library, Columbia University.

49. "Race Must Be Made Opera-Conscious," *Baltimore Afro-American,* July 2, 1932.

50. The piece also noted the "irony" that Bledsoe had sought to obtain the rights to compose the opera to no avail, because they had already been granted to Gruenberg; however, "Bledsoe's own version, according to those musicians who heard it, including Clarence Cameron White, the violinist, was far superior." While some sketches from Bledsoe's version are extant, the piece seems never to have been completed. "N.Y. Raves over Bledsoe's Debut in Opera," *Chicago Defender,* July 21, 1934.

51. Cosmopolitan Opera Association to Valdo Freeman, November 22, 1934, box 49, H. Lawrence Freeman Papers, Rare Book and Manuscript Library, Columbia University.

52. Edward Boatner, "Co-operative Opera Club," *New York Age,* May 31, 1941.

53. On the National Negro Opera Company, see Annegret Fauser, *Sounds of War: Music in the United States during World War II* (New York: Oxford University Press, 2013), 174–177; and C. Wells, "Grand Opera as Racial Uplift: The National Negro Opera Company, 1941–1962" (master's thesis, University of North Carolina at Chapel Hill, 2009). On Dawson's biography, see Karen Bryan, "Radiating a Hope: Mary Cardwell Dawson as Educator and Activist," *Journal of Historical Research in Music Education* 25, no. 1 (2003): 20–35.

54. Quoted in Wells, "Grand Opera as Racial Uplift," 4.

55. Carl Diton, "Grand Opera 'Aida' Brilliantly Enacted," *Baltimore Afro-American,* June 21, 1941; and Carl Diton, "Negro Opera Company Scores in New York," *New Journal and Guide,* April 8, 1944.

56. P. L. Prattis, "The Horizon," *Pittsburgh Courier,* February 5, 1944.

57. Annegret Fauser argues that several World War II–era operatic endeavors made similar ideological moves, motivated by a concern that opera's European connotations were undermining its cultural relevance under wartime conditions. Fauser, *Sounds of War,* 162–177.

58. "An Invitation to Opera Lovers," National Negro Opera Company Programs and Promotional Materials, Henry P. Whitehead Collection, Anacostia Community Museum Archives, Smithsonian Institution.

59. "Negroes to Present Opera Here," *Washington Post,* August 8, 1943.

60. Prattis, "The Horizon."

61. The company later expanded its programming to include works by Black composers, presenting Nathaniel Dett's oratorio *The Ordering of Moses* and Clarence Cameron White's *Ouanga.* But these remained exceptions rather than key works in its repertoire.

62. Fauser, *Sounds of War,* 176.

63. Nora Douglas Holt, "Are Negro Artists Ready for Opera? Will Public Back Them?" *New York Amsterdam News,* May 5, 1945.

64. Edgar T. Rouzeau, "Star Dust," *New Journal and Guide,* March 2, 1940.

65. Edgar T. Rouzeau, "'Met' Turns Down Negro Stars," *New Journal and Guide,* December 16, 1939.

66. Rouzeau, "'Met' Turns Down Negro Stars."

67. Edgar T. Rouzeau, "Star Dust," *New Journal and Guide,* October 14, 1939.

68. Nora Holt, "Long Island War Workers See Opera between Shifts," *New York Amsterdam News,* March 10, 1945.

69. Nora Holt, "Music: Metropolitan Opera Season," *New York Amsterdam News,* October 19, 1946.

70. Kira Thurman, *Singing Like Germans* (Ithaca, NY: Cornell University Press, 2021), 55. On Du Bois and Wagner, see Alex Ross, *Wagnerism: Art and Politics in the Shadow of Music* (New York: Farrar, Straus, and Giroux, 2020), 271–276.

71. W. E. B. Du Bois, "Forum of Fact and Opinion: Shrines," *Pittsburgh Courier,* October 17, 1936. Du Bois used the same phrase—"I know little of music"—to preface his writings on the sorrow songs in *The Souls of Black Folk* (1903).

72. Thurman, *Singing Like Germans,* 168–169.

73. W. E. B. Du Bois, "Forum of Fact and Opinion: Opera and the Negro Problem," *Pittsburgh Courier,* October 31, 1936.

74. Du Bois, "Opera and the Negro Problem." The echoes of Graham are particularly striking given that, in April 1936, she pleaded to accompany Du Bois on the trip: "Take me out into the air where I can breathe. I'm dying here. Every vision I ever had is trailing in the dust, every hope I ever had is being crushed." Shirley Graham to W. E. B. Du Bois, April 6, 1936, Du Bois Papers, https://credo.library.umass.edu/view/full/mums312-b078-i292. But Du Bois declined, citing a lack of funding. W. E. B. Du Bois to Shirley Graham, April 8, 1936, Du Bois Papers, https://credo.library.umass.edu/view/full/mums312-b078-i293.

75. "Revive *Abyssinia!*" *New York Amsterdam News,* October 26, 1935. Intriguingly, the article also claims that the Met stole the "gorgeous mountings" for its production of *Aida* from Williams and Walker.

76. Nora Holt, "Music," *New York Amsterdam News,* March 11, 1944.

77. Nora Holt, "Music," *New York Amsterdam News,* May 20, 1944.

78. See Heidi Waleson, *Mad Scenes and Exit Arias: The Death of the New York City Opera and the Future of Opera in America* (New York: Metropolitan Books, 2018).

79. Brown, *Hilltop,* 60.

80. Nora Holt, "Todd Duncan to Star in 'Pagliacci,'" *New York Amsterdam News,* September 15, 1945.

81. "Gets First Opera Call," *Baltimore Afro-American,* September 29, 1945.

82. James A. Standifer, "Reminiscences of Black Musicians," *American Music* 4, no. 2 (1986): 194–205, 198. Duncan made these comments in an interview conducted on February 20, 1980.

83. "Porgy to Pagli," *Newsweek,* October 8, 1945; Nora Holt, "Music: Duncan Eclipses Debut Performances in Roles of Tonio and Escamillo," *New York Amsterdam News,* October 27, 1945.

84. "Events in the World of Music," *New York Times,* September 9, 1945.

85. E. B. Rea, "Encores and Echoes," *Baltimore Afro-American,* September 29, 1945.

86. Thurman, *Singing Like Germans,* 190–203.

87. Luther P. Jackson, "Rights and Duties in a Democracy," *New Journal and Guide,* June 1, 1946.

88. Nora Holt, "Clod-Like Shoes Slowed Down Lyrical Camilla in Pagliacci," *New York Amsterdam News,* September 28, 1946.

89. John M. Lee, "The Showfront," *Cleveland Call and Post,* June 1, 1946.

90. Josephine Lee, *Oriental, Black, and White: The Formation of Racial Habits in American Theater* (Chapel Hill: University of North Carolina Press, 2022), 146.

91. Story, *And So I Sing,* 73. Kira Thurman, discussing Williams's performance of the same role in Vienna in 1956, suggests that "audiences were willing to make the racial leap and believe that a Black singer could play an Asian role," particularly a role that depicted an exotic, sexualized figure. Thurman, *Singing Like Germans,* 226. Similarly, Nina Sun Eidsheim writes that Williams's casting was a "compromised invitation" that shows how Black singers were "limited in artistic opportunities due to structural racism." Nina Sun Eidsheim, *The Race of Sound: Listening, Timbre, and Vocality in African American Music* (Durham, NC: Duke University Press, 2019), 63.

92. As Kunio Hara has documented, by 1946 Tamaki Miura was approaching the end of her life, and her final performance of Cio-Cio-San was recorded that spring. Her decline was often understood as analogous to that of the occupied nation. See Hara, "The Death of Tamaki Miura: Performing *Madama Butterfly* during the Allied Occupation of Japan," *Music and Politics* 11, no. 1 (2017): 1–26.

93. "Camilla Williams a Hit in City Opera," *New York Times,* May 16, 1946.

94. Camilla Williams and Stephanie Shonekan, *The Life of Camilla Williams: African American Classical Singer and Opera Diva* (Lewiston, NY: Edwin Mellen Press, 2011), 87.

95. Williams and Shonekan, *Camilla Williams,* 46.

96. Williams and Shonekan, *Camilla Williams,* 63.

97. Williams and Shonekan, *Camilla Williams,* 83.

98. Nora Holt, "Music: Unsung Music Teachers," *New York Amsterdam News,* January 18, 1947.

99. Nora Holt, "Major and Minor: Virginia State College Lists Artists for Concert Season," *New York Amsterdam News,* October 9, 1948.

100. See Annie Kim, "Bess Disembodied: Camilla Williams's (Re)Sounding Black Womanhood in *Porgy and Bess,*" *Women and Music: A Journal of Gender and Culture* 26, no. 1 (2022): 25–44, 36.

101. In 1946, Williams recorded "Summertime" as a standalone aria. The performance is stylistically quite different from her 1951 recording: she uses a wide vibrato, rolls her r's, and takes a more fluid approach to the tempo. The marked differences between the two suggest how much interpretive care and artistic decision-making informed each of Williams's recordings.

102. Williams and Shonekan, *Camilla Williams,* 116–117.

103. Daphne A. Brooks, "'A Woman Is a Sometime Thing': (Re)Covering Black Womanhood in *Porgy and Bess,*" *Daedalus* 150, no. 1 (2021): 98–117, 98.

104. My thinking here is indebted to Shane Vogel's description of Lena Horne's intentionally aloof "impersona." Vogel, *The Scene of Harlem Cabaret: Race, Sexuality, Performance* (Chicago: University of Chicago Press, 2009), 169–194.

105. This idea is informed by, but ultimately departs somewhat from, Annie Kim's interpretation, which posits that the recorded format enabled Williams to detach herself from the character via a process of "disembodiment." Kim, "Bess Disembodied."

7. Open Doors and Shadow Archives

1. Evelyn Cunningham, "There Was No Uproar at the Opera," *Pittsburgh Courier,* January 29, 1955.

2. Olin Downes, "A Door Opens," *New York Times,* October 17, 1954; "Greatest Musical Offer Ever," *New York Amsterdam News,* July 1, 1925; Salem Tutt Whitney, "Timely Topics: Caterina Jarboro and Jules Bledsoe," *Chicago Defender,* August 5, 1933; Richard Durant, "In the Realm of Music," *New York Age,* August 4, 1934; Nora Holt, "Negroes Eye Opera, But—," *New York Amsterdam News,* April 22, 1950.

3. Sylvia Olden Lee, "Pay Attention to the Words," *Fidelio Magazine* 7, no. 1 (Spring 1998).

4. Nina Sun Eidsheim, *The Race of Sound: Listening, Timbre, and Vocality in African American Music* (Durham, NC: Duke University Press, 2019), 61–90.

5. See Gerald Horne, *The Rise and Fall of the Associated Negro Press: Claude Barnett's Pan-African News and the Jim Crow Paradox* (Urbana: University of Illinois Press, 2017).

6. Dick Campbell, "'Troubled Island' Set for New York," *Pittsburgh Courier,* March 26, 1949.

7. Errol Hill and James Hatch write that opera was "the last bastion of American professional theatre from which Blacks were excluded, regardless of their proven competence, training, and talent." Errol Hill and James Hatch, *A History of African American Theatre* (New York: Cambridge University Press, 2003), 177.

8. Rosalyn Story, *And So I Sing: African-American Divas of Opera and Concert* (New York: Warner Books, 1990), 76.

9. Virgil Thomson, "The Last of the Divas," *New York Herald Tribune,* January 18, 1942.

10. "Negro Metropolitan Opera Singers Break Aida Pattern," *Atlanta Daily World,* December 19, 1951. The article is about four Black singers hired to sing in the chorus for *Cavalleria Rusticana.*

11. "Williams and Winters Superb in 'Aida,'" *New York Amsterdam News,* November 6, 1948.

12. The production, which featured four Black singers (Davis, Carol Brice, John Diggs, and Luther Saxon), prompted Howard Taubman to remark that "with the best will in the world toward them as artists, one felt that the Negroes and their fantastic get-ups were out of place . . . If they were meant to poke fun at the conventions of another day the purpose was only partly achieved. Too often there was the impression that the fun was at their expense." Taubman's critique recalls responses to *Four Saints in Three Acts* in its characterization of Black performers as inherently out of place. "Pastoral Opera Given at Museum," *New York Times,* December 11, 1941.

13. Davis's agent at this time was the impresario George Westerman, who also represented Dorothy Maynor, Carol Brice, and Camilla Williams. As Katherine

Zien observes, "one of [these artists'] primary reasons for taking to international concert stages was their exclusion from the domestic US opera stage." Zien, "Side-long Glances: Black Divas in Transit, 1945–1955," in *The Routledge Companion to African American Theatre and Performance* (New York: Routledge, 2018), 364.

14. Virginia Lee Warren, "Miss Davis Scores in Mexican Debut," *New York Times,* July 25, 1946.

15. Clipping from *Time,* July 29, 1946, Ellabelle Davis Collection, E. Azalia Hackley Collection of African Americans in the Performing Arts, Detroit Public Library (hereafter Ellabelle Davis Collection).

16. Eleanor Roosevelt, "My Day," July 31, 1946.

17. Promotional booklet, Ellabelle Davis Collection.

18. Press material on Ellabelle Davis, Soprano, Ellabelle Davis Collection.

19. Press material on Ellabelle Davis, Soprano, National Concert and Artists Corporation, undated, Ellabelle Davis Collection.

20. Quoted in Giulia Bonacci, "The Ethiopian World Federation: A Pan-African Organisation among the Rastafari in Jamaica," *Caribbean Quarterly* 59, no. 2 (2013): 73–95, 83.

21. Chatwood Hall, "Mayme Richardson in 'Farewell to Ethiopia,'" *Baltimore Afro-American,* September 11, 1948.

22. Intriguingly, Richardson had previously composed an original song, "Ethiopia," that was sung at events advocating anticolonial opposition to the Italo-Ethiopian War. Beginning with the lyrics "Ethiopia, land of the free," it called out to Ethiopia's "four hundred million children," urging transnational solidarity and a return to "our native land." Considered in tandem with her Addis Ababa performance, Richardson's composition might be seen as an extension of Aida's voice—linking the character's longing for and allegiance to her homeland to the plight of forcibly displaced African diasporic peoples, and reiterating the opera's enduring countercultural potential. Mayme Richardson, "Ethiopia," Leigh R. Whipper Papers, series G, box 114–5, Moorland Spingarn Research Center, Howard University.

23. "Entertainers Urged to Fight Discrimination," *Detroit Tribune,* October 18, 1947, Muriel Rahn Collection, E. Azalia Hackley Collection of African Americans in the Performing Arts, Detroit Public Library.

24. "Muriel Rahn Makes Bid for 'Met' Assignment," *Baltimore Afro-American,* November 13, 1948.

25. "The Met Bows Out as Salmaggi Soars," *Baltimore Afro-American,* August 28, 1948; "Singer Challenges Metropolitan Opera," *New Journal and Guide,* November 13, 1948; "Singer Seeks to Crash Metropolitan Opera Bias," *Los Angeles Sentinel,* November 18, 1948.

26. AGMA was the union representing operatic musicians. As Carol Oja notes, other artists, including Marian Anderson, pursued similar strategies, renting the Met as a way to access the space without having to be hired by the company. See Oja, "Jim Crow Segregation at the Metropolitan Opera: Revisiting Marian

Anderson's Premiere in 1955," paper presented at "Sound, Gender, and the Color Line: A Symposium and Celebration in Honor of Marian Anderson, Musician and Citizen of the World," Kislak Center for Special Collections, Rare Books, and Manuscripts, University of Pennsylvania Libraries, October 2018.

27. "Muriel Rahn among 15 to Be Honored by Women's Council," *Baltimore Afro-American,* June 18, 1949.

28. Billy Rowe, "Muriel Rahn Sings 'Aida' at Met for AGVA Fund," *Pittsburgh Courier,* January 1, 1949.

29. James L. Hicks, "Big Town," *Baltimore Afro-American,* February 5, 1949; "Muriel Rahn Among 15 to Be Honored by Women's Council."

30. Audition card, Muriel Rahn, Metropolitan Opera Archives. Rahn auditioned on December 20, 1949, February 22, 1951, June 12, 1952, and October 9, 1956.

31. Audition card, Caterina Jarboro, November 27, 1951, Metropolitan Opera Archives.

32. Jesse H. Walker, "AGMA Celebrating 20th Anniversary," *New York Amsterdam News,* June 8, 1957.

33. "Muriel Rahn Waging Fight for Negro Performers," *Atlanta Daily World,* November 8, 1951.

34. Muriel Rahn to Max Rudolf, May 5, 1952, Max Rudolf Correspondence, 1952–1958 R, Metropolitan Opera Archives.

35. George F. Brown, "The Exclusion Act of All Time," *Pittsburgh Courier,* March 15, 1947.

36. George F. Brown, "Public Opinion Could Change Metropolitan Policy," *Pittsburgh Courier,* April 26, 1947.

37. Rachel Leib to George Sloan, December 18, 1943; Dean Murem to Edward Johnson, May 13, 1944; Morris Carrell to Edward Johnson, January 25, 1944; Ernest Phillips to Edward Johnson, November 25, 1946; Reginald Farrow to Edward Johnson, March 15, 1949, all in Edward Johnson Correspondence, 1948–49 I–Z, 1949–50 A–M, Metropolitan Opera Archives (hereafter Johnson Correspondence).

38. Secretary to Mr. Johnson to Rachel Leib, December 31, 1944; Secretary to Mr. Johnson to Sylvia Golden, February 11, 1948, both in Johnson Correspondence. When I visited the Metropolitan Opera Archives in 2018, I found these materials while leafing through alphabetized correspondence. To my surprise, when I came to the letter N, there was a folder labeled "Negro question." The folder's obscure placement made it unlikely to be found. It also subsumed these letter writers into a category defined not alphabetically, but by their attention to race. This exception to the archive's rules parallels the Met's treatment of Black singers during these years.

39. Secretary to Mr. Johnson to Antonio Altamirano, April 8, 1948, Johnson Correspondence.

40. Secretary to Mr. Johnson to Mrs. E. B. Arnsten, November 27, 1946, Johnson Correspondence.

41. Olden Lee, "Pay Attention to the Words."

42. Elizabeth Nash, *The Memoirs of Sylvia Olden Lee, Premier African-American Classical Vocal Coach: Who Is Sylvia* (Lewiston, NY: Edward Mellen Press, 2001), 5.

43. Wallace Cheatham, ed., *Dialogues on Opera and the African-American Experience* (Lanham, MD: Scarecrow Press, 1997), 56. Olden Lee attests that she did not learn about this event until after her mother's death, when a family friend relayed it to her.

44. Upon moving to New York, the Lees rented a home owned by Sam Patterson, a jazz pianist who had inherited Joplin's piano. Edward Berlin, *King of Ragtime: Scott Joplin and His Era,* 2nd ed. (New York: Oxford University Press, 2016), 312.

45. Olden Lee, "Pay Attention to the Words."

46. Nash, *The Memoirs of Sylvia Olden Lee,* 75.

47. On Collins, see Yaël Tamar Lewin, *Night's Dancer: The Life of Janet Collins* (Middletown, CT: Wesleyan University Press, 2011). Carol Oja has shown how African American collective efforts, particularly those led by the NAACP's Walter White, facilitated Anderson's debut. See Oja, "Jim Crow Segregation at the Metropolitan Opera."

48. As Kira Thurman has argued, Anderson's "performative politics" began to develop prior to this event, when she performed in Nazi Germany and fascist Austria during the 1930s. Kira Thurman, *Singing Like Germans* (Ithaca, NY: Cornell University Press, 2021), 160.

49. Gayle Wald, "Soul Vibrations: Black Music and Black Freedom in Sound and Space," *American Quarterly* 63, no. 3 (2011): 673–696: 680, 674. To listen to Anderson's performance, see "Marian Anderson Sings at the Lincoln Memorial," April 9, 1939, newsreel, Hearst Metrotone News Collection, UCLA Film & Television Archive, https://www.youtube.com/watch?v=XF9Quk0QhSE.

50. Howard Taubman, *Music on My Beat: An Intimate Volume of Shop Talk* (New York: Simon and Schuster, 1943), 182.

51. See Oja, "Jim Crow Segregation at the Metropolitan Opera."

52. Harry S. Keelan, letter to the editor, *New York Times,* April 9, 1939. The letter was printed on the day of Anderson's Lincoln Memorial performance.

53. "Miss Anderson and the Met," *New York Amsterdam News,* October 30, 1954.

54. Marian Anderson, *My Lord, What a Morning: An Autobiography* (New York: Viking, 1956), 189.

55. Nora Douglas Holt, "Musicians Organize National Association," *Chicago Defender,* August 9, 1919.

56. Eidsheim, *Race of Sound,* 83.

57. Rudolf Bing, "American Export: Opera Stars," *New York Times,* December 26, 1954. In 1968, Bing engaged the African American soprano Martina Arroyo to sing Elsa—the first time a Black singer performed the role.

58. Quoted in C. Wells, "Grand Opera as Racial Uplift: The National Negro Opera Company 1941–1962" (master's thesis, University of North Carolina at Chapel Hill, 2009), 28.

59. Carl Diton, "Marian Anderson First for 'Met,' Not First in Interracial Opera," *Chicago Defender,* March 12, 1955.

60. "Move Underway to Help Negro Opera Hopefuls," *Pittsburgh Courier,* April 16, 1955.

61. Allan Keiler, *Marian Anderson: A Singer's Journey* (Urbana: University of Illinois Press, 2002), 273.

62. Olin Downes, "Opera: Masked Ball," *New York Times,* January 8, 1955; Howard Taubman, "Marian Anderson Wins Ovation in First Opera Role at the Met," *New York Times,* January 8, 1955.

63. Daphne A. Brooks, *Liner Notes for the Revolution: The Intellectual Life of Black Feminist Sound* (Cambridge, MA: Harvard University Press, 2021), 370.

64. MetOpera Database, Metropolitan Opera Archives, https://archives.metopera.org/MetOperaSearch/search.jsp?titles=Aida&sort=PDATE, https://archives.metopera.org/MetOperaSearch/search.jsp?titles=La%20Boh%C3%A8me&sort=PDATE, and https://archives.metopera.org/MetOperaSearch/search.jsp?titles=Carmen&sort=PDATE.

65. Poster for *The Martyr,* September 1947, box 36, H. Lawrence Freeman Papers, Rare Book and Manuscript Library, Columbia University (hereafter Freeman Papers).

66. Valdo Freeman, interview by Vivian Perlis, December 28, 1971, Major Figures in American Music Collection, Oral History of American Music, Music Library of Yale University.

67. "Notes About Week-end Music," *New York Amsterdam News,* September 27, 1947.

68. "'Martyr' Uncovers Star for Role in Met's 'Aida,'" *Baltimore Afro-American,* October 11, 1947.

69. Muriel Rahn, postcards to Harry Lawrence Freeman, box 49, Freeman Papers.

70. Paul Robinson to Edward Johnson, May 11, 1949, box 49, Freeman Papers.

71. On Still's heterogenous compositional aesthetic, see Gayle Murchison, "'Dean of Afro-American Composers' or 'Harlem Renaissance Man': The New Negro and the Musical Poetics of William Grant Still," in *William Grant Still: A Study in Contradictions,* ed. Catherine Parsons Smith (Berkeley: University of California Press, 2000); and Carol Oja, "New Music and the New Negro: The Background of William Grant Still's *Afro-American Symphony,*" *Black Music Research Journal* 22 (2002): 107–130.

72. William Grant Still, "The Composer Needs Determination and Faith," *The Etude* 67 (1949): 7.

73. William Grant Still to Clarence Cameron White, August 9, 1944, box 2, Clarence Cameron White Papers (Additions), 1906–1972, Sc MG 492, Schomburg Center for Research in Black Culture, Manuscripts Archives and Rare Books Division, New York Public Library. Hereafter White Papers (Additions).

74. William Grant Still to Clarence Cameron White, August 24, 1944, box 2, folder 21, White Papers (Additions).

75. William Grant Still to Clarence Cameron White, October 24, 1946, box 2, folder 21, White Papers (Additions).

76. Quoted in Beverly Soll, *I Dream a World: The Operas of William Grant Still* (Fayetteville: University of Arkansas Press, 2005), 47.

77. Tammy Kernodle, "Arias, Communists, and Conspiracies: The History of Still's *Troubled Island*," *Musical Quarterly* 83, no. 4 (1999): 487–508, 489.

78. Nora Holt, "New Opera Gets Green Light," *New York Amsterdam News*, February 5, 1949.

79. On Hughes's representation of Haitian history, see Nicole Waligora-Davis, *Sanctuary: African Americans and Empire* (New York: Oxford University Press, 2011), 110–134. See also Michael Largey, *Vodou Nation: Haitian Art Music and Cultural Nationalism* (Chicago: University of Chicago Press, 2006).

80. Radio interview with William Grant Still, March 19, 1949, in *Just Tell the Story: Troubled Island*, ed. Judith Anne Still and Lisa M. Headlee (Flagstaff, AZ: The Master-Player Library, 2006), 521.

81. Philip Kaisary, "Langston Hughes and the Haitian Revolution," in *Langston Hughes in Context*, ed. Vera Kutzinski and Anthony Reed (Cambridge: Cambridge University Press, 2022), 129.

82. C. James Trotman, "'For All the Kids to Come': The *Troubled Island* of William Grant Still and Langston Hughes," in *Langston Hughes: The Man, His Art, and His Continuing Influence* ed. C. James Trotman and Emery Wimbish Jr. (New York: Garland, 1995), 108.

83. Nora Holt, "Freedom the Theme in 'Troubled Island,'" *New York Amsterdam News*, April 9, 1949. "Old operatic patterns" is quoted in Kernodle, "Arias, Communists, and Conspiracies," 495.

84. "The World Premiere of 'Troubled Island,'" *New York Amsterdam News*, March 12, 1949.

85. Quoted in Kernodle, "Arias, Communists, and Conspiracies," 497.

86. This story was relayed by Verna Arvey in her memoirs; Still himself did not circulate it extensively. Kernodle concludes that although "one may never prove whether there was a critical conspiracy . . . there is evidence of other influences sabotaging interest in the opera after its initial performances." For instance, the State Department recorded the opera but declined to distribute it to foreign radio stations, eventually recalling it, possibly due to Hughes's involvement. Kernodle, "Arias, Communists, and Conspiracies," 500.

87. Langston Hughes, *The Collected Works of Langston Hughes,* ed. Leslie Catherine Sanders, vol. 6: *Gospel Plays, Operas, and Later Dramatic Works* (Columbia: University of Missouri Press, 2004), 30.

88. Tammy Kernodle, "'Sons of Africa, Come Forth': A Discussion of the Compositional Approaches of William Grant Still in the Opera *Troubled Island,*" *American Music Research Center Journal* 13 (2003): 25–36, 35.

89. See W. Jason Miller, *Origins of the Dream: Hughes's Poetry and King's Rhetoric* (Gainesville: University Press of Florida, 2016), 142–159.

90. Brent Hayes Edwards, *Epistrophies: Jazz and the Literary Imagination* (Cambridge, MA: Harvard University Press, 2017), 11–12.

91. Kevin Young, *The Grey Album: On the Blackness of Blackness* (Minneapolis: Graywolf Press, 2012), 11–20; Jean-Christophe Cloutier, *Shadow Archives: The Lifecycles of African American Literature* (New York: Columbia University Press, 2019).

92. J. Rosamond Johnson, "A Treasury of American Negro Music," typescript, 44–45, box 19, J. Rosamond Johnson Papers, MSS 21, Irving S. Gilmore Music Library, Yale University.

93. Nora Holt, "Opera, Ambition of Most Singers, Demands More Than Wistful Desire," *New York Amsterdam News,* September 23, 1950.

94. M. Marguerite Davenport, *Azalia: The Life of Madam E. Azalia Hackley* (Boston: Chapman and Grimes, 1947), 7.

95. The clipping is from a 1931 profile of Cato in the *Pittsburgh Courier.* Tellingly, the collage does not include parts of the profile that focus on her biography and musical theater experience. See Floyd G. Snelson Jr., "Harlem Limited Broadway Bound," *Pittsburgh Courier,* June 20, 1931.

96. Cloutier, *Shadow Archives,* 9.

97. "Cranbrook Loaned Hackley Memorial," *Michigan Chronicle,* February 5, 1944; see also Romie Minor, "Preserving the Black Performance for Posterity," *Michigan History Magazine* (2015): 50–55.

98. "The Hackley Memorial," *Michigan Chronicle,* December 8, 1951.

99. "Opera, Concert Stars at Johnson Collection," *New York Amsterdam News,* September 26, 1959.

100. Valdo Freeman, interview.

101. Edwards, *Epistrophies,* 14. "Its own story" is from Alessandro Portelli, "What Makes Oral History Different (1979)," in Portelli, *The Death of Luigi Trastulli and Other Stories: Form and Meaning in Oral History* (Albany: State University of New York Press, 1991), 52.

102. Nora Holt, "Father of Opera," *New York Amsterdam News,* November 11, 1944.

103. David Gutkin, "The Modernities of H. Lawrence Freeman," *Journal of the American Musicological Society* 72, no. 3 (2019): 719–779, 748–749.

104. Valdo Freeman, interview.

105. Holt, "Father of Opera."

106. Ellen Garvey, *Writing with Scissors: American Scrapbooks from the Civil War to the Harlem Renaissance* (New York: Oxford University Press, 2012).

107. Although Freeman seems to have been the primary creator of the scrapbooks, Valdo and Carlotta likely contributed as well, given their shared dedication to Freeman's legacy.

108. Valdo Freeman, interview.

109. H. Lawrence Freeman, *The Negro in Music and Drama,* 370, typescript, box 50, Freeman Papers.

110. Freeman, *The Negro in Music and Drama,* 372.

111. H. Lawrence Freeman to Eleanor Roosevelt, undated, box 49, Freeman Papers.

112. Kira Thurman, "Wagnerian Dreams, Grandiose Visions: Lawrence Freeman's *Voodoo* at the Miller Theater," *Opera Quarterly* 32, no. 2/3 (2016): 226–232, 226.

113. Freeman to Roosevelt, undated.

114. Freeman to Roosevelt, undated.

115. See Seth Colter Walls, "Voodoo Review—A Lost Harlem Renaissance Opera Soars," *The Guardian,* June 27, 2015, on the "audacious experimental textures" of Freeman's opera; and Michael Cooper, "Bringing an Opera Back to Life," *New York Times,* June 22, 2015.

116. Thurman, "Wagnerian Dreams," 230.

117. See Eidsheim, *The Race of Sound;* and Emily Thompson, *The Soundscape of Modernity: Architectural Acoustics and the Culture of Listening in America, 1900–1933* (Cambridge, MA: MIT Press, 2002).

Conclusion

1. Ralph Ellison, "The Little Man at Chehaw Station: The American Artist and His Audience," in *The Collected Essays of Ralph Ellison,* ed. John Callahan (New York: Random House, 2011), 520.

2. Ellison, "Chehaw Station," 523. Italics in original.

3. Leontyne Price, "Aida," in *The Metropolitan Opera Encyclopedia: A Comprehensive Guide to the World of Opera,* ed. David Hamilton (New York: Simon and Schuster, 1987), 16.

4. Harold Schonberg, "A Bravo for Opera's Black Voices," *New York Times,* January 17, 1982.

5. Dick Campbell, "Black Musicians in Symphony Orchestras: A Bad Scene," *Crisis,* January 1975, 12. Campbell, who was married to Muriel Rahn, had been a crucial voice in the fight for desegregation throughout the 1940s and 1950s. Although here he refers primarily to orchestral musicians, the sentiment applies to opera as well.

6. See Gerald Horne, *The Rise and Fall of the Associated Negro Press: Claude Barnett's Pan-African News and the Jim Crow Paradox* (Urbana: University of Illinois Press, 2017).

7. Farah Jasmine Griffin, *In Search of a Beautiful Freedom: New and Selected Essays* (New York: W.W. Norton, 2023).

8. See Tim Weiner, "Odetta, Voice of Civil Rights Movement, Dies at 77," *New York Times,* December 3, 2008.

9. See Samantha Ege, "Nora Douglas Holt's Teachings of a Black Classical Canon," in *The Oxford Handbook of Public Music Theory,* ed. J. Daniel Jenkins (New York: Oxford University Press, 2022). From 1953 to 1964, Holt also produced and hosted *Nora Holt's Concert Showcase* on Harlem's WLIB station, which similarly focused on Black classical musicians.

10. Samuel R. Delany, *Silent Interviews: On Language, Race, Sex, Science Fiction, and Some Comics* (Middletown, CT: Wesleyan University Press, 1994), 306. Italics in original.

11. "Action Line," *Chicago Tribune,* September 13, 1980. The paper published the letter with a response correcting Rhea's claim that she was the "first," citing predecessors including Elizabeth Taylor Greenfield, Sissieretta Jones, and Caterina Jarboro.

12. See, for example, Earl Calloway, "Black Opera Singers Getting Major Roles," *Chicago Defender,* January 20, 1968; and Raoul Abdul, "Celebrating the Legacy of Black Opera Pioneers," *New York Amsterdam News,* January 23, 2003.

13. Raoul Abdul, *Blacks in Classical Music: A Personal History* (New York: Dodd, Mead, 1977), 109.

14. Edward Berlin, *King of Ragtime: Scott Joplin and His Era,* 2nd ed. (New York: Oxford University Press, 2016), 275.

15. Elise Kirk, *American Opera* (Urbana: University of Illinois Press, 2001), 189.

16. John Kronenberger, "The Ragtime Revival," *New York Times,* August 11, 1974. On pre-1970s efforts to commemorate Joplin, see Berlin, *King of Ragtime,* 316–338. As Berlin details, excerpts from *Treemonisha* were performed in 1965, and plans for a full production were in place prior to the vogue of interest in Joplin's rags.

17. Martin Bernheimer, "From 'Porgy' to 'Harriet': Black Theme, White Composer," *Los Angeles Times,* March 10, 1985.

18. Daniel Paget, "The 'Treemonisha' That Broadway Left Behind," *New York Times,* December 1, 1991.

19. Abdul, *Blacks in Classical Music,* 126.

20. These included full productions by OperaCreóle in New Orleans and Opera NOVA in Arlington, Virginia, as well as a concert performance by the Mississippi Symphony Orchestra.

21. "The History and Mission of OperaCréole," OperaCréole.com, https://www.operacreole.com/about.

22. See Michael Andor Brodeur, "An Impresaria Rediscovered in 'The Passion of Mary Cardwell Dawson,'" *Washington Post,* January 21, 2023.

23. Jonnet Solomon, videoconference interview with the author, June 13, 2023.

24. On the transnational scope of Black opera in the twenty-first century, see Naomi André, *Black Opera: History, Power, Engagement* (Urbana: University of Illinois Press, 2018).

25. On the ensemble's previous productions, see André, *Black Opera*, 49–53.

26. See "Scott Joplin's *Treemonisha*," Volcano.ca, https://www.volcano.ca/treemonisha. See also Ryan Ebright, "Extraordinary Journey," *Opera News* 87, no. 12 (June 2023): 34–37.

27. Both Blanchard and Giddens first gained recognition in other genres, but neither is a newcomer to opera. Blanchard has described his father as an "opera fanatic," and Giddens trained as an opera singer at Oberlin Conservatory. See Michael Cooper, "The Met Will Stage Its First Opera by a Black Composer," *New York Times,* September 19, 2019.

28. While these events took place several years apart, they are compressed in the adaptation, such that Freddie dies just after the composer completes his work.

29. Karen Chilton, telephone interview with the author, June 2, 2023.

30. Karen Chilton, libretto for *Treemonisha* (Opera Theatre of Saint Louis, 2023), 21.

31. Chilton, *Treemonisha*, 55–57.

32. Chilton, *Treemonisha*, 18–19.

33. Chilton, *Treemonisha*, 56.

34. Harry Bradford, "What the Colored Vaudevillians Are Doing in New York City and the East," *Indianapolis Freeman,* November 13, 1909.

35. Valdo Freeman, interview by Vivian Perlis, December 28, 1971, Major Figures in American Music Collection, Oral History of American Music, Music Library of Yale University.

36. Justin Austin, Damien Sneed, and Brandie Inez Sutton, interview with the author, St. Louis, MO, June 12, 2023.

37. Brent Hayes Edwards argues that Langston Hughes's blues poems offer "an implied proposition that the spoken black vernacular can provide the material of a modernist lyric poetics—without mediation, without elevation, without any of the rarefied quirks that are so often taken to connote 'poetry.'" To my mind, Joplin makes a similar formal move, with similarly radical results. Brent Hayes Edwards, *The Practice of Diaspora: Literature, Translation, and the Rise of Black Internationalism* (Cambridge, MA: Harvard University Press, 2003), 60–61.

38. Russell, "The Futurity of American Music," *Indianapolis Freeman,* August 24, 1907.

39. These ideas are shaped by conversations with Will Liverman and Nicole Cabell, who I interviewed in 2021 in relation to their work on another Opera Theatre of Saint Louis project, a concert celebrating Juneteenth. See Lucy Caplan, "We Can Tell Our Own Stories," *Opera News* 85, no. 12 (June 2021): 24–27.

40. Karen Chilton, interview.

Acknowledgments

Like operas, books are made by ensembles. I am extraordinarily grateful for the teachers, colleagues, mentors, and friends who have made the writing of this book possible.

Librarians and archivists at repositories including the African American Museum and Library at Oakland, Anacostia Community Museum, Beinecke Rare Book and Manuscript Library, Carnegie Museum of Art, Center for Black Music Research, Columbia Rare Book and Manuscript Library, Detroit Public Library, Gilmore Music Library, Metropolitan Opera Archives, Moorland Spingarn Research Center, Musical America Archives, Peabody Institute, San Francisco Opera Archives, Schlesinger Library, Schomburg Center for Research in Black Culture, and the Texas Collection at Baylor University have provided crucial guidance and research support. I'm especially grateful to Melanie Zeck for being so generous with her time during my visit to Chicago in 2017, to Paul Fisher for sharing items from the Jules Bledsoe Collection with me digitally during the pandemic, to Barbara Rominski for digging through unprocessed collections in search of Julian Bagley's Signature Book, and to Matt Testa for sharing with me the English-language typescript of Anne Brown's memoir.

I have so much gratitude for my time at Yale, where I was lucky to be part of an incredible intellectual community. Daphne Brooks's creativity and brilliance were, and continue to be, transformative. I have endless appreciation and admiration for Jonathan Holloway's support, generosity, and kindness. I was also privileged to learn from many other wonderful teachers,

including Melissa Barton, Glenda Gilmore, Jacqueline Goldsby, Matt Jacobson, Gundula Kreuzer, Mary Lui, Sebastian Ruth, and Robert Stepto.

The first inklings of this project emerged when I was an undergraduate studying History and Literature at Harvard College. I benefited immensely from the encouragement of teachers, including Jeanne Follansbee; Jim Kloppenberg, an incredible mentor who introduced me to the joys of academic work; and Carol Oja, who has continued to be a wonderful adviser for many years. So it felt very fitting that I was able to return to H&L, this time as a lecturer, during the years when I wrote much of this book. Angela Allan, Tommy Conners, Thomas Dichter, Reed Gochberg, Rebecca Hogue, Karen Huang, Lauren Kaminsky, Emily Laase, Laura Quinton, Jessica Shires, Briana Smith, Duncan White, and many others created a collegial, supportive workplace. I am also grateful to the students with whom I was lucky to work during my time at Harvard—especially Anya Henry, a terrific research assistant.

I feel very fortunate to have joined the Department of Humanities and Arts at Worcester Polytechnic Institute. It is a pleasure to be part of such a vibrant community of devoted teachers and scholars. I'm especially grateful to Scott Barton, Joe Cullon, Lindsay Davis, Sarah Lucie, Mitchell Lutch, V. J. Manzo, Kate Moncrief, Rebecca Moody, Joshua Rohde, and Kara Parks Fontenot Sieczkiewicz for welcoming me to WPI with such warmth and enthusiasm.

Many other colleagues, including both scholars and artists, have offered vital feedback and support. For many illuminating conversations over the years, I thank Naomi André, Matt Aucoin, Mark Burford, Katie Callam, Alex Cowan, Ryan Ebright, Nina Sun Eidsheim, Glenda Goodman, Ashleigh Gordon, Carolyn Guzski, A. Kori Hill, Gwynne Kuhner Brown, Marti Newland Slaten, Guthrie Ramsey, Justin Randolph, Maria Ryan, Doug Shadle, Megan Steigerwald Ille, and Kira Thurman. For their feedback on drafts of various chapters, plus their camaraderie and moral support, I thank Allison Chu, Samantha M. Cooper, Monica Hershberger, Lily Kass, Isidora Miranda, Caitlin Schmid, and Kristen M. Turner. Samantha Ege provided perceptive comments on a draft of the entire book.

Helena Kopchick Spencer kindly invited me to participate in symposia hosted by the University of North Carolina, Wilmington / Opera Wilmington. In Wilmington, I met Richard Yarborough, and I am very thankful to him for speaking to me about his great-aunt, Caterina Jarboro. It was an honor to be part of a 2020 symposium celebrating Shirley Graham Du Bois at Oberlin College and Conservatory, facilitated by Courtney-Savali Andrews, Fredara Hadley, Caroline Jackson Smith, and Tamika Nunley.

A highlight of writing this book has been the opportunity to learn from and alongside musicians and practitioners. For their brilliant performances of music from *Tom-Tom,* I thank Jonathan P. Green, Candice Hoyes, Markel Reed, Davóne Tines, and Kyle Walker. Thank you to Fredara Hadley, Caroline Jackson Smith, and Chad Williams for lending their scholarly insight to those events, and to Matt Aucoin, Jen Chen, Zack Winokur, the American Modern Opera Company, the Harvard Office for the Arts, National Sawdust, and the Caramoor Center for Music and the Arts for their support. Thanks to the support of the Society of American Music's Virgil Thomson Fellowship, I was able to embark on a whirlwind research trip in the summer of 2023. Jonnet Solomon and Vallon Wallace of the National Opera House introduced me to Mary Cardwell Dawson's home in Pittsburgh. Chantal Incandela kindly organized conversations with several artists involved in Opera Theatre of Saint Louis's 2023 production of *Treemonisha,* including Justin Austin, Karen Chilton, Rajendra Ramoon Maharaj, Damien Sneed, and Brandie Inez Sutton.

It has been a joy to write this book under the auspices of Harvard University Press. I thank Sharmila Sen for her early trust in my work. Kate Brick, Jillian Quigley, and Stephanie Vyce have offered incredibly helpful guidance at various steps of the process. Two anonymous readers provided transformative, generous feedback on the manuscript. I sincerely appreciate Julie Carlson's superb copyediting. Emily Silk is an extraordinary editor—insightful, patient, and candid—and I am deeply grateful for her wisdom and expertise. I also appreciate the generous support of the AMS 75 PAYS Endowment of the American Musicological Society.

Some of the material in this book was developed in concert with work done for other publications. Chapters 2 and 3 build on ideas first presented in "'Strange What Cosmopolites Music Makes of Us': Classical Music, the Black Press, and Nora Douglas Holt's Black Feminist Audiotopia," which appeared in the *Journal of the Society for American Music* 14, no. 3 (August 2020): 308–336. And Chapter 4 includes text first published in "Race and History on the Operatic Stage: Caterina Jarboro Sings *Aida,*" my chapter in the collection *African American Arts: Activism, Aesthetics, and Futurity,* edited by Sharrell Luckett from Bucknell University Press in 2019. Please note that every effort has been made to identify copyright holders and obtain their permission for the use of copyrighted material. Notification of any additions or corrections that should be incorporated in future reprints or editions of this book would be greatly appreciated.

I owe my greatest thanks to my friends and family. Life in and around Cambridge is made better by Hillary Ditmars, Lin Georgis, Ian Kumekawa,

Hannah Lyons-Galante, and Sasha Sabherwal. A little farther afield, Christine Benador-Shen, Ellen Rim, Sarah Rosenwohl-Mack, and Michaela Ross are exceptionally kind and compassionate friends. Jessica Oddie is very far afield, but always close to my heart. My sister, Laurel, inspires me with her commitment to her values and fondness for abbrevs. Dona is a perfect, snuggly assistant. My husband, Chase Carpenter, has been by my side for more than a decade with an infinite supply of enthusiasm, patience, and kindness. Everything is made possible by my parents, Jeff Caplan and Emily Green Caplan. From the general (Remarkable! Interesting!) to the specific (proofreading every single word), they are always there for me. With inexpressibly deep gratitude for their love and support, I dedicate this book to them.

Illustration Credits

154   Box 23, Shirley Graham Du Bois Papers, Schlesinger Library, Harvard Radcliffe Institute.

160   "Opera Brings Glorious Negro Rhythm," *Cleveland Press.* Box 23, Shirley Graham Du Bois Papers, Schlesinger Library, Harvard Radcliffe Institute.

185   Carnegie Museum of Art, Pittsburgh: Heinz Family Fund, 2001.35.1374. © Carnegie Museum of Art, Pittsburgh.

186   Carnegie Museum of Art, Pittsburgh: Heinz Family Fund, 2001.35.1461. © Carnegie Museum of Art, Pittsburgh.

187   Carnegie Museum of Art, Pittsburgh: Heinz Family Fund, 2001.35.1469. © Carnegie Museum of Art, Pittsburgh.

194   Courtesy of the E. Azalia Hackley Collection of African Americans in the Performing Arts, Detroit Public Library.

205   Photography by Cecil Layne. Photographs and Prints Division, Schomburg Center for Research in Black Culture, New York Public Library.

210   Photo © Metropolitan Opera.

213   H. Lawrence Freeman Papers; Box 36; Rare Book and Manuscript Library, Columbia University Library.

220, 221 Courtesy of the E. Azalia Hackley Collection of African Americans in the Performing Arts, Detroit Public Library.

223   Photo by Ben Greenhaus. Courtesy of the E. Azalia Hackley Collection of African Americans in the Performing Arts, Detroit Public Library.

Index

Page numbers in italics refer to illustrations.

American Opera and Its Composers (Hipsher), 142, 284n42

American Romance (Freeman), 143, 285n51

Anderson, Marian, 4, 92; as activist, 208–209; in Chicago, 66; debut at Metropolitan Opera House, 2, 13, 197, 198, 208–209, 229; in Europe, 301n48; in People's Chorus, Philadelphia, 76; as Ulrica (character), 197, 208, 209–211, *210*

archival work of Black artists: Julian Elihu Bagley, 93–94, *94*; in Black press, 232; Minto Cato, 220–221, *221*, 304n95; communal efforts, 221–222, *223*; Harry Lawrence Freeman, 38, 222–227, 305n107; as history making, 16–17, 199; importance of, 218–220

Arroyo, Martina, 229, 302n57

Athalia (Freeman), 142

audiences: and activism, 14; as community, 88–89; composition of, 23, 51, 68, 251n13; contemporary, 237, 238–239; contributions to opera, 84–85; discriminatory policies, 86–87; experiences, accounts of, 87–89; in reviews, 45, 86

authenticity paradigm, 110–112

Avery, Marguerite, 1, 2, 103, 243n5

Bagley, Julian Elihu, 91–94

ballo in maschera, Un (Verdi), 196, 207–208. *See also* Ulrica (character)

Bizet, Georges, 41

Black artists in canonical roles: Aida, 105–106, 115–120, 123–126, 128–129, 131, 181; Cio-Cio-San, 192–193, 194, *194*, 297n92; importance in Black operatic counterculture, 40; Lakmé, 120–122, *121*; and social change, 131; Ulrica, 197, 208, 209–211, *210*

Black artists in Europe, 272n7; Jules Bledsoe, 132, *140*; Anne Wiggins Brown, 294n39; Florence Cole-Talbert, 18, 105, 116, 117, 119–120; Lillian Evanti, 120–122, 192; for greater opportunities, 104, 119, 120, 122, 197, 298–299n13; E. Azalia Hackley, 75, 77; Caterina Jarboro, 123, 127; vocal training, 60

Black artists in non-Black roles: Martina Arroyo, 302n57; Todd Duncan, 191; Lillian Evanti, *121*, 121–122; Camilla

Williams, 169, 192–193, 194, *194*, 201, 297n91

Black exceptionalism: arguments against, 6, 12, 16, 39, 58, 159; as consequence of inclusion, 190, 194, 198, 209, 218; as determined by white tastemakers, 58, 104, 261n13

Black exclusion from mainstream opera, 2; Black companies as alternatives, 40, 42, 256n95; Black operatic counterculture as alternative, 168; documentation of Black opera as response, 16–17; Sissieretta Jones, 6–7; as last area of racial exclusion, 200, 298n7; opera performances on Broadway, 171; popular music as alternative, 135–136

blackface in opera: *Aida* (Verdi), 115, 117, 126; in Metropolitan Opera Company, 138–139, 276n55; white supernumeraries, 100

blackface minstrelsy: legacy in opera, 137, 139, 172; opera as alternative to, 11–12, 43; popularity in nineteenth century, 8, 39

Black formalism, 6, 23–24

Black image in opera, 3–4; *Africaine, L'* (Meyerbeer), 82; *Aida* (Verdi), 96–98; as enslaved, 130–131; misrepresentations of, 137–139; parodies of operas, 8, 27; *Porgy and Bess* (Gershwin), 168; supernumeraries, *98*, 100, 228–229. *See also* exoticism

Black music scholarship, absence of opera in, 4

Blackness in opera: blackface minstrelsy, 139; canonical opera, 70–71; changes over time, 170–171; and colorism, 252n26; diversity of representation, 132; as expressed by choruses, 45; as international, 25–26, 33–35; as racialized novelty, 21; in scholarship of opera, 3–4; stereotypes, 137; as substitute for participation, 105; and supernumeraries, 100, 228–229

Blackness in Opera (collection), 5

Black opera companies: and canonical European operas, 44–46, 72–73, 180, 184; and collective sociality, 39, 184, 186–187; documentation in photographs, 185–187; early companies, 180; financial challenges, 184, 211; and indi-

Cato, Minto, 180, 181, *220,* 220–221, *221,* 304n95
Cavalleria Rusticana (Mascagni), 181, 191
Chicago's World Fair (1893), 24–25, 30
choruses, 41, 43, 44, 45–46, 158, 159
civil rights movement: and Black performers in canonical opera, 192, 201–202; and desegregation of opera, 18, 83, 85–86, 198; linking opera to, 7, 168–169, 183
Clorindy (Cook and Dunbar), as ragtime opera, 50
Clough, Estelle Pinckney, 60, 115
Coleridge-Taylor, Samuel: death of, 56; in early version of *Tom-Tom* (Graham), 150–151; influence on Clarence Cameron White, 145; *Thelma,* 145, 234
Cole-Talbert, Florence, 18, 116–120, 278n86
collaboration in Black opera. *See* collective nature of Black opera
collective nature of Black opera: archival work, 221–222, 232; and choruses, 44, 45–46; collective study of opera, 73–74; and creative collaboration, 12; as cultural practice, 3; and desegregation efforts, 170; and Drury Company, 39–40; E. Azalia Hackley's mass choral trainings, 77–79; necessity of, 22–23; as shared social experience, 3, 11, 65, 72, 159, 164, 184–186, *186*; and social change, 195, 198, 209–211; *Tom-Tom* (Graham), 155, 159
"Colored Actors' Declaration of Independence of 1898," 39–40
Colored American Opera Company, 9
commodification of black music, 7, 15, 22, 39, 136
composers: and Black history, 132–133, 282n2; symphonies, 137; and Black world-making, 134, 216; and creative ambition, 134–135; marginalization, 134; in 1970s and 1980s, 231. *See also* constraints on Black composers; *specific composers*
constraints on Black composers: exclusion from mainstream opera, 198, 199, 215, 294n50; financial challenges, 181, 212; lack of interest, 181–182, 211; as necessary for creative process, 165–166. *See also individual composers*

constraints on Black opera and artists, 30–31, 35; archival research, limits on, 161; educational opportunities, lack of, 66–67; financial, 8, 22, 39, 51, 134, 142, 163, 181, 184, 211–212; inaccessibility of opera, 137; Jim Crow, 7, 8, 12, 46, 53, 161; marginal status, 165; opportunities, lack of, 201; racist barriers, 2, 13, 23, 52, 62, 97, 135, 297n91; representational, 168. *See also* constraints on Black composers
Cook, Will Marion, 24, 50, 150, 251n17
Cooperative Opera Club, 182
costumes, 35–37, 124–125, *125,* 126
critics: on Black stereotypes by white composers, 137–139; on Drury Company production of *Carmen,* 44–45; in the early Black press, 46–47; on Harry Lawrence Freeman, 136, 144; on National Negro Opera Company (NNOC), 183; on *Porgy and Bess* (Gershwin), 175–176, 177–178; on the promise of Black opera, 141; on racial barriers in opera, 107–109, 111; role in bringing opera to the public, 17, 22, 69–71; role in shaping perceptions of opera, 67–68; and social critiques, 68–69; as social force, 47; on *Treemonisha* (Joplin), 238; white vs. Black critics, 45, 47, 50, 112, 126, 138–139, 144, 177–178. *See also* reviews; *specific critics*
cultural hegemony, 14, 21
cultural hierarchy, 9, 10, 21, 22, 50, 52, 228–229

Dance in Place Congo, The (Gilbert), 111–112
Davis, Anthony, 231, 244n12
Davis, Ellabelle, 18, 201–202, 215
Davy, Gloria, 229
Dawson, Mary Cardwell, 10–11, 182–183, 231, 235
de Lyon, Emma, 42, 104
de Reszke, Jean, 60, 75, 77
desegregation of opera: calls for improved access, 189–190; and casting of Black artists, 190–194, 201–204, 207–211; as collective effort, 169–170, 301n47; historic efforts, 197; limitations of, 131, 229–230; Metropolitan Opera House (New York City), 188–189, 197,

Freeman, Harry Lawrence (*continued*)
Black opera, 219; on *Porgy and Bess*
(Gershwin), 176; relationship to Black
culture and music, 23–24, 29, 136; as
vocal teacher, 59–60, 261n19; *Voodoo,*
143–145, 234. See also *Martyr, The*
(Freeman)

Garnes, Antoinette, 63–65, 76, 263n47,
264n49
Gershwin, George: adapting *Porgy* (Heyward), 174; *Blue Monday,* 137, 174; *Porgy
and Bess,* 13, 18, 66, 167–168; research
for *Porgy and Bess,* 174–175. See also
Porgy and Bess (Gershwin)
Graham, Shirley: as activist, 287n82; in
Africa, 164–165; and African diaspora,
133; composing *Tom-Tom,* 152, 159,
161–162; and W. E. B. Du Bois, 135,
296n74; early years, 149, 287n85,
287n86, 287n87, 287n88; ethnographic
approach to composition, 155–156, 163;
financial difficulties, 163; musical
training, 161; opera as refuge, 164; in
Paris, 149–150, 287n90; on *Porgy and
Bess* (Gershwin), 176; as a student,
149–150, 151; use of African music, 133,
148, 150. See also *Tom-Tom* (Graham)
Greenfield, Elizabeth Taylor, 9, 63
Gruenberg, Louis, 139, 294n50
Guest of Honor, A (Joplin), 55, 260n3

Hackley, E. Azalia: archival collection in
honor of, 221–222; mass choral train-
ings, 77–79, 78; as mentor to Florence
Cole-Talbert, 117; pedagogy, 76–77, 81;
as pioneer of Black opera, 219–220;
poor health, 267n109; singing career,
75; support of Black artists, 145;
transition to teaching, 75–76; writings,
79–80
Haiti in opera, 133, 145–147, 215–218
Hall Johnson Choir, 130–131, 292n12
Harlem Renaissance, 17, 83, 102, 104
Harris, Charles "Teenie," 185–187
Hayes, Roland, 14, 115
Heyward, DuBose, 174, 175
Higgins, Laurence, 151, 162, 291n149
Hipsher, Edward, 142
Hogan, Ernest, 30, 45, 56, 89–90

Holmes, Odetta, 14, 231
Holt, Nora, 17; audiences, accounts of, 88;
on Black opera companies, 184; on
Black stereotypes by white composers,
137; column in *Chicago Defender,*
70–71; contributions to opera criticism,
69–70, 222, 265n72; criticism of
blackface in *Aida* (Verdi), 100, 271n70;
on desegregation at Metropolitan Opera
House, 189; on exoticism, 71; on
Harry Lawrence Freeman, 224; later
work, 231, 306n9; on need for Black-
authored operas, 190; and Camilla
Williams, 193
Hotel Marshall, 40, 41, 45
Hughes, Langston, 215–218

In Dahomey (Williams and Walker), 33
Indianapolis Freeman, 47–48, 55
influence of opera on Black art, 14
institutionalization of opera: Black artists
within, 17–18, 180; and cultural hierarchy, 9–10; resistance to change, 81;
role of opera houses in, 7, 189, 247n35,
248n45

Jarboro, Caterina, 18; as Aida, 122–123,
124–126, *125,* 128–129, 130, 131; auditions at Metropolitan Opera House
(New York City), 204; debut as Aida,
122–123; early career, 123; as established
artist, 200–201; invented persona,
123–125, 127, 279n93, 281n120; vocal
characteristics, 127–128
Jim Crow: as barrier to Black participation
in opera, 7, 12, 53, 104, 161, 230; effect
on audiences, 86–89; "Jim Crow paradox," 199, 230; in opera houses, 69,
85–87, 97, 168, 180, 199, 268n11; and
Porgy and Bess (Gershwin), 175
Johnson, Edward "Black Carl," 89–91
Johnson, Hall, 172, 176, 292n11, 292n12
Johnson, J. Rosamond, 115, 141, 150, 219
Johnson, James Weldon, 254n74; archival
collection at Yale University, 222; discrimination complaint, 86; on Theodore
Drury, 45; translation of *Goyescas* (Granados), 95–96; works, opera in, 14
Jones, Sissieretta, 6–7, 23, 24–25, 114,
255n83

sacralization of opera. *See* institutionalization of opera

Salmaggi, Alfredo, 124, 127, 181

scholarship of Black opera, 3–6, 16, 43, 47

segregation in opera, 2, 7, 9–10, 16, 17

self-making: and Black women artists,
59–65, 123–124, 170, 178–180, 192–193;
despite racist barriers, 65; and *Treemonisha* (Joplin), 239; and vocality, 59,
62–63

"shadow archives." *See* archival work of
Black artists

Shanewis (Cadman), 111

Sheldon, Frederic, 42

Shuffle Along (Blake and Sissle), 110, 123,
136

Skyscrapers (Carpenter), 112

slavery, 8, 29; and Black artistry, 158; as
funding source for opera, 8, 247n36; in
operas, 29, 96–98, 111, 112, 130–131,
236

Souls of Black Folk, The (Du Bois), 14

Southern, Eileen, 5

South Side School of Grand Opera,
71–74

Star of Ethiopia, The (Du Bois), 128,
281n119

Stein, Gertrude, 170–173

Still, William Grant, 10, 137, 214–218,
303n86

supernumeraries, *98*; in *Aida* (Verdi),
96–98, 105, 228–229, 270n52; contributions to opera, 96, 102; limitations
on, 99, 100, 101–102, 198; as listeners,
100–101, 102; white supernumeraries,
97, 99–100

"Talented Tenth," 5, 15, 22, 25, 118.
See also Black exceptionalism

Thelma (Coleridge-Taylor), 145, 234

Thomson, Virgil, 170–173, 200–201

Tom-Tom (Graham), 18; and the African
diaspora, 133, 148–149, 152–153, 155,
157, 160–161; African music in, 150, 153,
155–156, 163; as archive, 160–161; as
Black music history, 148–149, 150–151,
156–157, 160; casting, 132, 158, *160,*
291n149; characters, 152–153, 156–157;
as collective, 159; as commissioned
opera, 151–152; ethnography, as in-

formed by, 155–156, 163; as expression
of Black experience, 156, 162; as historical counterknowledge, 149, 157–158;
as historical narrative, 134, 148–149;
inspiration for, 150; legacy of, 165–166;
musical elements, 153–154, 156–157,
161, 289n116; plot, 152–153; premiere,
148, 151; production issues, 162–163,
165–166, 291n149; reviews of, 158,
159–160; revisions of, 162, 163, 291n154;
score, *154*; tom-tom, use of and symbolism, 153, 154, 157, 159

Treemonisha (Joplin): contemporary response to, 239–240, 307n37; failed
production, 55–56; international productions, 235–236; and limitations of
mainstream inclusion, 234; revival,
1960s, 306n16; revival, 1970s, 233–234;
revival and contemporary politics, 236;
revival and reinterpretation, modern,
234, 236–240, 306n20, 307n28

Trotter, James Monroe, 5

Troubled Island (Still), 214–218, 303n86

Tryst, The (Freeman), 34

Ulrica (character), 197, 208, 209–211, *210.*
See also *ballo in maschera, Un* (Verdi)

Uncle Tom's Cabin (Stowe), 24

vaudeville, 7, 23, 42, 56, 89

Vendetta (Freeman), 142, 284n46

Virginia's Ball (Douglass), 21

"vocal culture" movement, 60–61

vocal training: of amateurs, 17, 60–61,
75–79, 180; by performers, 59–60; by
white teachers, 60; and working in other
genres, 135–136. *See also* pedagogy

Voodoo (Freeman), 143–145, 181–182, 227,
234

Wagner, Richard: and artistic transcendence, 189–190; influence on Black artists, 27, 31, 51, 143, 164

Walton, Lester, 17, 68–69, 90, 108, 111

White, Clarence Cameron, 133, 145–147,
151

White, Lucien, 138, 177

white artists in Black roles, 108, 115, 117

white managers, 39, 42, 255n83

whiteness of opera, 4, 10, 13, 16, 50, 100